THE AGGREGATE PRODUCTION FUNCTION AND THE MEASUREMENT OF TECHNICAL CHANGE

The Aggregate Production Function and the Measurement of Technical Change

'Not Even Wrong'

Jesus Felipe

Advisor in the Office of the Chief Economist, Economics and Research Department, Asian Development Bank, Manila, Philippines

and

John S.L. McCombie

Professor of Regional and Applied Economics and Director, Cambridge Centre for Economic and Public Policy, Department of Land Economy, University of Cambridge and Fellow of Downing College, Cambridge, UK

Edward Elgar
Cheltenham, UK • Northampton, MA, USA

Published by
Edward Elgar Publishing Limited
The Lypiatts
15 Lansdown Road
Cheltenham
Glos GL50 2JA
UK

Edward Elgar Publishing, Inc.
William Pratt House
9 Dewey Court
Northampton
Massachusetts 01060
USA

A catalogue record for this book
is available from the British Library

Library of Congress Control Number: 2013938059

This book is available electronically in the ElgarOnline.com
Economics Subject Collection, E-ISBN 978 1 78254 968 0

MIX
Paper from
responsible sources
FSC® C013056
www.fsc.org

ISBN 978 1 84064 255 1 (cased)

Typeset by Servis Filmsetting Ltd, Stockport, Cheshire
Printed and bound in Great Britain by T.J. International Ltd, Padstow

Contents

Prologue: 'Not even wrong'

The physicist Wolfgang Pauli was, with Heisenberg, Schrödinger and Dirac, one of the early leaders in the development of quantum mechanics. He was renowned for being a tough audience, exclaiming 'wrong' (*falsch*), or 'completely wrong' (*ganz falsch*) when he disagreed with a speaker. Near the end of his life, when asked his opinion of a recent article by a younger physicist, he sadly said 'it is not even wrong' (*Das ist nicht einmal falsch*) . . . *A scientific idea is 'not even wrong' if it is so incomplete that it cannot be used to make predictions that could be compared to observations to see if the idea is wrong.*
> (Peter Woit, 2006, p. 6, emphasis added; for a biography of Wolfgang Pauli, see Peierls, 1960)

This book shows that the aggregate production function suffers from this same problem, namely it is 'not even wrong'. Aggregate production functions are estimated using constant-price value (or monetary) data. This, together with an underlying accounting identity that by definition relates value added, or gross output, to the value of the total payments to the inputs, means that a near perfect statistical fit can always be obtained by estimating an aggregate production function. This is even though aggregation and other problems suggest that the aggregate production function does not exist. Furthermore, the estimated parameters, such as the 'output elasticities' and the aggregate 'elasticity of substitution' cannot be taken as being determined by the underlying technology. All that can be said with certainty is that the estimates reflect the mathematical transformation of the linear accounting identity.

Herbert Simon (1979a, p. 497) put it succinctly as follows in his Nobel Prize speech:

Fitted Cobb–Douglas functions are homogeneous, generally of degree close to unity and with a labor exponent of about the right magnitude. These findings, however, cannot be taken as strong evidence for the [neo]classical theory, for the identical results can readily be produced by mistakenly fitting a Cobb–Douglas function to data that were in fact generated by a linear accounting identity (value of goods equals labor cost plus capital cost), (see E.H. Phelps-Brown [1957]). The same comment applies to the SMAC production function (see Richard Cyert and Simon [1971]).

This book elaborates and extends the argument why the aggregate production function is 'not even wrong' in that, in Woit's words, predictions from it cannot be 'compared to observations to see if the idea is wrong'.

Acknowledgements

The authors and publisher are grateful to the publishers of *Eastern Economic Journal*, *Journal of Post Keynesian Economics*, *International Review of Applied Economics*, *Metroeconomica*, *Review of Political Economy* and the volume *Growth, Employment and Inflation: Essays in Honour of John Cornwall* for permission to use edited material previously published there. The authors would also like to thank (without in any way implicating) Paul Davidson, Robert Dixon, Frank Fisher, Geoff Harcourt, Marc Lavoie, Anwar Shaikh, Tony Thirlwall and the many others who have taken an interest in this work.

Disclaimer: The views expressed in this book are the authors', and not necessarily those of the Asian Development Bank, those of its Executive Directors, or those of the member countries that they represent.

Introduction

Begin at the beginning, and go until you come to the end: then stop.
(*Alice's Adventures in Wonderland*, Lewis Carroll)

The production function is undoubtedly one of the most widely used concepts in economics. Students of economics are normally introduced to the theory of production at an early stage of their studies. Introductory microeconomics textbooks outline the production function, isoquants, the conditions for cost minimisation, the demand for factors of production (based upon the marginal product theory of factor pricing) and so on. At the same time, the production function is extended seamlessly in first-year macroeconomic textbooks to encompass individual industries or, indeed, the whole economy. There is, however, little, or more usually no, discussion about the conditions under which it is legitimate to sum micro-production functions to give a well-defined aggregate production function. That this should be considered is not simply for mere intellectual curiosity. Indeed, since the 1940s, economists such as Leontief, Klein, or Nataf, among others, studied the aggregation problem, and for very good reasons. The same functional form is often assumed to hold irrespective of whether the production function refers to an individual plant, firm, industry, or to the whole economy. This, it turns out, has little or no theoretical justification. Sato and Fisher clarified and extended the work on aggregation during the 1960s and 1970s and obtained very damaging conclusions for the plausibility of aggregates such as output and capital.

The Cobb–Douglas production function is usually the first specific functional form that students encounter, partly because of its mathematical simplicity and the pedagogical advantage that this brings. But it is not merely useful for teaching purposes. It is also used in many theoretical and empirical research papers, as a perusal of the recent issues of any mainstream economics journal will confirm. Clearly, it is widely considered that the Cobb–Douglas is more than just a convenient teaching concept, but does indeed represent the actual production conditions of an industry or economy, albeit only as an approximation. Other more flexible functional forms, such as the constant elasticity of substitution (CES) or translogarithmic (translog) production functions, are also used. However, in many, but not all, cases it seems that relatively little is to be gained in the use of these more complex production functions. Moreover, the fact that factor shares are roughly constant is seen to provide an empirical justification for the use of the Cobb–Douglas production function. For example, Hoover (2012, p. 330) states in his intermediate macroeconomics textbook:

> The striking fact that, while there is some variation, the variation [in factor shares] is small and there is no trend. The approximate constancy of the labor share confirms the prediction of our model and provides a good reason to take the Cobb–Douglas production function as a reasonable approximation of aggregate supply in the U.S. economy.

Similar sentiments are expressed in Mankiw's (2010, pp. 56–9) more introductory macroeconomics textbook, where the Cobb–Douglas production function is uncritically introduced. As Kuhn (1962 [1970]) has shown, textbooks are important in that they inculcate the student into the prevailing paradigm and implicitly set the legitimate questions to be examined, through, for example, worked examples and the questions at the end of the chapters. These set the agenda for what are seen as the appropriate models and methodology for work at the frontiers of paradigm. Consequently, the erroneous impression that the aggregate production function is a useful approximation to the technological conditions of, say, the whole economy, is perpetuated.

The more flexible production functions suffer from other problems. For example, the CES production function is a non-linear form and its econometric estimation is more difficult. And the translog often suffers from severe multicollinearity. Indeed, the ubiquity of the Cobb–Douglas production function makes it a toss-up as to whether the names 'Cobb and Douglas' or 'Keynes' have been mentioned more frequently in the economics literature over the last few decades.

In fact, in spite of the criticisms that Cobb and Douglas's original empirical work received (Cobb and Douglas, 1928), so hostile that Douglas momentarily considered abandoning all further work on the production function, their article has subsequently been recognised as one of the top 20 papers published during the last hundred years in the *American Economic Review* (Arrow et al., 2011). The citation to their work reads:

> The cliché surely applies here: this paper needs no introduction. The convenience and success of the constant-elasticity Cobb–Douglas function has spread its use from representing production possibilities, which of course was its original use, to representing utility functions and to much else throughout empirical and theoretical economics. Cobb and Douglas explored elementary properties and implications of the functional form and pointed to the approximate constancy of the relative shares of labour and capital in total income as the validating empirical fact. (p. 2)

Ever since Solow's (1956, 1957) two seminal papers on growth theory, the aggregate production function has become the *sine qua non* of neoclassical growth models. The more recent developments in endogenous growth theory that began in the mid-1980s depend equally on the validity of the concept of the aggregate production function. Indeed, it is possible to go so far as to say that the core of neoclassical macroeconomics relies on the aggregate production function in one form or another, including, for example, real business-cycle theory and short-run models of unemployment. If we were compelled to dispense with the aggregate production function, then it is fair to say that little would remain of either short- or long-run neoclassical macroeconomic models. This would be a disconcerting prospect for many economists, to be resisted at any cost.

Nevertheless, notwithstanding its widespread use, there are a number of severe methodological problems facing the aggregate production function that make its use problematical. Most notably, there are the problems posed by both the Cambridge capital theory controversies and what may be generically termed the 'aggregation problems' that are to be found in the somewhat broader aggregation literature. While we discuss these in more detail in Chapter 1, it is useful to consider them briefly here.

The Cambridge capital theory controversies, as the name suggests, were concerned with the theoretical problems of aggregating heterogeneous individual capital goods into a single index that could be taken as a measure of 'capital' as a factor input. The debate started in earnest in the 1950s, and went through much of the 1960s and up to the early 1970s, although its origins can be traced back to the Classical economists. The outcome was that it was generally agreed that no such index could be constructed (Harcourt, 1972; Cohen and Harcourt, 2003, 2005). The debate further showed that, when comparing steady-state economies, there is no necessary inverse monotonic relationship between the rate of profit and the capital–labour ratio, as in the neoclassical schema, outside of the restrictive one-sector model.

However, there was a good deal more to the debate than a clash of ideologies (or paradigms, to use a less emotive word), as Solow, for example, retrospectively views it.[1] Even some neoclassical economists were disturbed by the conclusions of the controversies. Commenting on Brown's (1980) comprehensive survey of both the capital controversies and the aggregation problems, Burmeister (1980, p. 423) concluded, 'I agree fully with Brown's stated conclusion that "the neoclassical parable and its implications are generally untenable". ... Freak cases such as Samuelson's surrogate production function example are of little comfort'.

---

[1] 'The whole episode now seems to me to have been a waste of time, a playing-out of ideological games in the language of analytical economics' (Solow, 1988, p. 309).

He even made the radical suggestion that 'for the purpose of answering many macroeconomic questions – particularly about inflation and unemployment – we should disregard the concept of a production function at the microeconomic level' (pp. 427–8). If we follow this advice, then, of course, the concept of the production function at the macroeconomic level is also vitiated.

A second criticism is the 'aggregation problem'. This shows that the conditions under which it is possible to sum micro-production functions to give an aggregate relationship are so restrictive as to make the concept of the aggregate production function untenable (Brown, 1980; Fisher, 1992; Felipe and Fisher, 2003). It should be noted that this problem occurs in spite of the implausible assumption that there exist well-defined production functions at the firm level, where the inputs are all used optimally.

The technical literature on this is quite complicated and we review it briefly in the next chapter, but the problem is intuitively very straightforward. Consider, say, the manufacturing sector. This consists of such diverse industries as (to take as random examples) SIC 204, Grain Mill Products, and SIC 281, Industrial Organic Chemicals. Does it make any sense to combine the values of each of the outputs and the inputs of the two industries and estimate a production function that purportedly represents the underlying combined technology of these two industries? How do we even interpret the 'average' elasticity of substitution? In fact, the actual position is even worse than this, as estimating an aggregate production function for, say, manufacturing, combines many more disparate industries, and for the total economy, an even greater number.

Consider, for example, a less developed country such as the Philippines where, in Manila, a modern international banking system, complete with the latest information technology, coexists with small back-street enterprises, such as food stalls, located literally only a few streets away. Again, does it make sense to combine these activities in terms of both their outputs and inputs, as is implicitly done when an aggregate production function is estimated for the whole economy? Do we expect all these industries to be technically efficient, which is one of the necessary conditions for aggregation? As Leibenstein (1966) has shown empirically, producer or X-efficiency can differ greatly between firms making identical products.

Are workers in the informal or in the rural sectors in developing countries paid their marginal products and are they fully employed with no disguised unemployment? How do we measure the output of a marginal worker in the service sector, when the national accounts often use the deflated value of the remuneration of the inputs (especially labour) in these sectors as a measure of the real value of the output, with possibly some arbitrary allowance for productivity growth? These, to our way of thinking, are largely rhetorical questions, yet many studies uncritically use the aggregate production function, whether in a growth-accounting context (see, for example, the survey by Maddison, 1987) or in econometric analysis (for example, Mankiw et al., 1992), using data for both the advanced and the developing countries.

Fisher (2005, p. 490), who over the years has done more than most to determine the technical conditions under which one can aggregate micro-production functions into an aggregate production function, has summarised the conclusion to be drawn from this literature as follows: 'the conditions for aggregation are so very stringent as to make the existence of aggregate production functions in real economies a non-event'. He further argues that the conditions are such that aggregate production functions cannot even be regarded as *approximations*, as Solow (1957), for example, regarded them.

Yet, it is ironical that a consideration of these serious problems has all but totally disappeared from the textbooks, and the capital theory controversies have been relegated to the history of economic thought, which few economists bother with. Consequently, a whole new generation of economists uncritically use the aggregate production function with no appreciation of how tenuous its foundations are (Sylos Labini, 1995). It is indicative that Cohen and Harcourt felt compelled to write a reminder for the profession in the 2003 issue of the *Journal of Economic Perspectives* in the 'Retrospectives' section entitled 'Whatever Happened to the Cambridge Capital Theory Controversies?' and that Birner's 2002 volume, *The Cambridge Controversies in Capital Theory*, is part of the Routledge Studies in the History of Economics.[2] The aggregation problem has fared little better. In spite of Fisher's persistent warnings of its damaging implications for the aggregate production function, virtually none of the plethora of recent applied and theoretical papers on, for example, economic growth, pays even lip-service to the aggregation problem.

It is instructive to look at how the Cambridge capital theory controversies and the aggregation problem have been covered in the textbooks and survey articles on economic growth over the last 30 years, or so. We take 1971 as the starting year. This was chosen because by that date the main conclusions and implications of the Cambridge capital theory controversies had become established. Harcourt's (1969) accessible critique of the aggregate production function had been available for a couple of years.

---

[2]   Birner's book, while predominantly examining the Cambridge controversies from a methodological perspective, also contains a clear exposition of some of the developments in capital theory subsequent to Harcourt's (1972) survey.

The damaging problems for the aggregate production function posed by the required aggregation conditions should also have been widely appreciated by this time. Fisher (1992, p. xiii), for example, indicates that as far back as 1970 he had already called 'into question the use of aggregate production functions in macroeconomic applications such as Solow's famous 1957 paper'.

The standard textbooks on economic growth at this time, namely, Wan (1971), Jones (1975) and Hacche (1979), and the survey article by Nadiri (1970), all mentioned the capital controversies. Wan, Jones and Nadiri also mentioned the aggregation problem.

Wan (1971) was, for its time, a highly mathematical postgraduate textbook that comprehensively covered the state of neoclassical growth theory at that date: the Solow model, vintage capital goods growth models, optimal growth models and so on. Nevertheless, it also found space to include a chapter on the Robinson and Kaldor growth models. Chapter 4 of Wan's book presents a concise introduction to both the Cambridge controversies and the aggregation problems, and the damaging implications are clearly set out on page 110 of the volume. Indeed, it is ironical that Wan notes on that page that 'Mrs Robinson originally was not pessimistic enough. She still maintained the hope that techniques can generally be ranked by their "real" capital/labour ratio'. Jones (1975) and Hacche (1979) were popular and clearly written third-year undergraduate and/or postgraduate textbooks. Both authors dealt with the Cambridge controversies, but only the former with the aggregation problem. Both spent a considerable portion of their books elaborating the Kaldorian or neo-Keynesian theories of economic growth, which have now entirely disappeared from the more recent growth textbooks. Nadiri's (1970, p. 1146) article was a survey of the more applied aspects of growth theory, including the growth-accounting approach, but ended with the warning that 'the aggregate production function does not have a conceptual reality of its own'. Regarding total factor productivity (TFP), he added: 'without proper aggregation we cannot interpret the properties of an aggregate production function, which rules the behavior of total factor productivity' (p. 1144).

But by the 1990s all mention of these problems had disappeared from the growth theory textbooks, including Barro and Sala-i-Martin (1995 [2003]), Jones (1998 [2002]), Aghion and Howitt (1998, 2009), Weil (2005) and Acemoglu (2009). The survey on growth accounting by Maddison (1987) did not share any of Nadiri's reservations about the aggregate production function. However, to be fair, Temple (1999, p. 150) in his survey of the new growth theory evidence, notes briefly that 'arguably the aggregate production function is the least satisfactory element of macroeconomics, yet many economists seem to regard this clumsy device as essential to an understanding of national income levels and growth rates'. Nevertheless, Temple is more concerned about the importance of structural change, which one-sector models tend to abstract from, than about the legitimacy of the concept of aggregate production. Temple (2006) presents a defence of the use of the aggregate production function which is not compelling, as we shall show in this book.

Valdés (1999, p. xii) in the preface to his textbook on growth mentions that he hated, for example, the 'exaggeratedly heated "capital controversies"', but there is no further elaboration. He also mentions the need to 'accept that an aggregate production function exists' (p. 63), but there is no justification for this position. And on pages 105 to 106 of his textbook, he presents a model that does not satisfy the aggregation conditions.

After the substantial literature on neoclassical growth theory generated by Solow's (1956, 1957) path-breaking articles, the late 1970s and early 1980s were a relatively barren period for the subject.[3] But this was not because of any reservations about the use of the aggregate production function. It was simply because the important Kuhnian theoretical puzzles seemed to have been solved and it was thought that there was only some marginal tidying up to be done – the Solow growth model had been generalised to two sectors; optimal growth models had been constructed using the calculus of variations or optimal control theory; the golden rule of accumulation had been examined; the role of money in growth theory modelled; the implications of increasing returns for steady-state growth, although with diminishing returns to each factor of production, had been analysed. Indeed, the classic survey of Hahn and Matthews, although written in 1964, remained on many student reading lists for a good many years after its year of publication (complemented by the 1972 survey of the applied aspects of technical change by Kennedy and Thirlwall).

All this changed after the publication of Romer's 1986 paper, which presented the first of a new generation of endogenous growth models that attempted to explain technical progress.[4] Solow (1956) had treated this as exogenous, not because he believed that technical change appeared like 'manna from heaven', but simply for want of a satisfactory explanation.

---

[3] The growth-accounting approach of Denison (1967), and subsequent studies, had largely confirmed the quantitative importance of TFP growth, or the Solow residual (often misleadingly referred to as the rate of technical progress) found by Solow (1957) (see Solow, 1988). The claim by Jorgenson and Griliches (1967) to have fully explained away the residual was shown to be erroneous (Denison, 1972a and 1972b).

[4] Early endogenous growth models include Kaldor's (1957) 'technical progress function', Frankel's (1962) 'development modifier' and Arrow's (1962) 'learning-by-doing' model.

This, together with the rapid development of large databases (such as Summers and Heston's (1991) Penn World Tables) led to an explosion of both theoretical and applied neoclassical studies on economic growth. Consequently, there were new puzzles to solve (how to endogenise technical change and so on) and old puzzles became relevant again (Mankiw et al., 1992).

Given the normal lag between research publications and the inclusion of simplified versions of these models in textbooks, it was not until the mid-1990s that a new generation of growth textbooks became available. By now, neoclassical growth theory and, as we have seen, the use of the aggregate production functions were treated as uncontroversial and seen as useful for understanding the determinants of economic growth, even though at a high level of aggregation. This is not to say that there were (and still are) no disagreements of how best to solve the neoclassical growth 'puzzles', with the rehabilitation of Solow's approach by Mankiw et al. (1992) and the different approaches taken to endogenise technical change (Romer, 1994). Moreover, questions regarding the best econometric specifications and best statistical methods to be used in testing or estimating economic growth models remained. But the Cambridge capital theory controversies, aggregation problems and the alternative growth models of Joan Robinson and Nicholas Kaldor had been banished to the nether regions. Not all mention of the Cambridge controversies disappeared from the recent literature, but references were few and far between. Pasinetti (1994, p. 357), for example, felt compelled to remind the participants at a major IEA conference on economic growth:

> This result [that there is no unambiguous relationship between the rate of profit and the capital–labour ratio], however uncomfortable it may be for orthodox theory, still stands. Surprisingly, it is not mentioned. In almost all 'new growth theory' models, a neoclassical production function, which by itself implies a monotonic inverse relationship between the rate of profits and quantity of capital per man, is simply *assumed*. (Emphasis in the original)

Bernanke (1987, p. 203, emphasis in the original), commenting on the new endogenous growth models, also aired a similar concern: 'It would be useful, for example, to think a bit about the meaning of those artificial constructs "output", "capital" and "labor" when they are measured over such long time periods (*the Cambridge–Cambridge debate and all that*)'.

The aggregation problem, in contrast, has never been discussed in any great depth at the textbook level, and while neoclassical economists working on constructing capital stocks have inevitably encountered, and accepted, the various problems, it has never been seen as insurmountable in either theoretical or applied work.[5] Notable exceptions, noted above, are Brown (1980) and Burmeister (1980) and, of course, the extensive work of Fisher (1992, 2005).

The short-run aggregate production function, holding capital constant, has also been widely used in macroeconomics, especially since the development of the aggregate supply–aggregate demand (AS/AD) model in the neoclassical synthesis. A key tenet of this neoclassical theory is that unemployment is a consequence of real wage rigidity. The model assumes the existence of an inverse relationship between employment and the wage rate, namely, the labour demand function, in turn derivea from the aggregate production function. The more recent New Classical real business-cycle models also depend on the aggregate production function and productivity shocks to explain fluctuations in employment.

These arguments show that the theoretical foundations of the aggregate production function are so flawed that there is little justification for using it, *even as an approximation*. Moreover, these problems first became apparent decades ago. Yet, Walters (1963a), for example, who had written one of the early definitive studies on cost and production functions that included a discussion of the aggregation problem, and is still worth reading today, could not avoid the temptation of estimating aggregate production functions (Walters, 1963b). As he put it: 'the theoretical foundations of the aggregate production functions give one grounds for doubting whether the concept is at all useful. Nevertheless, the temptation to discuss movements in indices of input and output in terms of such a function is difficult to resist. And there is no doubt that it is useful to rationalize the data along these lines' (Walters, 1963a, p. 425). It is somewhat difficult to reconcile the last sentence with the conclusions of his survey of production and cost functions (both published the same year), to say the least. Today, economists seem to be largely unaware of the seriousness of the aggregation problem.

Solow (1957, p. 312) argued that the aggregate production function is merely a (heroic) simplification and like any model will have unrealistic assumptions. As he put it: 'it takes something more than the usual "willing suspension of disbelief" to talk seriously of the aggregate production function', but, even so, he is willing to suspend disbelief. At the end of

---

[5] For example, Hulten (1980, p. 124) accepts that 'capital aggregation must therefore be regarded as an approximate, or as applying in exact form only under exceptional circumstances. Applied economists can either accept this unfortunate situation or try to work directly with a disaggregated form of their model'. But he then cites Fisher (1965) as saying that the problem may, in fact, be insoluble. Nevertheless, Hulten, *inter alios*, is one of the leading exponents of the growth-accounting approach, which assumes the existence of an aggregate production function together with the usual neoclassical conditions.

the day, the question is whether or not the aggregate production function provides a reasonable approximation to the underlying technology of an economy, notwithstanding all its underlying problems; and whether it provides useful insights into, say, the growth process. This does raise the question as to how we are to judge whether or not the insights that it supposedly provides have any verisimilitude. A standard defence of the aggregate production function, for example, compares capital reswitching to the anomalous case of the Giffen good in consumer theory, the existence of which has not led to the abandonment of the law of demand. This, however, largely begs the question as it is not clear whether capital reswitching is the rule or the exception. Simulation exercises suggest that perhaps it is the latter, but such results depend upon the exact structure of the simulation models used, and it is doubtful if they fully capture the complex production process of a modern economy. Moreover, others such as Sraffa, take this to be irrelevant – the problem is that one cannot work with a construct, such as the aggregate production function, that is *logically* flawed. The Giffen good is not a logical inconsistency in consumer theory.

The answer to why the production function continues to be widely used today seems to be that its estimation, ever since Douglas's work in the 1920s with Cobb and subsequently in the 1930s with other colleagues, generally, but not always, gives good statistical fits. Furthermore, the estimated output elasticities obtained by Douglas using cross-sectional data were often very close to the factor shares obtained from the national accounts, as predicted by the aggregate marginal productivity theory of factor pricing. As Solow once remarked to Fisher, 'had Douglas found labor's share to be 25 per cent and capital's 75 per cent instead of the other way around, we would not now be discussing aggregate production function' (cited by Fisher, 1971b, p. 305).

The good statistical fit that the aggregate production function can give was forcibly brought home to one of the authors (McCombie), who, while estimating the Verdoorn law in the 1970s at Cambridge, UK, constructed estimates of regional capital stocks for the US.[6] Almost as an afterthought, he used these to estimate a conventional Cobb–Douglas production function for the two-digit SIC manufacturing industries for the US states' cross-regional data. Given the prevailing view at Cambridge, UK, at that time (namely, that it had been conclusively proved that the concept of aggregate production function was logically untenable), it came as quite

---

[6]   The Verdoorn law is the relationship between the growth of industrial productivity and output and came to prominence in Kaldor's (1966) inaugural lecture as an explanation of the UK's slow rate of economic growth in the early postwar period. See McCombie et al. (2002).

a shock to find estimates of the output elasticities of labour and capital usually around 0.75 and 0.25, and R^2s of over 0.9. It immediately led to a careful check to see if an error in the estimation or the punching of the data on computer cards had been made; it had not. This was a puzzle at the time, as, given all the problems associated with the aggregate production function, these results seemed too good to be true. It was not until much later that he found the beginnings of a convincing answer to this conundrum, almost by serendipity, in the form of articles by Phelps Brown (1957) and Shaikh (1974, 1980).

But we are getting ahead of ourselves. In retrospect, McCombie's results merely confirmed the earlier cross-sectional results of Douglas (1948) and those of Hildebrand and Liu (1965). At about the same time, Moroney (1972) published a detailed neoclassical study estimating the production function using US state data that found similar good fits. In the early 1990s, something similar happened to Felipe, trying to estimate endogenous growth models using cointegration methods.

Time-series data do not always give good statistical fits to the aggregate production function, although adjusting the capital stock for the level of capacity utilisation generally improves the results and gives putatively plausible results. Douglas (1976, p.914), in reviewing his studies on the aggregate production function commented, 'a considerable body of independent work tends to corroborate the original Cobb–Douglas formula, but, more important, the approximate coincidence of the estimated coefficients with the actual shares received also strengthens the competitive theory of distribution and disproves the Marxian'.

Consequently, the defence of the use of the aggregate production function rests largely on a methodological instrumental argument. All models involve unrealistic assumptions; after all, as Joan Robinson once remarked, a map on a scale of one to one is of no use to anyone. What matters is the explanatory power of the model, which is taken to be synonymous with its predictive power – the symmetry thesis (Friedman, 1953). Wan (1971, p.71), for example, views the aggregate production function as an empirical law in its own right which is capable of statistical refutation, a view shared by Solow (1974). Ferguson (1969, p.xvii) explicitly made this instrumental defence with respect to the criticism about the measurement of capital as a single index in Cambridge capital theory controversies:

> Its validity is unquestionable, *but its importance is an empirical or an econometric matter* that depends upon the amount of substitution there is in the system. Until the econometricians have the answer for us, placing reliance upon [aggregate] neoclassical economic theory is a matter of faith. I personally have faith. (Emphasis added)

But all this does not explain *why* aggregate production functions generally give such good statistical results, especially in the light of Fisher's (2005, p. 490) warning:

> One cannot escape the force of these results [of the aggregation literature] by arguing that aggregate production functions are only approximations. While, over some restricted range of the data, approximations may appear to fit, good approximations to the true underlying technical relations require close approximation to the stringent aggregation conditions, and this is not a sensible thing to suppose.

The answer for cross-sectional data is to be partly found in an article by Phelps Brown (1957) 'The Meaning of the Fitted Cobb–Douglas Production Function', which ironically was published the same year as Solow's (1957) influential paper entitled 'Technical Change and the Aggregate Production Function'. Buried in Phelps Brown's paper is the argument that the regression estimates are not capturing any aggregate technological parameters of the economy (which almost certainly do not exist), but are merely picking up an underlying identity, namely, *that value added is, by definition, equal to the wage bill plus the total remuneration of capital.*

Theoretically, the aggregate production function represents a technological relationship and as such is a relationship between the output and inputs measured in *physical* terms. However, because of the problems of the heterogeneity of output and inputs, notably capital (but also labour, although it is often treated as being homogeneous), constant-price value measures have to be used. And therein lies the explanation of the good statistical fits. (Studies that actually use physical data, the so-called 'engineering production functions', are few and far between. See Wibe, 1984.)

There is an underlying accounting identity that holds for the ith firm and which is given by $V_i \equiv W_i + \Pi_i$, where V is constant-price value added, W is the total wage bill, and Π denotes total profits. This identity can also be written as $V_i \equiv w_i L_i + r_i J_i$, where w is the wage rate, L is the employment, r is the *ex post* or earned rate of profit and J is the constant-price value of the capital stock, usually calculated by the perpetual inventory method. The identity also holds for gross output, where the value of output also includes the cost of materials. Furthermore, it holds at any level of aggregation, that is, for a sector or for the national economy. In fact, the National Income and Product Accounts (NIPA) show how the economy's total output is divided between wages and profits (the operating surplus). There is no assumption or theory (for example, Euler's theorem) behind this identity. It is important to emphasise that throughout the book we use V and J to denote the constant-price value measures of output (value added) and the capital stock; while Q and K are the homogeneous physical measures of these variables.

This identity holds regardless of the state of competition, whether or not constant returns to scale prevail, and whether or not factors are paid their marginal products. In fact, it holds even if there is no well-defined production function at either the micro or aggregate level. One of Kaldor's (1961) stylised facts is that factor shares are constant over time. It is termed a stylised fact because while it is always possible to find exceptions to it, especially in the short run, these are rare. Constant shares can arise because firms pursue a constant mark-up pricing policy, for which there is a good deal of empirical evidence (Lee, 1998). They do not necessarily require an underlying Cobb–Douglas technology in physical terms, even if such a well-behaved production function actually exists. If we sum the individual firms' output arithmetically and, given that wages and the rate of profit are approximately constant across firms, we obtain for an industry the definition for value added that $V \equiv wL + rJ$, where $V = \sum V_i$, and so on. The aggregate factor shares are also likely to be roughly constant. (Solow (1958) has demonstrated that the aggregate factor shares may well be more stable than the individual sector shares.) It may be shown (see Chapter 3) that purely for arithmetical reasons, a close approximation to the linear accounting identity is given by:

$$V \equiv AL^a J^{(1-a)}, \tag{I.1}$$

where a and $(1-a)$ are the labour and capital shares in output, respectively, that is, $a = wL/V$ and $(1-a) = rJ/V$; and A equals $Bw^a r^{(1-a)}$, which is a constant provided that there is no variation in the wage rate or the profit rate across industries (or regions if we use spatial data). If equation (I.1) is estimated using cross-sectional or regional data with the coefficients unrestricted, then we are bound to get a near perfect statistical fit, and with the estimates of the coefficients equal to the factor shares. It is readily apparent that the equation is *formally identical* to the Cobb–Douglas 'aggregate production function' with constant returns to scale, and the 'output elasticities' equal to the observed factor shares, but it is not a production function. (If wages and the rate of profit show some variation, then this may bias the estimated parameters, although in practice this bias is likely to be small.) Thus the putative aggregate Cobb–Douglas production function will give a very close fit to the data, even though, for example, the aggregate production function may not exist, markets are not competitive and increasing returns to scale prevail.

The implications of this critique are far reaching. If good statistical fits to a functional form that resembles the Cobb–Douglas production function (or, indeed, a more flexible production function) can be obtained using aggregate data that merely track the underlying identity, then it is not possible to interpret the statistical evidence as supporting the view that the relationship that has been estimated represents the technical conditions of production (such as the aggregate elasticity of substitution).

However, even though Phelps Brown's article was published in a leading journal, namely, the *Quarterly Journal of Economics*, it had almost no impact on the economics profession. Simon (with Levy) six years later published a formalisation of what could be taken to be Phelps Brown's argument. Nevertheless, Simon and Levy (1963) themselves were not entirely sure whether or not this was the case, as Phelps Brown's argument was admittedly somewhat obscure. Later, Simon (1979b) generalised the argument to explain why estimations of aggregate production functions using time-series data also give such good results and he also showed that the critique holds for other production functions, such as the CES. He thought these criticisms sufficiently important to mention them explicitly in his Nobel prize lecture (Simon, 1979a), but the message still fell on deaf ears. Simon was deeply sceptical of the marginal productivity theory of factor pricing as his correspondence in the early 1970s with Solow, recently unearthed by Carter (2011b), shows. In this correspondence, Simon pointed out to Solow the damaging implications of the accounting identity. (See also Felipe and McCombie, 2011–12.) To the best of our knowledge, there have been only three textbooks that have considered the argument, and only in so far as it relates to the cross-sectional (regional) data. These are Cramer (1969), Intriligator (1978) and Wallis (1979), but even here the full implications of the critique seem to have escaped these authors, who were perhaps more concerned with technical econometric issues. Intriligator, for example, merely notes that the identity will bias the estimates towards constant returns to scale, but not that it totally undermines the justification of the estimation of the aggregate production function in the first place.

Independently, Shaikh (1974) published an important short note similarly generalising the argument for the Cobb–Douglas to time-series data. This was, unfortunately and erroneously, dismissed by Solow (1974) in a one-page rejoinder, which began 'Mr Shaikh is wrong pure and simple'. This probably explains why little notice was ever paid to the paper. Shaikh's (1980) convincing rejoinder was eventually published in a book and not in the original journal, the *Review of Economics and Statistics*, which is why it is probably generally overlooked. The 2005 symposium on the aggregate production function published by the *Eastern Economic Journal* clarifies many of these issues.

The argument concerning the accounting identity is deceptively simple, but these arguments made in the above articles are not the whole story. The criticism has also been subject to a number of serious misunderstandings and erroneous objections including Solow (1974, 1987) and Temple (2006, 2010). In this book, the critique is examined in some length, given its undoubted importance, and new arguments and evidence are presented that provide additional support for it. While in many cases attention is confined to the Cobb–Douglas for expositional ease, it is also shown that the critique applies to *all* aggregate production functions. *Moreover, it should also be stressed that even if there were no aggregation problems and output and capital could be accurately measured in value terms, the critique would still apply.* The only solution is to use physical magnitudes, and even then some insurmountable problems still remain, namely the correct specification of TFP and the level and rate of growth of technology.

Of course, macroeconomics abounds with identities, but these are explicitly recognised for what they are; namely, definitionally true relationships. Take the simple national expenditure identity, $Y \equiv C + I + G + Z$, where Y is national income, C is consumption, I is investment, G is government expenditure and Z is net exports. No one would regress the growth of income on the growth of these variables, find a remarkably close statistical fit with the estimate coefficients having highly significant *t*-ratios (which would depend solely on the degree of stability of the share of the relevant variable in income) and contend that these results confirm the Keynesian theory of the importance of the role of the growth of demand in determining the growth of income.

Solow (1957, p. 312) comments that 'the aggregate production function is only a little less legitimate a concept than, say, the aggregate consumption function'. But this overstates the case. Let us take the simplest specification of the consumption function, $C = C_0 + b_1 Y^d$, where C_0 is autonomous consumption and Y^d is private disposable income. However, there is also an underlying identity that relates consumption to savings and income, namely, $C \equiv S + Y^d$, where S is private savings. It would be pointless to estimate either this or the transformation $\ln C = b_2 \ln S + b_3 \ln Y^d$. One reason for estimating the consumption function is to determine the value and the degree of stability of the marginal propensity to consume. This is based on the assumption that autonomous consumption is roughly constant (or grows at roughly a constant rate when time-series data are used). But it is usually fully appreciated that there is an underlying identity.

There are, of course, aggregation problems in constructing the data by summing over the individuals' income and expenditure. But these are much less severe than aggregating the diverse and complex production processes implicit in the aggregate production function. There is also the important difference that theoretically the consumption function is a relationship between the deflated values of consumption and income. We are interested, for example, in estimating the increase in expenditure (in money terms) on consumption goods when disposable income increases by a certain value. However, in estimating the aggregate production function, as we have stressed and will discuss more fully in the book, we are using these value measures as a proxy for physical magnitudes. The parameters of the aggregate production function arise theoretically from engineering relationships, and the use of value data vitiates this interpretation of the estimates. Moreover, the aggregate production function has a number of implications, such as the marginal productivity theory of factor pricing and the distinction between the contribution to output growth of the growth of factor inputs and the rate of technical change, that are absent from the consumption function.

The content of this volume is as follows. Chapter 1, 'Some problems with the concept of the aggregate production function', summarises the problems underlying the concept of the aggregate production function, namely the aggregation problem and the Cambridge capital theory controversies. For reasons of space, these are dealt with only briefly.

Chapter 2, 'The aggregate production function: behavioural relationship or accounting identity?', outlines the central tenet of the book, namely that the aggregate production function is best regarded as nothing more than the mathematical transformation of an identity. This is the accounting identity that defines value added in terms of total wages and profits, or gross output when the value of intermediate inputs is taken into account. The question posed in the title of the chapter is, therefore, largely rhetorical. As we have mentioned, the basic tenet is deceptively simple, and in this chapter we set out the theoretical arguments in some detail. It is shown that it is not only the underlying identity that poses problems, but also the fact that constant-price value data are almost invariably used in estimating production functions. The problem is that while neoclassical production theory explicitly refers to a technological relationship between *physical* units of output, labour and capital (strictly speaking the flow of labour and capital services), applied work almost invariably relies on value measures which pose the insuperable problem. Because of the underlying identity, it can be shown theoretically that the best statistical fit to a supposed aggregate production function will be given when there are constant returns to scale and the 'output elasticities' equal the respective factor shares. Of course, many statistical estimates of supposed aggregate production functions do not give perfect statistical fits. However, from the accounting identity and the Kaldorian stylised facts we can show, a priori, why this is the case. Moreover, in some circumstances, we can determine the direction of bias of the estimated coefficients before a single regression has been run. It is also possible to find the transformation of the identity that will give a perfect fit to the data.

In this chapter we also deal briefly with some common objections that have been made to us (both in seminars and in some referees' reports) and show that they are all based on fundamental misunderstandings of the argument. Temple (2006, 2010) is the only person who has considered the argument in print in any detail. While he sees some merit in the argument, he does not find it convincing. However, his comments are not compelling but, nevertheless, are instructive to the extent that if they are implicitly shared by other economists, they go a long way to explain why the critique has not had the impact it should have had. We reflect briefly on his comments in this chapter, but save a detailed consideration until Chapter 12. In the appendix to Chapter 2, we present an example using regression analysis that illustrates empirically the problems posed by the accounting identity. We also show explicitly that the critique applies to more flexible functional forms including the CES and the translog. Temple erroneously maintains that it applies only to the Cobb–Douglas production function, and hence that the argument has to rely on the *ad hoc* assumption (actually a stylised fact), *inter alia*, that factor shares are constant.

One of the problems is that the researcher can, for the vast majority of the estimations of production functions, only use value data and hence has no idea of the true underlying technological relationships. No one would deny that production functions exist in the sense that the volume of physical output is determined by the inputs of materials, labour of various skills and the vast number of different types of capital. (There are, of course, other problems associated with those large sectors of the economy, such as finance, services, government and local authority services, where there is no measure of output totally independent of the inputs. But we ignore this complication for the moment.)

Production relationships are likely to be very complex and differ from firm to firm, even those making the same product or producing the same service. However, as we have already noted, the problem is that the researcher simply does not have these physical data. One way out of this impasse is to use simulated data where, by construct, we do know the hypothetical underlying technology. This has the advantage of allowing us to demonstrate explicitly the extent of the problem. This is what Chapter 3, 'Simulation studies, the aggregate production function and the accounting identity', does. We start with some simulations of our own. To begin with, we assume that there are 'true' underlying Cobb–Douglas micro-production functions expressed in physical terms, but where the output elasticities of labour and capital are constructed to be 0.25 and 0.75, respectively. In other words, they differ from labour's and capital's factor shares (0.75 and 0.25, respectively). However, if firms follow a mark-up pricing where the mark-up is 1.333, the statistical results produce erroneous estimates of the factor shares equal to the observed output elasticities. This is even true when the underlying micro-production functions exhibit increasing returns to scale or where there is no well-defined relationship between output, labour and capital. The chapter also considers a number of other simulation studies where the hypothetical data give good statistical fits to the data, even though the underlying micro-production functions are nowhere near being of the Cobb–Douglas form.

Chapter 4, '"Are there laws of production?" The work of Cobb–Douglas and its early reception', is a step back in time and as the title suggests looks at the early reception of Cobb and Douglas's initial work. Today, it is often forgotten just how critical was this reception of their early studies, on both econometric and other grounds. This reception was so hostile that Douglas admitted that he almost lost heart and nearly gave up entirely his work estimating aggregate production functions. This chapter, though, is more than just an exercise in the history of economic thought, as it is shown that the accounting identity critique goes back, albeit in a rudimentary form, many years.

Chapter 5, 'Solow's 'Technical change and the aggregate production function' and the accounting identity', and Chapter 6, 'What does total factor productivity actually measure? Further observations on the Solow model', continues this theme. Solow's (1957) paper, along with his companion theoretical paper (Solow, 1956),[7] proved to be immensely influential in the subsequent development of neoclassical growth theory. But it is not generally realised how shaky are the foundations of Solow's model. We discuss Shaikh's (1974) provocative Humbug critique, where he shows that the method Solow used to 'correct' the production function for technical change is essentially tautological. As such, the resulting specification cannot but give a near perfect fit to the data. Shaikh showed that this was the case even using a hypothetical dataset where the scattergram of productivity on the capital–labour ratio spells out the word 'HUMBUG'. Perhaps more importantly, Shaikh also shows that Solow's model is subject to the accounting identity critique using time-series data. Chapter 6 shows how the identity is responsible for the evidence that has been used by a leading growth theory textbook to justify the empirical relevance of the Solow model. This chapter shows that the high explanatory power of Solow's model is very misleading.

---

[7]   Swan (1956) also independently developed a similar model.

The next five chapters provide empirical examples of where the accounting identity is largely, or entirely, responsible for generating the results of the estimation of the theoretical model. The Mankiw–Romer–Weil model (1992) was an influential extension of the Solow model. Chapter 7, 'Why are some countries richer than others? A sceptical view of Mankiw–Romer–Weil's test of the neoclassical growth model' shows why. It will come as little surprise to learn that all that the statistical fits of the world aggregate production function are capturing are the underlying accounting identity and the Kaldorian stylised facts. Chapter 8, 'Some problems with the neoclassical dual-sector growth model' demonstrates how the accounting identity, together with the national expenditure identity, is responsible for the empirical results that suggest that there are substantial externalities to the growth of exports and/or government expenditure. In fact, the regression results, because of the accounting identity, can shed no light on the existence, or otherwise, of externalities.

Oulton and O'Mahony (1994) use a large database of UK manufacturing industries to test whether or not capital is special. By 'special', they mean whether the output elasticity of the capital stock exceeds its factor share. If this is the case, they argue that it lends credence to the endogenous growth model where the growth of capital has a substantial externality effect. They find it doesn't but this should come as no surprise, as Chapter 9, 'Is capital special? The role of the growth of capital and its externality effect in economic growth' shows, given the existence of the accounting identity and the fact that they are using value data. In Chapter 10, 'Problems posed by the accounting identity for the estimation of the degree of market power and the mark-up', we consider Hall's work, where he attempts to estimate the degree of market power using the aggregate production function and the Solow residual. Hall finds that the estimate of labour's output elasticity exceeds its observed factor share, which he interprets as evidence of market power. We know, a priori, that because of the accounting identity, Hall should not have found this discrepancy, and the intriguing question is why? The answer is that he assumes that technical progress occurs at a constant rate. From the identity we know that the rate of technical progress is nothing more than the growth of the weighted wage rate and the rate of profit, which has a strong cyclical component. This causes the estimate of the mark-up to exceed unity. The last example we look at is in Chapter 11, 'Are estimates of labour demand functions mere statistical artefacts?', which considers various estimations of the neoclassical labour demand functions. It is shown that the negative relationship between the logarithm of employment and the logarithm of the real wage is likewise driven by the underlying identity and has obvious policy implications.

These examples are drawn from previously published articles of the authors and we have condensed and somewhat simplified the various arguments for this volume. Consequently, the reader is invited to consult the originals for a more detailed analysis.

We can liken these chapters to the game of 'Where's Waldo?'. This is a children's game where the character Waldo in his distinctive red and white shirt is hidden in a picture among a large number of other colourful characters and the task is to find him. Our examples are, of necessity, eclectic, and we leave it to the reader, having read the book, to see if he/she can spot Waldo (the accounting identity that drives the estimates), in other papers that use the aggregate production function. We close the book with Chapter 12, 'Why have the criticisms of the aggregate production function generally been ignored? On further misunderstandings and misinterpretations of the implications of the accounting identity'. The chapter also includes a detailed discussion of the ancillary issue of the persuasiveness of those few criticisms of our arguments that have been voiced. We have yet to find any such critiques, including those of Temple (2006, 2010), in the least bit compelling – but we are, of course, content to let the reader make up his or her own mind.

We have decided not to add a chapter on what to put in place of the aggregate production function. We have discussed this question in a number of seminars and presentations. Answering this sixty-four thousand dollar question would in itself take another book or, rather, several books. Other approaches to growth that do not rely on a production function do exist, including case studies and the insights provided by economic historians such as Landes (1998). The aim of this volume is much more limited – it is merely to show that the need for an alternative approach is long overdue. In other words, the above discussion is what Lawson (2004) terms 'an exercise in under-labouring'; or as John Locke (1690) put it: 'removing some of the rubbish that lies in the way of knowledge' (cited by Lawson, 2004, p. 317). But as Kuhn (1962 [1970]) pointed out, one paradigm, no matter how logically or empirically flawed, is only abandoned if it is replaced by another paradigm. Nevertheless, as we have mentioned above, it is beyond the scope of this volume to discuss alternative approaches. We merely hope to have made the case for serious consideration to be given to alternative approaches.

1. Some problems with the aggregate production function

> The production function has been a powerful instrument of miseducation.
>
> (Joan Robinson, 1953–54, p. 81)

INTRODUCTION

The heart of the neoclassical theory of production and price theory is the concept of the plant, or firm, production function. In its simplest form it expresses the maximum or optimal amount of output that can be produced with usually two factors of production, capital and labour, measured in physical terms.

The problem of whether these individual micro-production functions can be aggregated to give an aggregate production function for the industry, or even the whole economy, is sometimes, but not often, alluded to in the literature. For example, Estrin and Laidler (1995, p. 134) note that, notwithstanding the problems of constructing unambiguous indices of the quantities of capital and labour services, 'the results of the two input/one output special case are both useful and often capable of being generalised, and are therefore well worth the reader's attention'. Although not mentioned, there is also the problem of aggregating individual production functions with different functional forms to give an aggregate production function. Generally, the same functional form, commonly the Cobb–Douglas, is assumed at both the micro- and the macroeconomic levels as if one could move smoothly between the different levels of aggregation with no problems.

Unfortunately, this is not the case. There is now a large technical literature that examines the conditions under which this aggregation is possible. The results of this work conclude that these conditions are so restrictive that, as Fisher (1969, 1992) who has done more work on this topic than most, they are unlikely to be satisfied in reality; with the consequence that aggregate production functions most likely 'do not exist'. A more acrimonious exchange over the existence or otherwise of a well-behaved aggregate production function occurred generally in the 1960s and 1970s in the so-called 'Cambridge capital theory controversies', so named because the protagonists were based largely at Cambridge, Massachusetts, and Cambridge, UK. The debate could be viewed simply as a subset of the more general aggregation problem, as Fisher (2005) regards it, or as a more fundamental clash of paradigms, as Harcourt (1976) viewed it. Whatever the view taken, the capital theory controversies cast further doubt on the existence of a well-behaved production function.

In this chapter, we present a very brief overview of the substantial issues involved. It must be stressed that in this literature the micro-production functions (whether the technology has fixed coefficients or allows substitutability between capital and labour) are assumed to be well defined and unproblematic. They are very simple representations when compared with the actual production processes that occur in the real world. For example, the large differences between firms in what Leibenstein (1966) termed 'X-efficiency' are almost never mentioned and are relegated to business or industrial economics. There are strong grounds for suspecting that there are unlikely to be well-defined production functions at the plant or office level, even if we have physical data for the inputs and the outputs.

Brown (1966, p.11) provides a defence for the use of the production function largely on instrumentalist grounds:

> The objection is raised that the production function is a fiction. This is sometimes expressed by the statements that engineers do not work within a production function framework, and businessmen do not consider production functions as such within the set of constraints on their decisions. Since the production function is indirectly related to the physical–technical aspects of production, it is not directly measurable, and since it is foreign to the world of common sense, it is a fiction fabricated by marginalist economists. In one sense this argument is valid. . . . Yet . . . the employment of production functions can be justified simply on the ground that it produces highly useful and verifiable hypotheses.

This book challenges this view.

THE AGGREGATION PROBLEM: WHAT IS IT AND WHY DOES IT MATTER?

The aggregation problem is concerned with the conditions under which it is possible to sum micro-production functions to give an aggregate relationship. This work shows that these conditions are so restrictive as to make the concept of the aggregate production function problematical in the extreme. An underlying assumption is that there are well-defined micro-production functions that can be expressed in a simple mathematical form. In other words, the fact that the output of commodities of goods or services is physically determined by the flow of inputs is uncontroversial. Intuitively, we may think of an engineer designing a production process for, say, an oil refinery. The plans will indicate the efficient physical production techniques and combinations of labour (production engineers, administrative staff and so on) and physical capital (pipelines, fractionating columns, cooling towers) at different stages of the production process. The design will be dependent upon the relative scale of output and the relative costs, together with the level of technology.

Writing the micro-production function as a metaphor, a simple mathematical functional form can be used:

$$Q = f(\,L_1, L_2, L_i, \ldots, K_1, K_2, K_j, \ldots, M_1, M_2, M_k), \tag{1.1}$$

where Q is the volume of homogeneous output measured in *physical* terms, and L, K and M are the flows of labour services, *physical* heterogeneous capital services (broadly defined to include buildings and so on), proxied by capital stocks and materials. For practical purposes, the metaphor for these complex production processes of the firm is given by the familiar equation for a production function: $Q = Af(L, K)$ where Q is the maximum amount of output (number of homogeneous 'widgets') that can be produced from any combination of L and K (where capital K is measured as number of homogeneous 'leets', to use Joan Robinson's term). In other words, there is a unique mapping from L and K to Q. A necessary assumption for aggregation is that the inputs are used optimally. But already a further simplification has been made. It is assumed that, A denotes the level of technology, assumed to grow exponentially over time, but which is not directly observable.[1]

There are two technical, or mathematical issues, at stake here. The first is: under what conditions can the individual measures of, especially, the capital stock and output, but also labour, be aggregated into a single index? The second issue is: under what conditions can the functional forms representing the individual micro-production functions be summed to give a single aggregate production function that reflects the underlying properties of the micro-production functions? The technical literature on this is quite complicated and we can do no more than give a flavour of the issues involved. An accessible discussion is to be found in Felipe and Fisher (2003, 2006).

The aggregation problem is important in order to understand why aggregate production functions are such problematic constructs. In theory, the

---

[1]   This may be modelled as a knowledge production function, as in endogenous growth theory, but we shall not consider it here for reasons of space. It does not affect our argument.

production function is a representation of how a commodity (for example, a chair) is made. Output (Q), labour (L) and capital (K), as was emphasised earlier, are measured in physical terms. The production function corresponding to the chair denoted by the superscript i is, for expositional ease, $Q_t^i = f(L_t^i, K_t^i)$. We assume that there are no material inputs. (This simplifies the exposition but does not significantly affect the argument.) Each commodity (or service) that an economy produces is made up using a different production process, that is, a different technology, and with different machines and workers (and possibly with other additional inputs, different in each case). As far back as the 1940s and 1950s (Klein 1946a, 1946b; Leontief, 1947a, 1947b; Nataf, 1948; and Solow, 1955–56), economists started inquiring about the conditions under which so-called 'micro-production functions' like the one above could be 'summed up' so as to yield the aggregate production function of the form $Q_t = A_t F(L_t, K_t)$ representing the aggregate technology. This production function is supposed to show how 'aggregate output', the sum of the individual outputs, namely, carrots, chairs, ships, banking services, oil and millions of other products and services, is made up by transforming the aggregates capital and labour through the production process.

In one of the first works on aggregation, Klein (1946a) used Cobb–Douglas micro-production functions. He suggested that an aggregate (or strictly, an average) production function and aggregate marginal productivity relations analogous to the micro functions could be derived by constructing weighted geometric means of the corresponding micro variables, where the weights are proportional to the elasticities for each firm. The elasticities of the macro function are the weighted average of the micro elasticities, with weights proportional to expenditure on the factor. The macro revenue is the macro price multiplied by the macro quantity, which is defined as the arithmetic average of the micro revenues (similar definitions apply to the macro wage bill and macro capital expenditure). Klein's treatment of the problem, however, was rejected altogether by May (1947). Walters (1963a, pp. 8–9) also noted that Kleinian aggregation over firms had some serious consequences. The definition of the macro wage bill (that is, the product of the macro wage rate times the macro labour) is $wL = \frac{1}{n}\sum_{i=1}^{n} w_i L_i$, where w_i and L_i are the wage rate and homogeneous labour employed in the ith firm, and $L = \prod_{i=1}^{n} L^{\alpha_i / \Sigma \alpha_i}$ is the definition of the macro labour input, a geometric mean, where α_i is the labor elasticity of the ith firm. In a competitive market, all firms have the same wage rate $w^* = w_i$ for all i. Substituting the macro labour into the definition of the macro wage bill, and substituting w^* for w_i yields $w = (w^* \Sigma L_i)/(n \prod_{i=1}^{n} L^{\alpha_i / \Sigma \alpha_i})$. This implies that the macro wage rate will almost always differ from the common wage rate of the firms (similar issues apply to the prices of output and capital). It is therefore difficult to interpret w and to see why it should differ from w^*.

Leontief (1947a, 1947b) dealt with aggregation of variables into homogeneous groups. Leontief's (1947a) theorem provides the necessary and sufficient conditions for a twice-differentiable production function whose arguments are all non-negative, to be expressible as an aggregate. The theorem states that aggregation is possible if and only if the marginal rates of substitution among variables in the aggregate are independent of the variables left out of it. For the three-variable function $g(x_1, x_2, x_3)$ Leontief's theorem says that this function can be written as $G[h(x_1, x_2), x_3]$ if and only if $\partial(g_1/g_2)/\partial x_3 \equiv 0$ where g_1 and g_2 denote the partial derivatives of g with respect to x_1 and x_2, respectively. That is, aggregation is possible if and only if the marginal rate of substitution between x_1 and x_2 is independent of x_3. In general, the theorem states that a necessary and sufficient condition for the weak separability of the variables is that the marginal rate of substitution between any two variables in a group be a function only of the variables in that group, and therefore independent of the value of any variable in any other group.

In the context of aggregation in production theory (in the simplest case of capital aggregation), the theorem means that aggregation over capital is possible if and only if the marginal rate of substitution between every pair of capital items is independent of labour. Think of the production function $Q = Q(k_1, \ldots, k_n, L)$. This function can be written as $Q = F(L, K)$, where $K = \varphi(k_1, \ldots, k_n)$ is the aggregator of capital, if and only if $\partial[(\partial Q/\partial k_i)/(\partial Q/\partial k_j)]/\partial L = 0$ for every $i \neq j$. That is, the theorem requires that changes in labour, the non-capital input, do not affect the substitution possibilities between the capital inputs. This way, the invariance of the intra-capital substitution possibilities against changes in the labour input is equivalent to the possibility of finding an index of the quantity of capital. This condition seems to be natural, in the sense that if it were possible to reduce the n-dimensionality of capital to one, then it must be true that what happens in those dimensions does not depend on the position along the other axes (for example, labour).

Note that Leontief's condition is for aggregation within a firm, or within the economy as a whole assuming that aggregation over firms is possible. Is Leontief's condition stringent assuming aggregation over firms? It will hold for cases such as brick and wooden buildings, or aluminium and steel fixtures. But most likely this condition is not satisfied in the real world, since in most cases the technical substitution possibilities will depend on the amount of labour. Think for example of bulldozers and trucks, or one- and two-ton trucks. In these cases no quantity of capital in general can be defined (Solow, 1955–56, p. 103).

Solow argued that there is a class of situations where Leontief's condition may be expected to hold. This is the case of three factors of production partitioned into two groups. For example, suppose $y_j = f^j(x_{0j}, x_j)$, $j = 1,2$ where x_j is produced as $x_j = g^j(x_{1j}, x_{2j})$, so that the production of y_j can be decomposed into two stages: in the first one x_j is produced with x_{1j} and x_{2j}, and in the second stage x_j is combined with x_{0j} to make y_j. An example of this class of situations is that x_{1j} and x_{2j} are two kinds of electricity-generating equipment and x_j is electric power. In this case, the g^j functions are capital index functions (Brown, 1980, p. 389).[2]

We immediately run into the problem that if Q and K are not measured in homogeneous units, then how do we aggregate heterogeneous measures? But let us pass this by for the moment and regard capital as being measured in common units of leets, and output as numbers of widgets. In this aggregation process, it is important to emphasise that the function F has to be what economists refer to as 'well behaved', that is, with positive and diminishing marginal products.

To understand what an aggregate production function is, one must understand what the aggregation problem involves. The issue is how economic quantities are measured, in particular those quantities that represent by a single number a collection of heterogeneous objects; in other words, what is the legitimacy of aggregates such as investment, GDP, labour and capital in the context of production theory?

Consider the following problem. Suppose we have two production functions $Q^A = f^A(K_1^A, K_2^A, L^A)$ and $Q^B = f^B(K_1^B, K_2^B, L^B)$ for firms A and B. Define $K_1 = K_1^A + K_1^B$, $K_2 = K_2^A + K_2^B$ and $L = L^A + L^B$ (where K refers to capital – two types – and L to labour which is assumed to be homogeneous). The problem is to determine whether and in what circumstances there exists a function $K = h(K_1, K_2)$ where the aggregator function $h(\bullet)$ has the property that:

$$G(K,L) = G[h(K_1, K_2), L] = \Psi(Q^A, Q^B) \qquad (1.2)$$

and the function Ψ is the production possibility curve for the economy.

It will be noted that above we have already assumed that a production function exists at the level of the firm. If an enterprise assigns the use of its various factors to different techniques of production so as to maximise output, then maximised output will depend only on the total amount of such factors, and that dependence can be written as a functional relation-

---

[2]   However, if there are more than two groups, Gorman (1959) showed that not only must the weak separability condition hold, but also each quantity index must be a function homogeneous of degree one in its inputs. This condition is termed 'strong separability'.

ship. However, if the outputs and inputs are measured in physical units, this is likely to be a very complex function form as in our example of the oil refinery above. However, whether firms do maximise output is another (empirical) question. Leibenstein (1966), as we mentioned above, provides the classic evidence that they do not, as does much of the business studies literature. See, for example, the seminal study of Cyert and March (1963 [1992]). This does not mean that one can necessarily aggregate over factors. This is just one part of the aggregation problem. The other one is aggregation over firms – aggregation where factors are not all efficiently assigned.

Fisher, among others, worked out in the 1960s, 1970s and 1980s very comprehensively different aspects of the problem (see the collected papers in Fisher, 1992). The conclusion is that the conditions under which aggregate production functions can be derived by aggregating micro-production functions are so stringent that it is difficult to believe that actual economies satisfy them. For example, a labour aggregate L (to aggregate workers of different types) will exist if, and only if, a given set of relative wages induces all firms to employ different types of identical workers in the same proportion. Note that this condition requires the complete absence of specialisation in employment. Similarly, where there are many outputs, an output aggregate will exist if and only if a given set of relative output prices induces all firms to produce all outputs in the same proportion. This condition requires the absence of specialisation in production: all firms must produce the same market basket of outputs differing only in their scale. And finally, aggregate production functions exist if and only if all micro-production functions are identical except for the capital-efficiency coefficient. It is important to note that these conditions are derived under the assumption of constant returns to scale. Outside this case, it is virtually impossible to derive aggregation conditions. Are these conditions true in the real world? It is highly implausible that they are. They mean that, for all practical purposes, aggregate production functions do not exist, as they are constructs without sound theoretical foundations.

To see what the aggregation problem involves, consider the following simple case. If one could simply add the machines, and the exponents of the production functions were the same across firms, then we could construct an aggregate production function provided that certain optimising conditions are assumed. It is useful to digress briefly on this point. Consider two firms each exhibiting a Cobb–Douglas production function with identical exponents, and assume for the moment that capital is homogeneous (all are heroic and implausible assumptions, to say the least):

$$Q_1 = AL_1^\alpha K_1^{(1-\alpha)}, \tag{1.3}$$

$$Q_2 = AL_2^\alpha K_2^{(1-\alpha)}. \tag{1.4}$$

The crucial assumption is that *aggregate* output is optimised so that the maximum level of aggregate output (Q^*) as well as the optimised wage rate (w^*) and profit rate (r^*) are obtained. If we did not impose this condition, and we summed arithmetically, we would have:

$$Q = Q_1 + Q_2 = A(L_1^\alpha K_1^{(1-\alpha)} + L_2^\alpha K_2^{(1-\alpha)}), \tag{1.5}$$

which is a linear homogeneous production function, but is *not* a Cobb–Douglas. Moreover, it is not really an *aggregate* production function as the various inputs enter into the function separately.

Therefore, it is also assumed that the individual firms are technically efficient. This assumption implies that for each individual firm:

$$\frac{\partial Q_i^*}{\partial L_i} = w^* = \alpha \frac{Q_i^*}{L_i} \qquad (i = 1, 2) \tag{1.6}$$

$$\frac{\partial Q_i^*}{\partial K_i} = r^* = (1 - \alpha)\frac{Q_i^*}{K_i}. \tag{1.7}$$

Let us assume that the output of firm 1 is some arbitrary multiple (n) of the output of firm 2, that is, $Q_1^* = nQ_2^*$. As $w_1^* = w_2^*$ and $r_1^* = r_2^*$, it follows from equations (1.3) and (1.4) that $L_1 = nL_2$ and $K_1 = nK_2$. This is not a surprising result, as faced with a common set of factor prices, the two firms will have the same capital–labour ratios. If we now arithmetically sum the two micro-production functions, we obtain:

$$Q^* = Q_1 + Q_2 = A(1 + n)^\alpha L_1^\alpha (1 + n)^{(1-\alpha)} K_1^{(1-\alpha)}$$

$$= AL^\alpha K^{(1-\alpha)}, \tag{1.8}$$

where $L = (1+n)L_1$ and $K = (1+n)K_1$. This is now an aggregate Cobb–Douglas production function. This merely demonstrates why in practice we should *not* expect to find that an aggregate Cobb–Douglas production function exists, even if there are well-defined micro Cobb–Douglas production functions.

First, the derivation above depends on the assumption of competitive markets and the fact that inputs are efficiently allocated *between* firms as well as used technically efficiently *within* the firm. This is unlikely to occur given the presence of oligopolistic market structures and that individual firms are likely to be subject to substantial

X-inefficiencies. Second, it is implausible that firms have identical production functions.

Alternatively, from equations (1.3) and (1.4) we can calculate the geometric mean of the two firms' production functions as:

$$\sqrt{Q_1 Q_2} = A (\sqrt{L_1^\alpha L_2^\alpha})(\sqrt{K_1^{(1-\alpha)} K_2^{(1-\alpha)}}), \tag{1.9}$$

and measure total output as:

$$Q = 2\sqrt{Q_1 Q_2} = AL^\alpha K^{(1-\alpha)}, \tag{1.10}$$

where $Q = 2\sqrt{Q_1 Q_2}$, $L = 2\sqrt{L_1 L_2}$ and $K = 2\sqrt{K_1 K_2}$ and which may
be generalised to n firms. However, output and input data for individual
products or firms are not calculated in, say, the national income and
product accounts or the census of production in this way.

Consequently, to summarise, there are a number of reasons for anticipating that the aggregate Cobb–Douglas production function will not
give a good fit to the generated data. First, the exponents of the individual
Cobb–Douglas micro-production functions differ. Second, capital is firm
specific and not allocated optimally between firms. Third, the heterogeneity of the capital stock means that an index of capital has to be constructed, with the attendant aggregation problems. Moreover, the data are
summed arithmetically to give the aggregate variables.

Finally, we have the intractable problem that for much of the service
sector there are no unambiguous physical or indeed constant-price value
measures of output – just think of the health service, education, government administration, defence and so on.

Wilson (2009) provides a test of the Leontief–Solow–Fisher conditions
for the existence of a single aggregate capital stock, for any unit of production (firm, industry, economy), formed of separate quantities of heterogeneous capital. Wilson focuses on the relationship between heterogeneous
capital services and productivity at the firm level. The paper first derives
an empirical, firm-level production function specification incorporating
heterogeneous capital services *based on standard neoclassical production
theory*.

Wilson then directly tested the Leontief–Solow–Fisher conditions for a
single aggregate capital stock. The ability to express a firm's total capital
services with a single measure, even if that measure weights heterogeneous
capital goods by their relative marginal products, requires that individual
capital services each be weakly separable with labour (Solow, 1955–56)
and that their services be expressed in common units (Fisher, 1965). These

two conditions together require that different capital services be perfectly substitutable. These conditions have long been viewed by many economists as unrealistic. Solow himself, referring to the first of the two, commented that it 'will not often be even approximately satisfied in the real world' (1955–56, p. 103).

Wilson's results strongly rejected both conditions. First, he found strong evidence of complementarities and substitutabilities between capital types. In fact, there seems to be a particular pattern in these complementarities and substitutabilities: using any reasonable division of types of capital into 'high-tech' and 'low-tech' categories, the data indicate that high-tech capital goods tend to be complementary with low-tech capital goods, and substitutable with other high-tech capital. He also found complementarities and substitutabilities between a number of capital types and labour. For instance, software was found to be especially labour saving, while general-purpose machinery and trucks were especially labour augmenting.

It is important to emphasise that the aggregation problem does not deny that output and inputs are linked. Certainly, a chair is made with labour, capital and intermediate materials. And we are not saying either that aggregate output (Q) does not exist when measured in constant-price value terms. Aggregate output is the sum of private consumption, investment, government expenditures and net exports (from the demand side of the economy). Rather, the implication of this discussion is that the representation of an economy's aggregate technology as $Q_t = F(L_t, K_t)$ is fictitious. There is no such a thing as the physical output of the economy (Q) from the point of view of neoclassical production theory, that is, a function that transforms aggregate capital (K) and aggregate labour (L) into aggregate output (Q).

It is instructive to quote Fisher (2005, pp. 489–90) on the conclusions that can be drawn from this work:

> Briefly, an examination of the conditions required for aggregation yields results such as:
>
> - Except under constant returns, aggregate production functions are unlikely to exist at all.
> - Even under constant returns, the conditions for aggregation are so very stringent as to make the existence of aggregate production functions in real economies a non-event. This is true not only for the existence of an aggregate capital stock but also for the existence of such constructs as aggregate labour or even aggregate output.
> - One cannot escape the force of these results by arguing that aggregate production functions are only approximations. While, over some restricted range of the data, approximations may appear to fit, good approximations

to the true underlying technical relations require close approximation to the stringent aggregation conditions, and this is not a sensible thing to suppose.

In retrospect, these conclusions are hardly surprising. Take a simple example, the retail sector and the production function of a supermarket. Capital includes the structures, in other words, the buildings. If one were to increase the size of the building by a certain fraction, does it make sense to ask the question: how many check-out workers could be saved? Consider, a check-out till. The process of registering the cost of the purchases is clearly fixed technology – one check-out worker per till. But now technology has developed so that there are automated check-out tills, so there is technology that makes the elasticity of substitution between the check-out machine and the cashier infinite. Yet both procedures are used due to customer preferences, so even in this very narrow case there are 'production' processes producing identical output services, but with very different elasticities of substitution. So what sense does an aggregate elasticity of substitution between check-out machines and cashiers make in even this limited case? Even the smallest plant or office is likely to consist of a range of techniques with different elasticities of substitution and hence there are problems of aggregation even here.

THE CAMBRIDGE CAPITAL THEORY CONTROVERSIES

While the aggregation problems deal with issues aggregating both inputs (of all types) and production functions at different levels, the scope of the Cambridge debates is different. The Cambridge capital theory controversies, as the name suggests, were concerned with the theoretical problems of aggregating heterogeneous individual capital goods into a single index that could be taken as a measure of 'capital' as a factor input. Perhaps a useful and clarifying way to think about the Cambridge debates and the aggregation problem is to consider whether the problem of measuring capital relates to the interdependence of prices and distribution (the Cambridge–Cambridge debates), or whether it emerges out of the need to justify the use of the neoclassical aggregate production function in building theoretical models, and in empirical testing (the aggregation problem). Both problems can be present at once, of course, but they are not the same. Also, the Cambridge debates extended to other macro debates, such as the determinants of the interest rate, the causality between savings and investment, and so on, which we do not deal with here.

The debate started in earnest in the 1950s, and went through much of the 1960s and up to the mid-1970s, although its origins can be traced back to the Classical economists. The outcome was that it was agreed that no such index could be satisfactorily constructed (Harcourt, 1972; Cohen and Harcourt, 2003, 2005). The debate further showed that, when comparing steady-state economies, there is no necessary inverse monotonic relationship between the rate of profit and the capital–labour ratio, as in the neoclassical schema, outside of the restrictive one-sector model. In other words, the standard results from the aggregate production function as taught in the introductory textbooks could not be generalised to a multi-sector world. The main results are referred to as 'reswitching' and 'capital reversing'.

There is not space to go into the Cambridge capital theory controversies in detail here.[3] In this book, we are primarily interested in the problems affecting the use of the aggregate production function and hence our attention is primarily focused on the problems posed by the Cambridge controversies for the aggregate production function, *per se*, rather than the wider methodological implications.

The Problem of Measuring Capital

The problems of the measurement of capital had been known to the Classical economists (for example, Ricardo, 1821; Wicksell, 1893), but it was not until the early 1950s that Joan Robinson began to ask some awkward questions concerning the meaning and measurement of capital that the issue became prominent. It was her 1953–54 article 'Production Function and the Theory of Capital' that largely set the scene for the subsequent capital theory debate.

Joan Robinson was particularly critical of the use of the aggregate production function and the marginal productivity theory of distribution to determine factor returns and hence distributive shares, using what we may call the John Bates Clark neoclassical parable. The two awkward

---

[3]   They have been chronicled by Harcourt (1972), Cohen and Harcourt (2003, 2005), Pasinetti and Scazzieri (2008), and Lazzarini (2011), all of whom find the Cambridge, UK arguments convincing, and by Bliss (1975) and Bliss in Bliss et al. (2005) who found them less so. Recent assessments also are provided by Birner (2002), who provides both a survey of the more recent developments and a methodological assessment. Bliss et al. (2005) is the definitive three-volume collection of 77 of the key articles on the subject. Dow (1980) and Cohen (1984) provide methodological assessments of why the outcome of the debate failed to have any lasting effect on the economics profession. After the mid-1970s, the impact of the Cambridge capital theory controversies waned: the economics profession lost interest and it was business as before.

questions that Robinson asked were as follows. First, in what units is (aggregate) capital to be measured if it is to be used, along with labour and the level of technology, within the confines of the aggregate production function to determine the level of output? Second, is it possible to find a measure of the value of capital that is independent of the way output is distributed between the factors of production, labour and capital? If the aggregate neoclassical approach needs the rate of profit (or what comes to the same thing, the rate of interest in long-run equilibrium) to construct an index of capital, as Robinson argued it does, how can we use this 'measure' in the form of capital's marginal product to determine the rate of return to capital? For Robinson (1956), these were not rhetorical questions and her *Accumulation of Capital* is an attempt to find an answer.

One way to measure the capital stock could be to calculate its net present value. If the returns to a machine measured in monetary units were known, then its net present value could be estimated as the discounted stream of its net earnings. But this was not a satisfactory answer to Robinson's question, as it is necessary to begin by taking the rate of interest (the discount rate) as given, which is precisely what she wished to determine. There is a lack of causality which Cambridge, UK, took to be important: in order to determine the rate of profit, it is necessary to know the value of capital, but to determine the value of capital, it is necessary to use the rate of interest.

Rather than this 'forward-looking' measure of capital, capital goods could be valued by their cost of production. One approach, Robinson (1953–54, p. 82) suggested, was to measure capital in terms of wage units, 'that is, in effect, to measure their cost in terms of a unit of standard labour'. But there are problems here: labour makes machines with other machines and so 'the cost of capital includes the cost of capital goods, and since they must be constructed before they can be used, part of the cost of capital is interest over the period of time between the moment when work was done in constructing capital goods and the time they are producing a stream of output' (p. 82).

The response of the neoclassical economists to this line of argument was that Robinson had failed to understand the nature of a simultaneous equation system. This was the view of, for example, von Weizsacker (1971, pp. 97–8) and Stiglitz (1974). Harcourt's (1976) response was brief and to the point. It was that it is difficult to see how anyone familiar with the work of Joan Robinson, Kaldor and Sraffa could argue that they did not know about simultaneous equations:

> When marginal products are spoken of as key determinants of equilibrium values, what is meant is that the relationships which are being partially differentiated in order to obtain the marginal products need to be technical

relationships, formally akin to psychological ones like utility functions, so that they exist *before*, and are *independent* of, the equilibrium values which are the solutions of the sets of simultaneous equations. (The equalities (or inequalities) themselves between (say) marginal products and equilibrium prices are characteristics of the equilibrium solutions. They are therefore the *consequences* of the ultimate causes – preferences, technical endowments, and maximising behaviour. Yet even though there has been looseness of expression, the thrust of the argument is perfectly clear.) Clearly, the marginal product of 'social' or aggregate 'capital' cannot be fitted into this mould because it cannot be measured in a unit which is independent of distribution and prices. (Ibid. p. 37, omitting a footnote, emphasis in the original)

Joan Robinson, at least in the early years, was not nihilistic in her conclusions as to the possible usefulness of the aggregate production function. Although she argued that it 'has a very limited reference to actual problems', Robinson (1953–54, p. 100) did concede the 'platitude' that if in a country 'more capital had been accumulated in the past relative to the labour available for employment, the level of real wages would probably have been higher and the technique of production more mechanized, and, given the amount of capital accumulated, the more mechanised the technique of production, the smaller the amount of employment would have been', a concession Sen (1974, p. 334) readily seized on.

There is a methodological parting of the ways over the aggregate production function. The neoclassical path takes the view that any theory is a necessary abstraction from reality, with the assumptions emphasising the key factors with which the model is concerned. Different models may be needed to analyse different aspects of a class of problems. Indeed, as Joan Robinson herself said, a map on a scale of one to one is of no use to anybody. Just as Newtonian physics is only an approximation, it is perfectly satisfactory for introductory mechanics courses, so 'similarly, an aggregative growth model may do perfectly well in explaining long-term movements in certain macroeconomic variables' (Stiglitz, 1974, p. 901). This is adopting an almost instrumentalist view of science, where predictive ability is the deciding criterion of the usefulness of a theory.

The second path argues that one cannot have a theory that is logically flawed. This was the view of, for example, Sraffa who remarked at the 1958 Corfu conference on capital theory (Lutz and Hague, 1961, p. 305) 'theoretical measures [require] absolute precision'. If a theory can be shown under some circumstances to have perverse results, then one cannot continue as if these were non-existent or empirically trivial.

Samuelson's Surrogate Production Function and Reswitching and Capital Reversing

As noted above, the problems of the valuation and measurement of capital had been debated since the time of the Classical economists. However, it was paradoxically Samuelson's (1962) attempt to show that the one-sector aggregate production function could be viewed as an acceptable approximation, or 'parable', to a world where there are heterogeneous capital goods that led to the debate in the mid-1960s that attracted the attention of the wider community of economists. Ironically, the eventual outcome was the opposite of that put forward by Samuelson.

Samuelson posed the following question: given the properties of the one-sector aggregate production function with homogeneous physical capital goods, could it be a useful approximation, or parable, for a more complex set of underlying technical relationships with heterogeneous capital goods? For a short time, Samuelson thought he had succeeded in proving that this was indeed the case with his 1962 paper on the surrogate production function. A core relationship of his analysis was the *factor–price frontier* or the *wage–profit rate frontier* and so it is useful to derive it in the context of the one-sector model.

The aggregate production function (assuming, for expositional ease, no technical change) is theoretically given by:

$$Q = F(L, K), \tag{1.11}$$

where Q, L, K are the numbers of units of output, identical employees, and the physical units of capital (measured in, say, 'leets'), respectively. For consistency, L and K should be the flow of services provided by the stocks of labour and capital, but, as is usual in the literature, we shall assume that they are in fixed proportion to L and K and ignore the complication.

We may write the aggregate production function, under the assumption of constant returns to scale, in per capita terms as:

$$q = f(1, k), \tag{1.12}$$

where $q = Q/L$ and $k = K/L$. As we are dealing with a one-sector model, the value of the capital is in homogeneous physical units, but the implicit assumption is that this can also uniquely represent heterogeneous capital goods valued by their rental prices, and hence expressed in value terms.

Whether this is the case or not is at the heart of the capital theory controversies. From the usual optimisation assumptions, the optimal capital–labour ratio will occur where the isocost line, namely, $q = w + rk$, is tangent to the production function. In Figure 1.1(a), for the capital–labour ratio k_1, this occurs at point a. It can be seen that as the wage rate falls and the rate of profit increases, the point of tangency moves along the production function to the right. For example, at the higher capital–labour ratio, k_2, this occurs at point b. It follows that there is a monotonic inverse relationship between the rate of profit and the capital–labour ratio (see Figure 1.1(b)) and a positive monotonic relationship between the wage rate and the capital–labour ratio (Figure 1.1(c)).

The isocost line can be expressed as the linear equation, $w = q - rk$, which represents the wage–profit rate trade-off. At point a in Figure 1.1(d), the capital–labour ratio is k_1 and the wage–profit rate trade-off is $w_1 = q_1 - r_1 k_1$. This is depicted again by the line AA. As the capital–labour ratio increases, it can be seen from Figure 1.1(a), the rate of profit falls, and so a *linear* wage–profit rate trade-off at the greater capital–labour ratio k_2 is given by the line BB in Figure 1.1(d). Consequently, the envelope of the wage–profit rate trade-off, or the wage–profit rate frontier, is the *concave* function depicted in Figure 1.1(d).

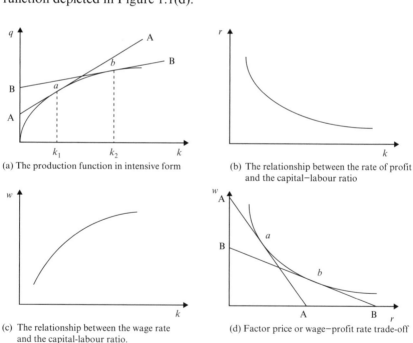

(a) The production function in intensive form

(b) The relationship between the rate of profit and the capital–labour ratio

(c) The relationship between the wage rate and the capital-labour ratio.

(d) Factor price or wage–profit rate trade-off

Figure 1.1   The one-sector aggregate production function

The slope of the wage–profit rate frontier at any point is given by the capital–labour ratio, and the measure of the quantity of capital does *not* alter with variation in the wage and rate of profit. In other words, the index of capital behaves as if capital were measured in physical units of 'leets'.

At the risk of repetition, we may summarise the results as follows:

- The rental price of capital (and rate of profit) declines with an increase in the capital–labour ratio, but at a decreasing rate, because of diminishing returns.
- The wage rate increases with an increase in the capital–labour ratio, but at a decreasing rate.
- From the above two results, it follows that there is an *inverse* relationship between the wage rate and the rental price of capital (and rate of profit) which is the factor-price frontier (or the wage–profit trade-off).
- At any point on the factor-price frontier, the slope of the curve is equal to the capital–labour ratio.
- The elasticity of the factor-price frontier equals the ratio of the factor shares (and the output elasticities).[4]

These results hold for a one-sector model and the key question is whether or not they can be generalised to the case where there are heterogeneous capital goods. In other words, can the results from the one-sector model act as an approximation, or a parable, for the more complex underlying technology? This is what Samuelson (1962) thought, erroneously as it turned out, that he had shown.

Samuelson assumed that a good can be made from a single technique 1, which comprises two separate production relationships. The first is for the production of the consumption good, say, corn which is produced by a specific capital good, for example, a plough and labour. The second, again with a fixed-coefficients technology, produces the plough using labour and ploughs. But technique 2 could use an entirely different capital good. As Samuelson put it 'any one capital good, call it alpha, looks entirely different from a second beta capital good. Thus, think of one as a plough; another as a machine tool or loom, or as a much more "mechanized" plough. No alchemist can turn one capital good into another' (p. 196).

---

4   To these results, Cohen and Harcourt (2005, p. xxxi) add that the approach grounds the 'return on capital (rate of interest) in the natural or technical properties diminishing marginal productivity of capital or roundabout production' and it explains 'the distribution of income between capitalists and labourers from a knowledge of relative factor scarcities/supplies and marginal products'.

It is assumed that there is perfect competition, and so the wage rate and the rate of profit are the same in both sectors. Instead of using two prices, one for corn and the other for machines, the price of corn is chosen as the numéraire and is set equal to unity. The equations for the two techniques of production may be solved to give a single relationship between the real wage rate and the profit rate. In other words, it is a *single* wage–profit rate trade-off. (See, for example, Jones (1975, ch. 4) and Lazzarini (2011, ch. 3) for formal expositions of this derivation.)

For expositional ease (but it actually turns out to be crucial for the results), Samuelson assumed that the capital intensities were the same in the consumption and the machine-good industry, which gives a *straight-line* wage–profit rate trade-off for each technique. Thus, if we take the wage–profit rate ratios for the various techniques, 1, 2, 3, and so on, we find that the envelope of these lines (the wage–profit rate trade-offs) takes a concave form similar to that given by the one-sector model. Consequently, if a continuum of different techniques exists, then we have arrived at the same predictions as the one-sector aggregate production which incorporates malleable homogeneous capital. Hence, this provides the rationale for Samuelson's contention that the aggregate production function may be seen as a parable for an economy with heterogeneous goods.

For a brief period, Samuelson was seen as providing a compelling justification for the use of the simple aggregate production function. Even if we use discrete and different technologies and capital goods, in the steady state high wage rates are associated with high capital–labour ratios. Moreover, if a technique is profitable at a given rate of interest, but becomes unprofitable at a lower rate of interest, it can never become profitable again at an even lower rate of interest.

The problem is that Samuelson's result depends on the assumption that both sectors making up the single technique have *identical* capital–labour ratios. This means that, to all intents and purposes, we are still in a one-commodity world. As soon as any attempt is made to generalise this assumption, the neoclassical parable breaks down. The factor-price frontier may be concave from below, or above, and two factor-price frontiers may intersect twice. In particular, a technique may be the most profitable at a high rate of interest and a low rate of interest, while another technique may be the most profitable at intermediate interest rates – a phenomenon known as 'reswitching'.

This is shown in Figure 1.2. The top panel of the figure shows the wage–profit rate trade-off for two techniques, 1 and 2, given by the lines CC and DD, respectively. It can be seen that at low and high interest rates, technique 1 with the wage–profit rate line CC dominates, whereas at intermediate interest rates, technique 2 with the convex from above wage–profit

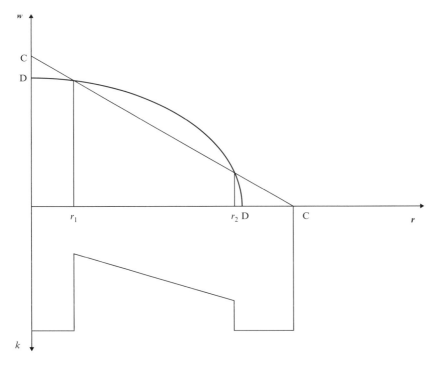

Figure 1.2   Reswitching and capital reversing

line DD is the more profitable. It is not linear because the capital intensities differ between the two sectors comprising technique 2. The lower half
of the figure shows the relationship between the value of the capital stock
and the rate of interest. In the case of technique 1, it may be seen that the
capital–labour ratio expressed in value terms is constant. However, with
technique 2, the value of the capital–labour ratio (and hence the value of
capital) varies as the rate of profit changes and there are discontinuities
at r_1 and r_2. Capital reversing occurs because as the rate of profit falls and
the economy switches at profit r_1 from techniques 1 and 2, so the value of
the given physical stock of capital falls. However, at the switch point r_2 the
value of the capital stock now *increases*, reverting back to its original value
(Figure 1.2, lower panel). In other words, this example is at variance with
the results of the simple aggregate production function.

The importance of reswitching was really brought home when Levhari
(1965) thought that he proved Samuelson's conjecture that reswitching cannot take place in a situation where every output requires every
other output as an input, either indirectly or directly, into its production

process. A symposium was held in 1965 to consider Levhari's results with the papers published in the *Quarterly Journal of Economics* in 1965. Levhari's conclusion, however, was shown to be false, except under a few special circumstances (see Birner, 2002, ch. 7 for a clear exposition).

Controversies often never seem to come to an unambiguous and conclusive end and this is the case with the Cambridge capital theory controversies. This is notwithstanding the summing up by Samuelson (1966), where he conceded the logical validity of reswitching.[5]

In the immediate aftermath of the *Quarterly Journal of Economics* symposium, there were further attempts to defend the neoclassical aggregate production function. See, for example, Ferguson and Allen (1970), Gallaway and Shukla (1974), Sato (1975) and Garegnani (1976). Burmeister (1977) also attempted to rescue the neoclassical position using the concept of the 'regular economy' but see Baldone's (1984) criticism. Ahmad (1991) and Birner (2002) give detailed expositions of these arguments. The latter views much of this subsequent literature as 'proof driven' with little or no economic content.

The final neoclassical response was to shift the debate into general equilibrium theory, which lies at the core of the neoclassical theory and explains prices in terms of preferences, endowments, technology and scarcity. No aggregation of capital is required. 'But the switch to general equilibrium, rather than saving the neoclassical parables, abandoned them for simultaneous equation price systems, and correct statements about factor returns being equal to or measured by disaggregated marginal products' (Cohen and Harcourt, 2003, p. 206).

There have been attempts to determine by simulations the likelihood of reswitching occurring. This, ironically, is almost entirely the preserve of the critics of the neoclassical analysis. For example, Pertz (1980) attempted to show that the likelihood of reswitching progressively declines as the number of sectors in an economy increases, but Ahmad (1991) finds no support for this – if anything, the converse is true. Mainwaring and Steedman (2000), in a simple two-sector single product scheme, find by means of simulation analysis that the probability of reswitching is very low, less than 1 per cent, although their method of determining this has been criticised by Salvadori (2000). Zambelli's (2004) simulation results confirm that the likelihood of reswitching is 'sporadic', but he finds that

---

[5]   In this article, he provides a very neat example of the causes of reswitching using a simple model for the production of a good using two different techniques that consist solely of different amounts of labour, which are applied at different periods of time. He shows that the same technique has the cheaper cost of production at both high and low interest rates, but not at intermediate values. (See also Cohen and Harcourt, 2003, pp. 202–3.)

the likelihood that the capital–labour ratio is negatively related to rate of profit (that is, there is no capital reversing) is only 40 per cent. He concludes that 'for the artificial economies described here, the results indicate there is a-not-too-small [world] for which the neoclassical postulates, in particular the "real Wicksell effect" . . . do not hold' (p. 115).

Petri (2000) notes that the probability of reswitching occurring in simulation models depends very much on the (arbitrary) underlying assumptions:

> There is the danger that, by changing them, one may obtain nearly any result. . . . Still, if one believes the kind of exercises attempted here, then the message appears to be that the Samuelson–Hicks–Garegnani model supplies no basis at all for believing that the likelihood of 'perverse' switches can be considered negligible, rather the opposite. (pp. 23–4)

Han and Schefold (2006) use input–output tables for the OECD countries to test empirically the possibility of reswitching. They find that the existence of at least three switch points between two wage curves is negligible; it occurs only 0.73 per cent of the time. This would, at face value, seem to confirm the Giffen good critique of the reswitching debate – it may be theoretically correct, but of sufficient minor importance empirically that it does not invalidate the use of the surrogate production function as a good approximation to the underlying production technology of a firm or economy.

Gandolfo (2008) in a comment on Schefold's (2008) application of the surrogate production function to the CES makes a number of important points concerning the Cambridge critique, the use of input–output tables and the aggregate production function (in this case the CES). First, he questions the assumption made by both parties that the underlying techniques are linear and perfect competition prevails, which is certainly not the case for many production processes. Once the assumption of perfect competition is dropped, then the assumption that the rate of interest is identical to the rate of profit becomes untenable. The rate of interest is a component of the cost of production and prices are no longer determined as in the standard Sraffian model.

Gandolfo makes the further point that all these models assume that there can be substitutability both *ex ante* and *ex post* where, once a technique is installed, there is no substitutability. He comments:

> [T]he data used, being based on real-life observations, presumably include nonlinearities and non-uniformity, as well as putty-clay phenomena. If so, they are not suitable to either confirm or disprove the theory behind the controversy. In particular, I feel that the debate on reswitching and reverse capital

deepening makes sense only *ex ante*. *Ex post*, changes in the real wage rate (for example determined by bargains between firms and trade unions) do not lead to changes in technique, but to changes in the rate of profit, at least in the short run. (p. 799)

Consequently, while the use of the actual (rather than hypothetical) input–output tables may seem to have the advantage of being more realistic, care must be taken in interpreting the results. In fact, this comes to the same conclusion as empirical estimations of aggregate production functions using value data, which also have been used to justify their continued use. However, the input–output approach shares the same limitations as estimates of the aggregate production function. The input–output table is a snapshot in time of the various flows between industries, measured in *value* terms. The data include the value of materials, wages and profit and there are no prices associated with the tables, just aggregate price deflators. Furthermore, the use of value data in the input–output tables as proxies for the technical coefficients of production, which are *assumed* to be fixed, is not an innocuous procedure. These 'coefficients' will change with changes in wages and the rate of profit. The justification by Han and Schefold (2006, p. 750) for using monetary values is not convincing. They argue that as distribution and relative prices change little at a constant rate of profit 'monetary coefficients do reflect physical structure'. It is similar to the implicit assumption in the neoclassical production function that one can move smoothly from output and capital in terms of physical magnitudes (which is the correct specification) to one where they are measured in value terms. Indeed, it takes but a small step to argue that the good fits often obtained by estimating aggregate production functions confirm the relevance of the surrogate production function. The problem is that the coefficients of production that may be derived from an input–output table are *not* technological coefficients as used in the Sraffian system, but are value measures and hence suffer from the problems outlined in this book.

Logical versus Historical Time

The debate about reswitching and capital reversing concerns comparisons of steady states or comparative statics. It does not involve *historical* time. Cohen and Harcourt (2005) emphasise the importance of this through a simple example. Imagine the simple textbook diagram of the isoquant with labour (measured in standard hours worked) on one axis and the *value* of capital on the other. (It must be the value of capital given the heterogeneity of the capital goods.) The optimal choice of technique is given by the tangency of the isocost line to the isoquant. Let us take a particular solution to this problem where the current prices are in long-run equilibrium. They have been constant in the past and will remain so for the foreseeable future. At this point all three measures of the value of capital – whether it is the cost of investment, the cost of production or the expected net present value – give the same result. Let us call this situation A. Similarly if we take another long-run situation where the factor prices are different, situation B, then again all three measures of capital are equivalent. But what happens if we are at situation A and then the relative prices change in historical time? As Cohen and Harcourt (p. xxxvi) put it: 'With different values of the interest rate, the net present value will no longer be equal to the initial investment or cost of production. A measure of the firm's capital can have three different quantitative values'. Moreover, the isoquant becomes incoherent as a movement along it will cause it to shift because it is not clear whether, or to what extent, the quantities of the heterogeneous capital stock or the value of capital stock are changing. Consequently, there are serious problems to the measurement of capital beyond those exposed by the reswitching debate.

CONCLUDING COMMENTS

We have only barely scratched the technical issues concerning the aggregation problems involving the aggregate production function. These suggest theoretically that the existence of the aggregate production function is highly unlikely. But in a sense, the problems are far more serious than these results suggest. This is because these arguments, damaging though they may be, still assume a very simple well-defined micro-production function at the plant or, when the output are services, organisation level. Consider the Cobb–Douglas micro-production functions or the fixed coefficients of the Sraffian system (even when proxied by input–output coefficients) and compare them with the heterogeneous labour skills and different types of capital goods, including structures, that go into the micro-production function, be it confectionery production or aircraft manufacturing, tax revenue collection or hospital services. Following Gandolfo, consider the various *ex ante* degrees of substitution between different types of ('putty') capital (personal computers and desks) or between labour and capital. These will differ once the capital equipment has been installed ('clay capital'). There is also substantial variation in the degree of efficiency between firms and organisations. Even if we had a complete description, or blueprint, of the various heterogeneous machines, computers, buildings and other capital goods and all the workers of different skills, or, in other words, a complete blueprint of the production process, it would be highly unlikely that we could find a simple mathematical equation linking the output(s) to the inputs. Actually, in most cases, it would not be a blueprint because it is a palimpsest of past investments and hirings. We shall not labour the issue, but simply point out the difficulty, or indeed impossibility, of finding any well-defined mathematical function that relates inputs to outputs even using physical measures at the microeconomic level.

It is thus all the more remarkable that, for example, Douglas (1948), in estimating the aggregate production function and relying on very crude measures of the value of the capital stock[6] and numbers employed, or man-hours and using numerous cross-industry datasets, should have found such extraordinarily good statistical fits. He invariably found correlation coefficients of over 0.9 and the 'output elasticities' as near to the values of the factor shares as makes no difference. In the subsequent chapters we explain why.

---

[6] They were seen as so problematical that shortly after Douglas published his first results the US statistical authorities ceased calculating them for many years.

2. The aggregate production function: behavioural relationship or accounting identity?

> If aggregate production functions did exist, then it would be easy to explain why one gets roughly correct factor share implications from using them; since I believe aggregate productions are not generally even good approximate descriptions of the technical production possibilities of a diverse economy, the question of what lies behind their apparent success at explaining factor shares is not a trivial one.
>
> (Franklin Fisher, 1971a, p. 405)

INTRODUCTION

In spite of the severe problems concerning the aggregate production function, as we briefly mentioned in the last chapter, the defence by those who continue to use it is that it is a parable, or approximation, that gives plausible estimates of the coefficients and good statistical fits. While what is meant by 'plausible estimates' somewhat begs the question, it is generally understood to mean that the estimated output elasticities are close to the factor shares, although statistically significant estimates that display increasing returns to scale would also be considered to be satisfactory. This instrumentalist defence of estimating aggregate production functions has been eloquently put forward by Solow, who can hardly be accused of not being fully aware of the aggregation problems underlying the concept of the aggregate production function:[1]

> I have never thought of the macroeconomic production function as a rigorously justifiable concept. In my mind, it is either an illuminating parable, or else a mere device for handling data, to be used so long as it gives good empirical results, and to be abandoned as soon as it doesn't, or as soon as something better comes along. (Solow, 1966, pp. 1259–60)

Throughout this book we define an aggregate production function to be one where output and the capital stock are expressed in constant-price

---

[1] See, for example, Solow (1955–56) and Fisher et al. (1977).

value terms. This is because the aggregation of the heterogeneous physical units of output and capital requires the use of prices. Consequently, production functions ranging for one for the whole economy to those of, say, industries at the three- or four-digit standard industrial classification (SIC) fall within our definition. Nearly all statistical estimations of production functions are undertaken using value data. This stands in contrast to those very few 'engineering' production functions which are estimated using *physical*, rather than value, data. These are not the concern of this book.

This chapter outlines the central tenet of the argument in this book. This is the critique that, notwithstanding the potentially serious issues arising from the aggregation problem and the Cambridge capital theory controversies, it is always possible, with a little ingenuity, to get a near perfect statistical fit to estimating a putative aggregate production function with the estimated output elasticities being very close to the respective factor shares.

The reason is that in empirical estimations of aggregate production functions, constant-price value (and not physical) data have to be used, as we have mentioned, because of the heterogeneity of output and capital goods, broadly defined. This is not an innocuous change as it means that there is an underlying accounting identity, namely the value of output is definitionally related to the total labour and capital costs, which determines the regression results. Specifications of aggregate production functions turn out to be nothing more than mathematical transformations of this identity, where, with the closest statistical fit, the estimated 'output elasticities' *must* always take a value that is close to the observed factor shares. (This is notwithstanding that some estimates of aggregate production functions, with relatively poor statistical fits, report different results.) The identity is compatible with any degree of competition, with both increasing and constant returns at the firm/plant level and whether or not an aggregate production function actually exists. Consequently, we can never be sure whether or not estimations of aggregate production functions tell us anything about the underlying technological parameters of the economy (such as the aggregate elasticity of substitution, which, in all probability, as Fisher et al. (1977) show, does not exist) or, for example, whether or not factors are paid their marginal products. The argument is deceptively simple, although no less devastating for that and, as we shall see, has been subject to a number of serious and puzzling misinterpretations that have resulted in some economists dismissing it altogether or downplaying its implications (for example, Temple, 2006, 2010).

THE NEOCLASSICAL PRODUCTION FUNCTION

Theoretically, the production function is a microeconomic concept and, as such, should be specified in physical terms. Ferguson, the author of the comprehensive *Neoclassical Theory of Production and Distribution* published in 1969 and a contributor to the debate about the paradoxes inherent in capital theory, put the position as follows:

> My book was intended chiefly to be an exposition and extension of the *microeconomic* theory of production, cost, and factor demand. . . . I assumed a production function relating physical output to the physical inputs of heterogeneous machines, and heterogeneous raw materials . . . Assuming variable proportions, each physical input has a well-defined marginal physical product. If profit maximising is also assumed, which does not seem to be objectionable to any of the participants in this debate [the Cambridge capital theory controversies], each entrepreneur will hire units of each physical input until the *value* of its marginal physical product is equal to its market-determined and parametrically-given input price. In essence, this is what I called the neoclassical, or the marginal productivity, theory of input pricing. (Ferguson, 1971, p. 250, omitting footnotes; emphasis in the original)

No one would deny that the output of goods or services is in some way determined by the flow of inputs. In this sense, some sort of a production relationship must exist, albeit of a complex nature. As we noted in the previous chapter, intuitively, we may think of an engineer designing a production process for, say, an oil refinery. The plans will indicate the efficient techniques and combinations of labour and machines at different stages of the production process, dependent upon the relative scale of output and the relative costs. Thus, the production function exists, so what is the controversy?

The first point is that even if we can enumerate all the heterogeneous outputs and inputs, the relationship must be stable. This is normally assumed to be the case in microeconomic theory (there is producer efficiency) and is a necessary condition for aggregation. But as Leibenstein (1966) has demonstrated, variations in the level of inefficiency with which inputs are used are an order of magnitude greater than losses due to allocative inefficiency. Indeed, casual empiricism and numerous management studies all attest to the large inefficiencies in organisations in both the private and public sectors and between countries. Leibenstein, on the basis of the large differences in productivity that exist between firms in the same industry and how simple changes in production measures can greatly increase productivity, came to the following conclusion:

> One idea that emerges from this study is that firms and economies do not operate on an out-bound production possibility surface consistent with their

resources. Rather they actually work on a production surface that is well within that outer bound. . . . The data suggest that in a great many instances the amount to be gained by increasing allocative efficiency is trivial while the amount to be gained by increasing X-efficiency is frequently significant. (p. 413)

But let us ignore these problems for the moment.

The concept of production function then moves seamlessly in the literature from the narrow engineering definition to a macroeconomic concept relating the inputs to the output of the whole economy, total manufacturing or individual industries. As Ferguson (1971, p.252) continues, 'neoclassical theory deals with macroeconomic aggregates, usually by constructing the aggregate theory by analogy with the corresponding microeconomic concepts. Whether or not this is useful is an empirical question to which I believe an empirical answer can be given'. Thus, the 'aggregation by analogy' is a parable and as such is 'important to those who are interested in empirical work at the aggregate level'.

In other words, these complex production processes of the various firms are given by the familiar equation for an aggregate production function:

$$Q = Af(L, K) \text{ or } Q = F(L, K, t), \qquad (2.1)$$

where in terms of the theory Q is the maximum amount of output (the numbers of homogeneous 'widgets') that can be produced from any combination of L and K (where L is employment and capital, K, is measured in homogeneous units). For simplicity, we follow the standard procedure and ignore the input of materials and also, for the moment, human capital. In other words, there is a unique mapping from L and K to Q. A is the level of technology and not independently measurable and so one problem is to correctly specify it in empirical analysis (Temple, 2006). A is sometimes termed 'total factor productivity' (TFP) and in time-series analysis it is often proxied by time. (Recent developments in endogenous growth theory seek to explain A in terms of a 'knowledge' or 'R&D' production function. But, as will be shown, this does not affect our argument.)

We have seen that this approach encounters a number of serious aggregation problems. While most economists are not overly enamoured with methodological questions, the standard defence of the use of equation (2.1) in empirical analysis is Friedman's (1953) instrumental position. Any theory, by definition requires abstractions and involves assumptions that may be unrealistic to a greater or lesser extent, but what matters is the predictive ability of the model. In other words, how well does it stand up to empirical testing or econometric estimation?

The notion of the analogy is reinforced by referring to constant-price measures of output in terms of physical dimensions, such as 'volume' or 'quantity'. Indeed, this was first done in the introduction to Cobb and Douglas's (1928) classic paper:

> The progressive refinement during the recent years in the measurement of the *volume* of physical production in manufacturing suggests the possibility of attempting (1) to measure the changes in the *amount* of labour and capital which have been used to turn out this *volume* of goods, and (2) to determine what relationships existed between the three factors of labor, capital, and product. (p. 139, emphasis added)

Thus, the production function may be written in value terms $pQ = pF(L, K, t)$ where p is the price of output in £s. Again, for definitional reasons, in this schema the value of output must equal the value of the inputs or $pQ \equiv wL + \rho K$. w is the wage rate and ρ is the (rental) price of capital both measured in £s per physical unit. However, it is readily apparent that theoretically it is possible to recover the physical quantities from the identity. In other words, $Q \equiv (w/p)L + (\rho/p)K$ where w/p and ρ/p are the factor payments expressed in units of output. Under certain circumstances, it is possible to estimate a production function and to test the marginal productivity theory of distribution.

To see this, consider the neoclassical approach that uses a micro-production function specified in *physical* terms where there is no technical change, namely $Q = A_0 f(L,K)$. (Alternatively, the data could be of a cross-sectional nature – either cross-regional or cross-industry – where there is the same technology.) Partially differentiating the micro-production function with respect to L and K gives $\partial Q/\partial L = f_L$ and $\partial Q/\partial K = f_K$, where f_L is the marginal product of labour and f_K is the marginal product of capital, both measured in physical units. By Euler's theorem which, of course, has no economic content, *per se*, we have, assuming constant returns to scale, the following equation: $Q = f_L L + f_K K$ or $pQ = pf_L L + pf_K K$ where p, it will be recalled, is the price per unit output, measured in, say, £s.[2]

Let us assume that the marginal products are roughly constant. Regressing Q on L and K will provide an estimate of the average values of f_L and f_K.[3] It does not make any difference if we use the monetary values as we are just multiplying all the variables by p; we shall still obtain the marginal products, although now measured in monetary

---

[2]   Euler's theorem does not, of course, require linear homogeneity. It is necessary for the production function to exhibit this if there is to be no 'adding-up' problem.
[3]   In these thought experiments we ignore any problems such as lack of variability in the data.

units. Of course, there is no reason why factors should be paid their marginal products and so a comparison of pf_L and pf_K with the actual factor payments would constitute a test of the marginal productivity theory of factor pricing. This is an important point, because the coefficients of the estimated linear equation $pQ = b_1 L + b_2 K$ are determined by the underlying production function and they will differ from the observed wages and rate of profit if factors are not paid their marginal products. This is because Q is a physical measure and is independent of the distribution of the product. For example, in the case of the Cobb–Douglas production function, $Q = AL^{\alpha}K^{\beta}$, we have $f_L = \alpha Q/L$ and $f_K = \beta Q/K$. If the distribution of output between labour and capital is different from that implied by the marginal productivity conditions, so that the factor shares differ from α and β, estimating the production function using physical data will still produce estimates of the output elasticities of labour and capital, namely α and β, when they are not constrained to equal unity.

If, however, we use value-added data, then, as we shall see below, the estimates of the supposed output elasticities must take the values of the shares and not the true output elasticities.

Alternatively, if we were to, say, estimate the Cobb–Douglas production function using physical data the specification then would be:

$$\ln Q = \ln A_0 + \lambda t + \alpha \ln L + \beta \ln K. \tag{2.2}$$

Again, under these assumptions there is no necessary reason why α should equal a and β should equal $(1 - a)$, where a is labour's share and $(1 - a)$ is capital's share.

Consequently, in these circumstances, the discussions concerning the appropriate estimation procedures of estimating the production function (whether it should be part of a simultaneous equation framework and so on) become relevant. The major problem with physical data is that as both the level and growth of TFP are unknown and have to be proxied by the use of dummies (in cross-sectional data) or a linear or non-linear time trend (with time-series data), we can never be sure that the correct specification is being estimated.

The 'unobtrusive postulate' is that for applied purposes it is assumed that the constant-price value of output (V) and capital (J) are excellent proxies of the physical quantities (Q) and (K). But the major problem is that they are conceptually very different. The confusion arises because output may be written for any time t as:

$$P_t V_t^0 \equiv P_t \sum_i p_i^0 Q_{it} \equiv w_t^n L_t + r_t J_t^n. \tag{2.3}$$

V_t^0 is value added at time t measured at base-year prices, 0. The base-year price of the ith industry (or firm) is p_i^0, Q_{it} is the physical quantity of the ith industry at time t, w_t^n is the nominal or current price wage at time t, r_t is the rate of profit, and J_t^n is current price value of the capital stock, usually calculated by the perpetual inventory method cumulating net investment. P is not a *price* but a *price deflator* and, for example, $w^n/P = w$ is the real wage measured in monetary (and not physical) units, that is, it is measured at base-year prices.

As an example, let us assume that firms pursue a mark-up pricing policy where the price is determined by a fixed mark-up on unit labour costs. We have assumed for simplicity that no materials are used in production, but, in practice, firms mark-up on normal unit costs. See Lee (1998) for a detailed discussion. Thus $p_i = (1+\pi_i)w_iL_i/Q_i$ where π is the size of the mark-up. Value added is $V_i = p_iQ_i = (1+\pi_i)w_iL_i$ and for industry as a whole $V = \Sigma\ p_iQ_i = \Sigma(1+\pi_i)w_iL_i$, or, approximately, $V = (1+\pi)wL$, where π is the average mark-up and w is the average wage rate. Labour's share is $a = 1/(1+\pi)$ and this will be constant to the extent that the mark-up does not vary. In practice, it is likely to vary to the degree that the composition of firms with differing mark-ups alter and there are changes in the individual mark-ups, which may be temporary, as a result of the wage-bargaining process. Solow (1958) has shown, however, that aggregation may well *decrease* the variability of the aggregate factor shares compared with the shares of the individual firms or industries.

We have the accounting identity $V \equiv W + \Pi \equiv wL + rJ$. $W = wL$ is labour's total compensation and $\Pi = rJ$ is total profits, including any monopoly profits (the operating surplus). rJ is equal to πwL and capital's share is given by $(1-a) = \pi/(1+\pi)$.[4] Suppose that w and r are the same across the units of observation in cross-sectional data, or do not change over time when time-series data are used. If we were to estimate $V = b_3L + b_4J$, then the estimates of b_3 and b_4 will *always* be w and r, respectively. If w and r do vary, the estimated coefficients will each be their average values. Compare this with the regression of pQ on L and K, discussed above, when the estimated coefficients can differ from the factor payments.

It is consequently the existence of the accounting identity specified in constant-price value terms, namely $V \equiv wL + rJ$ that poses the problem, and we next turn to a consideration of why this is the case. We start for expositional ease by considering the case of the Cobb–Douglas production function, but it should be emphasised that the critique applies to any

---

4    $V = (1+\pi)wL$ and $V - wL = rJ = \pi wL$.

specification. More flexible aggregate production functions, such as the CES and the translog are discussed in Appendix 2A1.

THE ACCOUNTING IDENTITY AND THE COBB–DOUGLAS PRODUCTION FUNCTION

A version of the argument was first brought to the fore by Phelps Brown (1957) in his seminal paper 'The Meaning of the Fitted Cobb–Douglas Function'. (A discussion of Phelps Brown's argument, placing it in its historical context, is to be found in Chapter 4.) It is one of the ironies of the history of economic theory that this article, which challenged the whole rationale for estimating aggregate production functions, was published in the same year as Solow's (1957) 'Technical Change and the Aggregate Production Function'. The latter, of course, was largely responsible for beginning the neoclassical approach to the empirical analysis of economic growth and the widespread use of the aggregate production function that has persisted to date.

One aspect of Phelps Brown's critique was addressed to the fitting of production functions using cross-sectional data and was specifically directed at Douglas's various studies (see Douglas, 1948). It is useful to consider this first, as it avoids the complication of technical change. We consider the latter next when we look at time-series data.

Cross-section Data

Phelps Brown (1957) noted that there always exists an underlying accounting identity noted above for the ith firm given by:

$$V_i \equiv w_i L_i + r_i J_i, \tag{2.4}$$

where again V, L, J, w and r are output (value added at constant prices), the labour input, the constant-price value of the capital stock, the wage rate, and the observed rate of return.[5] Because of the existence of the identity, Phelps Brown (p. 557) concluded that the 'Cobb–Douglas [α] and the share of earnings in income will be only two sides of the same penny', where α is the output elasticity of labour.

The argument seems to be this. The elasticity of output with respect to

---

[5]   It will be recalled that we use V and J to refer to the value measures; Q and K are used to denote the physical measures of output and capital.

labour of the constant-returns-to-scale Cobb–Douglas production function measured in value terms,

$$V_i = A_0 L_i^\alpha J_i^{(1-\alpha)} \tag{2.5}$$

is defined as $\alpha = (\partial V_i / \partial L_i)(L_i / V_i)$. ($A_0$ is assumed to be constant across the units of observation.) Given the assumptions of the neoclassical theory of factor pricing, from the first-order conditions, the marginal product of labour equals the wage rate, that is, $\partial V_i / \partial L_i = w_i$. Consequently, it also follows that $\alpha = a_i = w_i L_i / V_i$; the share of labour in value added. Likewise, $\partial V_i / \partial J_i = r_i$ and $(1-\alpha) = (1-a_i) = r_i J_i / V_i$.

The mainstream approach sees these as testable predictions of the neoclassical theory of factor pricing. However, the accounting identity given by equation (2.4), defines the measure of value added for all units of observation, whether they are at the level of, say, the firm or the whole economy. It should be emphasised once again that there are no behavioural assumptions underlying this equation, in that it is compatible with any degree of competition, increasing or decreasing returns to scale and whether or not a well-behaved underlying aggregate production function actually exists.

Consequently, partially differentiating the accounting identity, $V_i \equiv w_i L_i + r_i J_i$, with respect to L_i gives $\partial V_i / \partial L_i = w_i$ and it follows that $(\partial V_i / \partial L_i)(L_i / V_i) = a_i = w_i L_i / V_i$. This is identical to the result obtained from the aggregate production function and the first-order conditions, as shown above. The problem is that as it is derived from an identity, this result is always true, that is, it is impossible to reject it by statistical testing. As the argument stemming from the identity has not made any economic assumptions at all, the finding that the putative output elasticities equal the observed factor shares cannot be taken as a test of whether or not factors of production are paid their marginal products. This is a position, however, that was not accepted by Douglas (1976, p. 914) himself who took the contrary position arguing that it is a test of the marginal productivity theory of factor pricing, although without considering Phelps Brown's critique.[6]

If the (aggregate) output elasticity of labour and the share of labour's total compensation are merely 'two sides of the same penny', could it be that the Cobb–Douglas is simply an alternative way of expressing the income identity and, as such, has no implications for the underlying

---

[6] As Phelps Brown's argument was directed at Douglas's work, *per se*, and was published in the *Quarterly Journal of Economics*, it is difficult to believe that Douglas was not aware of it.

technology of the economy? This was the proposition that Simon and Levy (1963) proved some eight years later.

Following Simon and Levy, and Intriligator (1978), the isomorphism between the Cobb–Douglas production function and the underlying accounting identity may be simply shown. The Cobb–Douglas, when estimated using cross-section (firm, industry or regional) data, is specified as the more general form of equation (2.5) where increasing returns to scale are allowed for:

$$V_i = A_0 L_i^\alpha J_i^\beta. \tag{2.6}$$

Dividing this by $V_i' = A_0 L_i'^\alpha K_i'^\beta$ and taking logarithms gives:

$$\ln \frac{V_i}{V_i'} = \alpha \ln \frac{L_i}{L_i'} + \beta \ln \frac{J_i}{J_i'}, \tag{2.7}$$

where the X_i' denotes that the value of the variable in the neighbourhood of X_i where X is V, L and J. Hence, the ratio between X_i and X_i' is arbitrarily close to unity.

Using the Taylor-series approximation that $\ln \frac{X_i}{X_i'} \approx (\frac{X_i}{X_i'} - 1)$, at the tangency of a plane to equation (2.6) this equation may be expressed as:

$$V_i = \left(\alpha \frac{V_i'}{L_i'}\right) L_i + \left(\beta \frac{V_i'}{J_i'}\right) J_i + (1 - \alpha - \beta) V_i'. \tag{2.8}$$

Using a Taylor-series expansion for equation (2.4), the accounting identity, and assuming that wages and the rate of profit are constant gives:

$$V_i = V_i' + w(L_i - L_i') + r(J_i - J_i') = wL_i + rJ_i + [1 - a - (1 - a)]V_i'. \tag{2.9}$$

Hence, it may be seen from a comparison of equations (2.8) and (2.9) that $\alpha = w'L_i'/V_i'$ and $\beta = rJ_i'/V_i'$. Moreover, it follows that $(1 - \alpha - \beta) V_i'$ must equal zero, which implies that $\alpha + \beta = 1$. Consequently, the data will always suggest the existence of 'constant returns to scale', whatever the true technological relationships of the individual production processes. This result shows that the linear accounting identity will ensure that the data for the *i*th unit of observation give a close statistical fit to the Cobb–Douglas, even though the Cobb–Douglas does not exist as an aggregate production function. The equivalence between the two equations (2.4) and (2.5) may be most easily seen by considering them expressed as:

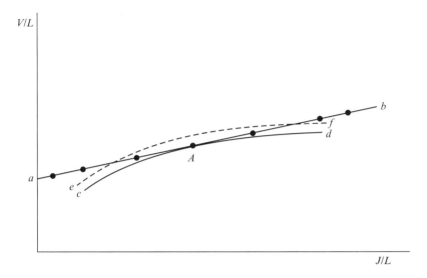

Figure 2.1   The Cobb-Douglas approximation to the linear accounting identity

$$\frac{V_i}{L_i} = w + r\frac{J_i}{L_i} \approx A\left(\frac{J_i}{L_i}\right)^{(1-a)}. \qquad (2.10)$$

If we use cross-section data and mistakenly estimate a Cobb–Douglas function, we can see that we are likely to obtain a good statistical fit because of the underlying accounting identity. The position is shown in Figure 2.1 where the line *ab* is the accounting identity. The curve *cd* is the Cobb–Douglas approximation tangential to *ab* at A for the *i*th firm (or region) that, for example, has the average capital–labour ratio.

However, *J/L* is likely to show some variation between the units of observation and so the observed cross-sectional data points will lie along *ab*. (In practice, there is likely to be a scatter of observations both above and below *ab* and a series of roughly parallel lines representing different firm accounting identities.) Mistakenly fitting a single Cobb–Douglas function to these data along *ab* will give the best statistical fit shown by the dotted line *ef*, where it will slightly overpredict the value of output near the average value of the *J/L* ratio and underpredict it elsewhere.

As the fitted Cobb–Douglas is an approximation to the accounting identity, the question arises as to how good is the statistical fit, given the variation to the capital–labour ratio. Fortunately, Simon (1979b) has calculated the relative error of the estimated output as the ratio of the value of output predicted by using a Cobb–Douglas function to the actual value given by the accounting identity. In his calculations, he 'allowed an extreme range of 25 to 1 from the lowest to the highest ratio of L to $[J]$ (from 0.2 to 5). Even over this wide range, far wider than anything encountered in the literature, the fitted C–D [Cobb–Douglas] function approximates to data on the plane [equation (2.4)] with a maximum error of less than 15 per cent' (p. 466). When the range of the capital–labour ratio is restricted to that actually observed, the estimating error is less than 5 per cent. This is not surprising as estimates of the Cobb–Douglas using actual cross-industry or cross-region data often give an R^2 that exceeds 0.9 (Douglas, 1976).

We confirmed this with a simple simulation exercise. The accounting identity may be written in index form as $\tilde{V} \equiv a\tilde{L} + (1 - a)\tilde{J}$ where the tilde denotes an index. We constructed an artificial dataset of 25 observations with L/J increasing from 0.20 to 5, similar to Simon (1979b) in increments of 0.20. The index of value added per unit of capital, $\tilde{V}/\tilde{J}$, was constructed from the identity using the equation:

$$\tilde{V}/\tilde{J} \equiv a(\tilde{L}/\tilde{J}) + (1 - a). \tag{2.11}$$

The share of wages in value added was taken to be 0.75. The share was not assumed to be constant, but was constructed so that it varied as if drawn from a normal distribution with a standard error of 0.02, which is plausible when compared with actual values of labour's share. (The simulated value of a ranges from 0.80 to 0.72.) These data were used to estimate both the linear identity and the Cobb–Douglas specification. The results of estimating the relationships between indices of output per worker and the capital–labour ratio are as follows:

$$\tilde{V}/\tilde{L} = 0.757 + 0.240(\tilde{J}/\tilde{L}) \quad \overline{R}^2 = 0.997 \ SER = 0.015, \tag{i}$$
$$(200.51) \quad (80.42)$$

$$\ln(\tilde{V}/\tilde{L}) = 0.079 + 0.231\ln(\tilde{J}/\tilde{L}) \quad \overline{R}^2 = 0.888 \ SER = 0.068. \tag{ii}$$
$$(4.35) \quad (13.87)$$

The identity, equation (i), not surprisingly, gives an almost perfect fit. The shares of labour and capital are 0.757 and 0.240, respectively, and sum to 0.997. But what is interesting is the very good fit that the Cobb–Douglas function, equation (ii), gives in log form, notwithstanding the substantial variation in the capital–labour ratio. If the underlying artificial nature of the data which generated this result were overlooked, the statistical results of equation (ii) could be interpreted as not refuting the hypothesis that the manufacturing sector (or the whole economy) could be represented by an aggregate Cobb–Douglas production function. It would also be possible to infer, as Douglas did, that the equality of factor shares and the output elasticities support the marginal productivity theory. But, of course, there is no justification for either of these conclusions.

As the linear income identity exists for *any* underlying technology, we cannot be sure that all that the estimates are picking up is not simply the identity. The fact that a good fit to the Cobb–Douglas relationship is found implies nothing, *per se*, about such technological parameters as the elasticity of substitution.

The good approximation of the Cobb–Douglas to the accounting identity is also likely to carry through even when we allow w and r to change, provided now that the factor shares do not show very much variation. To see this, using cross-firm data, let us assume a continuum of firms and differentiate the accounting identity to give:

$$dV_i = (dw_i)L_i + w_i dL_i + (dr_i)J_i + r_i dJ_i \qquad (2.12)$$

or

$$\frac{dV_i}{V_i} = a_i \frac{dw_i}{w_i} + a_i \frac{dL_i}{L_i} + (1 - a_i)\frac{dr_i}{r_i} + (1 - a_i)\frac{dJ_i}{J_i}. \qquad (2.13)$$

Let us assume that factor shares are constant. There are many reasons why this should occur other than because there is a Cobb–Douglas production function. For example, we have seen that this will occur if firms pursue a constant mark-up pricing policy regardless of the form of the underlying production function in engineering terms. The Keynesian/Kaleckian/Kaldorian macroeconomic theory of distribution will also give the same result without using the construct of the aggregate production function. See Kaldor (1955–56, section IV). Equation (2.13) may be integrated to give:

$$V_i = Bw_i^a r_i^{(1-a)} L_i^a J_i^{(1-a)} = AL_i^a J_i^{(1-a)}, \qquad (2.14)$$

where B is the constant of integration and equals $a^{-a}(1 - a)^{-(1-a)}$.

For any one unit of observation, for any single time period, equation (2.14) is an *exact* transformation of the accounting identity. This is illustrated by Table 2.1 which reports the values for the relevant macroeconomic values for UK industry in 1990. We should emphasise

*Table 2.1   UK total industry: selected macroeconomic variables for 1990
(current prices)*

Value added (V)	£519,089 million
Wage rate (w)	£13,017.72
Total persons employed (L)	28.189 million
Rate of profit (r)	0.0988
Capital stock (J)	£1,540,000 million
Capital–output ratio (J/V)	2.9667
Labour's share (a)	0.7069
Capital's share ($1-a$)	0.2931
a^{-a}	1.2779
$(1-a)^{-(1-a)}$	1.4329

The Two Accounting Identities

(i) $V \equiv L + rJ$

£519,089m $\equiv$ £13,017.72*28.189m + 0.0988*£1,540,000m

(ii) $V \equiv [a^{-a}(1 - a)^{-(1-a)}w^a r^{(1-a)}]L^a J^{(1-a)} = AL^a J^{(1-a)}$

£519,089m $\equiv$ 1.28*1.43*£810.33*0.51*184,774.58*£3,731.31

Notes: m in equations (i) and (ii) denotes millions. Figures for equation (ii) are not exact because of rounding.

Sources: OECD Database, *Flows and Stocks of Fixed Capital, 1971–1996*, OECD, and authors' estimates.

that this argument is applicable to any country or industry and for any particular date.

As may be seen, the total value added for UK industry in 1990 was about £520 billion, with total employment of a little over 28 million and an average wage of about £13,000. Data are available for the total compensation of workers from the national accounts and profits (the gross operating surplus) were calculated as the difference between value added and the total wage bill. Given the estimates of the gross capital stocks, the derived rate of profit is just under 10 per cent per annum. The share of labour in total output is 0.71 and the share of capital is 0.29, which accords with the stylised facts for the values of aggregate factor shares for the advanced countries. Because of the way the data have been constructed, the (linear) accounting identity given by equation (2.4) holds exactly. In other words, there is no statistical discrepancy and this is confirmed by equation (i) in Table 2.1 where it can be seen that value added is exactly the sum of the factor incomes. What is important, though, is that equation (ii) in Table 2.1 shows that equation (2.14) is an exact approximation (if this is not a contradiction in terms!) to the linear accounting identity. Just as the linear accounting identity is compatible with any state of competition, increasing, decreasing or constant returns to scale, the existence or non-existence of the aggregate production function, so this is true for the putative Cobb–Douglas relationship (not production function) which is given by equation (2.6).

What are the wider implications of this? To answer this, suppose that we were to use cross-section data (say, regional data) to estimate the Cobb–Douglas 'production function'. If factor shares[7] and the wage rate and rate of profit do not differ greatly between regions (so A in equation (2.6) is roughly constant), it can be seen that the Cobb–Douglas multiplicative power function will give a very good approximation to a linear function. The corollary is that the linear accounting identity will likewise give a good approximation to the Cobb–Douglas relationship. As the linear income identity exists for *any* underlying technology, we cannot be sure that all that the estimates are picking up is not simply the identity. The fact that a good fit to the Cobb–Douglas relationship is found implies nothing, *per se*, about such technological parameters as the elasticity of substitution.

However, using cross-country data such as that from the Penn World Table that includes both developed and less developed countries should not give such a good fit, because of the international variability in, especially, w. This indeed proves the case. In other words, in this case the Cobb–Douglas is a poor approximation to the linear accounting identity, unless, for example, regional, or national, dummies are used to capture the variability in w. (See the discussion of the Mankiw–Romer–Weil (1992) model in Chapter 7.)

It should be noted that this critique of the aggregate production function is not just confined to the Cobb–Douglas production function. Simon (1979b) explicitly considers the CES production function given by $V = A[\delta L^{-\theta} + (1 - \delta)J^{-\theta}]^{-1/\theta}$ where A is interpreted as an efficiency parameter and δ is a distributional parameter, and the elasticity of substitution is given by $\sigma = 1/(1+\theta)$. It is assumed that there are constant returns to scale, but we have seen that the data and accounting identity, which must always be satisfied, implies this, so it is not an arbitrary assumption.

Simon argues that if the true relationship were given by the accounting identity and we were mistakenly to estimate the CES production function, then if θ goes to zero, the function becomes a Cobb–Douglas. He cites

---

[7] In fact, the simulations above show that the factor shares can vary randomly by quite a margin and the Cobb–Douglas will still give a reasonably good fit to the data.

Jorgenson (1974) as suggesting that most estimates give θ close to zero and so the argument still applies. However, more recent studies find that the putative aggregate elasticity of substitution is less than unity. But the argument is more general than Simon implies, and applies directly to any supposed production function, as we demonstrate below. (See Appendix 2A2.)

If we were to express *any* production function of the form $V_i = f(L_i, J_i)$ (such as the translog) in proportionate rates of change and use the marginal productivity conditions, we would find that $dV_i/V_i = c + a_i dL_i/L_i + (1-a_i)dJ_i/J_i$, where c is a constant. This is formally exactly equivalent to the accounting identity expressed in proportionate rates of change, provided that $a_i dw_i/w_i + (1-a_i)dr_i/r_i$ is again constant or it will give a good approximation provided that $a_i dw_i/w_i + (1-a_i)dr_i/r$ is orthogonal to $a_i dL_i/L_i + (1 - a_i) dJ_i/J_i$. This may be seen from a comparison of equations (2.6) and (2.13), from which it follows that $\alpha_i = a_i$ and $\beta_i = (1 - \alpha_i) = (1 - a_i)$. If shares do vary, then we may be able find to an explicit functional form that is more flexible than the Cobb–Douglas that gives a good fit to the accounting identity; but, of course, this does not mean that the estimated coefficients can now be interpreted as technological parameters.[8] If $a_i dw_i/w_i + (1 - a_i)dr_i/r$ does not meet the assumptions noted above, all this means is that the estimated functional form will be misspecified and the goodness of fit will be reduced. (See Appendix 2A1.)

Time-series Data

The fact that the identity precludes interpreting the cross-section Cobb–Douglas or more flexible functional forms as unambiguously reflecting the underlying technology of the economy implicitly suggests that this is true of estimations using time-series data.[9] This is, in fact, the case as Shaikh (1974, 1980) has shown. Differentiating the income identity, $V_t \equiv w_t L_t + r_t J_t$, with respect to time, we obtain:[10]

$$\hat{V}_t \equiv a_t \hat{w}_t + (1 - a_t)\hat{r}_t + a_t \hat{L}_t + (1-a_t)\hat{J}_t, \tag{2.15}$$

where $\hat{V}$, $\hat{L}$, $\hat{J}$, $\hat{w}$ and $\hat{r}$ denote exponential growth rates. $a_t \equiv w_t L_t /V_t$ is labour's share in output and $(1 - a_t) \equiv r_t J_t /V_t$ is capital's share.

---

[8]   The CES function may be regarded akin to a Box–Cox transformation which is simply a mathematical transformation that attempts to find the best fit for the identity when w and r vary.

[9]   Phelps Brown (1957) does consider time-series data, but mainly when there is no time trend included (that is, the data are not de-trended). He shows that, in these circumstances, the estimated coefficients will merely reflect the historical growth rates of the various variables.

[10]   The case of gross output is discussed in Appendix 2A2.

The general form of an aggregate production function with exogenous technical change is given by $V = F(L, J, t)$ and in growth rate form:

$$\hat{V}_t = \lambda_t + \alpha_t \hat{L}_t + \beta_t \hat{J}_t, \tag{2.16}$$

where α and β are the output elasticities that may change over time. λ_t is the rate of technical progress that also may vary temporally. (There is nothing in neoclassical production theory that says it must be at a constant rate, with, say, a random component.)

Compare equation (2.16) with the accounting identity expressed in growth rate form in equation (2.15). If the neoclassical economist assumes constant returns to scale, perfect competition and that the marginal productivity theory of factor pricing holds, then equations (2.15) and (2.16) in neoclassical production theory are formally equivalent. But as equation (2.15) is an identity, it is true *irrespective* of these assumptions and, as in the case of cross-sectional data, it holds even when the aggregate production function does not exist. Consequently, the argument follows through *whether or not* factor shares and the weighted growth of the wage rate and the rate of profit are constant. In practice, researchers will attempt to find an explicit functional form that will give a good fit to the data generated by equation (2.16) such as that given by a Box–Cox transformation or the translog.

Thus, to summarise, we have:

$$V_t \equiv w_t L_t + r_t J_t \Rightarrow \hat{V}_t \equiv a_t \hat{w}_t + (1 - a_t)\hat{r}_t + a_t \hat{L}_t + (1 - a_t)\hat{J}_t \Rightarrow$$
$$\hat{V}_t \equiv \lambda_t + \alpha_t \hat{L}_t + \beta_t \hat{J}_t \Rightarrow V_t = f(L_t, J_t, t),$$

where the arrows show the direction of 'causation'. This implies once again that $a_t \equiv \alpha_t$ and $(1 - a_t) \equiv \beta_t \equiv (1 - \alpha_t)$. As we have noted, economists try to find a specific mathematical functional form that will closely fit the data generated by equation (2.16) and, hence, unwittingly, the underlying identity, equation (2.15). If, and only if, the weighted average of the growth rates of the wage and profit rates are a constant, and factor shares are also constant, will a conventional Cobb–Douglas relationship fit this criterion. If they are not constant, then, as we emphasised above, a more flexible functional form that contains the Cobb–Douglas as a special case, such as a Box–Cox transformation or the translog, will be required. But these mathematical isomorphisms should not be regarded as aggregate production functions. Consequently, the argument does not apply solely to the case where the aforementioned assumptions hold, as, for example, Temple (2006) assumes.

In fact, while the cross-region or cross-industry studies normally give a very good fit to the Cobb–Douglas (and other) production functions, the time-series estimations sometimes produce implausible estimates with, for example, the coefficient of capital being negative. Sylos Labini (1995, Table 1, p. 490) provides a useful summary of some time-series studies that give poor statistical fits. The fact that the results are often so poor may ironically give the impression that the estimated equation is actually a behavioural equation.[11] However, the failure to obtain plausible estimates will occur if either the factor shares are not sufficiently constant or the approximation $a_t \hat{w}_t + (1 - a_t)\hat{r}_t \approx \lambda$ (that is, a constant) is not sufficiently accurate. In practice, it is the latter that proves to be the case, as estimations of equation (2.16) with a variety of datasets produce well-determined estimates of the coefficients which equal the relevant factor shares. It is found that the rate of profit, especially, has a pronounced cyclical component and so proxying the sum of the weighted logarithms of w and r by a linear time trend (or their growth rates by a constant) biases the estimated coefficients of $\ln L$ and $\ln J$.[12]

The conventional neoclassical approach, which is based on the assumption that an aggregate production function is, in fact, being estimated, usually attributes a poor fit to the failure to adjust the growth of factor inputs for the changes in capacity utilisation. As $a_t \hat{w}_t + (1 - a_t)\hat{r}_t \equiv \lambda_t$ tends to vary procyclically, the inclusion of a capacity utilisation variable will tend to improve the goodness of fit and cause the estimated coefficients to approximate more closely the relevant factor shares. While $\hat{r}$ has a pronounced procyclical fluctuation, the growth of the capital stock generally shows little variation. Adjusting $\hat{J}$ for changes in capacity utilisation increases its cyclical fluctuation and at the same time reduces that in $\hat{r}$.[13] The weighted sum of the logarithms of the wage and profit rates is now more closely proxied by a linear time trend and the regression estimates more closely reflect the identity. As Lucas (1970, p. 24), commented: 'some investigators have obtained "improved" empirical production functions (that is, have obtained labour elasticities closer to labour's share) by "correcting" measured capital stock for variations in utilisation rates'. (The same argument holds when the labour input is adjusted for changes in its intensity of use over the cycle.)

---

[11]   Ironically, Sylos Labini (1995) takes these poor statistical fits as a reason for abandoning the neoclassical aggregate production function altogether. This is precisely the opposite of our argument, whereby, in spite of implausible estimates of the coefficients of putative production functions in some studies, it is always possible with some ingenuity to find a specification that gives a near perfect statistical fit.

[12]   As we are dealing with an identity, we treat the regressions using either logarithms of the levels or exponential growth rates as equivalent.

[13]   This is because the two variables are related through capital's (roughly) constant share in output $(1-a) = rJ/V$.

An alternative procedure would be to introduce a sufficiently complex non-linear time trend more accurately to capture the variation of λ_t (Shaikh, 1980; Felipe and McCombie, 2003). With sufficient ingenuity, we should be able eventually to approximate closely the underlying identity, increasing both the R^2 and the values of the *t*-statistics, and hence find a very good fit for the 'production function'. Generally, as we have noted above, it is this problem, rather than the change in factor shares, that is of greater empirical importance. As in the case of cross-sectional data, the problem posed by the identity occurs even though the factor shares vary. Appendix 2A2 presents some estimates that illustrate the arguments concerning the identity and the aggregate production function with respect to both cross-section and time-series data.

THE OBSERVED AND 'VIRTUAL' ACCOUNTING IDENTITIES

In the above analysis, we have shown how the putative aggregate production function estimated using value data is nothing more than an approximation to the accounting identity. However, as the accounting identity is derived from data in the National Income and Product Accounts (NIPA), the rate of profit is an *ex post* measure and includes any economic or monopoly profits.

However, it has been shown above that the neoclassical approach also involves an accounting identity (what we may term a 'virtual' identity), but, under the standard neoclassical production theory assumptions, the rate of profit is the perfectly competitive 'rental price of capital'. In other words, the firm maximises production subject to a 'cost constraint' which excludes any economic rents. This can be a source of confusion because the 'virtual identity' assumes constant returns to scale and factors being paid their marginal products and it has been inferred that these assumptions are necessary for the above argument concerning the aggregate production function and the NIPA (accounting) identity, which is not correct. We may easily demonstrate this. The neoclassical identity is given by:

$$pQ \equiv wL + \rho_c K + \Omega, \tag{2.17}$$

with the usual notation and where ρ_c is the competitive rental price of capital (which differs from ρ used above which includes monopoly profits, if any) and Ω is the monetary value of 'economic profits'. The latter equals $\rho_{nc}K$, where ρ_{nc} is the non-competitive component of the rental price of capital. It is normally assumed that the labour market is competitive. If perfect competition is assumed, as is generally the case, identity (2.17) becomes $pQ \equiv wL + \rho_c K$, which is what might be termed the 'virtual' identity referred to above. This approach assumes that both labour and capital markets are competitive and thus the factor prices w and ρ_c equal their corresponding marginal revenue products, which measure their opportunity cost. This approach tries to draw a conceptual distinction between the imputed return to capital and the income of capitalists. The neoclassical cost identity is given by $C \equiv wL + \rho_c K$.[14] These are the *costs* to the firm (including the normal profits) and not its *revenues*. Consequently, it does not include economic profits, if any. It is the neoclassical total cost identity that appears in most microeconomics textbooks, rather than the value-added accounting identity.

However, the value-added accounting identity used in applied analysis is given by:

$$PV \equiv wL + rJ \equiv wL + r_c J + \Omega' \equiv wL + r_c J + r_{nc} J, \qquad (2.18)$$

where P is the price deflator, which for expositional ease, we may set equal to unity. In applied neoclassical analysis r_c is sometimes interpreted as the competitive rental price of capital, but is actually a pure number, the rate of return and r_{nc} is the corresponding non-competitive rate of return and $\Omega' = r_{nc} J$.

While equation (2.18) is correct from a definitional point of view, the assumption made is that it is the natural extension of the microeconomic identity to the aggregate level. It can be seen that it implicitly sums the terms $r_c J$ and Ω' to give rJ, that is, total profits.

The accounting identity must hold always by definition, as value added measured in the NIPA includes any economic profits under the category 'operating surplus' (Ω'). The concepts of the profit rate and the rental price of capital while analogous are subtly and importantly different.[15]

---

[14]   It should be noted that this differs from the neoclassical cost function which takes the general form $C = F(w, \rho_c, Q)$, and specific functional forms include, for example, the Cobb–Douglas and the translog cost function.

[15]   The rental price of capital, ρ_c, is a central concept in the neoclassical theory of productivity that has its origins in the neoclassical theory of investment developed by Jorgenson (1963). The rental price of capital is the implicit price that the firm charges itself for the assets that it owns, and is equal to the price that it would have to pay to rent an equivalent asset in a competitive market. However, there are no data on rental costs, except for a few markets (such as for aircraft). In most cases, firms have purchased and own the assets themselves. If well-developed competitive rental markets existed for all types of capital goods, it would be possible to observe the relevant rental rate on capital and, therefore, to calculate economic profits. But, as such data do not generally exist, one must typically infer indirectly the rental price of capital. The rental price of capital is often computed as $\rho_c = [p_K(i + d) - \dot{p}_K]/P$, where P is the output price deflator, p_K is the price of the capital goods, i is the nominal interest rate, d is the rate of depreciation and $\dot{p}_K$ is the capital gain or (if negative) loss. This

The profit rate is the firm's return on its capital, whereas the rental price of capital is the imputed cost to the firm on its capital. The former incorporates both the imputed cost of capital (in general, an unobservable variable) and oligopolistic, or economic, profits (rents), should these exist. The important point to note is that the assumptions of perfect competition in the capital markets and the optimisation behaviour of firms are made in the neoclassical literature to derive ρ_c, while the notion of the profit rate is theory independent. In other words, its derivation is not dependent upon any implicit theoretical assumptions, except that to the extent that it is defined as $r \equiv (V - wL)/J$. It should be noted that the argument does not depend upon this particular definition of r. All it requires is that the accounting identity is internally consistent and either one of the arguments is derived residually or that there is a statistical adjustment to ensure that this occurs if all the variables are derived independently.

It should be clear that the reason why this distinction matters is that as the neoclassical model usually assumes perfect competition and constant returns to scale, it might be erroneously thought that in using the NIPA identity as a critique of the aggregate production function, we also need to make the same assumption, namely that the value of the accounting identity should exclude any monopoly profits. A second important point, linked to the above, is that it is incorrect to argue that the NIPA identity is related to (or derived from) Euler's theorem. As argued above, the theoretical conditions to derive the concept of an aggregate production function make the existence of this concept a problematic issue, to say the least. Therefore, it cannot be argued that the identity follows from, or is a consequence of, Euler's theorem.

A major difference between the neoclassical parable and the accounting identity is, as we have shown, that the former assumes that output is a 'physical' magnitude and hence independent of the distribution of the output. But in applied work output is a monetary measure, namely value added, which does include any economic profits. In empirical work, if it is found that output does include monopoly profits, then in terms of equation (2.18), the value of monopoly profits should be deducted from both sides of the equation so that $V_c \equiv V - \Omega' \equiv wL + r_c J$ and this should be used in empirical production analysis, if one accepted the underlying neoclassical theoretical assumptions about the existence of an aggregate production function, and so on. This is because as V is a proxy for Q, it

---

formula indicates that the imputed rental price of capital is equivalent in competitive equilibrium to the marginal revenue product of capital services. The expected capital gain or loss is calculated, for example, as a three-year moving average of the annual price change of the capital good.

should not vary simply because the degree of competition differs. But once the adjustment has been made, the argument concerning the identity now follows through exactly.[16] The estimated 'output elasticities' will equal the factor shares, although capital's share will be larger than when monopoly profits are present.

ESTIMATING CROSS-SECTION PRODUCTION FUNCTIONS: A PROBLEM OF IDENTIFICATION OR INTERPRETATION?

The most likely explanation of why the existence of the accounting identity has not been thought normally to pose any difficulties for the estimation of the production function is, as we have suggested above, a conflation of the terms 'constant-price' output and the 'volume' of output. To see the difference this makes, it is useful to consider one of the few textbook explanations which does note the existence of the accounting identity and discusses the conditions under which it putatively does, and does not, pose a problem for the estimation of a production function.

Thomas (1993, pp. 311–12) considers the issue raised by the accounting identity and believes it to be a problem when factor prices do not vary when cross-firm data are used.[17] In these circumstances, he considers that there is also a separate identification problem. Nevertheless, given the existence of suitable identifying variables, such as variation in the factor prices, he contends that the technological parameters of the latter can be estimated. Both the problems posed by the accounting identity and the identification problem disappear. However, it will be shown that this is not the case – rather, there is what may be best described as a problem of interpretation of the estimates.

Thomas explicitly considers a cross-section production function; but the same arguments still hold for time-series estimation. It is useful to go in detail through his argument, turning first to the problems raised by the accounting identity.

Suppose the *physical* data used in estimation obeys the accounting identity:

$$p_i Q_i \equiv w_i^n L_i + \rho_i^n K_i. \tag{2.19}$$

---

[16]   The picture is complicated somewhat by the fact that some calculations of the rental price of capital deduct the corporate tax rate. We shall not pursue this issue here.

[17]   This exposition is chosen merely for convenience, as it is a standard result. See, for example, Wallis (1979).

Equation (2.19) may be written as:

$$Q_i \equiv (w_i^n/p_i) L_i + (\rho_i^n/p_i) K_i. \tag{2.20}$$

If p_i, ρ_i^n and w_i^n are constant over the cross-section, the identity (2.19) expresses Q_i simply as a function of L_i and K_i, as does the production function:

$$Q_i = A L_i^\alpha K_i^\beta. \tag{2.21}$$

Hence, in attempting to estimate (2.21), Thomas considers that we may merely be confusing it with the identity (2.19): 'A "good fit" may merely mean that we have rediscovered the identity that was artificially enforced on the data' (p. 312), especially if there is little variation in the factor prices. He does not, however, develop this argument further.[18]

Moreover, there are further problems when factor prices are constant. This is because the marginal productivity conditions can be written as:

$$\ln Q_i = \psi + \ln L_i \tag{2.22}$$

and

$$\ln Q_i = \psi' + \ln K_i, \tag{2.23}$$

where $\psi = \ln(w_i/\alpha)$ and $\psi' = \ln(\rho_i/\beta)$ are constants. The production function 'could be confused, for example, with a linear combination of the marginal productivity equations' (p. 310). The reason is as follows. Consider the case where only the production function has a disturbance term. 'Any attempt to relate output, $\ln Q$, to $\ln K$ and $\ln L$ will only yield an estimate of some linear combination of equations [2.22] and [2.23] such as:

$$\ln Q_i = \frac{\Lambda\psi + \Theta\psi'}{\Lambda + \Theta} + \left(\frac{\Lambda}{\Lambda + \Theta}\right) \ln L_i + \left(\frac{\Theta}{\Lambda + \Theta}\right) \ln K_i, \tag{2.24}$$

where Λ and Θ are any two constants' (p. 311).[19] Equation (2.24) is obtained by multiplying equation (2.22) by Λ and equation (2.23) by Θ

---

[18] It is not clear that this does pose a problem. If we were to estimate $Q = b_1 L + b_2 K$ using physical data then if there is an underlying true production function $b_1 = f_L$ and $b_2 = f_K$ and these will differ from w^n/p and ρ^n/p unless factors are paid their marginal products and the usual neoclassical assumptions hold.

[19] The notation has been altered to be consistent with that in the text.

and summing the resulting two equations. The coefficients of $\ln L$ and $\ln K$ are undetermined. However, this argument does *not* hold if we are using value data because of the underlying identity.

We begin with the definition of value added again as:

$$V_i \equiv w_i L_i + r_i J_i \equiv \ln B + a \ln w_i + (1 - a) \ln r_i + a \ln L_i + (1 - a) \ln J_i, \tag{2.25}$$

where $\ln B = - a \ln a - (1 - a) \ln (1 - a)$.

This may be expressed as:

$$V_i \equiv \ln A_i + a \ln L_i + (1 - a) \ln J_i, \tag{2.26}$$

and as $a \equiv w_i L_i / V_i$ and $(1 - a) \equiv r_i J_i / V_i$ it follows that:

$$\ln V_i \equiv -\ln a + \ln w_i + \ln L_i, \tag{2.27}$$

and

$$\ln V_i \equiv -\ln(1-a) + \ln r_i + \ln J_i. \tag{2.28}$$

Let us assume that $\ln w$ and $\ln r$ are indeed constant. If we multiply equations (2.27) and (2.28) by any two constants Λ and Θ and then sum the equations we obtain, analogously to equation (2.24), the following:

$$\ln V_i = -\frac{\Lambda}{\Lambda + \Theta} \ln a - \frac{\Theta}{\Lambda + \Theta} \ln (1 - a) + \frac{\Lambda}{\Lambda + \Theta} \ln w + \frac{\Theta}{\Lambda + \Theta} \ln r$$

$$+ \left(\frac{\Lambda}{\Lambda + \Theta}\right) \ln L_i + \left(\frac{\Theta}{\Lambda + \Theta}\right) \ln K_i. \tag{2.29}$$

But we know that equation (2.25) holds exactly even when $\ln w$ and $\ln r$ are constant, as it is an identity. It follows that $\Lambda/(\Lambda+\Theta)$ must equal a and $\Theta/(\Lambda+\Theta)$ must equal $(1 - a)$ and this is what the estimated values of the coefficients will be. This may be easily seen by comparing equations (2.25) and (2.29). Consequently, there is no identification problem, *per se*, as all that we are estimating is the underlying identity.

Let us turn to the case where there is variation in the factor prices and 'hence, there would be no question of confusing the production function with the marginal productivity equations and neither could it be confused with any accounting identity' (p. 312).

Under the conventional interpretation that we are estimating a production function, we have a three-equation system with by assumption Q_i, L_i and K_i endogenous and the factor prices exogenous. There is now no identification problem as supposedly the factor prices in the marginal productivity equations serve to identify the production function and presumably the variation in factor prices means that the results cannot be confused with equation (2.26).

However, as we have shown above, when we are using value data, the factor prices *do* appear in the 'production function' as shown by equation (2.25). In fact, with variation in factor prices, all we have are three identities, namely equations (2.25), (2.27) and (2.28). As such each can be estimated separately by OLS and the question of endogeneity and exogeneity does not arise. Moreover, as we have seen even with variation in factor prices, it is the accounting identity that is driving the results, although of course, estimating equation (2.26) with A assumed to be constant will cause a degree of misspecification error.

COST FUNCTIONS AND THE ACCOUNTING IDENTITY

We have seen how the existence of the underlying accounting identity means that we can always get a perfect fit to an aggregate production function and it is not surprising that the same applies to the cost function. The cost function shows how total costs vary as output varies, in the light of fixed factor prices, that is, $C = f(Q)$, where C is total costs. As the derivation is usually carried out at a particular point in time, the distinction between nominal costs and real costs is not normally made. It will, however, be necessary to make this distinction when we consider the cost function in a dynamic context. It is derived on the assumption that the firm chooses the optimum combination of the factors of production given the relative factor prices. It is perhaps easiest to demonstrate our argument with respect to the Cobb–Douglas and its cost function.

As any standard microeconomics textbook shows, the total cost function is obtained by maximising the output given by the production function, namely $Q = AL^\alpha K^\beta$, subject to the cost equation or accounting identity, $C = wL + \rho_c K$, where C is assumed to be constant, that is, the firm has a fixed budget to spend on both factors of production.

This procedure is not seen as tautological because Q is assumed to be a homogeneous quantity, independent of the costs of production, although, of course, $pQ = C$, where p is the price per unit of Q. Obtaining the first-order conditions from the constrained maximisation and setting them to zero, from some straightforward algebra, it may be shown that the cost equation is given by:

$$C = A^{-1/(\alpha+\beta)} \left[\left(\frac{\alpha}{\beta}\right)^{\beta} + \left(\frac{\beta}{\alpha}\right)^{\alpha} \right]^{1/(\alpha+\beta)} w^{\alpha/(\alpha+\beta)} \rho_c^{\beta/(\alpha+\beta)} Q^{1/(\alpha+\beta)}. \quad (2.30)$$

Thus, total costs depend upon the volume of output, the production coefficients, α, β and A and the prices of the factors of production, w and ρ_c. Equation (2.30) is interpreted as a behavioural relationship as it can be used to estimate the degree of returns to scale. Moreover, it is seen as a testable hypothesis because, according to this interpretation, if firms were not productively efficient, even if the production function were a Cobb–Douglas, the estimation could give a very poor statistical fit.

However, if value data are used for output so that $Q = V$, then it is straightforward to show that we have a tautology again. To see this, let us assume constant returns to scale so that $\alpha + \beta = 1$. Under these circumstances, the expression in square brackets, namely $[(\alpha/\beta)^{\beta} + (\beta/\alpha)^{\alpha}]$, is equal to $\alpha^{-\alpha}(1 - \alpha)^{-(1-\alpha)}$ and equation (2.30) becomes:

$$C = \alpha^{-\alpha}(1-\alpha)^{-(1-\alpha)} w^{\alpha} r^{(1-\alpha)} V/A. \quad (2.31)$$

As $V/A = L^{\alpha} J^{(1-\alpha)}$, it follows that equation (2.31) becomes:

$$C = \alpha^{-\alpha}(1-\alpha)^{-(1-\alpha)} w^{\alpha} r^{(1-\alpha)} L^{\alpha} J^{(1-\alpha)}, \quad (2.32)$$

which is identical to the accounting identity given by equation (2.14), where $\alpha = a$ and $(1 - \alpha) = (1 - a)$. Thus, if we use value data, equation (2.32) is definitionally true and does not need to be derived by the optimising procedure outlined above. The reason why equation (2.32), in logarithm form, is seen as a behavioural equation is that if $A(t)$ is proxied by a linear time trend, the statistical fit may be poor for reasons set out earlier in this chapter. That is to say, it does not adequately capture the path of $a\ln w + (1-a)\ln r$.

We can also see that one neoclassical procedure for deriving the rate of technical change also gives precisely the same result that we have derived from the accounting identity.

Total costs in neoclassical theory in nominal terms are given by:

$$C^n = A^{-1} B(w^n)^{\alpha} (\rho_c^n)^{(1-\alpha)} Q \quad (2.33)$$

and unit costs by:

$$c^n = A^{-1}B(w^n)^\alpha (\rho_c^n)^{(1-\alpha)}. \tag{2.34}$$

The superscript n denotes a nominal value. Suppose that there is no technical change. The growth of unit costs (which equals the growth of the price of Q) is given by:

$$\hat{c}_t^n = \alpha \hat{w}_t^n + (1 - \alpha)\hat{\rho}_{ct}^n = \hat{p}_t, \tag{2.35}$$

and there is no growth in the weighted average of the real wage rate and rental price of capital, that is,

$$\alpha(\hat{w}_t^n - \hat{p}_t) + (1 - \alpha)(\hat{\rho}_{ct}^n - \hat{p}_t) = \alpha \hat{w}_t + (1 - \alpha)\hat{\rho}_{ct} = 0. \tag{2.36}$$

If we allow for technical progress so that $\hat{A}_t = \lambda_t$, then the rate of cost diminution is given by:

$$\hat{c}_t^n = -\lambda_t + \alpha \hat{w}_t^n + (1 - \alpha)\hat{\rho}_{ct}^n = \hat{p}_t, \tag{2.37}$$

and the rate of technical change equals the weighted growth of the real wage and the real rental price of capital, that is,

$$\lambda_t = \alpha \hat{w}_t + (1 - \alpha)\hat{\rho}_{ct}. \tag{2.38}$$

This is exactly the same result that we get from just using the identity, when monopoly profits have been deducted, and where once again $\alpha = a$ and $(1 - \alpha) = (1 - a)$ but where p is the price index rather than a price, *per se*. In other words, $\lambda_t = \alpha \hat{w}_t + (1 - \alpha)\hat{r}_t$.

A Generalisation

We may generalise this argument about the rate of real cost diminution to other more complex cost functions. Following Whiteman (1988), consider first a production function with factor-augmenting technical change, namely $Q = F(A_L L, A_K K)$, where A_L and A_K are indices of labour and capital efficiency and the rates of labour- and capital-augmenting technical progress are given by λ_L and λ_K. Duality theory shows that the production function has a cost function of the form $C^n = f(w_E^n, \rho_{cE}^n, Q)$, where C^n is total nominal costs and w_E^n and ρ_{cE}^n are the efficiency adjusted or effective nominal wages and rental price of capital, that is, w^n/A_L and ρ_c^n/A_K, respectively. Assuming constant returns to scale, the cost function can be expressed as $c^n = g(w_E^n, \rho_{cE}^n) = g(w^n/A_L, \rho_c^n/A_K)$ where c^n is the unit cost of production. This may take an explicit functional form such as the Cobb–Douglas (as we have seen above)[20] or the translog cost function. Whiteman, for example, uses the translog unit cost function and differentiating this with respect to factor prices and using Sheppard's lemma gives an equation for each of the factor shares. Moreover, partially differentiating the unit cost function with respect to time and substituting in the equations for factor shares gives an expression for the dual rate of cost diminution as (Whiteman, 1988, p. 248):

$$\frac{\partial \ln c_n}{\partial t} = -\lambda_t = -[a_t \lambda_{Lt} + (1 - a_t)\lambda_{Kt}]. \tag{2.39}$$

If we totally differentiate the cost function with respect to time and equate the rate of change in product prices ($\hat{p}$) with the rate of change in unit costs ($\hat{c}^n$) we obtain an expression for the rate of technical change as:

$$\lambda_t = a_t \hat{w}_t^n + (1 - a_t)\hat{\rho}_{ct}^n - \hat{p}_t = a_t \hat{w}_t + (1 - a_t)\hat{\rho}_{ct}. \tag{2.40}$$

Thus, the conclusion from this general neoclassical analysis is that the rate of technical change is measured as the difference between the weighted sum of the growth of nominal wages and the rental price of capital and the rate of change in prices. This is precisely the same result we get from the accounting identity without any of the heroic neoclassical assumptions.

NEOCLASSICAL GROWTH ACCOUNTING AND THE IDENTITY

The use of value-added data also poses difficulties for the neoclassical growth-accounting approach. This *assumes* an aggregate production function, constant returns to scale, and the marginal productivity theory of factor pricing. Under these assumptions, from the 'dual' of the production function, the growth of TFP (the 'Solow residual' or, somewhat misleadingly, the rate of technical progress) is given by the weighted growth of the real wage rate and the rate of profit. Hence, the growth of TFP ($T\hat{F}P$) is equal to:

$$T\hat{F}P_t \equiv \lambda_t \equiv a_t \hat{w}_t + (1 - a_t)\hat{r}_t \equiv \hat{V}_t - [a_t \hat{L}_t + (1 - a_t)\hat{J}_t]. \tag{2.41}$$

The problem is that this is formally identical to the accounting identity in value terms and, hence, as we have noted, the neoclassical assumptions underlying the theory cannot be tested.

---

[20]   In this case, factor augmenting and neutral technical change are indistinguishable.

A 'startling' result (Solow, 1988, p. 313) of Solow's (1957) empirical analysis estimating the rate of technical progress was that over 87.5 per cent of the growth of productivity in the US private non-farm sector over the period from 1909 to 1949 could be attributable to technical change. The remainder 12.5 per cent was ascribed to the contribution of the growth of the factor inputs.

But it can easily be shown why the contribution of technical progress must, of necessity, be much greater than that of the growth of the factor inputs. If factor shares are constant, then $\hat{w}_t \equiv \hat{V}_t - \hat{L}_t$ and $\hat{V}_t - \hat{L}_t \equiv a\hat{w}_t + (1 - a_t)\hat{r}_t + a_t(\hat{J}_t - \hat{L}_t)$. As the share of labour, a, generally takes a value of between 0.65 (as in Solow's data) and 0.75, then if $\hat{r}_t = 0$, the rate of 'technical change' or $T\hat{F}P$, which consequently equals $a\hat{w}_t$, must generally account for between 65 and 75 per cent of the growth of labour productivity. It is startling that anybody should find this result 'startling'.

SOME FUNDAMENTAL MISCONCEPTIONS OF THE ARGUMENT

At the beginning of this chapter, we stated that the argument, although straightforward, was deceptively so. Consequently, we discuss briefly here some misconceptions that have been put to us[21] by economists working with production functions concerning the problems posed by the accounting identity. We shall consider some of them in greater detail in later chapters and, especially, Chapter 12.

1. Macroeconomics Abounds with Identities

It is undoubtedly true that there are many underlying identities in macroeconomics and, in nearly all cases, they are seen for what they are, definitional and not behavioural relationships. Take the example used in the Introduction. The national income accounting identity is given by $Y \equiv C + I + G + X - M$ (where Y is income; C is consumption; I is investment; X is exports; and M is imports). This equation may be differentiated, integrated and expressed in logarithmic form as $\ln Y \equiv \ln D + \phi_C \ln C + \phi_I \ln I + \phi_G \ln G + \phi_X \ln X - \phi_M \ln M$ (where the coefficients, the share of the relevant variable in income, sum to unity, and D is the constant of integration). This will give a perfect or near perfect statistical fit depending upon the

---

[21]   We assure the reader that they are not straw horses!

degree of variation of the coefficients (which are the shares in income of the particular variables) over time. But nobody would actually estimate the equation and interpret it as a statistical test of, say, the Keynesian theory of macroeconomics and the importance of demand in determining income.

As we have noted above, Solow (1957, p. 312) argues that the aggregate production function is 'only a little less legitimate a concept than say the aggregate consumption function'. However, the aggregation problems involved in the consumption function is *qualitatively* different from that of the aggregate production function. The estimated slope coefficient of the consumption function may be interpreted as some measure of the marginal propensity to consume. While it may be seriously biased because of the aggregation, it represents the change in the value of consumption due to a change in the *value* of income. The aggregate production function is estimated using, as a proxy, value data, purportedly to shed light on a *physical* or *technological* relationship between inputs and outputs. Therein lies the problem as discussed in this chapter.

2.   It is Merely a Problem of Aggregation

Some authors have suggested that the question at stake is merely one of aggregation. Typical of this is the view that aggregation at some level is unavoidable. Consider a production function for motor vehicle parts, made from hundreds of inputs. To refuse to aggregate even at the level of motor vehicle parts made from hundreds of inputs would be indefensible as science works with approximations, or so the argument goes.

However, it is not a question of simply refusing to aggregate. The problem, of course, is that to aggregate physical inputs and outputs requires prices, and so the use of these data to estimate a technological relationship runs into the problems outlined above. (Of course, there are cases where aggregation is necessary and justifiable, such as in the consumption function, but this is a different case from the production function and is discussed below.) In this vein, Temple (2006, 2010) suggests that the problem may be solved by sufficient disaggregation, and cites the work of Jorgenson and Griliches (1967). However, Temple seems to miss the fundamental point that Jorgenson and Griliches worked with *value* data and so disaggregation of the data does not remove the problem. We just have an accounting identity with more variables on the right-hand side. Jorgenson and Griliches's neoclassical procedure also requires the explicit assumption of a constant-returns-to-scale production function, competitive markets and the marginal productivity theory of factor pricing. Indeed, they themselves say that their disaggregated data cannot be used to test the theory of marginal productivity.

3. In Equilibrium, the Aggregate Production Function must be Closely Approximated by the Linear Accounting Identity

Some economists express no surprise that the Cobb–Douglas is an approximation of the linear accounting identity. For example, in the equilibrium of the model (that is, the point at which the production function is maximised subject to the linear cost constraint), the Cobb–Douglas production function and the linear constraint have the same slope and is an approximation of the national accounting identity. In this interpretation, the critique is merely restating, in another way, an equilibrium condition. An unstated postulate in this argument is that the aggregate production function actually exists; in other words this argument assumes *what is in dispute* or commits the error of *petitio principii*. The economy is also assumed to be in a state of equilibrium and empirically the economy is technically efficient (output is asserted as 'being maximised subject to a constraint'). This criticism of the accounting identity critique begs the question.

4. The Accounting Identity is Merely the Dual of the Production Function

This is a corollary of item (3), above. It has been argued that the argument is just a restatement of neoclassical optimisation conditions from the point of view of the 'dual' of the production function. In other words, the rate of technical change or, more accurately, the growth of TFP, as we discussed above, is given by $T\hat{F}P_t = \alpha_t \hat{w}_t + (1 - \alpha_t)\hat{r}_t$ and, given the usual neoclassical assumptions, this equals $a_t\hat{w}_t + (1 - a_t)\hat{r}_t$. For example, Hsieh (2002, p. 502) argues that 'It is useful to think this [growth-accounting identity] as an accounting identity'. He elaborates:

> [W]ith *only* the condition that output equals factor incomes, we have the results that the primal and dual measures of the Solow residual are equal. No other assumptions are needed for this result: we do not need any assumption about the form of the production function, bias of technological change or the relationship between factor prices and their social marginal products. (Hsieh, 1999, p.135, emphasis added; see also Barro (1999) for a similar view)

But this is very misleading. The growth-accounting approach requires the *existence* of a well-behaved aggregate production function together with optimising behaviour and the neoclassical theory of factor pricing. Hsieh's argument is surprising given our arguments above which shows that the growth-accounting results can be derived from the identity *without* the assumption of an aggregate production function, and if there is no well-behaved aggregate production function there is no dual to it.

5.   It is Merely a Problem of Correctly Identifying the Aggregate Production Function

Typical of this view is Bronfenbrenner (1971) who argues that as the aggregate production function includes time as an argument (as in $A(t)$), and the cost function (the accounting identity) does not, this serves to identify the production function. (Even if this were correct, which it is not, any shift in the production function would serve to identify the cost function, not the production function.) However, as we have shown in this chapter, it is not an identification problem; the aggregate production function is just an approximation to the accounting identity. They are in Phelps Brown's (1957) words, just different sides of the same penny. It is not a problem that can be solved by estimation in a series of simultaneous equations as our discussion above of Thomas (1993) shows. Temple (2006, 2010) also takes this view.

6.   Many Recent Studies have Examined the Problems of Correctly Specifying and Estimating the Aggregate Production Function

Sceptics of the arguments concerning the accounting identity often commit an *ignoratio elenchi*. This occurs, for example, when papers are cited as refuting the critique that actually have no bearing on the issue. It is held that examples where the accounting critique undermines the analysis relate to a now dated literature and do not take into account recent developments in the use and modern estimations of production functions. In subsequent chapters we show that a number of seminal papers suffer from the accounting identity problem, including Hall (1988a, 1988b) and Mankiw et al. (1992), and estimates of labour demand functions, for example, Hamermesh (1993). Given space constraints, we leave it to others to find 'Waldo' in more recent papers.[22]

For example, the following have been mentioned as undermining the critique. Antras (2004) finds that assuming Hicks-neutral technical change biases the estimation of aggregate production functions towards the Cobb–Douglas. However, this result is not relevant to the critique as it assumes in the first place that the aggregate production function can be estimated, which is what is being disputed. Another example of this problem is Hsieh and Klenow (2009). They construct heterogeneous agent economies that do not rely on the concept of aggregate production function, but on firm-level production technologies. Yet, even a cursory examination of this

---

[22]   As noted in the Introduction, Waldo is a character hidden in a colour picture with a large number of other characters. 'Where's Waldo?' is a child's game of trying to pick him out of this multitude.

paper shows that the micro-production functions do not have heterogeneous physical inputs, but instead use constant-price output and capital. Because the aggregate production function is still being used years after the original critique was advanced in a rudimentary form by Phelps Brown (1957), this in no way invalidates the criticism, as some seem to believe.

7. Estimates of Production Functions often Perform Badly and Sometimes Show Significant Increasing Returns to Scale

The reason why the aggregate production function does not always give a good statistical fit is nearly always because the weighted logarithm of the wage rate and the rate of profit (or their growth rates) is not adequately proxied by a linear time trend (or a constant). It could also be because, when a Cobb–Douglas is estimated, there is too much variation in the factor shares. However, the evidence suggests that the poor statistical fits are primarily due to the first reason.[23] In this case, it is possible to determine *precisely* the degree of bias involved through the estimation of the auxiliary relationship between the weighted logarithm of the factor prices and the logarithm of the inputs. This bias is often upwards, giving the impression that there are statistically significant increasing returns to scale. We discuss this further in Chapter 10 when we question what statistical estimates of market power actually mean. It is also possible to 'retrieve' the accounting identity through the use of a more flexible time trend or adjusting the capital stock for changes in 'capacity utilisation' as we noted above.

8. The BLS and OECD Routinely Calculate and Publish Tables of Estimates of Total Factor Productivity

Surprisingly, an argument frequently made is that the aggregation problem and the Cambridge capital theory controversies cannot be correct, or important, because value measures of the aggregate capital stock are routinely used in 'state-of-the-art' growth-accounting studies. This, it is argued, explicitly defines the relationship between aggregate inputs and outputs at the country or regional level. There are also routinely made calculations of TFP growth (or multi-factor productivity growth as it is sometimes called) by, for example, the OECD (the STAN database) and the US Bureau of Labor Statistics (BLS).[24] (See, for example, OECD,

---

[23] It is for this reason that Douglas undoubtedly changed in the 1930s from estimating time-series production functions to the use of cross-sectional data (where the wage and profit rates showed much smaller variation).

[24] Available at www.oecd.org/sti/stan/ and http://www.bls.gov/data/, respectively.

2004.) This is essentially an 'appeal to authority' type of justification. An implication of this argument is that as Cobb and Douglas (1928) had used value indices of the capital stock in their original regressions, and while there may have been statistical deficiencies in the way they were computed, this is still no reason to deny that the aggregate production function exists. However, use of the perpetual inventory method to estimate the constant-price value of the capital stock does not avoid the aggregation problem; and, of course, does not vitiate the problem of the accounting identity, which involves the inappropriate use of value instead of physical data.

9.   Some Further Issues

Kincaid (2009) has brought a philosopher's eye to neoclassical growth theory and provides a clear discussion of the nuances of causality in explaining economic growth within the neoclassical paradigm. Perhaps a philosopher of science untrammelled by any particular economic para-digm is the nearest we can get to Kuhn's 'uncommitted observer'. Kincaid is well aware of the seriousness of the problems of measuring capital and the capital theory controversies and aggregation problems *à la* Fisher (1992), unlike most economists trained within the neoclassical school. This leads him to conclude that 'there are serious doubts about neoclassi-cal growth models in so far as they are supposed to be providing a causal explanation based on marginal productivities' (p. 466).

Kincaid continues 'if the equations tested are just supporting the claim that there is some causal contribution and causal relationship from the *quantity* of capital a country has at its disposal and the total, then the doubts are less worrisome' (p. 466, emphasis added). This is correct to the extent that even a brief visit to a developing country will provide evidence that the observed physical capital stocks (the physical infrastructure, the types and quantities of machinery and the skills of teachers and their resources) are fewer and of poorer quality than in the advanced countries.

However, this does not mean that fitting an aggregate production func-tion using value data can tell us anything more than this casual empiricism. It cannot distinguish between the contributions to productivity growth made by technical progress and capital accumulation. The usual statistical diagnostic tools (such as the R^2, t-ratios, and tests for unit roots) are liter-ally meaningless in this case. No economic hypothesis is being tested. The accounting argument is that there is no point in estimating relationships based on the so-called 'aggregate production function'.

Moreover, Kincaid (footnote on p. 473) does not see the 'logical rela-tionship' between the argument made by Felipe and McCombie (2006) that the good fits to aggregate production functions are being caused simply by the accounting identity and Fisher's (1971b) point that the good fits are due to the factor shares being constant. It is useful to clarify the relationship between both arguments here. When factor shares are constant, the accounting identity will ensure that the Cobb–Douglas gives a good statistical fit to the data and hence explains Fisher's results. If factor shares are variable then we need to choose a more flexible transformation of the identity to get a good fit. Kincaid also asks: 'how do these aggregation issues bear on that work [growth accounting] and its evidential value?'. Our answer is that the growth-accounting approach has *no* evidential value. In fact, from the identity it has simply been shown above that the growth of so-called technical change must account for about three-quarters of productivity growth; a result Solow (1988) found 'startling', which itself is startling, as noted above.

Finally, Temple (2006, 2010) has presented a considered and detailed assessment of the critique, and while he accepts that it has some validity and needs to be more widely known, he argues that Felipe and McCombie make too much of it. Rebuttals of Temple's criticisms are to be found in Felipe and McCombie (2010a, 2012). Nevertheless, there are a number of serious misconceptions in Temple's argument that we shall briefly discuss here. A more detailed discussion is to be found in Chapter 12.

First, as we noted above, Temple believes that disaggregation will overcome the problem. We have argued that it will not so long as value data are used. Second, Temple assumes that the critique requires a number of *ad hoc* assumptions, such as constant factor shares and that the growth of the weighted wage rate and rate of profit is constant over time. Consequently, he considers that it only applies to the spurious Cobb–Douglas. Related to this, he seems, at times, to believe that it is simply an identification problem. For example, he argues that if value data were generated by a 'stable production function' and the researcher were capable, *inter alia*, of controlling for TFP, then there is no reason for 'the parameters to be unidentified'. Moreover, he argues that the 'dynamic version of the value added identity cannot do any better than this model' (Temple, 2010, p. 688). But, as our discussion of the critique has shown, it is not fundamentally an identification problem. Temple, like other critics, is guilty here of *petitio principii*. In other words, he *assumes* the existence of the aggregate production function that can be estimated with value data in defence of the criticism that it cannot.

Temple, nevertheless, accepts an important implication of the criticism:

[I]n particular, the argument shows that an applied researcher may appear to obtain meaningful results from estimating a production relationship, even when the researcher is making assumptions that do not hold in the data. One important instance arises when factors are not paid their marginal products. In that case, although researchers often interpret their results as if the estimated parameters can be used to derive output elasticities, the identity suggests that the estimates may be more closely related to factor shares. (p. 686)

This comes perilously close to conceding our arguments.

CONCLUDING COMMENTS

This chapter has presented the central argument as to why regression analysis of aggregate production functions can give no indication of the underlying aggregate technological parameters of the economy, which aggregation theory suggests do not exist. As we stated in the introduction, the argument while straightforward, is deceptively simple. It is a matter of logic rather than methodology and the plausibility or otherwise of assumptions. It is either correct or incorrect. We have argued that it is the former and have not yet seen any compelling formal proof to the contrary. (Solow (1987) has attempted to provide a refutation, but it is erroneous. This is discussed in Chapter 5.)

We outlined some major misunderstandings about the argument that go some way to explaining why it has not had more impact. It is not just that there is an underlying identity: it was shown that there is an identity in monetary terms even if we have physical data (that is, there is an accounting and a 'virtual' identity). It is the fact that it is not possible to recover the physical data from the value-added identity and hence it is not possible to interpret the regression results as reflecting technological parameters. In this sense Solow (1957, p. 312) is wrong when he argues that 'the aggregate production function is only a little less legitimate a concept than, say, the aggregate consumption function'. There are, of course, aggregation problems when individual consumption functions with separate marginal propensities to consume are summed and an estimate of the aggregate marginal propensity to consume is obtained. But at least the consumption function is correctly defined as a relationship between variables using constant-price value data and the marginal propensity to consume as the ratio of the absolute change of the *monetary value* of consumption to that of income (at least in the simplest specification of the consumption function). But this is not the case with the aggregate production function where using constant-price data as a proxy for physical data renders the interpretation of any estimated coefficients problematical.

Table 2.2 presents a summary of the relationship between the accounting

Table 2.2 *The relationship between the accounting identity and the aggregate production function using time-series data*

The Accounting Identity	The Neoclassical Production Function
Prices are a mark-up on unit labour costs	The micro-production function with constant returns to scale is given by:

$$p_i = (1 + \pi_i)\frac{w_i L_i}{Q_i}$$

$$Q_i = A_{0i}e^{\lambda t}L_i^\alpha K_i^{(1-a)}.$$

A constant mark-up gives constant shares of labour (a) and capital ($1-a$) in total value added, regardless of the underlying technology.

$$a_i = 1/(1 + \pi_i) \text{ and } (1 - a_i) = \pi_i/(1 + \pi_i).$$

The accounting identity is given by:

$$p_iQ_i \equiv w_iL_i + r_iJ_i$$

where $r_i = (p_iQ_i - w_iL_i)/J_i$

Summing over industries gives:

$$V = \sum p_iQ_i = wL + rJ$$

There are no serious aggregation problems. Aggregation may actually reduce the variability of the aggregate factor share compared with the individual factor shares.

By definition (and making *no* assumption about the state of competition or the mechanism by which factors are rewarded) the following conditions hold:

$$\frac{\partial V}{\partial L} \equiv w \text{ and } \frac{\partial V}{\partial J} \equiv r$$

Given constant factor shares, the accounting identity at time t may be written as:

$$V_t = Bw_t^a r_t^{(1-a)}L_t^a J_t^{(1-a)}$$

Aggregation problems and the Cambridge capital theory controversies show that theoretically the aggregate production function does not exist. Nevertheless, it is assumed that:

$$\sum Q_i = Q = A_0e^{\lambda t}L^\alpha K^{(1-a)}$$

Assuming (i) perfect competition and (ii) the aggregate marginal productivity theory of factor pricing gives:

$$p\frac{\partial Q}{\partial L} = pf_L = w \text{ and } p\frac{\partial Q}{\partial K} = pf_K = \rho.$$

From Euler's theorem:

$$Q = f_LL + f_KK$$

and the cost identity is:

$$pQ = wL + \rho K \text{ or}$$
$$Q = (w/p)L + (\rho/p)K$$

where w/p and ρ/p are physical measures and equal f_L and f_K.

It is assumed for empirical analysis that $Q = V$ and $K = J$.

Using time-series data and estimating $\ln V_t = c + b_1t + b_2 \ln L_t + b_3\ln J_t$ provides estimates of b_2 and b_3, which are the aggregate output elasticities of labour and capital. If a good statistical fit is found, it is

Table 2.2   (continued)

The Accounting Identity	The Neoclassical Production Function
or, assuming the stylised fact that $a\hat{w}_t + (1-a)\hat{r}_t = a\hat{w} = \lambda$, as:	inferred that the estimation has not refuted the hypothesis of the existence of the aggregate production function.
$$V_t = Be^{\lambda t} L_t^a J_t^{(1-a)}$$	The estimates of b_2 and b_3 equal the observed factor shares, i.e.,
Estimating $\ln V_t = c + b_1 t + b_2 \ln L_t + b_3 \ln J_t$ gives estimates of b_2 and b_3 exactly equal to the factor shares for *definitional* reasons: i.e. $b_2 = a$, and $b_3 = (1-a)$.	$b_2 = \alpha = a$ and $b_3 = (1-\alpha) = (1-a)$ if assumptions (i) and (ii) above hold. If this is found to occur, it constitutes a failure to refute the theory that markets are competitive and factors are paid their marginal products.
It is always possible to find an approximation that will give a perfect statistical fit to the data.	

The Equifinality Theorem

Estimating $\ln V = c + b_1 t + b_2 \ln L + b_3 \ln J$ will always give a perfect fit to the data, provided that factor shares are constant and the stylised fact $a\hat{w}_t + (1-a)\hat{r}_t = a\hat{w} = \lambda = $ a constant holds. This is the case irrespective of whether it is a 'true' underlying aggregate Cobb–Douglas production function (no matter how theoretically implausible this may be) or no aggregate production function exists at all. The data cannot discriminate between these two cases. (The same result holds using growth rates.) If the condition of constant factor shares and a constant growth of the weighted wage and profit rates is not met, it is still possible to obtain a perfect fit by a more flexible approximation to the accounting identity than that given by the Cobb–Douglas. It is therefore not possible empirically to test the existence of the aggregate production function or the aggregate marginal productivity theory of factor pricing.

---

identity and the Cobb–Douglas production function when time-series data are used (although as we emphasise again, *pace* Temple (2006, 2010), *inter alios*, the critique applies to any production function). We have termed the conclusion that a specification of the accounting identity that resembles an aggregate production function, can always be found to give a good fit to the data, the 'equifinality theorem'.

The implications of the equifinality theorem may be summarised as follows.

1. It is not possible to test statistically, and hence potentially refute, the hypothesis that the economy is representable by an aggregate production function.
2. The values of the factor shares determine the values of the output elasticities in a statistical sense, rather than the other way around for economic reasons (such as factors are paid their marginal products under competitive conditions).
3. The first-order conditions, which may be erroneously interpreted as derived from the marginal productivity theory of factor pricing, will always be statistically significant.

APPENDIX 2A1   THE CES PRODUCTION FUNCTION, THE TRANSLOG PRODUCTION FUNCTION, THE BOX–COX TRANSFORMATION AND THE ACCOUNTING IDENTITY

In this appendix we show explicitly the relationship between the accounting identity and the CES and translog production functions. We also show how the data of the accounting identity can through the Box–Cox transformation give a good fit to a linear relationship, the Cobb–Douglas or the CES 'production function' depending upon the variability of w and r and the factor shares. This illustrates how the aggregate 'production function' is nothing more than a mathematical transformation that satisfies the accounting identity and which accurately tracks the path of factor shares.

The CES Production Function

We have seen that the firm data may be summed arithmetically to give the familiar aggregate accounting identity, $V_t \equiv w_t L_t + r_t J_t$ or, in growth rates, $\hat{V}_t \equiv a_t \hat{w}_t + (1 - a_t)\hat{r}_t + a_t \hat{L}_t + (1 - a_t)\hat{J}_t$.

What we require is some mathematical functional form that will give a good prediction to V or to w at any specific time, t. In particular, we need some functional form that will accurately track the path of the a_ts and $(1 - a_t)$s. Suppose that over the period for which data are available, we find that labour's share is rising at a steady rate (and, consequently, capital's share is falling). It is a straightforward matter to show that the CES is likely to give a better approximation to the accounting identity than the Cobb–Douglas relationship.

The CES 'production function' with Hicks-neutral technical change is given by:

$$V_t = A(t)[\delta L_t^{-\theta} + (1 - \delta)J_t^{-\theta}]^{-1/\theta} \quad (1 \geq \delta \geq 0; \theta \geq -1), \quad (2A1.1)$$

where $A(t)$ is interpreted as an efficiency parameter and $A(t) = A_0 e^{\lambda t}$ is the measure of Hicks-neutral technical change when time-series data are used, δ is a distributional parameter, and the elasticity of substitution is given by $\sigma = 1/(1+\theta)$. It is assumed that there are constant returns to scale, but we have seen that the data and accounting identity, which must always be satisfied, implies this, so it is not an arbitrary assumption.

The growth of output is given by:

$$\hat{V} = \lambda + \left(\frac{\delta L_t^{-\theta}}{D_t}\right)\hat{L}_t + \left[\frac{(1-\delta)J_t^{-\theta}}{D_t}\right]\hat{J}_t, \tag{2A1.2}$$

where $D_t = [\delta L_t^{-\theta} + (1-\delta)J_t^{-\theta}]$.

The marginal productivity conditions are given by:

$$\frac{\partial V_t}{\partial L_t} = w_t = \frac{\delta L_t^{(-\theta-1)}V_t}{D_t} \tag{2A1.3}$$

and

$$\frac{\partial V_t}{\partial J_t} = r_t = \frac{(1-\delta)J_t^{(-\theta-1)}V_t}{D_t}. \tag{2A1.4}$$

Consequently, equation (2A1.4) may be expressed as:

$$\hat{V}_t = \lambda + a_t\hat{L}_t + (1-a_t)\hat{J}_t, \tag{2A1.5}$$

given that:

$$a_t = \frac{w_t L_t}{D_t} = \frac{\delta L_t^{-\theta}}{D_t} \tag{2A1.6}$$

and

$$(1-a_t) = \frac{r_t J_t}{D_t} = \frac{(1-\delta)J_t^{-\theta}}{D_t}. \tag{2A1.7}$$

The growth rate of labour's and capital's factor shares are given by:

$$\hat{a}_t = (1-a_t)\theta(\hat{J}_t - \hat{L}_t) = -(1-a_t)\left(1 - \frac{1}{\sigma}\right)(\hat{J}_t - \hat{L}_t) \tag{2A1.8}$$

and

$$(1-\hat{a}_t) = -a_t\theta(\hat{J}_t - \hat{L}_t) = a_t\left(1 - \frac{1}{\sigma}\right)(\hat{J}_t - \hat{L}_t). \tag{2A1.9}$$

Thus, as the capital–labour tends to grow at a roughly steady rate over time, it may well be a good proxy for the rates of change of the shares, if these growth rates are also at a constant rate.

Consequently, if we were to estimate:

$$\hat{a}_t = b_1(\hat{J}_t - \hat{L}_t), \qquad (2A1.10)$$

where the rate of change of labour's share was positive, as $\hat{J} - \hat{L}$ generally is also positive we would find an estimate of $b_1 > 0$ which implies that $\theta > 1$ and so $\sigma = 1/(1+\theta) < 1$, that is, the supposed aggregate elasticity of substitution is less than unity. Conversely, if labour's share were falling over the period concerned, this would imply that $\sigma > 1$. Thus, in these circumstances, the CES function would provide a better approximation to the data than the Cobb–Douglas. Because we have started with an aggregate production function which is assumed to exist with all the usual neoclassical properties, the rate of change of the shares is assumed to be *caused* by the rate of growth of the capital–labour ratio together with the technical parameters such as the aggregate elasticity of substitution. For example, up until 1973 factor shares were relatively stable, but for a period of time after the 1973 oil crisis there was a decline in the share of profits which, as we noted above, implies that the elasticity of substitution was less than unity, an argument advanced by Sargent (1985).

But suppose, for example, for some other reason such as the increasing bargaining strength of labour, labour's share increases over the time period under consideration, and equation (2A1.1) gives a good fit to the data. We know that given $a_t\hat{w}_t + (1 - a_t)\hat{r}_t$ is approximately a constant, equation (2A1.6) follows from the identity, without the need for factors to be paid their marginal products. Consequently, an alternative explanation is that the time path of the factor shares *causes* the CES to give a better fit to the data than the Cobb–Douglas (the CES is a better approximation to the accounting identity), through the 'coincidental' correlation with the growth of the capital-labour ratio, which, as we have mentioned, usually shows a positive trend rate of growth. If the change in the factor shares is actually determined by such factors as changes in the bargaining power of labour and capital,[1] this would have to be interpreted in terms of an aggregate production function as being caused by a change in the elasticity of substitution. It would, furthermore, imply highly unstable values for the elasticity of substitution. This is precisely what estimates of the variable-elasticities-of-substitution aggregate production functions find (Bairam, 1987). But

---

[1]   McCombie (1987) shows that if the mark-up on total unit costs (including intermediate products) is relatively stable, but firms in an inflationary environment (resulting from, say, the oil price increase in 1973/74) only pass on the increase in costs to the consumer without applying the mark-up to these extra costs, then the profit share will fall. Firms in the later upswing may seek to remedy this by learning to apply the mark-up to any increase and to increase the size of this mark-up. This will lead to a fall in labour's share. It has nothing to do with changes in either the elasticity of substitution or the degree of bias in the rate of technical change.

if one is committed to the aggregate production function, to find that its technological parameters change rapidly is disconcerting, to say the least.[2]

The Translog Production Function

The translog production function with the inputs measured in terms of efficiency units is given by:

$$\ln V_t = \ln A_0 + \alpha \ln A_{Lt}L_t + \beta \ln A_{Kt}J_t + \gamma (\ln A_{Lt}L_t \ln A_{Kt}J_t) + \omega (\ln A_{Lt}L_t)^2$$
$$+ \varepsilon (\ln A_{Kt}J_t)^2, \tag{2A1.11}$$

where A_{Lt} and A_{Kt} are the levels of factor-augmenting technology, termed the augmentation level parameters, which in pooled country data, are allowed to differ between countries and where λ_L and λ_J are the rates of labour and capital-augmenting technical change. Substituting $\ln A_{Lt} = \ln A_{L0} + \lambda_L t$ and $\ln A_{Jt} = \ln A_{J0} + \lambda_J t$, where A_{L0} and A_{J0} are the initial levels, the following estimating equation is derived:

$$\ln V_t = \ln A_0 + \delta(\ln A_{L0})^2 + \varepsilon(\ln A_{J0})^2 + \gamma(\ln A_{L0})(\ln A_{J0}) + \alpha \ln A_{L0} + \beta \ln A_{J0}$$
$$+ (\alpha + \gamma \ln A_{J0} + 2\delta \ln A_{L0}) \ln L_t + (\beta + \gamma \ln A_{L0} + 2\varepsilon \ln A_{J0}) \ln J_t$$
$$+ \omega (\ln L_t)^2 + \varepsilon(\ln J_t)^2 + \gamma(\ln L_t)(\ln J_t) + (2\varepsilon\lambda_K + \gamma\lambda_L)(t \ln J_t)$$
$$+ (2\omega\lambda_L + \gamma\lambda_J)(t \ln L_t) + [(\beta + \gamma \ln A_{L0} + 2\varepsilon \ln A_{J0})\lambda_J$$
$$+ (\alpha + \gamma \ln A_{J0} + 2\omega \ln A_{L0})\lambda_L]t + [\varepsilon(\lambda_J)^2 + \omega(\lambda_L)^2 + \gamma\lambda_L\lambda_J]t^2 \tag{2A1.12}$$

or, equivalently:

$$\ln V_t = c + b_1 \ln L_t + b_2 \ln J_t + b_3(\ln J_t)^2 + b_4(\ln L_t)^2 + b_5(\ln L_t \ln J_t)$$

$$+ b_6(t \ln J_t) + b_7(t \ln L_t) + b_8 t + b_9 t^2. \tag{2A1.13}$$

Equation (2A.13) was estimated by, for example, Kim and Lau (1994)[3] in first differences together with the corresponding first-order condition for labour, that is, a system of two equations reflecting the technical relations and the economic decisions of the firm. The reason is

---

[2] The CES production function is sometimes specified with labour and/or capital-augmenting technical progress. This does not affect the argument, except that under neoclassical assumptions the rate of change of the factor shares will also be functions of the degree of bias in the rate of 'technical change'.

[3] They used pooled time-series data for the G5 countries and for the four East Asian newly industrialised economies. Their study is discussed in Felipe and McCombie (2003).

that it is inappropriate to estimate the production function as a single regression equation treating capital and labour as exogenous variables. Consequently, as A_{L0} and A_{J0} differ between countries, the coefficients c, b_1 and b_2 are country-specific constants. Estimates of the rate of factor-augmenting technical change may be obtained by using the estimates of ε, ω, γ and the coefficients of $(t\ln J)$ and $(t\ln L)$ or their first differences if the growth rate specification is used. The coefficient of t^2 is not independent, but is determined by the estimates ε, ω, γ, λ_L and λ_J.

Expressions for the output elasticities may be obtained by differentiating $\ln V_t$ with respect to $\ln L_t$ and $\ln J_t$, respectively. If profit maximisation and perfect competition hold, these will equal the relevant factor shares:

$$\frac{\partial \ln V_t}{\partial \ln L_t} = \alpha + \gamma \ln A_{J0} + 2\omega \ln A_{L0} + (2\omega \lambda_L + \gamma \lambda_J)t + 2\omega \ln L_t + \gamma \ln J_t = a_t$$
(2A1.14)

and

$$\frac{\partial \ln V_t}{\partial \ln J_t} = \beta + \gamma \ln A_{L0} + 2\varepsilon \ln A_{J0} + (2\varepsilon \lambda_J + \gamma \lambda_L)t + 2\varepsilon \ln J_t + \gamma \ln L_t$$

$$= (1 - a_t).$$
(2A1.15)

Thus, the test of the assumption of a competitive labour market is to determine whether or not the coefficients in (2A1.14) and (2A1.15) are statistically significantly different from those in equation (2A1.12). If they are, the argument is that this is sufficient to reject the null hypothesis. Alternatively, we could test the hypothesis that the output elasticities equal the factor shares.

However, in the light of our earlier comments, it will come as no surprise to learn that these arguments are invalidated by the underlying identity, as will now be shown. To commence, let us differentiate equation (2A1.13), the 'production function', with respect to time. Denoting growth rates by the lower case, we obtain:

$$\hat{V}_t = \alpha'_t \lambda_L + \beta'_t \lambda_J + \alpha'_t \hat{L}_t + \beta'_t \hat{J}_t,$$
(2A1.16)

where

$$\alpha'_t = (\alpha + \gamma \ln A_{J0} + 2\delta \ln A_{L0}) + (2\delta \lambda_L + \gamma \lambda_J)t + 2\omega \ln L_t + \gamma \ln J_t$$
(2A1.17)

and

$$\beta'_t = (\beta + \gamma \ln A_{L0} + 2\varepsilon \ln A_{J0}) + (2\varepsilon\lambda_J + \gamma\lambda_L)t + 2\varepsilon \ln J_t + \gamma \ln L_t, \tag{2A1.18}$$

where the variables α'_t and β'_t are the respective output elasticities. From the marginal productivity conditions, equations (2A1.17) and (2A1.18), $\alpha'_t = a_t$ and $\beta'_t = (1 - a_t)$. Thus, if there is profit maximisation and perfect competition then, from equations (2A1.14) to (2A1.18) the following relationship must hold:

$$\hat{V}_t = \alpha_t\lambda_L + (1 - \alpha_t)\lambda_J + \alpha_t\hat{L}_t + (1 - \alpha_t)\hat{J}_t = \lambda_t + \alpha_t\hat{L}_t + (1 - \alpha_t)\hat{J}_t, \tag{2A1.19}$$

where α_t and $(1-\alpha_t)$ are labour's and capital's factor shares.

On the other hand, recall that differentiating the identity $V = wL + rJ$ with respect to time and expressing the result as growth rates, we obtain the familiar result:

$$\hat{V}_t = a_t\hat{w}_t + (1 - a_t)\hat{r}_t + a_t\hat{L}_t + (1 - a_t)\hat{J}_t = \lambda_t + a_t\hat{L}_t + (1 - a_t)\hat{J}_t. \tag{2A1.20}$$

Since the latter is obtained from an identity, it must *always* hold for any putative production function, and does not involve the assumption that factors are paid their marginal products.

Comparing equations (2A1.19) and (2A1.20) it can be seen that (2A1.19) will always hold by virtue of the underlying identity. Consequently, *labour's and capital's output elasticities must equal their respective factor shares, regardless of whether or not markets are competitive.* It is thus not possible to test this hypothesis by the procedure adopted by Kim and Lau. Moreover, constant returns to scale must prevail, as from equations (2A1.16) and (2A1.19), $\beta'_t = (1 - \alpha'_t)$. Thus doubling the growth rates of labour and capital will double the growth rate of output.

The translog form can be derived from the identity in a manner analogous to that for the Cobb–Douglas as follows. Assume that λ_t follows a linear time trend (as in the case of the Cobb–Douglas) or some more complex function of time, and that factor shares in this economy happen to be well tracked empirically by the expressions in equations (2A1.17) and (2A1.18). (This is comparable to the assumption of constant factor shares to derive the Cobb–Douglas.) If these equations are substituted into the identity (2A1.19) and the equation is integrated, the translog is derived.

The limitation with the Cobb–Douglas is that if shares vary too much over time, we may not obtain a very good fit to the data. The advantage of the translog is that by making factor shares a function of $\hat{L}$, $\hat{J}$, λ_L and λ_J, it allows for a better approximation (a more flexible functional form) than the Cobb–Douglas to the accounting identity. However, we should not necessarily expect the parameters ε, γ and ω to be very stable over time, since the values they take are merely coincidental, and do not necessarily reflect any underlying technology.[4] (See McCombie and Dixon, 1991 for a theoretical and empirical study of the accounting identity and 'biased technical change'.)

The Box–Cox Transformation

As we have established, an aggregate production function is theoretically merely a mathematical function that relates inputs to outputs. It is actually nothing more than a mathematical transformation that satisfies the accounting identity and which accurately tracks the path of the factor shares. Suppose, like Douglas, we have data on V, L and J. Cobb suggested to Douglas that he try estimating the familiar multiplicative power relationship that we now know as the Cobb–Douglas production function. But he might have suggested using the less restrictive Box–Cox transformation. Consider the transformation of a variable:

$$
Y(\eta) = \begin{cases} \dfrac{Y^{\eta} - 1}{\eta}, & \eta \neq 0 \\ \ln Y, & \eta = 0. \end{cases}
$$

The extended Box–Cox transformation of the accounting identity is therefore:

$$
V(\eta) = c + b_1 L(\eta) + b_2 J(\eta). \tag{2A1.21}
$$

If $\eta = 1$, and the regression goes through the origin, we have the linear accounting identity. If $\eta = 0$, we have the familiar Cobb–Douglas. What happens if $0 > \eta > 1$? Consider the CES production function given by equation (2A1.1), but let us, for expositional ease, assume that we are dealing with cross-section data so A is constant.

Equation (2A1.1) may be expressed as:

$$
V^{-\theta} = [A^{-\theta}\delta]L^{-\theta} + [A^{-\theta}(1 - \delta)]J^{-\theta}. \tag{2A1.22}
$$

---

[4]   The Cobb–Douglas is a special case of the translog (when the restriction $\gamma = \omega = \varepsilon = 0$ is imposed). As factor shares are constant, however, it is not possible to derive separately the estimates of the degree of labour- and capital-augmenting technical change.

Compare this with the extended Box-Cox transformation when $\eta \neq 0$ and the constant term equals zero:

$$V^\eta = b_3 L^\eta + b_4 J^\eta. \tag{2A1.23}$$

It follows that $\eta = -\rho$. It can be seen that the CES is nothing more than a Box–Cox transformation of the linear accounting identity and will give a better fit than the former if w and r and/or factor shares vary. This could be because the mark-up varies over time, either randomly or because of changes in the market power of firms and the bargaining power of labour.

Consequently, this provides a further illustration of the argument that it is the underlying identity that is determining the values of the coefficients when an aggregate production function is estimated. (See McCombie, 2000 for an example of the use of the Box–Cox transformation using cross–regional US state data.)

APPENDIX 2A2   AN EMPIRICAL ILLUSTRATION USING REGRESSION ANALYSIS. THE CASE OF THE INDIAN TEXTILE INDUSTRY[5]

In this appendix, we present empirical evidence that illustrates the theoretical arguments discussed above. While in later chapters we shall consider the problems that the identity poses for some well-known studies, it is useful here to illustrate the main points empirically using data for value added and gross output for publicly listed Indian textile industry firms. (The exact industry or data is not, of course, important.) We take the accounting identity as the primitive notion and corroborate that its estimation leads to the results discussed above and which we know *ex ante*. Then we compare these results with those of the misspecified identity which may be erroneously interpreted as a production function. We show why the latter often yields implausible statistical results.[6] First we show the results for the

---

    [5]   This draws on Felipe et al. (2008).

    [6]   We are grateful to the Institute for Studies in Industrial Development, New Delhi, for kindly making these data available to us. The data included the following firm-specific information: gross output, book value of plant and equipment, total wage bill, and expenditures on raw materials, intermediates, fuel and energy. Industry-specific wage rates were used to divide firms' total wage bill to arrive at the number of workers. Real values for gross output, capital stocks, and total intermediate inputs were derived by deflating gross output, the book value of plant and machinery, and total intermediates (raw materials plus intermediates plus fuel plus energy), respectively, by an industry-specific price deflator for total intermediates.

time-series case using these data for one firm, for both value added and gross output; and then for a cross-section of firms in the textile industry.[7]

Time-series and Value-added Data

Table 2A2.1 summarises the relevant results pertaining to value-added production data for the time-series case.

We first estimate the approximation to the identity when factor shares are constant, namely:

$$\ln V = c + b_1 \ln w + b_2 \ln r + b_3 \ln L + b_4 \ln J, \qquad (2A2.1)$$

where we expect the estimates of b_1 and b_3 to be equal and b_2 and b_4 also to be equal. The results are reported in Table 2A2.1, equation (i). It can be seen that there is a very good statistical fit with the estimated coefficients of labour and capital taking values of 0.29 and 0.71, respectively, and both are statistically significant at the 1 per cent confidence level. It can be seen that the estimates are very close to the actual factor shares, the values of which are reported in the notes to Table 2A2.1. The textile industry is relatively capital intensive and so the share of capital, and hence the estimate of its 'output elasticity', is much greater than the average for the whole economy. In other words, capital's share is about 0.7 whereas for the whole economy it is about 0.3. The R^2 is 0.999, and not unity, because there is some variability of the shares, but the estimates show that the factor shares are roughly constant.

Equation (ii) replaces $\ln w$ and $\ln r$ with a linear time trend. This corresponds to the putative Cobb–Douglas production function. A comparison between regressions (i) and (ii) is revealing. Now the estimates of the coefficients of labour and capital are negative. Given the results in regression (i), we know the reason for this. All that the time trend does in regression (ii) is to approximate the weighted average of the logarithms of the wage and profit rates, that is, $a \ln w_t + (1 - a) \ln r_t$. It was shown above that for this approximation to be close, the weighted wage and profit rates would have to grow at a constant rate. This regression shows that this is not true. Hence, this approximation to the identity turns out to be extremely poor. This is not an econometric problem in the standard sense, because all that

---

Because the industry-specific deflators pertain to calendar years while firms' data pertain to their fiscal years, each of the deflators was adjusted for the fiscal year of the firm.

[7]   The firm used in the estimation was chosen on the basis of the relative constancy of the factor shares. This choice is deliberate, of course, since the point of our exercise is to illustrate the argument made above.

Table 2A2.1   *The accounting identity and the Cobb-Douglas 'production function', Indian textile industry, 1976–1989 (Time series, value-added regressions, OLS estimates)*

	Log levels			Growth rates		
	(i)	(ii)	(iii)	(iv)	(v)	(vi)
Constant	0.588	14.716	0.000	0.035	−0.003	0.009
	(12.59)***	(4.60)***	(0.53)	(0.96)	(−3.57)	(1.38)
Trend		0.080				
		(3.78)***				
w	0.289		0.281			
	(43.19)		(25.35)***			
r	0.709		0.706			
	(168.00)***		(145.88)***			
L	0.292	−0.017	0.278	0.146	0.308	0.246
	(57.57)***	(−0.07)	(35.78)***	(0.40)	(36.94)***	(4.03)
J	0.710	−0.816	0.705	−0.202	0.744	0.697
	(127.30)***	(−2.17)*	(69.02)***	(−0.48)	(64.85)***	(8.38)***
$T\hat{F}P_r$						1.056
						(19.02)***
$T\hat{F}P$					1.019	
					(141.54)***	
No. obs	14	14	13	13	13	13
DW stat.	2.81	2.29	2.65	2.38	2.10	2.09
$\bar{R}^2$	0.999	0.83	0.999	−0.16	0.999	0.97

Note: *t*-statistics in parentheses; * denotes significant at the 10% confidence level; ** at the 5% confidence level; and *** at the 1% confidence level. The average factor shares are 0.70 for capital and $(1 - 0.70) = 0.30$ for labour; with ranges 0.67–0.74 for capital and 0.26–0.33 for labour.

Source: Felipe et al. (2008).

is required is to find a good approximation to the term $a\ln w_t + (1 - a)\ln r_t$. For a researcher faced with these poor results, there are two approaches that could be followed to 'rescue' the supposed production function.

The first is to include a non-linear time trend that more closely approximates $(1 - a)\ln w_t + a\ln r_t$ than does a linear time trend. The second is to adjust the capital stock for changes in capacity utilisation.[8] A visual inspection of the data (not shown here) indicates that the fluctuation in

---

[8]   The theoretical justification for this in production function analysis is that it is the flow of capital services that enter into the production function. Estimates of the capital stock calculated by the perpetual inventory method do not make any allowances for changes in the intensity of use of the capital stock over the cycle.

$a \ln w_t + (1 - a) \ln r_t$ is almost entirely driven by the cyclical fluctuation in r_t. As $r_t = (1 - a)V_t/J_t$, it can be seen that if J is multiplied by an index of capacity utilisation that imparts a cyclical fluctuation to this series, this will have the effect of dampening the cyclical fluctuation in r. In other words, $r/U = (1 - a)V/(JU)$. This is, in practice, the most usual procedure adopted and has, not surprisingly, proved to be remarkably successful (see Lucas, 1970).

Turning now to the regression in growth rates, regression (iii) again corroborates that all that is being estimated is an identity and results are virtually identical to those in regression (i). Regression (iv) corresponds to the supposed Cobb–Douglas production function, expressed in growth rates and where the intercept is the putative (constant) rate of technical progress. Once again, the results are very poor, with the estimates of the coefficients of labour and capital statistically insignificant, and the latter again negative. In regression (v), we have constructed the variable $T\hat{F}P_t \equiv a_t\hat{w}_t + (1 - a_t)\hat{r}_t$, which, if all the neoclassical assumptions are correct, should, in this framework, equal the rate of technical progress. In other words, we are, in effect, following the first method discussed above for rescuing the production function. There is nothing in neoclassical production theory that requires this growth rate to be constant. $T\hat{F}P_t$, by construction, must theoretically enter the regression with a coefficient of unity. The estimates of labour and capital are, again, equal to the average factor shares and the coefficient of $T\hat{F}P_t$ is very close to unity. This regression confirms empirically that all that is needed is to find a variable that tracks correctly the path of $T\hat{F}P_t$ (for example, an appropriate trigonometric function).

Finally, regression (vi) uses as a regressor the term $(1 - a_t)\hat{r}_t$, that is, $T\hat{F}P_{rt}$ which excludes the term $a_t\hat{w}_t$. As we have noted, this proves to be the most volatile component of $T\hat{F}P_t$, and the one that largely determines its fluctuation. This can be seen from Table 2A2.1, equation (vi), where using $T\hat{F}P_r$ instead of $T\hat{F}P$ still gives the estimated output elasticities close to the factor shares, although the goodness of fit in terms of the t-ratios is not so good.

Time-series, Gross-output Data

We use next gross-output data for the same firm to prove the generality of the argument. In this case, the accounting identity is given by:

$$Y_t \equiv W_t + \Pi_t + M_t \equiv w_t L_t + r_t J_t + m_t M_t, \qquad (2A2.2)$$

where Y_t denotes real gross output, J_t is the constant-price value of the capital stock and M_t is the constant prices value of materials (to simplify we aggregate intermediate materials and energy). m_t denotes the price of materials, strictly speaking the price deflator. Denoting the shares of labour, capital, and materials in gross output as θ_L, θ_J and θ_M and proceeding as above, equation (2A2.2) can be rewritten as:

$$Y_t \equiv B_0 w_t^{\theta_L} r_t^{\theta_J} m_t^{\theta_M} L_t^{\theta_L} J_t^{\theta_J} M_t^{\theta_M}. \tag{2A2.3}$$

One can derive similar expressions to the ones derived above in growth rates. Now the weighted average of the growth rates of the factor prices is given by:

$$T\hat{F}P_t' \equiv \theta_{Lt}\hat{w}_t + \theta_{Jt}\hat{r}_t + \theta_{Mt}\hat{m}_t. \tag{2A2.4}$$

Table 2A2.2 shows the estimation of equation (2A2.3), the approximation to the gross output identity under the sole hypothesis that factor shares are constant, both in levels (regression (vi)) and growth rates (regression (viii)). The result that the estimates are close to the three shares (and of approximately equal magnitude for each of w and L; r and J; and m and M) together with the extremely close fit can only be interpreted as empirical validation of the hypothesis that all that is being estimated is the accounting identity. Indeed, the results indicate that factor shares must be sufficiently constant in the dataset so that equation (2A2.3), whether estimated in log-levels (equation (vi)) or in growth rates (regression (vii)) – both regressions yield virtually the same estimates – provides an excellent approximation to the accounting identity. The R^2 is virtually unity, and very importantly, there is no econometric problem that needs to be taken care of, such as endogeneity of the regressors.

We now discuss the results that researchers obtain estimating the standard production function for gross output as $Y_t = B_0 e^{\lambda t} L_t^\alpha J_t^\beta M_t^\gamma$ (regression (vii) in log-levels and regression (ix) in growth rates). As we found with value-added data, the differences with the previous results are startling. The estimates are now not plausible and include negative values. The coefficients are substantially different depending upon whether levels or growth rates are used. Most researchers would perhaps argue that these estimates are the result of endogeneity bias and spuriousness due to the presence of unit roots. Hence they would search for econometric solutions such as finding a suitable instrumental variable. Alternatively, they would search for a better proxy for the 'rate of technical progress'.

What has happened? As argued above, our parsimonious explanation is that the weighted average of the factor prices has not been correctly proxied thus causing an omitted variable bias. It is not a case of true endogeneity bias. An inspection of the fluctuation path of $T\hat{F}P_t' \equiv \theta_{Lt}\hat{w}_t + \theta_{Jt}\hat{r}_t + \theta_{Mt}\hat{m}_t$

Table 2A2.2   *The accounting identity and the Cobb–Douglas 'Production*
Function', Indian textile industry, 1976–1989 (time series,
gross-output data, OLS estimates)

	Log levels		Growth rates			
	(vi)	(vii)	(viii)	(ix)	(x)	(xi)
Constant	1.071	8.764	−0.001	0.019	−0.002	0.009
	(19.30)***	(4.86)***	(−0.90)	(1.07)	(−1.97)*	(1.01)
Trend		0.052				
		(4.42)***				
w	0.162		0.166			
	(14.72)***		(12.93)***			
r	0.328		0.330			
	(59.98)***		(52.20)***			
m	0.518		0.508			
	(27.26)***		(25.59)***			
L	0.142	−0.038	0.135	0.021	0.158	0.152
	(21.33)***	(−0.24)	(17.46)***	(0.11)	(16.50)***	(1.59)
J	0.315	−0.513	0.329	−0.124	0.349	0.388
	(32.78)***	(−2.32)**	(28.42)***	(−0.61)	(26.20)***	(2.69)**
M	0.535	0.547	0.532	0.673	0.535	0.429
	(65.28)***	(2.97)**	(64.49)***	(4.67)***	(68.31)***	(4.89)***
$T\hat{F}P'_r$						1.076
						(5.14)***
$T\hat{F}P'$					1.040	
					(57.98)***	
No. obs	14	14	13	13	13	13
DW stat.	2.406	2.255	1.874	1.777	2.324	2.330
$\overline{R}^2$	0.99	0.95	0.99	0.63	0.99	0.90

Note: *t*-statistics in parentheses; * denotes significant at the 10% confidence level; ** at the 5% confidence level; and *** at the 1% confidence level. The average factor shares are 0.33 for capital, 0.53 for materials and (1 − 0.33 − 0.53) = 0.14 for labour; with ranges 0.30–0.38 for capital, 0.47–0.56 for materials and 0.13–0.16 for labour.

over time, and which is being proxied by the constant term in the regression in growth rates, shows that that induces substantial omitted bias. Hence the other coefficients are biased. Regression (x) in growth rates introduces the variable $T\hat{F}P'_t \equiv \theta_{Lt}\hat{w}_t + \theta_{Jt}\hat{r}_t + \theta_{Mt}\hat{m}_t$ explicitly as a regressor. Because of the identity, the coefficient of this variable has to take a value of unity as it does in practice. This indicates that all that is needed is to search for a variable highly correlated with $T\hat{F}P'_t$ such as a non-linear time trend or to adjust the capital stock for changes in capacity utilisation.

It is worth noting that the variable driving the movements in $T\hat{F}P'_t$ is again the growth rate of the rate of profit weighted by capital's factor share $(\theta_{Jt}\hat{r}_t)$, while the other two variables contribute very little of its variation. Moreover, given the constancy of the shares, movements in $\theta_{Jt}\hat{r}_t$ are driven basically by $\hat{r}_t$.[9] By introducing in the regression $\theta_{Jt}\hat{r}_t\,(T\hat{F}P'_{rt})$ (regression (xi)), the results improve dramatically and once again are close to the expected factor shares.

Cross-sectional Data

Finally, and to dispel any doubts about the generality of the argument, we now discuss the empirical evidence using cross-sectional data.

It must be noted that, in general, it is easier to obtain plausible results with cross-sectional than with time-series data. The reason is that, often, wage and profit rates in a cross-section (for example, regions in a country, firms in a sector) vary relatively little. This implies that the term A_i in the equation $V_i \equiv Bw_i^a r_i^{(1-a)} L_i^a J_i^{(1-a)} \equiv A_i L_i^a J_i^{(1-a)}$ will be closely approximated by a constant term, so that $A_i \approx A$ will be, effectively, the constant in the regression. This means that the cross-sectional regression $V_i = A_0 L_i^\alpha J_i^\beta$ produces a good statistical fit, provided only that factor shares in the cross-section do not vary excessively.

Table 2A2.3 reports the results based on value-added production data using a cross-section of 48 Indian firms for 1980.[10] As before, we show first the full approximation to the identity in regression (xii), and then the production function, regression (xiii). The results for the full regression corroborate that equation (xii) provides a good approximation to the accounting identity. It is virtually a perfect fit with the estimated coefficients highly significant and approximately equal to the average factor shares. The important difference between this specification and the ones using time-series data is that the Cobb–Douglas regression now works very well, with estimates that look plausible for production function parameters. The reason must be that the term $A_i = \bar{a}\ln w_i + (1-\bar{a})\ln r_i$, where $\bar{a}$ denotes the average value, is sufficiently (though not perfectly) approximated by the constant term, although its omission does bias the coefficients of $\ln L$ and $\ln J$ to some degree.[11]

---

[9] The correlation between $T\hat{F}P'_t$ and $\theta_{Jt}\hat{r}_t$ is 0.91; between $T\hat{F}P'_t$ and $\hat{r}_t$ is 0.92; and between $\theta_{Jt}\hat{r}_t$ and $\hat{r}_t$ is 0.99. On the other hand, the correlations between $T\hat{F}P'_t$ and $\theta_{Lt}\hat{w}_t$, and between $T\hat{F}P'_t$ and $\theta_{Mt}\hat{m}_t$ are much lower (0.58 and 0.10, respectively).

[10] These are firms producing textiles, the industry with the largest number of firms in the data available to us.

[11] The regression of A_i on a constant yields a value of 7.31, the mean, statistically significant at the 1% level. The maximum value of the series is 8.99 and the minimum is 6.05.

Table 2A2.3   The accounting identity and the Cobb–Douglas 'production function' Indian textile firms (cross-section value-added data, OLS estimates, log-levels)

	(xii)	(xiii)
Constant	0.578	0.282
	(2.94)***	(1.37)
w	0.257	
	(1.52)	
r	0.736	
	(71.41)***	
L	0.281	0.529
	(44.12)***	(9.15)***
J	0.720	0.440
	(105.31)***	(7.27)***
No. obs	48	48
$\overline{R}^2$	0.999	0.960

Note: Absolute value of t-statistics in parentheses; * denotes significant at the 10% confidence level; ** significant at 5%; and *** at the 1% confidence level. The average factor shares are 0.69 for capital and 0.31 for labour; with ranges 0.57–0.85 for capital and 0.14–0.42 for labour.

3. Simulation studies, the aggregate production function and the accounting identity

> As a purely theoretical matter, aggregate production functions exist only under conditions too stringent to be believed satisfied by the diverse relationships of actual economies. . . . Indeed, the problem is sufficiently complicated that perhaps the most promising mode of attack on it is through the construction and analysis of simulation experiments.
>
> (Fisher, Solow and Kearl, 1977, p. 305)

INTRODUCTION[1]

In the previous chapter, it was shown why the existence of an underlying accounting identity is responsible for the good statistical fits of aggregate production functions, even though the latter in all probability do not theoretically exist. In this chapter, we consider some simulation studies that illustrate the problems associated with the estimation, and interpretation, of aggregate production functions. The advantage of simulation experiments is that they allow us to know precisely what the underlying technological structure of the economy is. If the Cobb–Douglas production function gives a good fit to the aggregated data when we know that either the underlying technology of the firms in no way resembles the Cobb–Douglas production function, or, if it does, the conditions for successful aggregation are (deliberately) violated, then this should at least give us reason to pause for thought.

We start with a simulation exercise that we undertook to determine what precisely conventional regressions of production functions using value data are actually estimating. We also consider the extent to which we can be confident that estimates of total factor productivity (TFP) are approximating the rate of technical progress, or the rate of increase in efficiency of an economy. The advantage of this simulation approach is that we know by construct what the true micro-production relations are, and which are not known to the researcher.[2] The latter can only draw

---

[1]   This draws on Felipe and McCombie (2006, 2010b).
[2]   For the purpose of this exercise, we implausibly assume that a well-defined micro production exists.

inferences resulting from the use of value data, which is often at a highly aggregate level. By comparing these estimates with the true underlying parameters of the firms we are able to show the potential degree of discrepancy between the two – which turns out to be considerable.

We next consider the seminal studies of Fisher (1971b) and Fisher et al. (1977) where aggregate production functions (the Cobb–Douglas and the CES, respectively) seem to work in that they give good statistical fits, although we know from the aggregation conditions that there are no well-defined aggregate production functions. It is shown how this apparent paradox can be resolved by a consideration of the accounting identity.

We next present some simulation results which show, *inter alia*, that the poor fits to the Cobb–Douglas that are often obtained using actual time-series data are largely due to the poor approximation that a linear time trend gives to the weighted growth of the wage rate and rate of profit, rather than the variability of the factor shares. It is also shown again that such econometric issues that are often stressed as important in the literature (such as the question of endogeneity and the stationarity of the data) are very much of a second order of importance.

The next simulation study that we consider is that of Nelson and Winter (1982). They assume that firms have a fixed-coefficients technology and are satisficers, not optimisers. Nevertheless, the aggregate data generated by their simulations closely approximate the US data used by Solow (1957) in his seminal paper, and give a good fit to the Cobb–Douglas production function.

Shaikh (2005) undertakes some simulations using the Goodwin growth model, where again it is illustrated that the data will give a good fit to the Cobb–Douglas production function, even though the underlying technology is fixed coefficients. The study by Hartley (2000) is another important simulation contribution. This uses the production function employed in the dynamic general equilibrium model of Hansen and Sargent (1990, 1991). This is a real business-cycle model which is quintessentially neoclassical with, *inter alia*, inter-temporal optimisation of agents. He shows that estimates of the Solow residual bear little or no resemblance to the true rate of technical progress, known by construction of the data. Finally, we conclude by mentioning Houthakker's (1955–56) early note demonstrating that it is possible that a Pareto distribution of firms with fixed coefficients can generate a production function that resembles a Cobb–Douglas production function with decreasing returns to scale.

THE TYRANNY OF THE ACCOUNTING IDENTITY: THE STUDY OF FELIPE AND MCCOMBIE (2006)

To illustrate the problems posed by the accounting identity and the use of value data which we have discussed in earlier chapters, we undertook some simple simulations with a view to determining what the estimation of production functions and growth accounting is actually measuring. The key question behind the exercise is the following: if an aggregate production function does not exist, what is being measured as productivity growth, in particular as TFP growth, in exercises that use aggregate data? This has the following implications: first, if the answer is that it is some average of individual firms' productivities, then, does the aggregate method still yield such an average? If not, why not? Second, and more generally, how and to what extent are we misled by the results of aggregate growth accounting? It should be emphasised that we do not undertake any Monte Carlo simulations. The purpose of this exercise is merely to generate a dataset whose underlying structure is known, in both physical and value terms, in order to highlight the different results that the two types of data lead to in growth-accounting exercises.

The importance of this simulation compared with others discussed in this chapter is that it explicitly considers the relationship between the inputs and output measured in physical terms and the different relationship when value data are used. As creators of the hypothetical economy, we, and the reader, know the values of both the physical and the value data, but the researcher knows only the latter.

Box 3.1 summarises the assumptions of the simulations. We assume for the sake of argument that there are well-defined micro-production functions, which are specified in physical terms, as theoretically they should be. The constant-price value of output is calculated through a mark-up and the value of the capital stocks is generated residually through the National Income and Product Accounts (NIPA) identity. It is assumed that each firm produces a homogeneous output, which may or may not be the same for all firms. The analysis does not depend on this assumption so long as, in the former case, it is not possible to recover the physical quantities from the value data. In the latter case, that is, output is not homogeneous across firms, we cannot, of course, estimate a cross-section production function using physical data. It is important to emphasise that we generate two types of data, namely, in physical and in value terms. The former are constructed to give a good fit to the Cobb–Douglas function. Value data, as indicated above, are generated through the accounting identity. The investigator knows all the value data, but cannot recover the physical data from them.

BOX 3.1   SUMMARY OF THE ASSUMPTIONS OF THE SIMULATIONS

Cross-firm Estimation of the Production Function

- There are 10 firms, one period.
- Identical production functions are of the form $Q_i = A_0 L_i^\alpha K_i^{(1-\alpha)}$, where Q_i and K_i are generated as random variables. L_i is calculated through the production function. These are physical data. A_0 is the same across firms and normalised to 1.
- Output elasticities are (i) labour, $\alpha = 0.25$; (ii) capital, $(1-\alpha) = 0.75$, with a random error to avoid multicollinearity.
- Value data: firms set prices as a mark-up on unit labour costs, that is, $p_i = (1+\pi)w_i L_i/Q_i$, where $\pi = 0.333$ is the same across firms.
- Money wage rate is $w_i = w$ and is the same across firms.
- Profit rate is $r_i = r = 0.10$ and is the same across firms.
- Output in value terms is $V_i = p_i Q_i$.
- Capital stock in value terms is $J_i = (V_i - w_i L_i)/r_i = (V_i - wL_i)/0.1$.
- Labour share in value terms is $a_i = (wL_i)/V_i = 1/(1+\pi) = 0.75$.
- Capital share in value terms is $(1-a_i) = \pi/(1+\pi) = 0.25$.
- Mean of a_i is 0.744 (range 0.698–0.795).

Rate of Technical Progress and Growth of Total Factor Productivity

- Outputs of the 10 firms grow at different rates over the period, but $\hat{Q}_i = \hat{K}_i$.
- Same rate of technical progress for all firms, $\varphi_i = \alpha(\hat{Q}_i - \hat{L}_i)$, assumed to be $0.5 = 0.25\,(\hat{Q}_i - \hat{L}_i)$ % p.a.
- Growth of employment $\hat{L}_i = \hat{Q}_i - (\varphi_i/\alpha)$.
- Output elasticities (physical terms) and average shares (value terms) are, labour, $\alpha = 0.25$, $a = 0.75$ and capital, $(1-\alpha) = 0.75$, $(1-a) = 0.25$.
- True rate of technical progress (firm level): $\varphi_i = \hat{Q}_i - 0.25\hat{L}_i - 0.75\hat{K}_i$.
- Total factor productivity growth: $T\hat{F}P_i = \hat{V}_i - 0.75\hat{L}_i - 0.25\hat{J}_i$

Increasing Returns to Scale

- *Q, L* and *K* and their growth rates as above.
- Output elasticities are labour, $\alpha = 0.3$, and capital, $\beta = 0.9$. Degree of returns to scale = 1.2.
- Value data calculated as before and mark-up π is also 0.33.
- Factor shares are labour, $a = 0.75$, and capital, $(1 - a)$ = 0.25.

It should also be noted that in the case where a cross-firm production function is estimated, no aggregation problem *à la* Fisher is involved. This is an important point. If we need to estimate a production function using outputs and inputs summed over different firms, we encounter all the well-known aggregation problems. As value data have to be used in estimating this aggregate production function, we have shown in Chapter 2 why regressions using these data give a good fit to the aggregate data when theoretically they should not. But the problem is even more fundamental than this. As will be demonstrated, the accounting identity presents insurmountable problems of interpretation, even when there are no aggregation problems of any kind regarding functional forms, or affecting output, labour or capital or problems of the type discussed in the context of the Cambridge debates regarding the nature and construction of capital stocks.

The important aspect of our simulations is that they show how the use of value data can give results at variance with the true magnitudes of the underlying production functions and, therefore, misleading numerical estimates of both the parameters of the production function and of the 'rate of technical progress'. For clarity purposes, we shall confine the term 'technical progress' to that calculated using physical data; and the term 'total factor productivity' to that calculated using value data.

Cross-firm Estimation of the Production Function

In the first example, data in physical units were generated for 10 firms for one period under the assumption that they all have identical Cobb–Douglas constant-returns-to-scale production functions given by:

$$Q_i = A_0 L_i^\alpha K_i^{(1-\alpha)}, \tag{3.1}$$

where Q_i is the number of units of homogeneous output, generated as a random variable; K_i is the number of identical machines which are specific to the particular industry, also generated as a random variable; L_i is the level of labour input, generated through the production function, equation (3.1); A_0 takes the same value for all firms and was normalised to unity. The parameters α and $(1 - \alpha)$ are the output elasticities of labour and capital, respectively, and are constructed to take values of 0.25 and 0.75.[3] *The output elasticities were deliberately chosen to be the converse of the factor shares found in the NIPA.*

In order to generate the constant-price monetary values of the data, each firm sets prices as a mark-up on unit labour costs, that is,

$$p_i = (1 + \pi) w_i L_i / Q_i. \tag{3.2}$$

The mark-up (π) is the same for all firms and takes a value of one-third, so $(1+\pi) = 1.333$. The wage rate is the same across firms, the same as the profit rate r, which takes a value of 0.10. The *value* of the capital stock was calculated residually through the accounting identity as $J_i \equiv (V_i - wL_i)/r$, where V_i is value added, constructed as $V_i = p_i Q_i$ for each firm using equation (3.2). The values of the factor shares are directly calculated using these value data. Labour's share is calculated as $a_i = wL_i/V_i$ and capital's share as $(1-a_i)$. It should also be noted that $a_i = 1/(1+\pi)$, and so it takes a value of 0.75 for each firm, with a small variation due to the error term added. The mean value of labour's share for the 10 firms is 0.744 (with a range of 0.698–0.795).

The mean value of the capital–output ratios in value terms (J_i/V_i) is 2.57 with a range of 2.24–3.18. These values are very close to what are observed empirically for a wide range of industries and economies, and are the result of a roughly constant rate of profit and constant factor shares. As $J/V = (1-a)/r$, where $(1-a)$ is capital's share and, as noted above, is approximately equal to 0.25 and the profit rate is 0.10, the capital–output ratio will not differ much from 2.50. As we are dealing with individual firms and we design the simulations, we know both the physical data and the values, as we know the prices. But let us assume that the prices are unknown to the researcher, as is usually the case, because the output and capital stocks for different firms are aggregated in the NIPA using value measures. Consequently, V and J (in constant prices, although since we only have one period, the distinction between current and constant prices does not arise) were taken as proxies for Q and K.

---

[3]   To prevent perfect multicollinearity, a small random variable was added to these and, where necessary, other variables used in the simulation.

These value data were then used to estimate a cross-firm production function. The results of the estimation are:

$$\ln V = 2.867 + 0.750\ln L_i + 0.250\ln J_i \quad \overline{R}^2 = 0.999$$
$$(478.77) \quad (136.40) \quad (45.41) \quad SER = 0.0025.$$

This gives a remarkably close fit to the Cobb–Douglas production function, which is to be expected given the method used to construct the data. However, some of Douglas and his colleagues' early studies, which used real, as opposed to simulated, cross-state data, also found similarly close statistical fits.[4] The sum of the estimated coefficients is 1.00 and this is not significantly different from unity (the value of the t-ratio testing this hypothesis is 0.02). With the close correspondence between the supposed 'output elasticities' and factor shares calculated from the data (0.750 and 0.744, and 0.250 and 0.256), it is little wonder that such results could be interpreted as providing evidence in favour of competitive markets and disproving the Marxian argument, as Douglas (1976, p. 914) claimed.

This is notwithstanding the fact that factors are *not* paid their marginal products in physical terms in our simulation data. Competition could force firms to be X-efficient so that firms do hire the factors of production up to the point where their physical returns equal their factor rewards in terms of the commodity produced. This would determine the optimal L_i/Q_i, which is used in the mark-up pricing equation. However, using value data would still give estimates of the 'output elasticities' of labour and capital equal to $1/(1+\pi)$ and $\pi/(1+\pi)$, respectively. Thus, the fact that the value of 'output elasticities' is close to their factor shares would always give the impression that factors are paid their marginal value products, although this would vary depending upon the size of the mark-up.

However, it should be emphasised that the estimated 'output elasticities'

---

[4]   For example, Douglas (1976, p. 906) reports the following results for a production function based on American cross-section studies, 1904, 1909, 1914 and 1919.

Year	α	β	$\alpha + \beta$
1904	0.65 (32.5)	0.31 (15.5)	0.96
1909	0.63 (31.5)	0.34 (17.0)	0.97
1914	0.61 (30.5)	0.37 (18.5)	0.98
1919	0.76 (38.0)	0.25 (12.5)	1.01
Average	0.66 (33.0)	0.32 (16.0)	0.98

Note: t-values in parentheses. Total number of observations: 1,490.

are, of course, not the same as the 'true' output elasticities of the micro-production function. In other words, the true output elasticity of labour is 0.25, but the estimate using value data is 0.75.

The goodness of fit is dependent upon the degree of variation in the mark-up. With identical mark-ups which give identical factor shares, the fit is exact and estimation is not possible because of perfect multicollinearity (Felipe, 1998). Indeed, it is the constant mark-up that is solely responsible for generating the 'spurious' Cobb–Douglas.

To demonstrate this, the physical values of the three series Q, L and K were next generated as random numbers. V and J were calculated as before. The estimation using value data yielded a very good fit to the Cobb–Douglas with the values of the 'output elasticities' the same as before (the result is not reported here). This does not necessarily mean that we are postulating that output is actually a random function of the inputs.

However, when one considers the complex production processes of any modern firm, there may be some individual parts of the process subject to fixed coefficients, whereas others may be subject to differing elasticities of substitution, to say nothing of differences between plants in managerial and technical efficiencies. Thus, the 'randomness' may simply be a reflection of the severe misspecification error inherent in specifying the micro-production function as a Cobb–Douglas. But the important point to note is that even in this case, where there is no well-defined micro-production function, the use of value-added data will give the impression that there exists a well-behaved aggregate Cobb–Douglas production function.

The Rate of Technological Progress and Total Factor Productivity Growth

In order to calculate the TFP growth, we need the growth rates of output, capital and labour. We assumed that output of the 10 hypothetical firms grows at different rates (we only have one growth period), but, for expositional purposes only, the series were constructed such that the growth rate of the physical capital–output ratio is zero (that is, output and capital grow at the same rate) for all firms. It was also assumed that each firm experiences the same rate of technical progress (φ_i), 0.5 per cent per annum, equal to $\varphi_i = \alpha(\hat{Q}_i - \hat{L}_i)$. This is due to the fact that the underlying production functions are Cobb–Douglas and that the growth of output equals the growth rate of capital. Hence, the growth rate of employment for each firm was constructed as $\hat{L}_i = \hat{Q}_i - (\varphi_i/\alpha)$, where $\varphi_i = 0.5\%$, as noted above. The output elasticities of labour and capital in *physical terms* are again 0.25 and 0.75, the average *value shares* are 0.744 (with a range from 0.698 to 0.795) and 0.256, and the aggregate shares are 0.744 and

0.256 as each firm has the same mark-up, which means that the labour share of each firm is the same and if we aggregate over firms, the aggregate share is about the same.

The rate of technical progress using the physical simulated data would be calculated by the investigator unaware of its value (although *we* know it by construction, 0.5 per cent per annum) for each hypothetical firm separately using the standard growth-accounting equation, that is,

$$\varphi_i \equiv \hat{Q}_i - \alpha \hat{L}_i - (1 - \alpha) \hat{K}_i, \tag{3.3}$$

where the output elasticities α and $(1 - \alpha)$ are 0.25 and 0.75, respectively.

As the rate of technical progress is the same for each firm, we can talk about the rate of technical progress being 0.5 per cent per annum, even in the case where we assume that the physical outputs of the various firms are not homogeneous.

However, let us assume, once again, that the individual prices of the various firms are not available and so it is not possible to extract data on the physical units of output. All that can be used in empirical work, as is usually true in practice, is the constant-price value of output and of the capital stock. The TFP growth is given by:

$$\hat{TFP}_i \equiv \hat{V}_i - a\hat{L}_i - (1 - a)\hat{J}_i, \tag{3.4}$$

where the shares of labour and capital are 0.75 and 0.25, respectively.

The unweighted mean rate of TFP growth of the individual firms is 1.49 per cent per annum, which, not surprisingly, is almost identical to the rate of TFP growth obtained by aggregating the value data over all 10 firms and using these in equation (3.4) (1.48 per cent per annum).

Thus, the use of physical data yields technical progress accounting, on average (the unweighted mean), for $\varphi_i = 0.25(\hat{Q}_i - \hat{L}_i)$, that is, 25 per cent of labour productivity growth, with a very small difference between firms due to the small random element introduced for the reasons noted above.[5] On the other hand, the use of value data for each of the 10 firms gives a mean value of the rate of TFP; that is, $\hat{TFP}_i = 0.75(\hat{V}_i - \hat{L}_i)$, or 75 per cent of the growth of labour productivity, with a range from 80 to 70 per cent. And the figure using the aggregate data (that is, using the aggregate values of output, labour and capital) is 74 per cent. The reason for the marked difference between these values and the 'true' rate of technical progress is

---

[5]   This is because there is no growth in the physical capital–output ratio, $\varphi_i \equiv \alpha(\hat{Q}_i - \hat{L}_i)$ and α, the physical output elasticity of labour, is equal to 0.25. Hence the rate of technical progress equals one-quarter of the growth of labour productivity.

that labour's share of output in value terms is 0.75, while the 'true' output elasticity of the firms' production functions is 0.25.

It is worth noting that the TFP growth can be written as

$$T\hat{F}P_t \equiv \hat{V}_t - a_t\hat{L}_t - (1-a_t)\hat{J}_t \equiv a_t(\hat{V}_t - \hat{L}_t) + (1-a_t)(\hat{V}_t - \hat{J}_t).$$

This is a weighted average of the growth rates of labour and capital productivity. Therefore, it could be argued that $T\hat{F}P$ is an aggregate measure of productivity growth. This interpretation, however, faces the problems discussed in this subsection, namely, that the figure computed is not equivalent to the true rate of technical progress.

Consequently, the use of value data produces an estimate of TFP growth that is significantly different from the rate of technical progress obtained using physical data. Even with well-defined underlying Cobb–Douglas production functions expressed in physical terms, the use of value data as a proxy for output can give very misleading estimates of the rate of 'technical progress'.

Increasing Returns to Scale and Total Factor Productivity Growth

What happens if the individual firms are subject to increasing returns to scale when physical data are used? To examine this question, we first estimated the cross-firm production functions using value data when the micro-production functions exhibit the same degree of increasing returns to scale. The data for the inputs in physical terms were the same as those used in the previous simulation, with the exception that now the elasticities were multiplied by 1.20, so $\alpha' = 0.30$ and $\beta' = 0.90$. This represents a substantial degree of returns to scale and results in a value of output that is significantly larger than when constant returns to scale are imposed. The value data were calculated the same way as before, with a mark-up once again of 1.333.

Estimating the unrestricted Cobb–Douglas production function gives a result that is virtually identical to that for constant returns to scale, as reported above, except for a change in the value of the intercept. Consequently, we do not report the results here.

The estimates of the putative output elasticities are once again very close to the observed (value) factor shares and sum to unity, thereby erroneously suggesting that the production process of the various firms are subject to constant returns to scale. The reason for this seemingly paradoxical result is that the calculation of value added is given by $pQ = V = (1+\pi)wL$ and as nominal wages and the level of employment are the same as before, so is the constant price measure of value added, although the price per unit is now lower (there is no inflation in the simulated data). Recall that with value data, estimation of the production function would yield elasticities equal to the factor shares.

Next, we calculated the rate of technical progress and the TFP growth. For comparability with the constant-returns-to-scale case, the growth rates of physical output, capital and labour were the same as before. The rate of technical progress was calculated using the physical data as:

$$\varphi_i = \hat{Q}_i - \alpha'\hat{L}_i - \beta'\hat{K}_i, \tag{3.5}$$

where $\alpha' = 1.2\alpha$ and $\beta' = 1.2(1 - \alpha)$. It can be seen that the rate of technical progress calculated using equation (3.5) will differ from the 0.5 per cent in the case of constant returns to scale. In fact, it will be on average lower, given the larger weights of the growth of the factor inputs. The rate of technical progress, calculated using equation (3.5) for each firm now varies considerably across firms (for reasons of space we do not report the full results).[6] The unweighted mean is (coincidentally) 0.00 per cent per annum, with a range of ± 0.4 percentage points per annum.[7]

On the other hand, the growth rates of TFP of the individual industries, calculated using equation (3.4) and value data, are again all approximately 1.5 per cent per annum. This is because the shares of labour and capital in value terms are once again 0.75 and 0.25, and the growth rates of V, L and J are the same as before.[8] Thus, the use of value data can give a very misleading estimate of the true rate of technical progress. The use of value data erroneously ascribes the effect of increasing returns on increasing the efficiency of the factors of production to the rate of technical progress.

Temple's (2010) Misunderstanding

In the course of a wide-ranging and erroneous criticism of the accounting identity critique (which we deal with in detail in Chapter 12), Temple (2010) argues that as the estimated coefficients of the logarithm of labour and capital in the simulations differ markedly from the true output elasticities, there must be large differences between the rewards to factors and their marginal products: 'Those are not the usual assumptions made in

---

[6]   This is because while the growth rates of Q and K are the same between firms, employment growth rates differ and so the change in weighting causes the rate of technical change now to differ across firms.

[7]   As we cannot sum across the physical quantities, we cannot calculate a meaningful average rate of technical progress, as the individual rates cannot be unambiguously or uniquely weighted. Nevertheless, we did calculate the unweighted mean.

[8]   With a constant mark-up of 1.33, the shares will be always 0.75 and 0.25, regardless of the technical conditions of production (for example, the degree of returns to scale).

interpreting the results from estimated production functions' (p. 690). But any researcher (or entrepreneur) with only access to the value data and interpreting the results of the estimated 'production function' would find that the estimated 'output elasticities' equal the observed factor shares. The researcher does not know what the true marginal products are in *physical* terms. Thus, as we have demonstrated, the researcher would erroneously conclude that markets are perfectly competitive, constant returns to scale prevail, and that factors are paid their marginal products. This would also be the case, as we show in our simulations above, when the true micro-production function displays increasing returns, or, indeed, there is no well-defined relationship between the outputs and inputs. In the model we use, prices are determined by a mark-up on unit costs, which in turn is determined by, for example, the state of competition in the industry and the relative power of labour and capital in the wage-bargaining process. The marginal product of labour in value terms may well differ from the physical marginal productivity of labour if the firm (but not the researcher) knows the true micro-production function, but so what?[9] Firms, under neoclassical assumptions, will set the rewards equal to the marginal product measured in value terms and are unlikely even to know a worker's physical marginal product. There are vast sectors of the economy where there is no reliable independent measure of output even in constant-price value terms or where a worker, or a group of workers, does not contribute to producing a single homogeneous physical output.

Summary

We can draw the following conclusions from these simulations.

- The TFP growth depends crucially on the weights attached to the growth of capital and labour. The growth-accounting approach assumes that factors are paid their marginal products and hence the technologically determined output elasticities will equal the factor shares. However, when value data are used we have shown that the factor shares will *always* equal the putative output elasticities and both are determined by $1/(1+\pi)$ (labour) and $\pi/(1+\pi)$ (capital),

---

[9] Temple further argues that some argue that 'no firm knows its production function' but he considers it knows its costs and that well-behaved cost functions are mirrored by the existence of production functions. But a cost function is also derived from the accounting identity and will be mirrored by a 'spurious' production function (see Chapter 2). A cost function expressed in value terms does not guarantee the existence of a well-behaved neoclassical production function.

where $(1+\pi)$, it will be recalled, is the mark-up. The estimates of the output elasticities using value data will almost certainly differ from the true ones (always assuming that there is a well-defined micro-production function in physical terms).

- Where it is possible to compare the 'true' growth rate of technical progress with the TFP growth in value terms (namely at the firm level here), the two values will probably differ markedly. In general, it is not possible to recover the physical quantities (of both output and capital) from the value data through the individual prices, and so resort is made to value data with potentially very misleading results. Where the physical data can be inferred, it can only be done at a very low level of aggregation. It requires each output and capital good to be measured separately in physical terms.

- The problems posed by the accounting identity are independent from, and in a sense more fundamental than, either the aggregation problem or the Cambridge capital theory controversies. This is because the problems arise even if they do not pose any problems.

FISHER'S (1971B) SIMULATION EXPERIMENTS

For many years Franklin Fisher has played a leading role in determining the exact conditions necessary for the consistent aggregation of capital (and labour and output) and for the aggregation of micro-production functions to give well-behaved aggregate production functions. (See, for example, the collection of his seminal papers published as Fisher, 1992). As a result of his work, Fisher considers that the concept of the aggregate production function makes no theoretical sense at all. In two classic papers, Fisher (1971b) and Fisher et al. (1977), he sought to shed light, through a series of simulation experiments, on the conundrum as to why aggregate production functions appear to work. The 1971 paper addressed the question as it relates to the Cobb–Douglas production function. The later article generalised the Cobb–Douglas to the CES production function.

Simulating the Aggregate Cobb-Douglas Production Function[10]

Fisher's (1971b) approach in his simulation experiments was to start with well-defined Cobb–Douglas micro-production functions at the firm or

---

[10]   This draws heavily on the exposition in Shaikh (1980) and Felipe and McCombie (2010b).

individual industry level. Having constructed the data for these separate firm production functions annually over a 20-year period, the statistics were then summed and used to estimate an aggregate production function. A proxy for the aggregate capital stock was constructed, but this suffered from an aggregation problem. When the macroeconomic data were used to estimate an aggregate production function, Fisher, to his evident surprise, found that the results were remarkably well determined and the data gave a good prediction of the wage rate, even though the aggregate production function did not exist.

To elaborate: Fisher proceeded by constructing a large number of hypothetical economies, each comprising 2, 4 or 8 'firms', depending upon the experiment. The micro-Cobb–Douglas production functions of each firm exhibited constant returns to scale. Perfect competition was assumed to prevail. Hence, the underlying economy was quintessentially neoclassical. The individual firms had different output elasticities; in one series of experiments the values of labour's output elasticities were chosen to be uniformly spread over the range of 0.7 to 0.8 and, in the other, over the range of 0.6 to 0.9, so that in the four-firm case the values were 0.6, 0.7, 0.8 and 0.9. The unweighted average in all cases was 0.75.

The labour force and the capital stock were constructed to grow at predetermined rates over the 20-year period. Technical change occurred at a constant rate that differed between firms, or was absent. Output was homogeneous and capital was heterogeneous and firm specific. Given this latter constraint, labour was allocated between firms such that the marginal product of labour was constant across firms. The heterogeneous capital was *not* allocated between firms so that the marginal dollar invested in each firm was the same. Moreover, as the capital stocks were heterogeneous, they could not be simply added together, so an index, with all its attendant aggregation problems, had to be constructed.

Consequently, there were a number of reasons for anticipating that the aggregate Cobb–Douglas production function would not give a good fit to the generated data:

- The exponents of the individual Cobb–Douglas micro-production functions differed.
- Capital was firm specific and not allocated optimally between firms.
- The heterogeneity of the capital stock meant that an index of capital had to be constructed, with the consequent aggregation problems.
- The firm data were summed arithmetically to give the aggregate variables.

Fisher ran 830 simulations using a number of different assumptions and estimated the following relationships using time-series data aggregated across the individual firms:

$$\ln V_t = c + b_1 t + b_2 \ln J_t^* + b_3 \ln L_t, \qquad (3.6)$$

$$\ln(V_t/L_t) = c + b_1 t + b_4 \ln(J_t^*/L_t), \qquad (3.7)$$

where V is aggregate value added[11] and J^* is an index of capital, which will be discussed below. (The time trend was dropped for the experiments where no technical change was introduced.)

Fisher found uniformly high R^2s of generally around 0.99, a value not untypical of R^2s found using real, as opposed to hypothetical, data as we have seen. Generally speaking, the aggregate production functions gave well-defined estimates, especially when constant returns were imposed to remove the multicollinearity between $\ln L$ and $\ln J^*$ as in equation (3.7).

However, the main focus of the study was on the degree to which the aggregate production function succeeded in explaining the generated wage data. It was found that, in the main, there were exceptionally good statistical fits, much to Fisher's surprise.

We should not expect the prediction of wages to be very accurate if the variance of labour's share is large, but 'while it is thus obvious that a low variance of labour's share is a necessary condition for a good set of wage predictions, it is by no means obvious that this is also a sufficient condition. Yet, by and large, we find this to be the case' (Fisher, 1971b, p. 314). This result occurs even when it can be shown unequivocally that the 'underlying technical relationships do not look anything like an aggregate Cobb–Douglas (or indeed *any* aggregate production function) in any sense' (p. 314, emphasis in the original). Fisher came to the following conclusion:

> The point of our results, however, is not that an aggregate Cobb–Douglas fails to work well when labor's share ceases to be roughly constant, it is that an aggregate Cobb–Douglas will continue to work well so long as labor's share continues to be roughly constant, *even though that rough constancy is not itself a consequence of the economy having a technology that is truly summarised by an aggregate Cobb–Douglas.* (p. 307, emphasis added)

Why did Fisher get such surprising results? We may explain this as follows.[12] Consider *n* firms or industries, each of which has a 'true'

---

[11]   Note that as output is assumed to be homogeneous by Fisher, we could equally have used the notation Q.

[12]   See Shaikh (1980) for an explanation along different lines.

production function given by $Q_{it} = A_{it}L_{it}^{\alpha_i}K_{it}^{(1-\alpha_i)}$ where $i = 1, \ldots, n$, and the output elasticities differ. K is the firm-specific capital stock (in terms, of say, numbers of identical machines). To generate an aggregate capital stock, Fisher notes that Euler's theorem holds:[13]

$$V_t \equiv w_t L_t + \sum_{i=1}^{n} \rho_{it} K_{it},$$

(3.8)

where ρ_t is again the rental price of capital, that is, the competitive cost of hiring a machine for one period. 'This means that at any moment of time, the sum of the right-hand side of [3.8] makes an excellent capital index' (p. 308).[14] Fisher, therefore, runs the model for the individual firms over the 20-year period, and then obtains the sum of gross profits from the accounting identity for the firm. Then summing the number of machines for each firm, he obtains an average rental price of capital for each firm, which by definition is constant over the period:

$$\bar{\rho}_i \equiv \frac{\sum_{t=1}^{20} \rho_{it} K_{it}}{\sum_{t=1}^{20} K_{it}}.$$

(3.9)

The index of the aggregate capital stock is then given by:

$$J_t^* \equiv \sum_{i=1}^{n} \bar{\rho}_i K_{it}.$$

(3.10)

It should be noted that this index does not fulfil the necessary aggregation conditions:

> The problem, of course, occurs because the relative magnitudes of the $[\rho_i(t)]$ not only do not remain constant over time but also are not independent of the magnitude of $L(t)$; this is the essence of the capital-aggregation problem. ...
> Nevertheless, it seems clear that an aggregate production function will do best if its capital index comes as close as possible to weighting different capital goods by their rentals. (Fisher, 1971a, p. 308, omitting a footnote)

The definition of value added for the *i*th firm is:

---

[13]   Note that as equation (3.8) is an accounting identity, it will hold under all circumstances.
[14]   Fisher clearly means 'on the right-hand side' here rather than 'of'.

$$V_{it} \equiv w_{it}L_{it} + \rho_{it}K_{it} \equiv w_{it}L_{it} + \frac{\rho_{it}}{\bar{\rho}_{it}}J^*_{it}. \tag{3.11}$$

We may sum equation (3.11) over the n firms to give:

$$V_t \equiv \sum_i^n V_{it} \equiv w_t L_t + \xi_t J^*_t, \tag{3.12}$$

where w_t is the (weighted) average wage rate and $\xi_t \equiv (V_t - w_t L_t)/J^*_t$. The variable ξ_t will be approximately equal to unity to the extent that the deviations of ρ_{it} from $\bar{\rho}_{it}$ tend to wash out when aggregated across firms. In other words, for every firm for which $\bar{\rho}_{it}$ overstates ρ_{it} there is a firm (or group of firms) where the ρ_{it} understates the rental price by approximately the same amount. A stronger assumption that gives the same result is that the rental price of capital for each firm does not greatly vary over time so $\rho_{it} \approx \bar{\rho}_{it}$.[15] It may be seen that the aggregate share of labour will be $a_t = \sum_{i=1}^n a_i \omega_{it}$ where $\omega_{it} = V_{it}/V_t$ and a_i is constant over time. a_t will be constant if ω_{it} is assumed either to be roughly constant or to vary in such a way as to make a_t constant.[16] We can now explain why an aggregate production function will give a good fit to the data. Even though the factor shares differ between firms, if in aggregate they are roughly constant, then assuming $\xi = 1$ or is constant over time, differentiating the accounting identity $V_t \equiv w_t L_t + r_t J_t$ and integrating will give:

$$V_t \equiv B w_t^a r_t^{(1-a)} L_t^a J_t^{(1-a)} \tag{3.13}$$

and as $r_t^{(1-a)} J_t^{(1-a)} \approx J_t^{*(1-a)}$, this may be expressed as:

$$V_t = B w_t^a L_t^a J_t^{*(1-a)} = A_0 e^{\lambda t} L_t^a J_t^{*(1-a)}, \tag{3.14}$$

---

[15] Equation (3.12) differs from the identity derived from the national accounts $V_t \equiv w_t L_t + r_t J_t$, where r_t is the rate of profit. J_t is the value of the capital stock calculated by the perpetual inventory method and equals the number of machines multiplied by their purchase price appropriately deflated (not their rental price, which is the price per period). As we demonstrated above, if we assume for expositional purposes that r_t equals the rate of interest, then $J_{it} = (\rho_{it}/r_{it})K_{it}$ and $V_t \equiv w_t L_t + \xi_t J^*_t \approx w_t L_t + r_t J_t$. (For expositional ease, we again abstract from capital gains and depreciation.) Consequently, if $\xi_t \approx 1$ then $J^*_t \approx r_t J_t$ or the total compensation of capital.

[16] With two firms, the firms' shares in total output have to be constant for aggregate labour's share (or the aggregate output elasticity of labour) to be constant. (This assumes that the individual firm's labour shares are constant, but differ between firms.) But this is not true if there are more than two firms. Take the four-firm case where the labour shares are 0.6, 0.7, 0.8 and 0.9. At time t, if the firms' shares in total output are 0.25, 0.25, 0.25 and 0.25, the aggregate value of labour's share will be 0.75. It will, however, still take the same value at time $t+1$ if the firms' shares change to 0.167, 0.333, 0.333 and 0.167.

where λ' is the constant growth rate of w_t weighted by a.[17] This is where the relationship between the accounting identity and the aggregate production function comes into play. Thus, as Fisher (p. 325) concludes,

> [It is] very plausible that in these experiments rough constancy of labour's share should lead to a situation in which an aggregate Cobb–Douglas gives generally good results including good wage predictions, even though the underlying technical relationships are not consistent with the existence of any aggregate production function and even though there is considerable relative movement of the underlying firm variables.

However, our interpretation is that the underlying micro-production functions could give constant firm-level factor shares for purely neoclassical reasons. It will be recalled that the firms are assumed to have Cobb–Douglas production functions which will give constant factor shares. Although the weights (the firms' shares in total output) attached to them for aggregation may change over time, this does not prevent the shares from being roughly constant. Solow (1958b) discusses why an aggregate factor share often shows less volatility than the individual shares that constitute it. However, Fisher himself does not find this explanation convincing (1971b, p. 325, fn. 23).[18]

Fisher et al.'s (1977) CES Simulation Experiments

In a follow-up paper, Fisher et al. (1977) extended the simulation approach to the CES production function. The methodology was basically the same as before, including the method for the calculation of the index of the capital stock. The only difference was that this time the firms' technologies were represented by CES production functions, although without an allowance for technical change. The ith firm's output is given by:

$$Q_i = A(\delta_i L_i^{-\theta_i} + (1-\delta_i) K_i^{-\theta_i})^{-\left(\frac{1}{\theta_i}\right)}, \tag{3.15}$$

where A is the level of technology, δ is a distribution parameter and θ is a technological parameter. The elasticity of substitution is given by $\sigma_i = 1/(1+\theta_i)$.

Labour was again allocated between firms in such a way as to max-

---

[17]   This may be obtained by differentiating equation (3.12) and integrating, noting that $J*/V \approx (1-a)$.

[18]   Fisher argues that in his simulations 'relative outputs do not seem to be very constant', but as we have seen in note 16, this is not necessary for aggregate labour's share to be constant if the number of firms exceeds 2.

imise aggregate output. Fisher et al. used three firms in the simulations (although in one case this was increased to five). There were 11 experiments or 'cases' (labelled A to K in their paper) with each case having a total of 22 runs over 20 periods. In each experiment, each firm had a fixed elasticity of substitution with the greatest disparity being Case J with values of 0.25, 0.95 and 1.65 (see Table 1, p. 309). The distribution parameter δ, the initial capital stock and employment varied depending upon the run under consideration, as did the growth of the firms' capital stocks. Parameter values were chosen so that labour's share was between 0.65 and 0.85 with an average of 0.75. The total labour force was constructed to grow at 2 per cent per period, together with a small random element.

For each case, the 22 runs were divided into two groups. In the first group, the firms with the larger elasticities of substitution had the larger distribution parameters. In the second group, a larger elasticity of substitution was associated with a smaller distribution parameter. Within each group, the 11 runs were associated with different growth rates of the firms' capital stocks. An aggregate Cobb–Douglas and a CES production function were estimated using the summed data that had been generated over the 20 periods.

Equation (3.15) was estimated by non-linear least squares but, as often happens in practice, this did not give a well-defined value of θ, and hence of the elasticity of substitution. While this did not seriously affect the ability of equation (3.15) accurately to predict aggregate output, this could not be said for the predicted wage rate. In other words, the predicted marginal product of labour was not close to the actual wage.

Consequently, the wage relation of the CES,

$$\ln(Q/L)_t = H + \sigma \ln w_t, \tag{3.16}$$

was also estimated, where H is a combination of the production function parameters. The estimate of σ was then imposed on equation (3.15) and the resulting CES 'hybrid' equation used to estimate the distribution parameter, δ, the efficiency parameter, A, and the predicted wage. While equation (3.16) does not explicitly require an estimate of the aggregate capital stock, it nevertheless requires one implicitly for its derivation from the CES production function.

The results of estimating the production function were good in terms of the R^2, although once again this was not the main focus of the study, which again was on how well the aggregate production function predicted the wage rate. As with the Cobb–Douglas simulation study, the predictions were very close, with the hybrid CES equation outperforming the CES production function. The Cobb–Douglas production function, not surprisingly, was a good predictor whenever the shares were roughly constant.

The simulations also generated estimates of the elasticity of substitution. Nevertheless, as Fisher et al. point out, 'the elasticity of substitution in these production functions is an "estimate" of nothing; there is no "true" aggregate parameter to which it corresponds' (p. 312).

Considering the first group of runs, the main results may be summarised as follows: the averages of each of the 11 runs (eight in one case) gave the aggregate 'elasticity of substitution' (which, it will be recalled, does not theoretically exist) and were within the range of the individual firms' values nine times out of a total of 17 for the CES and 12 times out of 17 for the CES hybrid production function. Hence, as Fisher et al. (p. 316) put it, the estimates were within the 'ballpark'. Moreover, some of these aggregate elasticity results did distinguish between groups of firms where the individual elasticities were low and those where they were high. There were exceptions, however. For example, in cases A and K the average CES elasticity of runs 1–11 was 3.12 and 3.30 respectively, while the highest firm elasticity in both cases was 1.66.

However, when we consider what occurred *within* the individual cases there were sometimes great discrepancies. The largest was where there was an estimate of the aggregate elasticity of substitution of 17.18 (Case A, run 10) with the individual elasticities ranging from 0.6 to 1.66. These discrepancies were due to the changing output shares of the various firms over time, especially when the firm with the extreme elasticity of substitution and/or values of the distribution parameters gained a substantially larger share of the total output.

Thus, while the aggregated data gave good predictions for the wage rate,

> the estimated parameters themselves are sometimes quite far from anything one could sensibly describe as roughly characterizing the real – i.e., the model – world. The aggregated data themselves do not tell you very clearly whether the estimated parameters are likely to have average meaning or not. (p. 319)

Consequently, studies that attempt to estimate an aggregate elasticity of substitution in an effort to determine, for example, the effects of investment grants and subsidies on the level of employment, have to be treated with extreme caution on two grounds. First, even if it is conceded that there are well-defined micro-production functions, there exists no aggregate production function. Second, even if well-determined estimates of the parameters of the putative aggregate production function are obtained, they may bear no correspondence to the average of the individual firms' elasticities. Hence, any calculations using the aggregate elasticity could be entirely meaningless.

Fisher et al. were unable to find any simple rule that could explain the aggregate results, as Fisher did for the Cobb–Douglas (that is, the constancy of the factor share). However, we have shown that as value data are used, the accounting identity will mean that reasonably good statistical fits will be given to the aggregated data.

WHY DOES THE COBB–DOUGLAS PRODUCTION FUNCTION WORK? THE STUDY OF FELIPE AND HOLZ (2001)

With the developments in time-series econometrics during the last decades it has been appreciated that regression analyses may give spurious results if the data are not stationary or cointegrated. The analysis of Felipe and Holz (2001) focuses on two questions that arise from this consideration.

How Far Does Spuriousness Explain the Fit of the Cobb–Douglas Production Function?

The classic papers of Nelson and Kang (1984) and Durlauf and Phillips (1988) discussed the econometric implications of including a linear time trend as one of the right-hand-side variables in the regression where output, labour and capital were not stationary but were required to be first differenced to make them so (in other words they were I(1)). Using simulation analysis, Nelson and Kang showed that the high R^2 values and significant t-values of the coefficients are due to spurious detrending by including a time trend, rather than due to the existence of any economic relationship among the variables. From the economic point of view, the trend is included in the specification of the production function as a measure of technological progress. From the econometric point of view, however, if output and inputs are difference stationary processes (DSP or I(1)), the regression is spurious and should therefore be run in first differences. Only if all the time series are trend stationary processes (TSP) is the inclusion of a time trend econometrically acceptable.

Nelson and Kang explicitly considered estimating the production function. They ran the regression $Y_t = c + b_1 t + b_2 X_t + u_t$,

> where $[Y_t]$ is a nonstationary variable such as output, $[X_t]$ is a nonstationary independent variable (or set of such variables) such as a production input, and $[u_t]$ is a sequence of disturbances. The role of time is to account for growth in Y not attributable to X, for example, the impact of technological change on output. (p. 78)

Ironically, the data were constructed so that the true values of b_1 and b_2 were zero or there was no true relationship between the variables.

Using one thousand simulation runs, they obtained a mean R^2 value of 0.501, the estimate of the time coefficient, b_1, was statistically significant at the 5 per cent confidence level in 83 per cent of the runs, and the coefficient of X, b_2, was significant at the 5 per cent (1 per cent) level 64 per cent (55 per cent) of the runs. This is notwithstanding, of course, that there was no true relationship between the variables.

Felipe and Holz (2001) extend Nelson and Kang's simulations to take into account that the output and inputs series used to estimate the production function $V_t = A_i f(L_i, J_i)$ are linked through the accounting identity, $V_t \equiv w_t L_t + r_t J_t$. They set up three simulations.

The first set of simulations simply extended Nelson and Kang's analysis for the case of three unrelated random walks (the three variables in logarithms). Consequently, V, L and J were all generated as random walks. This constitutes the 'lower bound' case where there are three unrelated random walks (two explanatory variables). Compared to Nelson and Kang's regression with one explanatory random walk, the R^2 value was up slightly at 0.575 (compared with Nelson and Kang's value of 0.501). All the other results resemble those in Nelson and Kang's regression: the parameter estimates are unsurprisingly not close to any realistic factor share; there are clearly no constant returns to scale; and, as we would expect, differencing leads to an insignificant R^2 value.

In the second set of simulations, w, r and L were random walks and values for V and J were obtained through the accounting-identity equation $V_t \equiv w_t L_t + r_t J_t$ and the definition of the labour share, that is, $a_t = (w_t L_t)/V_t$, which was set equal to 0.60. Felipe and Holz estimated $\ln V_t = c + b_1 t + b_2 \ln L_t + b_3 \ln J_t$. Note that if the data exactly satisfied the assumptions that the factor shares and the grown rates of the wage and profit rates were all constant, and a Cobb–Douglas production function with a time trend was estimated, it follows that perfect multicollinearity among the variables would have prevented the estimation. However, as the growth rates of the wage and profit rates in this set are not constant (w_t and r_t are random walks), the equation $V_t = A_0 e^{\lambda t} L_t^\alpha J_t^{(1-\alpha)}$ is *not* the correct functional form that corresponds to the accounting identity. Consequently, the R^2 value is not equal to one and there is still some scope for spuriousness to improve the R^2 value (by 0.12) when going from the non-spurious regression in first differences (R^2 value of 0.7522) to the spurious regression in levels (R^2 value of 0.8735).

The regression results from 1,000 simulations give a mean value of the coefficient of $\ln L$ of 0.500 and of $\ln J$ of 0.494 and their sum equals 0.985 with a range from 2.097 to 0.008. The null hypothesis of constant returns to scale is rejected in just over 60 per cent of the simulations. If the data are differenced so that the correct specification is estimated, then the sum of the mean values of the output elasticities is 0.9995 (the range is from 1.235 to 0.763). The null hypothesis of constant returns to scale is rejected only 5.5 per cent of the time. The effect of the spuriousness is indicated by the low Durbin–Watson statistic in the regression in levels, 0.322, compared with 2 when first-difference data is used. Moreover, although the rate of technical progress is zero, it is statistically significantly different from zero in 40 per cent of the runs, whereas in the first-difference case this only occurred in less that 2.5 per cent of the cases. Consequently, as is to be expected, first differencing the data gives the more reliable estimates.

The third set of simulations extends the regressions (in log levels) to the case where all the variables are trend stationary processes. As all variables now are TSP, the time trend is correctly included in the regression, and, unlike in the previous sets, the two regressions are not subject to the problems of spurious detrending. The effects of imposing the accounting identity link are similar to those obtained for DSP variables. Once the accounting identity link has been instituted, the R^2 improves from 0.684 (that is, the lower bound for the non-spurious regression, but where there is no relationship through the accounting identity) to 0.953, constant returns to scale can no longer be rejected, and, again crucially, the coefficient estimates turn highly significant and 'credible' in terms of a factor-share interpretation.

The conclusion of these Monte Carlo simulations is that if the profit rate, wage rate, and labour are difference stationary processes, then spuriousness may explain a *small* part of the good fit of a production function estimation, but obscures some issues such as constant returns to scale. The accounting identity link in the simulations turns out to be the major force leading to a high R^2 value, independent of the issue of spuriousness, and only the accounting identity link can explain the proximity of the values of the estimated parameters to the factor shares, and thus the emergence of constant returns to scale. The importance of this last point must be stressed. Only the link of the variables through the identity gives rise to parameter values close to the factor shares. This is why the generation of 'independent' random walks (as in Nelson and Kang, 1984) or trend stationary variables yields parameter values that cannot be interpreted in terms of a Cobb–Douglas production function.

Therefore, the existence of the underlying identity causes the problem of non-stationarity to be very much of a second order of magnitude when the Cobb–Douglas is estimated with a time trend to capture the weighted growth of the wage and profit rate.

When Will the Cobb–Douglas Production Function give Poor Statistical Results?

Felipe and Holz's second question was as follows: to what extent do the two assumptions of constant factor shares and constant growth rates of the wage and profit rates have to be relaxed for the regression estimation results to no longer be 'good?'. In other words, are the poor fits to the Cobb–Douglas that are sometimes found primarily due to the variability in the weighted wage and profit rates (and hence inappropriately proxied by a linear time trend) or to the fluctuations in the factor shares ('output elasticities')?

To answer this question, the data were simulated allowing the weighted average of the growth rates of the wage and profit rates and of the labour share (and hence of the capital share) to vary independently, so that their separate effects could be seen in the estimations. The accounting identity constraint was imposed by calculating the level of output as $V_t = w_t L_t / a_t$ and the value of the capital stock as $J_t = (V_t - w_t L_t)/r_t$. A large number of simulations were run and the reader is referred to Felipe and Holz (2001) for a detailed discussion.

Overall, the most remarkable feature is that relatively small variations in the growth rates of the wage and profit rates make the Cobb–Douglas production function with a time trend yield poor results with coefficient estimates that are far from the factor shares (but the R^2 value remains high due to the presence of the identity). Only a low variation in the growth rates of the wage and profit rates, as well as very specific combinations of higher variation in these growth rates, lead to good Cobb–Douglas production function estimation results.

THE EVOLUTIONARY GROWTH MODEL OF NELSON AND WINTER (1982)

The next example we shall consider is the evolutionary model of Nelson and Winter (1982). Nelson and Winter consider that 'the weakness of the [neoclassical] theoretical structure is that it provides a grossly inadequate vehicle for analysing technical change' (p. 206). What is particularly interesting is that they develop a model where individual firms have fixed-coefficient production functions and, as we shall see, their underlying behaviour is far from the usual neoclassical assumptions of the theory of the firm. Nevertheless, by a suitable calibration of the model, Nelson and Winter are able to generate a time path of the aggregate economy that very closely approximates the actual US data used in Solow's (1957) paper, 'Technical Change and the Aggregate Production Function'. Indeed,

Nelson and Winter see that one of the major requirements of any simulation model is that it should be compatible with the historical record.

Their simulation model is one where a hypothetical economy is made up of a number of firms producing a homogeneous good. The technology available to each firm is one of fixed coefficients, but with a large number of possible ways of producing the good given by different input coefficients (ϕ_L, ϕ_K) of differing efficiencies. However, the firm does not know the complete set of the input–output coefficients that are available to it, and so cannot immediately choose the best-practice technology. It only learns about the different techniques by engaging in a search procedure. The firms are not profit maximisers, but are satisficers and will only engage in such a search for a more-efficient technique if the actual rate of profit falls below a certain satisfactory minimum, set at 16 per cent.

There are two ways by which the firm may learn of other fixed-coefficient techniques. The first is the *innovation* process. The firm engages in a localised search in the input-coefficient space. This potentially comprises the complete set of possible existing techniques, but the firm will only be concerned with a particular subset. This is because it is assumed that the probability of a firm identifying a new technique is a declining function of the 'distance' in terms of efficiency between any particular new technique and the firm's existing technology. Consequently, the firm only searches locally in the input-coefficient space near its existing technique. The 'distance' between the efficiency of a technique h' compared with the current technique h is a weighted average of $\ln(\phi_K^h/\phi_K^{h'})$ and $\ln(\phi_L^h/\phi_L^{h'})$ with the weights summing to unity. Consequently, if the weight of $\ln(\phi_K^h/\phi_K^{h'})$ is greater than 0.5, the result will be that it is more difficult to find a given percentage reduction in the output–capital ratio than in the output–labour ratio. The converse is true if the weight is less than one-half.

Second, there is the *imitation* process where the firm discovers the existence of, and adopts, a more efficient technique because other firms are already using it. It is assumed that the probability of discovering this technique is positively related to the share of output produced by all the firms using this technique. This is similar to diffusion models where a firm that is not using the current best-practice technique learns of it with an increasing probability as more and more firms adopt it.

The overall probability of a firm finding a new technique h' is modelled as a weighted average of the probability of finding the technique by local search and by imitation. The exact values of the weights chosen in calibrating the model will determine whether the firm engages in local search or in imitation. The firm will adopt h' only if it gives a higher rate of profit than that obtained by the existing technique, but it is also possible for the firm to misjudge the input coefficients of an alternative technique. The model is sufficiently flexible for new firms to appear.

The wage rate is endogenously determined by labour demand and supply conditions in each time period. The labour supply is constructed to grow at 1.25 per cent per annum. The prevailing wage rate affects the profitability of each firm, given the technique it is using. The behaviour of the industry as a whole also affects the wage rate. Each firm is assumed to always operate at full capacity, and so in effect Say's law operates and there is no lack of effective demand.

The simulations show that the increase in wages has the effect of moving firms towards techniques that are relatively capital intensive. When the firms check the profitability of the technique, when there is a higher wage rate, it will be the more capital-intensive techniques that will pass the test. While a rising wage rate will make all techniques less profitable, those that are labour intensive will be more adversely affected. However, as Nelson and Winter (1982, p. 227) point out, 'while the explanation has a neoclassical ring, it is not based on neoclassical premises'. The firms are not maximising profits. 'The observed constellations of inputs and outputs cannot be regarded as optimal in the Paretian sense: there are always better techniques not being used because they have not yet been found and always laggard firms using technologies less economical than current best practice'.

As we have noted above, the model was simulated with a view to comparing the outcome with Solow's (1957) results from fitting an aggregate production function for US data. To achieve this, the input-coefficient pairs space was derived from Solow's historical data – the US non-farm private business sector from 1909 to 1949. The simulation results produce industry data very similar to Solow's historical data. Indeed, if an aggregate Cobb–Douglas production function is fitted to the data generated by the model using Solow's procedure, very good fits are obtained with the R^2s often over 0.99 and the estimated aggregate 'output elasticity with respect to capital' (which, in fact, does not exist) very close to capital's share. As Nelson and Winter (1982, p. 227) observe, 'the fact that there is no production function in the simulated economy is clearly no barrier to a high degree of success in using such a function to describe the aggregate series it generates'.

Solow's (1957) procedure was to estimate a number of 'technologically deflated' production functions including the Cobb–Douglas with constant returns to scale imposed (see Chapter 5 for a detailed discussion).

$$\ln\left(\frac{V_t/L_t}{A_t}\right) = c + b_1\ln\left(\frac{J_t}{L_t}\right),$$ (3.17)

*Table 3.1   Cobb–Douglas regressions with time trend (equation (3.18)):
simulation-generated data*

b_1	b_2	b_3	$b_2 + b_4$	R^2
0.012	0.649	0.336	0.985	0.999
0.011	0.541	0.681	1.222	0.999
0.016	0.764	0.201	0.965	0.998
0.017	0.158	0.728	0.886	0.997
0.016	0.654	0.281	0.935	0.999
0.017	0.833	0.222	1.055	0.999
0.009	0.593	0.405	0.998	0.998
0.013	0.658	0.075	0.733	0.999
0.008	0.550	0.505	1.055	0.998
0.011	0.360	0.648	1.008	0.999
0.009	0.336	0.723	1.059	0.999
0.015	0.505	0.532	1.037	0.998
0.008	0.444	0.637	1.081	0.999
0.010	0.448	0.669	1.117	0.999
0.013	0.545	0.479	1.024	0.999
0.007	0.547	0.641	1.188	0.998

Note: Standard errors not reported in the original table.

Source: Nelson and Winter (1982, Table 9.4).

where V, L, A and J are value added, labour, the index of technology calculated à la Solow,[19] and the value of the capital stock. Nelson and Winter (1982, Table 9.3, p. 225) report the results of estimating this equation using the results from 16 runs. The statistical fit is very high with the R^2s ranged from 0.942 to 0.999 and the estimate of b_2 (capital's share) took a plausible mean value of 0.245 with a range from 0.193 to 0.313.

Using the same data, they also freely estimate the Cobb–Douglas without using the observed factor shares to derive A as in the previous specification. This took the form:

$$\ln V_t = c + b_1 t + b_2 \ln L_t + b_3 \ln J_t. \tag{3.18}$$

Their results are reported in Table 3.1.

---

[19]   The growth of A is calculated, in effect, as $\hat{A}_t \equiv \hat{V}_t - a_t \hat{L}_t - (1 - a_t)\hat{J}_t$. The index of A is calculated by setting A_{1909} equal to unity and using $\hat{A}_t$ to calculate the values for subsequent years. If labour and capital's share (a_t and $(1 - a_t)$) are constant, equation (3.17) is nothing more than a tautology, that is, true by definition, and cannot be regarded as a test of the Cobb–Douglas production function. (See Chapter 5 for a further discussion.)

These results are actually considerably better than freely estimating the Cobb–Douglas production function with Solow's data. Indeed, the latter results showed that the coefficient of the capital stock was statistically insignificant. As the study of Felipe and Holz (2001) suggests, the reason for Solow's poor results is the procyclical fluctuation in the weighted growth of the wage and profit rates and hence they are poorly proxied by a linear time trend. In the case of Nelson and Winter's data, we can infer that the path of the weighted growth of the wage rate and the rate of profit shows less fluctuation around its trend. Nevertheless, there are one or two implausible results in Table 3.1 where one simulation gives a labour coefficient as low as 0.075. The mean values of capital's and labour's output elasticities are 0.485 and 0.537.

For our purposes, it is worth emphasising that the simulated macroeconomic data suggest an economy characterised by factors being paid their marginal products and an elasticity of substitution of unity, even though we know that every firm is subject to a fixed-coefficients technology. The reason why the good fit to the Cobb–Douglas production function is found is once again because the factor shares produced by the simulation are relatively constant (see Nelson and Winter, 1982, Table 9.1, pp. 218–19).

Nelson and Winter (p. 227) summarise their findings as follows:

> On our reading, at least, the neoclassical interpretation of long-run productivity growth is sharply different from our own. It is based on a clean distinction between 'moving along' an existing production function and shifting to a new one. In the evolutionary theory, substitution of the 'search and selection' metaphor for the maximization and equilibrium metaphor, plus the assumption of the basic improvability of procedures, blurs the notion of a production function. In the simulation model discussed above, there was no production function – only a set of physically possible activities. The production function did not emerge from that set because it was not assumed that a particular subset of the possible techniques would be 'known' at each particular time. The exploitation of the set was treated as a historical, incremental process in which non-market information flows among firms played a major role and in which firms really 'know' only one technique at a time.

SHAIKH'S (2005) NON-LINEAR GOODWIN MODEL AND THE COBB–DOUGLAS PRODUCTION FUNCTION

Shaikh (2005) provides further evidence of the difficulty of estimating an aggregate production function by extending his 1987 entry in the *New Palgrave*. He generates data by simulating a slightly modified version of the Goodwin (1967) model, which is based on a fixed-coefficients production function with Harrod-neutral technical change. However, as the dataset has the property that factor shares are roughly constant, not surprisingly, he is able, eventually, with a judicious choice of a time path for technical change, to show that the Cobb–Douglas production function gives a good fit to the data. The generated data are also compared with actual data for the US economy over the postwar period (taken from the US Bureau of Economic Analysis National Income and Product Accounts). The generated data show marked similarities to the actual data and, again, because of the constancy of the factor shares, the latter give a good fit to the Cobb–Douglas production function.

The simulation model may be described as follows. The level of output is given by a fixed-coefficients production function:

$$Q = \min\left(\frac{L}{\phi_L(t)}, \frac{K}{\phi_K}\right), \tag{3.19}$$

where $\phi_L(t) = \phi_{L0}e^{-\lambda t}$. Consequently, over time, the amount of labour required to produce a given volume of output falls at the rate λ, or, what comes to the same thing, labour productivity increases at the rate λ, which is taken to be 2 per cent per annum. Thus, machines of more recent vintages require less labour, but the same amount of capital, as earlier machines. The capital coefficient, however, is constant over time so technical change is labour augmenting. It follows from the conditions of production that $\hat{Q}_t - \hat{L}_t = \lambda$ and $\hat{Q}_t - \hat{K}_t = 0$ and as $\hat{L}_t$ is assumed to grow at 2 per cent per annum, output and capital grow in equilibrium at 4 per cent. This assumes that production is at full capacity and that the economy is moving along its warranted path. Thus, we have two of Kaldor's stylised facts, namely, a constant growth of labour productivity and a constant capital–output ratio.

A property of the production function is that a change in the wage rate will not affect the choice of technique; all it will do is alter the distribution of income. The fact that we are dealing with a fixed-coefficients technology means that the marginal products cannot be defined. As Shaikh (2005, p. 451, original italics) emphasises,

> *It follows that the technological structure of this control group [Goodwin] model is entirely distinct from that of neoclassical aggregate production function theory and associated marginal productivity rules.*

The growth of the real wage rate is determined by the employment ratio (the ratio of employment to the labour force) and labour's share. The rationale is that as the labour market becomes tighter (the employment ratio rises) so the growth of the real wage increases. On the other hand, as labour's share increases, the employers' resistance to granting real wage increases hardens. In equilibrium the parameters of the equation are such that the growth of the real wage is 2 per cent per annum, that is, equal to the growth of labour productivity, and this means that labour's (and hence capital's) share is constant. The advantage of this specification is that the growth of the real wage is determined by institutional factors and relative bargaining power between capital and labour and has nothing to do with the technical conditions of production (as in the marginal productivity theory of factor pricing).

The model is stable in that after a shock the growth of output converges to 4 per cent per annum and labour's share to a constant (≈ 0.84) and the employment ratio to a steady 95 per cent. Consequently, the simulated data series, like the actual US data, have factor shares that do not vary greatly over time. Nevertheless when a Cobb–Douglas is estimated with a linear time trend (in the log-level specification) or with a constant intercept (in the growth-rate form), the results are poor regardless of whether the simulated or the actual US data are used and whether the Cobb–Douglas is freely estimated or has constant returns to scale imposed on the coefficients.

The reason is that, as we have seen in this and earlier chapters, notwithstanding the constancy of the factor shares, if the growth of the weighted wage and profit rates is not sufficiently constant, this can lead to poorly determined and biased coefficients of the factor inputs. In fact, both datasets show a pronounced fluctuation in the rate of profit, which has generally been found to be the main cause of other poor fits of the Cobb–Douglas (the wage rate is not so volatile around its trend). Shaikh notes that the Solow residual is nothing other than the weighted average of the growth of the wage and profit rates, so that $\hat{A}_t = a\hat{w}_t + (1-a)\hat{r}_t$ and $A_t = B_0 w_t^a r_t^{(1-a)}$. Consequently, the only difference between the Cobb–Douglas and the identity is the restriction usually imposed on the Cobb–Douglas that the weighted growth of the wage and profit rates is a linear function of time with a random error term. (If shares are not exactly constant then this will provide another difference.) But even in the neoclassical schema, there is no reason why this should be the case. The actual time path of A_t can be approximated to any required degree of precision by a complex time trend. Shaikh uses a Fourier series to approximate A_t and, not surprisingly, he gets a good fit to the data with the estimated coefficients equal to the factor shares.

HARTLEY (2000), THE PRODUCTION FUNCTION AND THE REAL BUSINESS-CYCLE MODEL

Hartley (2000) assesses the recursive dynamic equilibrium model of Hansen and Sargent (1990, 1991) which forms the framework of a real business-cycle model. The model is a representative agent model. The production process consists of two types of firms. The first type produces consumption and investment goods for sale, and intermediate goods, which they do not sell, but use in the next period. The type 2 firms purchase investment goods and rent physical capital to the type 1 firms. The actual production processes are not Cobb–Douglas but are linear and are quite restrictive in their specifications. Hartley used the model to generate a number of different types of shocks of varying intensity, including changes in labour productivity, changes in the depreciation rate of capital and changes in the exogenous technology level. The last is the mechanism that largely drives the typical real business-cycle model. Because the model is a simulation, the intensity and type of these shocks are known precisely.

What is interesting is that for a large range of plausible values the correlation between the 'true' technological shock and the Solow residual (calculated in the usual way) was low or even negative.

Although Hartley puts forward a number of reasons as to why the Solow residual sometimes acts perversely, the main reason would seem to be one of aggregation. The factor shares in the simulation data are roughly constant and the calculation of the Solow residual and its interpretation as a measure of technical change is only legitimate if these are the output elasticities of the aggregate production function. In the case of constant factor shares, this would suggest an aggregate Cobb–Douglas production function.

However, from the underlying structure of the model we know that the technology cannot be represented by an aggregate Cobb–Douglas and so the factor shares do not represent the output elasticities. An advocate of real business-cycle models would simply dismiss these anomalous results on the grounds that if the underlying technology is not an aggregate Cobb–Douglas production function (or more strictly, if the factor shares do not reflect the various output elasticities) then the Solow residual does not theoretically reflect the rate of disembodied technical change. Consequently, it should come as no surprise in the first place if it is not highly correlated with the 'true' rate of technical change. The Solow residual is only taken as a measure of technical change in real business-cycle models as the aggregate production function is assumed to be a Cobb–Douglas production function. If the production function is of the type in the Hansen–Sargent model then there is no disagreement with Hartley – the Solow residual is not the appropriate measure.

This does not diminish the importance of Hartley's argument though. An economist faced with the generated data of the Hansen–Sargent model would be tempted to fit a Cobb–Douglas to the data.[20] If there is no way of knowing what the true underlying production function is, the temptation would be to assume that if the statistical fit is good and the estimated 'output elasticities' are close to the factor shares, then it would be reasonable to assume that the aggregate production function is indeed a Cobb–Douglas. Hence, the Solow residual would be taken to be a good measure of technological shocks. Hartley's study shows that such an assumption could be both unwarranted and very misleading.

THE HOUTHAKKER MODEL (1955–56): AN AGGREGATE COBB–DOUGLAS PRODUCTION FUNCTION IS COMPATIBLE WITH A FIXED-COEFFICIENTS MICRO-PRODUCTION FUNCTION

In an important article, Houthakker (1955–56) showed dramatically that it is possible for the data to give a good fit to a Cobb–Douglas production function, even though the underlying technology of the firms is given by a fixed-coefficients technology. While Houthakker does not undertake any simulations, we have included it in this section as the researcher with only knowledge of the aggregate data will erroneously assume that the aggregate production function is a Cobb–Douglas.

Suppose each firm has a fixed-coefficients technology given by:

$$Q_i = \min \left[L_i/\phi_{Li}, K_i/\phi_{Ki} \right], \tag{3.20}$$

It is assumed that the ϕ_L, ϕ_K space is dense and so there is a production process for every combination of ϕ_L and ϕ_K. As production is based on this technology, no firm is capable of producing without both inputs and the larger are ϕ_L and ϕ_K, the greater is productive capacity. A key assumption is that the distribution of capacity is given by the Pareto distribution:

$$Q_i(\phi_L, \phi_K) = A\phi_L^{\gamma_1 - 1}\phi_K^{\gamma_2 - 1} \qquad (\gamma_1 \geq 1, \gamma_2 \geq 1). \tag{3.21}$$

---

[20]   Hartley does not, in fact, undertake this.

This is not an unreasonable assumption given that firm sizes empirically follow a Pareto distribution.

Given this distribution, it is necessary to know which machines are in use and which are idle before the 'mean' production function can be determined from the set of fixed-coefficient micro units. This can be done by using the profit function, where profits are equal to $pQ_i = wL_i - rK_i$. Only where this is positive will there be machines earning positive or zero quasirents. Thus, the set of machines in operation will be determined by the distribution of capacities over ϕ_L and ϕ_K and the relative prices of labour and capital. Houthakker proves that aggregate output will be given by:

$$Q = CL^{\gamma_1/(\gamma_1+\gamma_2+1)}K^{\gamma_2/(\gamma_1+\gamma_2+1)}, \tag{3.22}$$

which is similar to the Cobb–Douglas production function with decreasing returns to scale.

The value of the factor rewards of each input is a constant fraction of the total value of output, the remainder going to the fixed inputs.

Heathfield and Wibe (1987, p. 152) summarise the implications as follows: 'The burden of this is that a fixed (micro) coefficient world can give rise to an aggregate production function if the micro units are distributed in a particular way (Pareto distribution) and if the zero quasi-rent moves about depending upon [factor] prices'.

But the researcher with access only to the macroeconomic data would conclude from the good fit the data give to equation (3.22), that the technology of the economy was representable by an aggregate Cobb–Douglas production function.

CONCLUSIONS

This chapter has considered the insights that the use of simulation data can give to the unreliability of using aggregate data to estimate an aggregate production function, and the dangers of drawing misleading inferences from the estimated coefficients. Felipe and McCombie (2006) showed explicitly the problems posed by using value data. Even though they assumed well-behaved micro-Cobb–Douglas production functions expressed in physical terms, because of the mark-up pricing policy, the 'output elasticities' estimated using value data were always equal to the observed factor shares. But the estimates were diametrically opposite to the true elasticities known from the construction of the hypothetical data (0.75 as opposed to 0.25, in the case of the labour's output elasticity).

They also show that the accounting identity would ensure a good fit to the data even when Q, L and K were random variables. Moreover, another simulation showed that the estimates would also give constant returns to scale, even though all the underlying micro-production functions displayed strong increasing returns to scale.

Fisher (1971b) and Fisher et al. (1977) demonstrate that reasonably good statistical fits could be given to the aggregate Cobb–Douglas and the CES production functions (and wage equations) even though the aggregation of the underlying production functions suggested that this should be highly unlikely. The organising principle behind these results is again the existence of the accounting identity.

Felipe and Holz (2001) find that econometric problems of spuriousness and lack of integration of the data are of a second order compared with the constraint imposed on the data by the accounting identity. Poor statistical fits to the Cobb–Douglas are far more likely to be caused by proxying the variations in the logarithm of the weighted wage rate and the rate of profit by a linear time trend, rather than by fluctuations in the factor shares.

Nelson and Winter (1982) show that a model with firms exhibiting fixed coefficients and satisificing behaviour can give a good fit to the Cobb–Douglas production function using Solow's (1957) data. Hartley (2000) shows how the Solow residual can give a very misleading estimate of the rate of technical progress. Shaikh's (2005) simulation study and Houthakker's (1955–56) theoretical analysis both also demonstrate how a fixed-coefficient micro-production function can also lead to the erroneous impression that the technology of the economy is given by an aggregate Cobb–Douglas production function.

These studies all conclusively show how misleading are the inferences that can be drawn about the technology of the representative firm from a good statistical fit to an aggregate production function. The problem is that the researcher using value data will never know just how misleading are the results.

4. 'Are there laws of production?' The work of Cobb and Douglas and its early reception

> The [aggregate production function] must have needed an even tougher hide to survive Phelps Brown's [1957] article on 'The Meaning of the Fitted Cobb–Douglas Function' than to ward off Cambridge Criticism of the marginal productivity theory of distribution.
>
> (Joan Robinson, 1970, p. 317)

INTRODUCTION[1]

The year 1927 represents a landmark in the development of economics. It ranks alongside 1871 (the year of publication of Jevons's *Theory of Political Economy* and Carl Menger's *Grundsätz*), 1936 (the year of Keynes's *General Theory*) and 1961 (Muth's 'Rational Expectations and the Theory of Price Movements'). It was in 1927 that, at the annual meeting of the American Economic Association, Charles Cobb and Paul Douglas first promulgated the results of the estimation of their now famous aggregate production function. Here, for the first time, was found supposedly empirical support for both the existence of a well-defined aggregate production function and the marginal productivity theory of distribution. Their initially controversial paper was published the following year in the *American Economic Review*.

The importance of some seminal works is immediately apparent on (or even prior to) their publication. The *General Theory* and the discussions of the Cambridge Circus come readily to mind. Some have never really lived up to their initial promise (for example, Joan Robinson's (1933) *Economics of Imperfect Competition* – as conceded by Robinson, herself. Her colleague, Dobb (1973, p. 212) considered that 'it affected very little of the general corpus of economic theory', although there was a revival of interest in this approach decades later).[2] With others, such as Walras's *Éléments d'Économie Politique Pure: Ou Théorie de la Richesse Sociale*

---

[1] This chapter draws on McCombie (1998a) and Felipe and Adams (2005).
[2] The Dixit–Stiglitz (1977) mathematical formulation of imperfect competition enabled increasing returns to be modelled on rigorous micro foundations.

(1874) and Muth's (1961) article on rational expectations, it took years, if not decades, for the importance to become fully appreciated. But it would be difficult to find a path-breaking study that was received initially with such outright hostility and scorn as that of Cobb and Douglas. 'Our paper met with a very hostile reception, and the next few years were full of the most caustic criticism. I think no one said a good word about what we had tried to do' (Douglas, 1967, p. 17). What was especially discouraging for Douglas, in particular, was that from none was the criticism more vehement than his own senior colleagues at the University of Chicago. Eventual vindication and recognition, though, came in December 1947 when Douglas gave the sixtieth presidential address to the American Economic Association at Chicago (published subsequently with the rhetorical title 'Are There Laws of Production?' in the 1948 *American Economic Review*). The ultimate accolade of their work came in 2012 when it was included in the top 20 articles to be published in the *American Economic Review* in the last hundred years (Arrow et al., 2011).

As we have seen, the phrase 'laws of production' refers to the mathematical function that represents the technological relationship between the maximum value of output and the factor inputs (together with a time trend, if time-series data are used). When regression methods are used to estimate a specific functional form, it is to be expected that the factor inputs, usually labour and capital (and the time trend, if appropriate), result in a predicted value of output that is often very close to the observed value. Indeed, it has been argued that the production function is the nearest economics comes to a law comparable to those found in the physical sciences. However, as we have shown earlier, there are no grounds for such a view. It is worth repeating that this is not to deny that there are 'laws of production' in the general sense that for a particular individual production process the volume of output is related in some systematic way to the physical quantities of inputs. What is denied is that empirical evidence using constant-price value data can determine whether or not a well-defined aggregate production function actually exists. Today, when the Cobb–Douglas production function and its subsequent generalisations such as the CES and translog production functions are, rightly or wrongly, such indispensable tools for the majority of economists, it is easy to overlook the initial unflattering reception Cobb and Douglas's work received.

In this chapter, the development of the Cobb–Douglas production function is traced from its inception, and the early criticisms are assessed. This is an interesting exercise in the history of economic thought in its own right; but it also demonstrates the continuing relevance of some of these criticisms. With the renaissance of the aggregate production function after Solow's seminal growth paper in 1957, most of the unresolved criticisms were largely forgotten, occasionally to be rediscovered (sometimes more than once). To take just one example: Samuelson (1979), in his far from hagiographic tribute to Douglas on the latter's death, raised some perceptive and fundamental criticisms of the specification and estimation of, especially, the cross-industry production function regressions. He concluded that 'it is a late hour to raise these doubts about the Emperor's clothes, but not until undertaking the present assignment did this child give the matter of across-industry fitting the careful attention it deserves and does not appear to have received' (p. 933, omitting a footnote). Samuelson seems to have been unaware that virtually identical criticisms had been raised in an important paper by Phelps Brown (1957), elegantly formalised by Simon and Levy (1963) and restated and extended by Shaikh (1974) and Simon (1979b). These papers were not published in obscure journals, but in prestigious periodicals, which makes their neglect by not only Samuelson, but also the profession at large all the more surprising.

It may be that the subsequent debates concerning the aggregate production function, most notably the Cambridge capital theory controversies (Harcourt, 1972) and the stringent assumptions needed for aggregation (Fisher, 1969) discussed in Chapter 2 overshadowed these earlier reservations.

There were a number of early critiques of Douglas's work. Some of these were satisfactorily dealt with by Douglas and his collaborators, but others remain and are just as damaging as the better-known capital controversies and aggregation issues.

In this chapter, we summarise the original results of Cobb and Douglas (1928). These seemed to be later confirmed by their subsequent time-series results for Massachusetts and New South Wales. We discuss the negative reactions that their paper had when it was published. A reworking of Douglas's original data by Mendershausen (1938) and by us shows that the estimates are not robust and, in fact, offer no support for the marginal productivity theory, as Douglas (1976) argued, even by his own criteria. Indeed, ironically these revised results would lead one to doubt the empirical existence of an aggregate production function.

There is exegetical evidence that Douglas (1934, 1948) began to realise that his results using time-series data would not bear the interpretation he originally placed on them, although not surprisingly he played down his reservations. The outcome was that he increasingly shifted the emphasis to regression analysis using cross-industry data, especially as the results appeared to be considerably more stable. We discuss this in the next section. Indeed, for the two decades of the 1930s and 1940s there was an impressive amount of replication of the estimation of the Cobb–Douglas production function, using a variety of different cross-industry datasets.

(See, *inter alios*, Handsaker and Douglas, 1937; Bronfenbrenner and Douglas, 1939; Gunn and Douglas, 1941, 1942; Daly and Douglas, 1943; and Daly et al., 1943.)

Nevertheless, as we have noted above and shall show below, these results are not immune to very serious criticisms. It will become clear that some of these early criticisms, and their subsequent elaborations, have never been satisfactorily answered and are as relevant today as they were several decades ago.

THE INITIAL DEVELOPMENT AND ESTIMATION OF THE AGGREGATE PRODUCTION FUNCTION

Before these and other criticisms are pursued further, it is useful to consider the original study of Cobb and Douglas. It is difficult to do better than to quote Douglas (1948, p. 6) as to how they came to settle on the Cobb–Douglas relationship:

> It was twenty years ago last spring that, having computed indexes for American manufacturing of the numbers of workers employed by years from 1899 to 1922, as well as indexes of the amounts of fixed capital in manufacturing deflated to dollars of approximately constant purchasing power, and then plotting these on a log scale together with the Day index of physical production for manufacturing, I observed that the product curve lay consistently between the two curves for the factors of production and tended to be approximately a quarter of the relative distance between the curve of the index for labor, which showed the least increase over the period and that of the index for capital, which showed the most. Since I was lecturing at Amherst College at the time, I suggested to my friend, Charles W. Cobb, that we seek to develop a formula which would measure the relative effect of labour and capital upon product during this period. We were both familiar with the Wicksteed analysis and Cobb was, of course, well versed in the history of the Euler theorem. At his suggestion, therefore, the sum of exponents was tentatively made equal to unity in the formula[3]

$$V = AL^\alpha J^{(1-\alpha)}$$

> Here it was only necessary to find the values of A and α. This was done by the method of least squares and the value of α was found to be .75. This was almost precisely what we had expected to find because of the relative distance of the product curve from those of the two factors. The value of the capital exponent, or $1 - \alpha$, was, of course, then taken as .25. Using these values, we then computed indexes of what we would theoretically have expected the product to be

---

[3]   We have changed the notation to be consistent with that in the book.

in each of the years had it conformed precisely to the formula. We found that the divergences between the actual and theoretical product were not great since in only one year did they amount to more than 11 per cent, and that except for two years, the deviation of the differences was precisely what we would expect from the imperfect nature of the indexes of capital and labour.

The Cobb–Douglas production function also putatively provides a joint test of the aggregate marginal productivity theory of factor pricing and perfect competition. It will be recalled that this production function is given by $V = AL^\alpha J^{(1-\alpha)}$. If factors are paid their marginal products, then the real wage is given by $w = \partial V/\partial L = \alpha V/L$. Similarly, the rate of profit is given by $r = \partial V/\partial L = (1-\alpha) V/L$. Given the underlying accounting definition of value added, namely, $V = wL + rJ$, it can be seen that, by substituting in the marginal productivity conditions, the product will be exactly exhausted by the factor payments (that is, by Euler's theorem). It follows that the elasticities of output with respect to labour and capital will equal their respective shares in output, that is, $\alpha = a$ and $(1 - \alpha) = (1 - a)$ where $a = wL/V$ and $(1 - a) = rJ/V$.

The studies of the National Bureau of Economic Research on income were available in 1927 and these showed that labour's share in value added over the 1909–19 period was almost constant and the average was 74.1 per cent. This was virtually identical to the estimate of α obtained by Cobb and Douglas (1928), a fact that convinced Douglas that he was on the right track. A major rationale for his work on the aggregate production function was explicitly to test and quantify the neoclassical marginal productivity theory of distribution. For example, Douglas complained, in his 1948 address, that he had observed an 'experienced instructor' drawing marginal productivity curves on the blackboard without the faintest idea of what the slope of the curve should look like. Now, for the first time, there was some empirical evidence. The estimates of the production function implied an elasticity of demand for labour of −4 and for capital of −1⅓.[4] As Samuelson (1979) points out, Douglas was reassured to find that the former was close to Pigou's (1933) 'deductive estimate' of −3 (see Douglas, 1934, *Addendum*, pp. xvii–xviii). These findings gave Cobb and Douglas the confidence to proceed and present their paper to the December 1927 meeting of the American Economic Association.

The impetus for Douglas's research may be traced back to 1899 when John Bates Clark effectively rediscovered von Thünen's principle of marginal productivity (first outlined in the latter's *Der Isolierte Staat*

---

[4] These are the constant-capital elasticities of the demand for labour and capital and are equal to $-1/(1 - \alpha)$ and $-1/\alpha$, respectively.

(1826)). Clark's definitive statement of the principle appeared in his book *The Distribution of Wealth* published in 1899. At about this time, Wicksteed and Wicksell were also elaborating on distribution theory. Douglas, in fact, mistakenly gave priority for the discovery of the 'Cobb–Douglas' production function to Wicksteed (rather than Wicksell) citing Wicksteed's *Essay on the Co-ordination of the Laws of Distribution* (1894). In choosing the multiplicative specification of the production function, Cobb and Douglas (1928) also referred to the theory as being 'due to J.B. Clark, Wicksteed et al.'

Wicksteed, it is true, did extend the marginal principle from the utility function and the determination of the pricing of commodities to the pricing of factors of production. Furthermore, he discussed the linear homogeneous production function in general terms: 'If we have $\pi = \phi(\Lambda, K)$, then we also have $m\pi = \phi(m\Lambda, mK)$' (where π, Λ and K are output, labour and capital). From here, he demonstrated Euler's theorem 'without knowing that Euler had done it more than a hundred years before' (Sandelin, 1976, p. 118).

Wicksteed, however, unsuccessfully tried to demonstrate the 'adding-up problem'; namely, that if there is perfect competition, then only if the production function is homogeneous and of the first degree will the payment to factors of their marginal products exactly exhaust total output. It was left to Flux (1894) in his review of Wicksteed to 'give an elementary but elegant proof of Wicksteed's contention' (Blaug, 1978, p. 463). Moreover, Wicksteed did not explicitly specify a Cobb–Douglas production function. In fact, he describes a production function where as more and more labour is added to a fixed amount of land, the volume of total output eventually actually diminishes. 'That is, the marginal product of labour switches from positive to negative, a property which excludes the Cobb–Douglas function as a possible description of the "laws of production", at any rate in the neighbourhood of the switching point' (Sandelin, 1976, p. 119). As Sandelin (1976) and Samuelson (1979) point out, it is clear that the credit should have gone to Wicksell instead. In his classic paper 'Marginal Productivity as the Basis for Distribution in Economics', published in *Ekonomisk Tidskrift* in 1900, Wicksell also considered the adding-up problem and it was here that the function used by Cobb and Douglas was alluded to for the first time.[5]

---

[5] Sandelin (1976, p. 119) has also noted that the origins of the Cobb–Douglas production function can be traced back even further, namely to Wicksell's (1895) *Zur Lehre von der Steuerincidenz*. However, the production function is implicit, rather than explicit, in this work.

Wicksell (1900 [1958], footnote 1, p. 98) presented the argument so succinctly that it is worth quoting him:

> The matter is quite simple from the mathematical viewpoint. If we consider the product *P* as a function of the number of workers *a* and the number of acres of land, *b* [these being the only two factors of production] the marginal productivities are the partial differential coefficients of *P* with respect to *a* and *b*, so that we have

$$a\frac{\delta P}{\delta a} + b\frac{\delta P}{\delta b} = P.$$

> The general solution to this equation is

$$P = a \cdot f\left(\frac{b}{a}\right),$$

> where *f*( ) is an arbitrary function. In other words, *P* must be a *homogeneous* and *linear* function of *a* and *b*. Among the infinite number of functions with these properties we may select: $P = a^{\alpha}b^{\beta}$, where α and β are two constant fractions whose sum is 1. (Emphasis in the original)

It was perhaps natural that Cobb should suggest fitting the data to such a function as $P = a^{\alpha}b^{\beta}$ ($V = AL^{\alpha}J^{(1-\alpha)}$ in our notation) not least that it already had recognition as 'a well-known theory' (Cobb and Douglas, 1928, p. 151). As Samuelson notes (1979, p. 927), Wicksell seemed to have discovered the relationship by backing into it, 'beginning with the simplest square-root examples such as $bL^{1/2}$'.[6]

THE FIRST REACTIONS TO THE COBB–DOUGLAS PRODUCTION FUNCTION

We have noted that much of the early reaction to Douglas's first paper was hostile. Reflecting on this early denigration (which is not too strong a word) of his work, Douglas (1948) considered that the critics could be divided into three camps. First, there were the 'institutionalists' who decried any type of statistical or econometric work. It should be

---

[6] Douglas was well aware of other possible specifications. One of his associates, Sidney Wilcox, suggested as early as 1926 the relationship $V = AR^{(1-\alpha-\beta)}L^{\alpha}J^{\beta}$ where *R* is defined as the combination of inputs given by $(L^2 + J^2)^{1/2}$. When $\beta = 1 - \alpha$, this specification reduces to the Cobb–Douglas. Douglas (1934) found that the estimation of this relationship gave the result $V = 1.063R^{-0.146}L^{0.788}J^{0.358}$. There are, however, two disadvantages to this formulation. First, the estimate of the coefficient of *R* is not independent of the units of measurement and, second, the production function does not everywhere exhibit convex isoquants when $(1 - \alpha - \beta) \neq 0$ (Samuelson, 1979).

remembered that econometrics was then in its infancy and was still far from being generally accepted as a useful tool. While the Econometric Society had been founded in 1930, the major impetus for statistical analysis can be traced to the work of the Cowles Commission in the 1940s and, in particular, to Haavelmo's 'methodological manifesto', 'The Probability Approach in Econometrics' (1944) (de Marchi and Gilbert, 1989, p. 2).

Second, there were the theorists who believed that it was fruitless to try to assign numerical values to the parameters of a theory that they regarded as intrinsically unquantifiable. The 1930s saw the attempt to establish a quantitative revolution in economics:

> The econometricians of the 1930s had a strong sense that it was part of their mission to make economics 'operational'. . . . However, the extended conflict over the desirability of mathematical economics, while vociferous, probably involved philosophical prejudices less deep-seated than the proposition that statistical methods are applicable in economics. (Ibid., pp. 1–2)

Thus, it is not so strange to find Douglas having to justify his attempts at quantification, *per se*. As he wrote in 1934 (p. 106):

> Any inductive study dealing with the problems of distribution or of value is almost invariably either brushed aside or attacked by the devotees of 'pure' theory on the ground that since statistical analysis is necessarily based on comparisons between time or space its units can never be identical with those timeless concepts which characterize 'pure' theory. . . . When statistical series dealing with time sequences or even relative distributions in space are brought forward, the armchair theorists brush these aside on the ground that they may include either shiftings of the curves or different curves. These series are then dismissed as being merely historical or empirical.

Yet, on reflection, this reaction to his work is perhaps not so strange. Similar sentiments were also expressed by no less an authority than Keynes (1939) in his review of Tinbergen's (1939) econometric study, although the latter is now seen as one of the pioneering attempts at econometric model building. Keynes held that Tinbergen's work was merely 'a piece of historical curve fitting and description'; so at least Douglas was in good company. (Morgan (1990) has argued that not only was Keynes unaware of the new developments in econometrics that were used by Tinbergen, but had also clearly not read the book carefully.) Douglas (1934, p. 106) felt it necessary to ask, even if there were some force to the criticisms mentioned above,

> should we abandon all efforts at the inductive determination of economic – theory and remain in the ivory tower of 'pure' theory? If this is what is done, we may as well abandon all hope of further developing the science of economics

and content ourselves with merely the elaboration of hypothetical assumptions which will be of little aid in solving problems since we will not know the values. Or shall we try to make economics a progressive science?

Finally, in the third camp, and to be taken the most seriously, were those econometricians who disputed the interpretation of the results, primarily for statistical reasons. Most notable of these were the distinguished pioneering econometrician Frisch and his former pupil, Mendershausen. The latter considered the whole study so specious that 'all past work should be torn up and consigned to the wastepaper basket' (quoted by Douglas, 1976, p. 905). This bitter comment must have left a deep impression on Douglas as he also had mentioned it in his earlier work when he remarked: 'My friends thought the better part of valour was to ignore the whole subject and never mention it, but others were not so kind' (Douglas, 1967, p. 18).

Consequently, it is not surprising that Douglas was so discouraged and disheartened by such criticism that, at one stage, he had thought of giving up the effort entirely (1967, p. 18 and 1976, p. 905). Nevertheless, he persevered and undertook, in conjunction with a number of assistants and collaborators, more and more estimations of production functions, with increasing emphasis on the use of cross-industry data which were more plentiful, especially statistics for the capital stock, for example, for the Australian states. (The year 1931 was the last one until the postwar period for which the US statistical authorities and Congress, on the advice of American economists and statisticians, collected US capital stock statistics. It was felt that the data were too unreliable to be of any use.) Douglas (1934) incorporated the original 1928 study into his book, *The Theory of Wages*, along with two further time-series studies (of Massachusetts and New South Wales) which seemed to confirm the early results. As has been noted, Douglas's 1947 presidential address was a lengthy survey and defence of his procedure for estimating production functions:

> By this time we had accumulated about 2,100 observations for the United States and about 1,400 for countries other than the United States. We found that the deviations of the actual observations from the theoretical values for the United States were relatively minor. They were much less than one would expect from the normal distribution measures of statistical error, and this was true also of the British Commonwealths. (Douglas, 1967, p. 19)

But it was not until 1957, with the publication of Solow's classic paper on technical change and the aggregate production function, that Douglas's work received universal recognition. Indeed Samuelson, one of Douglas's pupils, considers that Douglas never fully appreciated the ultimate impact

which the Cobb–Douglas production function (and the subsequent generalisations such as the CES and translog production functions) had on the
profession.[7]

CRITICISMS OF THE INITIAL TIME-SERIES DATA

Econometrics was in its infancy when Cobb and Douglas (1928) published their results so it is not surprising that many of the usual statistical
diagnostics, including the R^2 were absent. We re-estimated the production
function using Cobb and Douglas's data in intensive form, that is to say
regressing:[8]

$$\ln(V/L)_t = c + (1 - \alpha) \ln(J/L)_t. \tag{4.1}$$

The estimate of $(1 - \alpha)$, capital's output elasticity was 0.251, not surprisingly close to Cobb and Douglas's original estimate, with a t-ratio of
4.25. (This is based on White's heteroscedastic-consistent standard errors.)
The $\bar{R}^2$ is just under 0.6. Durand (1937) and Mendershausen (1938) both
pointed out that rather than imposing the constraint that the output elasticities summed to unity (that is, assuming that constant returns to scale
prevail), the output elasticities should be freely estimated. This was easily
remedied by Douglas and the outcome reported in his presidential address
(published in 1948). He found that the sum of the coefficients was close to
unity, although as no standard errors were reported, this was not statistically tested. Re-estimating the specification by OLS and not constraining
the coefficients to unity gives a value of the sum of the coefficients equal
to 1.011, which is not statistically significant at the 99 per cent confidence

---

[7]   Douglas's main academic interest was in labour economics, especially the history of
wage theories, the effect of the elasticity of supply on wages and occupational and geographi-
cal differences in wages. His magnum opus was *The Theory of Wages* (1934) and it was as
part of this study that Douglas became interested in production theory and the marginal
productivity theory of factor pricing. 'It began as an analysis of the relative elasticities of
supply of both labor and capital and the effect of varying rates of change in these upon the
distribution of the product. But without a theory of production, elasticities did not themselves explain much' (Douglas, 1972, p.46). A first draft of his book won a prestigious prize
in 1927, but extensive revisions and elaborations meant that its publication was delayed until
1934. Douglas went on to have a distinguished role in public life, being elected to the US
Senate in 1948. What is surprising is how little emphasis he placed in later life on his academic
work. In his autobiography of over 600 pages, *In the Fullness of Time* (Douglas, 1972), barely
two pages are devoted to the Cobb–Douglas production function and only one short chapter
documents his academic career.

[8]   We used Douglas's original dataset, although we used his revised (1934) employment
series.

level. These results, of course, merely serve to confirm those of Cobb and Douglas (1928) and Douglas (1934).

Criticisms of the results and specification of the model, from those who did not simply dismiss the whole endeavour out of hand, were not slow in forthcoming. Several issues were raised by J.M. Clark (1928) in a comment published at the same time as Cobb and Douglas's original paper. Another major criticism that deserves explicit mention was Mendershausen's (1938) predominantly econometric critique.

It is possible to identify three main strands in these early criticisms, some of which were easily disposed of by Douglas, but others were not. First, it was held, notably by Mendershausen, that the original results were plagued by the problem of serious multicollinearity and the undue influence of outliers. Consequently, the results were spurious, notwithstanding the fact that the estimates took plausible values, with the output elasticities being close to the relevant factor shares. Second, there was the complete absence of any allowance for technical change, a fact which so shocked Joseph Schumpeter (Samuelson, 1979). Indeed, the remarkable goodness-of-fit suggested that, in fact, there was very little left for technical change to explain. Third, and indeed related to the second problem, was the objection that the estimates were only capturing the historical trend growth rates of output, labour and capital which had no implications for the form of the production function. Each of these criticisms will be considered in turn.

The Problem of Multicollinearity

Mendershausen (1938) argued that there was very nearly perfect multicollinearity between the three variables $\ln V$, $\ln L$ and $\ln J$ with partial correlation coefficients between pairs of the variables of over 0.8. He demonstrated this by performing two additional multiple regressions, minimising the sum of squares in each direction of $\ln L$ and $\ln J$, in other words using these variables as the regressors. He found that implied estimates of α and β differed considerably depending upon the method of normalisation.[9] He argued that the reason for these discrepancies

---

[9] Mendershausen's (1938, p. 147) estimates were:

Direction of Minimisation	α	β
$\ln V$	0.76	0.25
$\ln L$	−1.06	−1.14
$\ln J$	2.23	−0.34

was the presence of multicollinearity and the excessive leverage from three observations, 1908, 1921 and 1922. (The 1920–21 period saw a fall in output of just under 30 per cent and 1921–22 a recovery of a similar magnitude.)

From a modern perspective, Mendershausen's statistical procedure is unusual, since if we assume that $\ln L$ and $\ln J$ are the independent variables, then the other specifications violate the exogeneity assumption of OLS as $\ln V$, which is endogenous, is specified as exogenous in the two other regressions. Moreover, at first glance, the multicollinearity in Cobb and Douglas's original specification (that is, with $\ln V$ as the regressand) does not seem to be a problem; the partial correlation between $\ln J$ and $\ln L$ is less than the multiple R^2 and the standard errors of the coefficients are low. While these findings are suggestive, rather than conclusive, $\alpha + \beta$ can be estimated with precision and as we have seen it is not significantly different from unity. Thus, to gain an estimate of α the restricted regression is appropriate.

Mendershausen's discussion opens an interesting window on the methodological debates in econometrics that were going on in the 1930s. One school of thought, which is implicit in Mendershausen's argument, assumed that statistical specifications were exact relationships, especially after the data had been pre-adjusted to take account of other influences. The reason why perfect fits were not obtained was the presence of measurement errors and the object was to choose the method of normalisation that would minimise the impact of these errors.

The other view was the one that is generally accepted today, namely that the direction of causation is important and that the residuals capture the effect of the inevitable missing variables, as well as measurement errors and errors induced by averaging or aggregating the data (Morgan, 1990). (The former approach is now largely forgotten, although a vestige remains in the method of indirect least squares.) If the conventional approach is adopted, and it is assumed that the appropriate specification is to regress $\ln V$ on $\ln L$ and $\ln J$, then Mendershausen's critique becomes obviated. Zellner et al. (1966) provided a theoretical justification for this procedure.

Nevertheless, further analysis of Cobb and Douglas's specification, that is, with $\ln V$ as the regressand, shows that the results are extremely unstable. We performed a rolling regression with a window of size 10. The size of the window is to a certain extent arbitrary and the value of 10 was chosen as providing an acceptable trade-off between the degrees of freedom and the number of regressions. The instability of the coefficients was such that the value of α for many of periods was negative and generally the coefficient was statistically insignificant (Table 4.1). The good

Table 4.1   Estimates of α, β and (1 − α) from a rolling regression:
American manufacturing, 1899–1908 to 1913–1922

Period	α (t-value)	β (t-value)	α + β	(1 − α) (t-value)
1899/1908	1.476 (5.16)	−0.051 (−0.36)	1.425	0.180 (1.31)
1900/1909	1.450 (5.00)	−0.065 (−0.46)	1.385	0.161 (1.22)
1901/1910	1.381 (4.76)	−0.076 (−0.56)	1.305	0.078 (0.70)
1902/1911	1.314 (4.11)	−0.112 (−0.75)	1.202	−0.144 (−0.13)
1903/1912	1.422 (4.37)	−0.154 (−0.91)	1.268	−0.007 (−0.05)
1904/1913	1.652 (5.09)	−0.291 (−1.58)	1.361	−0.053 (−0.31)
1905/1914	1.588 (4.80)	−0.250 (−1.46)	1.338	−0.901 (−0.58)
1906/1915	1.453 (4.13)	0.004 (0.02)	1.457	0.168 (0.94)
1907/1916	1.270 (4.93)	0.181 (1.13)	1.451	0.432 (2.12)
1908/1917	0.978 (2.52)	0.268 (0.99)	1.246	0.535 (2.30)
1909/1918	0.701 (1.24)	0.290 (0.85)	0.991	0.280 (1.51)
1910/1919	1.000 (1.86)	0.054 (0.17)	1.054	0.109 (0.64)
1911/1920	0.940 (2.05)	0.080 (0.32)	1.020	0.096 (0.67)
1912/1921	0.839 (6.52)	0.062 (0.89)	0.901	0.062 (0.89)
1913/1922	0.612 (2.81)	0.216 (1.79)	0.828	0.237 (2.04)

Notes: α and β are the unconstrained output elasticities of labour and capital and α + β is the degree of returns to scale. (1 − α) is the output elasticity of capital when constant returns to scale are imposed.

Source: Douglas (1934).

results that Cobb and Douglas obtained were due to the inclusion of the outlier years of 1921 and 1922.

It also turns out that the other datasets (for Massachusetts and New South Wales) which Cobb and Douglas used to support their conjectures also suffer from similar problems of instability. Thus, it is difficult not to agree with Mendershausen's (1938, p. 152) conclusion, although for different reasons, that 'it is now obvious that the empirical relation found between the coefficients α and β cannot be taken as a verification of the *pari passu* law. . . . The nature of the production law cannot be ascertained at all from this set of variates'. To be fair, Douglas (1948), himself, does allude, although understandably briefly, to the problems posed by omitting a few of the terminal years of his data, but does not report the regression results. Subsequent to his 1928 paper, Douglas, with his colleagues, confined his attention to cross-sectional data which gave much better results. It is thus somewhat of an irony that his original paper gives no support to the existence of 'laws of production'.

The Absence of Technical Progress

From a modern perspective, a glaring omission from Cobb and Douglas's specification is the assumption of a constant technology (the A in the equation for the production function $V_t = AL_t^\alpha J_t^\beta$ does not vary over time).

Their critics were quick to seize on this point. Mendershausen (1938, p. 145) commented 'these assumptions are manifestly in contradiction to all that economists know about the industrial development during this period'. Clark (1928, p. 463), likewise, expressed concern:

> One of the striking things in this study as presented is the fact that it seems to allow no room for the natural effect of advances in the 'state of the arts'. To one accustomed to crediting our increase in per capita output to triumphs of inventive genius, it must be a rude shock to see the whole increase calmly attributed to increased capital; while even on this basis the share of capital is only one-fourth of the whole, which seems too modest to leave room for any deductions. What, then, has become of our boasted progress?

Phelps Brown (1957, p. 550) also pointed out that an implication of Douglas's estimates was that the marginal product of capital in American manufacturing fell by one-half over the 1899–1922 period, which seems implausible.[10] Douglas (1934, pp. 209–16) did discuss the problems posed by technical progress in some depth, but, as we shall see, did not come up with a satisfactory solution.

To a modern reader, with the benefit of the hindsight of Solow's (1957) classic paper (where technical progress explained over 85 per cent of the growth of GNP per head in the US private non-farm sector from 1909 to 1949) and the experience of the plethora of neoclassical 'growth accounting' studies that have attempted, with limited success to explain this 'residual', such criticisms of Cobb and Douglas's specification are not only pertinent, but also have a certain irony. Clark (1928, p. 464) argued that growth, *per se*, together with rising labour costs, induced technical progress. In a statement that has a modern ring to it and is reminiscent of endogenous growth theory, he argued:

> [I]t is typical of present-day methods of management to set a research department to work definitely on the problem created by changing cost conditions. The result is that any such changes will call forth a crop of new devices or cause

---

   [10]   This was based on the observation that the rate of change of the rate of profit is equal to the growth of the output–capital ratio, as the marginal product of capital is given by $(1 - \alpha)(V/J)$. Hence, its rate of growth is $\hat{V}_t - \hat{J}_t$, where the circumflex denotes a proportionate growth rate. From 1899 to 1922, the marginal product of capital was declining at an exponential rate of 2.88 per cent per annum, which implies a fall of 48 per cent over the period.

others to be quickly developed which would otherwise have been very slow in getting past the experimental stage.

Clark, however, does not suggest how an allowance for technical progress could be included in the regression analysis. Rather, he comes close to advocating a growth-accounting procedure:

> In inquiring whether these figures offer any evidence of the existence of 'pure progress', the only available method seems to be to make all reasonable adjust-ments in the direction which would tend to indicate such progress, and then to see if the resulting trend of product is higher, relative to those of capital and labour, than can be plausibly explained by the actions of labour and capital alone. (p. 465)

Douglas (1934, p. 209) certainly conceded that the omission of any allowance for technical change was 'disconcerting'. As he pointed out, the growth of productivity in his formula was almost entirely explained by the growth of the tangible factors of production: 'But this is not really progress in any dynamic sense. It is a mere accumulation of greater quan-tities of the factors rather than a greater effectiveness of each unit'. How can the approach allow for technical change? Douglas made some not very convincing suggestions.

First, he argued that a greater role for technical change may be found in the subperiods and especially during the boom years of 1921–26, although much of the rapid increase in productivity was likely to have been the result of the economy coming out of a severe recession and, hence, the effect of a greater utilisation of the factor inputs. Second, he had sympathy with Clark's suggestion, anticipating the new growth theory by several decades that 'the product apparently attributable to capital alone is also in a sense attributable as well to progress'. One possibility, Douglas advanced, was that an improvement in the quality of the capital stock is likely to have been matched by an increase in the quality of the labour force:

> If this be the case, then the improvement in the quality of the workers has served to balance the qualitative improvement of the capital instruments with the result that while 'progress' would have affected the joint product through each of the factors it will not be reflected in the formula. (p. 209)

Douglas's interpretation seems to be something along the following lines. The production function may be written in intensive form as:

$$(V/L)_t = A(J/L)_t^{(1-\alpha)}. \tag{4.2}$$

Define the quality-adjusted capital and skill-adjusted labour as $J_t' = J_t\exp(\lambda_J t)$ and $L_t' = L_t\exp(\lambda_L t)$ where λ_J and λ_L are the rates of improvement in the efficiency of capital and labour. Let us assume that J'_t/L'_t is approximately equal to J_t/L_t so that $\lambda_J \approx \lambda_L$.

Consequently, if equation (4.2) is expressed as (dropping the time subscripts for notational ease):

$$V/L = A(J'/L')^{(1-\alpha)},\qquad(4.3)$$

then the contribution of technical progress is being captured by the *observed* capital–labour ratio. The difficulty with this line of reasoning is that it is only correct if the level of productivity is also measured in terms of efficiency labour units, that is, V/L', which is not the case. In other words, equation (4.3) should be:

$$V/L = A_0 e^{\lambda_L t}(J'/L')^{(1-\alpha)}.\qquad(4.4)$$

But of course, it is J and L that is observed and not J' and L'. Improvements in the quality of labour and capital are not offsetting but rather are reinforcing since equation (4.3) should be written as in the now standard form:

$$V/L = A_0 e^{\lambda t}(J/L)^{(1-\alpha)},\qquad(4.5)$$

where $\lambda = \alpha\lambda_L + (1-\alpha)\lambda_J$.

Moreover, even if the whole of the residual is attributed to technical progress, as we have seen above, it has quantitatively a small role to play. Nevertheless, Douglas made no explicit justification for a constant, or time-invariant, production function except by pointing to the good fit such a function gave to the data. Mendershausen (1938, p. 145) dismissed this as *petitio principii*, since 'only if this hypothesis [of a constant production function] is justified can the function claim to be taken as a production function'.

One solution to the problem of the absence of technical progress is the inclusion of a time trend in the regression to capture the exogenous shift of the production function. As Brown (1966) notes, one of the first economists to undertake this was Tinbergen (1942). Tinbergen, in fact, constrained the coefficients, a priori, to be 0.75 and 0.25 on the basis of Douglas's findings, but as Brown points out, this is an unnecessary restriction:

'In retrospect, Professor Tinbergen's introduction of a trend term appears so obvious that one wonders why it was not done before. The obviousness of the innovation should not detract from its importance: it provides an operational means of quantifying neutral changes in the production process'. (Brown, 1966, p. 112)

In fact, a hint as to how to proceed was given to Douglas by Copeland who, in correspondence, informed him that he (Copeland) had assumed that the whole of the growth of productivity was the result of technical progress and had consequently attempted to explain the growth of V/L solely in terms of a log-linear time trend. He found that the fit was as good as that achieved by Cobb and Douglas. It is a short step to combine the two methods and to incorporate a time trend as in equation (4.4); but for some reason Douglas never took it. Including a time trend to capture exogenous technical change also has the advantage that it detrends the data (the Frisch–Waugh theorem).

However, in *The Theory of Wages* Douglas reported that two of his students had estimated the Cobb–Douglas function using detrended data. They somewhat unconventionally fitted a log–log time trend to J (that is, $\ln J = a_1 + b_1 \ln t$) and linear trends to L and V (that is, $L = a_2 + b_2 t$), rather than using the more usual log-linear relationships. They found that α took a value of 0.84, when the sum of the output elasticities was constrained to equal unity, and the value of the constant was to all intents unity when the detrended data were used. Douglas considered that the results were more or less in accord with the original results: 'The equation of trend ratios can be treated as $V' = L^{0.84} J^{0.16}$ [where V' is the predicted value of V]. The value of α is only 9 points or 12 per cent more than the value of .75 as computed from the original data' (1934, p. 144).

This is misleading and is not the whole story. We re-estimated the production function using the same data with the coefficients unconstrained. The estimate of α was 0.864 (with a t-ratio of 5.72), but β took a value of -0.464 (-1.31). The sum of α and β is 0.400 with a large standard error of 0.309. This would tend to refute Douglas's contention, not lend it support.

But the problems do not stop there. We estimated the production function using Cobb and Douglas's data but now explicitly including a linear time trend. Using the full sample, 1899–1922, the estimate of the coefficient of the capital stock (its output elasticity) was negative, -0.449 (with a t-ratio of -1.26).[11] If we estimated the restricted specification, the estimate of the coefficient of $\ln(J/L)$ was likewise negative and taking a value that was not significantly different from zero.

Thus, ironically, including a linear time trend as a proxy for technical change gives no support for there being 'laws of production'. As Phelps Brown (1957) noted, this problem plagued other early studies as when a time trend had been included in the studies of, for example, Wall (1948) and Leser (1954), 'the results have not been acceptable' (p. 550).

---

[11]   The estimate of α is 0.849 (t-ratio 6.01).

THE CROSS-SECTION STUDIES

Douglas's reaction to all the hostile criticism to his original studies was, in collaboration with a number of colleagues, to undertake even more statistical analyses using American and Australian data. There was obviously a limit to the amount of replication that could be achieved using time-series data given the limited data then available. Moreover, the anomalies were beginning to mount up, as we have noted:

> One persistent area of difficulty in these last months has been the Massachusetts time-series. We tried to improve on Professor Cobb's series of capital and product with the result that the more we refined the basic series, the more nonsensical the results became. . . . Secondly, it is disconcerting to observe if we shorten our time periods by dropping off a number of terminal years, we appreciably alter our results. We observed this fact earlier, as did Professor Williams in New Zealand, but this paradox has been most manifest when we omit the war years from 1916 on in our United States time series. (Douglas, 1948, p. 21)

Consequently, with the help especially of Grace Gunn, Douglas turned his attention to estimating production functions using inter-industry data, the results of which, he considered, supported his earlier time-series results. Douglas (1948, Table I, p. 12), for example, reports cross-industry regression results for six years between 1889 and 1919 using US manufacturing data. The smallest number of observations was 258 (for 1909) and the average estimate of α was 0.63, while that for β was 0.34. Table 4.2 reports the similar results Douglas obtained using Australian data.

The subsequent multitude of results certainly removed the objections that the first estimates were either merely the consequence of coincidental historical growth rates or plagued by multicollinearity, or both. As Douglas (1948, pp. 40–41) argued:

> It is hard to believe that these results can be purely accidental, as some critics have maintained. . . . The deviations of the actual or observed values from those which we would theoretically expect to prevail under the formula are not large and indeed are slightly less than we would expect under the random distribution of errors and of measurement. It is submitted that the total number of observations, namely over 3,500, is sufficiently large so that if the results had been purely accidental, this degree of agreement would not have occurred.

What may be regarded as the seminal paper using cross-industry results was written by Douglas in collaboration with Grace Gunn and published in 1941. Here, they threw down the challenge – 'On the whole, the results of this study tend to corroborate the findings of early ones. We invite comment and criticisms' (Gunn and Douglas, 1941, p. 80).

Table 4.2   Production function for Australia, selected fiscal years

Cross-section studies and fiscal year	Observations (N)	Values of α	SE of α	Values of β	SE of β	α + β
Australia						
1913	85	0.52	0.05	0.47	0.05	0.99
1923	87	0.55	0.05	0.49	0.05	1.02
1927	85	0.59	0.05	0.34	0.04	0.93
1935	138	0.64	0.04	0.36	0.04	1.00
1937	87	0.49	0.04	0.49	0.04	0.98
Victoria						
1911	34	0.74	0.08	0.25	0.11	0.99
1924	38	0.62	0.08	0.31	0.10	0.93
1928	35	0.59	0.07	0.27	0.09	0.86
New South Wales						
1934	125	0.64	0.04	0.34	0.03	0.99
Average of all common- wealth and state studies	714	0.60	0.06	0.37	0.06	0.97
Average of common- wealth studies only	482	0.55	0.04	0.43	0.04	0.98
Average of state studies only	232	0.65	0.07	0.29	0.08	0.94

Source: Douglas (1976, Table 2, p. 907).

But once again, objections were not slow in forthcoming. The consensus today, ignoring the problem of the accounting identity, is that the estimation of inter-industry production functions makes little theoretical sense. First, it is highly unlikely that each industry is subject to the same production function and, if this is the case, the regression analyses are likely to suffer substantial misspecification errors. Or, to put this in another way, there is only one observation for each potential production function and the data are drawn from as many different production functions as there were observations. Of course, nothing about a production function can be inferred from only one observation. (See Bronfenbrenner (1944) who interpreted the aggregate production function as the envelope of the differing micro-production functions of the various firms.)

Second, even if there were a common production function, the fact that, in equilibrium, firms would face the same factor prices means that all the observations would be on the same point on the production function. Thus, if we were to estimate $V/L = A(J/L)^{(1-\alpha)}$ we should find that there was no systematic variation in the capital–labour ratio (since this is a function of relative factor prices, which are constant). The only variation in the data would come from the disturbance term. Hence, the results could not be interpreted with confidence as reflecting the parameters of the production function.

THE ACCOUNTING IDENTITY CRITIQUE MAKES A FIRST APPEARANCE

This leads to Phelps Brown's (1957) major criticism. All that is being captured by Douglas's regressions is the familiar accounting identity $V \equiv wL + rJ$ and he was not estimating a technological relationship, in the form of a production function, at all. This is a significant criticism which we have discussed above in Chapter 2. We shall return in later chapters to this critique as we elaborate on the insurmountable problems that it poses for estimating aggregate production functions. The point was not new at that time but had been made, often in a not very clear way, in papers in the 1940s that addressed the fitting of the Cobb–Douglas function, by especially Reder (1943) and Bronfenbrenner (1944).

A useful discussion of these papers is to be found in Marshak and Andrews (1944, Appendix 2, p.192). Marshak and Andrews seemed to take the view that, on the whole, Douglas and his co-workers had been fitting a hybrid of a cost and production function and had confused it with the true production function. The implication is that there is an identification problem, similar to that exemplified by the familiar textbook example of supply and demand curves. A consequence of this is that all is not lost, however, as it should be theoretically possible to find exogenous variables to identify the production function.

But Phelps Brown (1957) suggested that the problem is, in fact, insoluble. There is no identification problem; the estimates are unambiguously of the accounting identity (see Chapter 2). The Phelps Brown critique was subsequently formalised by Simon and Levy (1963) and Cramer (1969), but the full importance of the criticism went largely unnoticed. For example, Intriligator (1978, p.270), while discussing Cramer's argument, only notes that it will lead to a bias in the estimates towards constant returns to scale and that factor shares will be approximately equal to the output elasticities. It is not mentioned that the problem removes entirely the possibility of interpreting the result of estimating a production function as a test of a technological relationship. To be fair, though, Cramer himself does not push his argument to its logical conclusion.

One reason for the relative neglect of this argument may be partly due to the fact that it was originally applied to inter-firm production functions and, as we have noted, these were already suspect on theoretical grounds.[12] But perhaps more importantly, it was (erroneously) not seen to be applicable to time-series estimations. We return to this important point below. In view of the significance of the Phelps Brown criticism, it is worth quoting him on this point:

> For on this assumption [that we can write $V \equiv wL + rJ$ for any industry], the net products to which the Cobb–Douglas is fitted would be made of just the same rates of return to productive factors, and quantities of those factors, as also make up the income statistics; and when we calculate α by fitting the Cobb–Douglas function we are bound to arrive at the same value as when we reckon up total earnings and compare them with the total net product. In α we have a measure of the percentage change in net product that goes with a 1 per cent change in the intake of labour, when the intake of capital is constant; but when we try to trace such changes by comparing one industry with another, and the net products of the two industries approximately satisfy $V_i \equiv w_i L_i + r_i J_i$ the difference between them will always approximate to the compensation at the wage rate w of the difference in labour intake. The Cobb–Douglas α, and the share of earnings, will be only two sides of the same penny. (1957, p. 557)[13]

The message of the cited passage is, in fact, simple; but no less devastating for that. Phelps Brown's argument implicitly starts with the definition of the output elasticity with respect to labour as $\alpha = (\partial V/\partial L)/(L/V)$. Consequently, α is equal to the percentage change in output when the labour input increases by 1 per cent, *ceteris paribus*. The accounting identity is given by $V \equiv wL + rJ$ from which it may be seen that the difference in output between two firms that differ only in their labour input is $\Delta V = w \Delta L$ and

$$\frac{\Delta V}{\Delta L} \cdot \frac{L}{V} = \frac{wL}{V} = \alpha. \tag{4.6}$$

Consequently, α must, *by definition*, equal labour's share in output.

We have demonstrated in Chapter 2 that the accounting identity $V = wL + rJ$ will give a good approximation to $V = AL^\alpha J^{(1-\alpha)}$ provided that factor shares are constant and, using cross-sectional data, the wage and profit rates do not greatly vary. As this occurs with the cross-sectional

---

12   In the postwar period, a number of studies were undertaken for individual industries using US state data (for example, Hildebrand and Liu, 1965, and Moroney, 1972). This specification using cross-state data avoids the objection to the cross-industry studies that it was unlikely that all industries could be represented by the same production function. Nevertheless, the good statistical fits that were usually obtained using the regional data must be attributable to the accounting identity.

13   The notation has been changed to make it consistent with that in the text.

data, it is little wonder that such good statistical fits are found with the estimated 'output elasticities' close to the factor shares.

SAMUELSON (1979) 'REDISCOVERS THE WHEEL'

We close this chapter by noting that the critique has occasionally been rediscovered. Samuelson (1979), for example, in reviewing Douglas's academic contribution on the latter's death, became yet another to discover, to his evident surprise, that the Emperor had no clothes. He noted the fact that there is an underlying accounting identity and that all that is being estimated is this identity because of the tautology induced by computing r as a residual by defining it as $(V - wL)/J$. As he put it: 'No one can prevent us from labelling this last vector as (rJ), as J.B. Clark's model would permit – even though we have no warrant for believing that non-competitive industries have a common profit rate r and use leets capital . . . in proportion to the $(V - wL)$ elements!' (p. 932).

Commenting on the cross-sectional results of Douglas and his colleagues, he noted:

> Should I not concede that, at the least, these cross-sectional investigations have tested – and verified triumphantly – the hypothesis that the C–D exponents do sum to unity to a good approximation as the neoclassical marginal-productivity wants them to do? On examination I find, when one specifies $V = AL^{\alpha}J^{\beta}$ and lets the cross-sectional data decide whether $\alpha + \beta = 1$, that results tend to follow purely as a cross-sectional *tautology* based on the *residual* computation of the nonwage share. (p. 932, emphasis in the original. The notation in all of the quotations from Samuelson has been changed to make it consistent with that in the book.)

Samuelson gives an example of why Douglas's estimates will always give constant returns to scale using hypothetical data for four industries and calculating the coefficients α and β in the equation:

$$\ln V_i = \alpha \ln(wL_i) + \beta \ln(V_i - wL_i). \qquad (4.7)$$

He uses this specification, even though his previous discussion had been in terms of the Cobb–Douglas production function, $V_i = AL_i^{\alpha}J_i^{\beta}$, because he only generates hypothetical data for the factor shares.[14] Samuelson's hypothetical data are given by Table 4.3.

---

[14]   Note that equation (4.7) can be written as: $\ln V \equiv \alpha \ln w + \beta \ln r + \alpha \ln L + \beta \ln J \equiv a \ln(wL) + (1 - a) \ln(rJ)$.

Table 4.3 Samuelson's data

Firm	1	2	3	4
V	10	20	30	40
wL	6	12	24	32
rJ	4	8	6	8
α	0.6	0.6	0.8	0.8

Samuelson next averages the data for firms 1 and 2 and also for firms 3 and 4. This gives him only two observations for each variable (let us call them 1 and 2) so a regression will give a perfect fit. Equation (4.7) may be written as:

$$\frac{\ln V}{\ln(rJ)} = \alpha \frac{\ln(wL)}{\ln(rJ)} + \beta. \tag{4.8}$$

Consequently, α may be calculated arithmetically as the slope of equation (4.8), which with two observations is given by:

$$\alpha = \frac{\Delta \ln(V/rJ)}{\Delta \ln(wL/rJ)}$$

or

$$\alpha = \frac{\ln(V/rJ)_1 - \ln(V/rJ)_2}{\ln(wL/rJ)_1 - \ln(wL/rJ)_2}. \tag{4.9}$$

This gives a value of 0.707 for α and 0.293 for β, compared with labour's average share of 0.74.

Finding that the sum of the estimated coefficients equal unity, Samuelson (p. 933) concludes that 'profit and wages add up to total *V* along any fixed ray not because Euler's theorem is revealed to apply on that ray but rather because of the accounting identity involved in the residual definition of profit'.

Samuelson (pp. 934–6) also discusses time-series estimation of 'production functions' (especially Solow, 1957) and even with careful reading, it is not clear whether or not he appreciates the fact that the accounting identity also undermines the unambiguous interpretation of these regression results. For example, he argues:

Solow (1957) showed that U.S. GNP data for 1909–49 were consistent with Hicks-neutral [and Harrod-neutral] technical change ... Solow not only validated

> Abramovitz's pragmatic [growth-accounting] picture, he provided it with a shiny
> new theoretical frame, and thereby launched a hundred studies of the 'residual',
> the factor $A(t)$ . . . in front of neoclassical production functions (p. 935).

But given that factor shares are constant, the accounting identity shows that the residual is merely the weighted growth of the real wage and the rate of profit. He seems to fail to realise the 'Catch–22' situation that to interpret the estimates as parameters of a production function, we have to *assume*, in spite of all the arguments outlined in previous chapters, that the aggregate production function actually exists and that there is no way to test this assumption, even indirectly.

Nevertheless, Samuelson raises the question as to whether 'Kaldor and the neo-Keynesians are right in suggesting that the Cobb–Douglas results are a cooked-up forgone conclusion from the nature of the statistical methodology!'. While he concedes that this is a possibility, he does not emphasise the underlying accounting identity in this case. Rather he discusses it in terms of the plausibility or otherwise of labour- and capital-saving technical change and if J/L varied in terms of efficiency units. He does note, however, even though the data may give a good fit to the production function, 'we cannot rule out the possibility that some other model could generate the same observations' (p. 936). Precisely: it is the accounting identity.

COBB AND DOUGLAS'S STUDIES REVISITED

Time-series Data and Cobb and Douglas (1928)

We have seen above that, paradoxically, the initial Cobb and Douglas results are, on closer inspection, extremely poor and if this had been pointed out at the time, it is doubtful that the paper would have had the impact that it did. As we have shown, first, the production function made no allowance for technical change and hence did not include a time trend. While the results for the whole 1899–1922 period were good with the estimates of the output elasticities being close to the factor shares, this was the result of the inclusion of two outliers, namely the years 1921 and 1922. We have seen that the results are otherwise extremely poor. However, the inclusion of a linear time trend does not rescue the situation. The problem is that from the accounting identity we know that a linear time trend will only be a good proxy if $a\hat{w}_t + (1-a)\hat{r}_t = \lambda_t$ is constant. If it shows even moderate cyclical variation over time, then the goodness of fit can break down dramatically. (The other explanation is that the factor shares vary significantly over time, but while they did exhibit some fluctuation this is not sufficient to cause the breakdown in the statistical relationship.)

Given the existence of the identity, it may seem at first somewhat paradoxical that introducing a time trend actually worsens the goodness of fit and the estimated output elasticities diverge from the factor shares, markedly so in the case of capital. However, we may easily see why this is the case. The cyclical path of λ_t is simply an empirical issue. Once we find a good mathematical approximation to use as a proxy, it will take us back to the identity. Given the cyclical fluctuation of the weighted growth of the factor inputs, a trigonometric function with sines and cosines, for example, should provide a much better approximation than that provided by the simple linear time trend (nothing in neoclassical economics says that 'technical progress' must be approximated through a linear time trend). Using the dataset of Cobb and Douglas (1928), the best statistical fit was given by the Cobb–Douglas, which includes as a regressor the time trend given by the variable:

$$\Gamma(t) = [\sin(T^5) + \cos(T^4) - \cos(T^2) - \sin(T^2)], \qquad (4.10)$$

(where T denotes time, 'sin' is the sine function, and 'cos' is the cosine function) rather than simply by t. Γ has an estimated coefficient of $\lambda = 0.032$ that is statistically significant. The other two estimates are very close to the factor shares and the fit is very good. The estimation results are reported as equation (i) in Table 4.4.

Table 4.4   Cobb–Douglas regressions (OLS estimates unless otherwise indicated)

(i) $\ln V_t = 0.032\Gamma_t + 0.726\ln L_t + 0.274\ln J_t$ $\quad\quad\quad (3.48) \quad\quad (18.83) \quad\quad (7.71)$	$R^2 = 0.973; DW = 1.95; \chi_i^2 = 0.02$
(ii) $\ln V_t = 0.023\Gamma_t + 0.756\ln L_t + 0.246\ln J_t$ $\quad\quad\quad\; (2.50) \quad\quad (15.84) \quad\quad (5.52)$	$R^2 = 0.977; DW = 1.76; \chi_i^2 = 0.43$
(iii) $\ln(V_t/L_t) = 0.029\Gamma_t + 0.001\ln L_t + 0.259\ln(J_t/L_t)$ $\quad\quad\quad\quad\; (2.39) \quad\;\; (0.43) \quad\quad\; (2.59)$	$R^2 = 0.768; DW = 1.95; \chi_i^2 = \text{n.a.}$
(iv) $V_t = e^{\lambda\Gamma t}L_t^\alpha J_t^\beta + u_t: \lambda = 0.333; \; \alpha = 0.722; \; \beta = 0.277$ $\quad\quad\quad\quad\quad\quad\quad\quad (3.65) \quad\quad (16.12) \quad\quad (6.80)$	$R^2 = 0.964; DW = 1.90; \chi_i^2 = 0.00012$

Notes: Period 1899–1992, except for equation (ii) which is 1899–1920; chi-square test (χ_i^2) $H_0: \alpha + \beta = 1$ (critical value 5% significance level: 3.84); *t*-statistics in parentheses; n.a. denotes not applicable; u_t in equation (iv) is the error term; Initial values for non-linear least squares: $\lambda = 0.03; \alpha = 0.75; \beta = 0.25$.

We noted above that Cobb and Douglas's initially plausible results with a time trend depended on the inclusion of 1921 and 1922. When these years are excluded the relationship broke down. However, this no longer happens with the cyclical time trend. As may be seen from equation (ii) the fit is still very good with the estimated coefficients very stable. Equation (iii) reports the results when the coefficients are constrained to unity and equation (iv) is estimated by non-linear least squares. Not surprisingly, all the regressions give very similar results.

Why does $\Gamma(t)$ work? With constant factor shares, the identity may be written as $V_t \equiv Bw_t^a r_t^{(1-a)} L_t^a J_t^{(1-a)}$. If, indeed, factor shares were exactly constant, this expression would be the identity, and so all that $\Gamma(t)$ in regression (i) in Table 4.4 does is to approximate the term $Bw_t^a r_t^{(1-a)}$. Therefore, we can compute the value of $Bw_t^a r_t^{(1-a)}$ as the ratio $V_t / L_t^a J_t^{(1-a)}$. Although the approximation is not perfect (the correlation between $\Gamma(t)$ and $V_t / L_t^a J_t^{(1-a)}$ is 0.588), it is certainly much better than that provided by the exponential time trend, and as argued above, it suggests that finding the exact path is simply a matter of trial and error, and a dose of patience in front of a computer.[15]

CONCLUDING COMMENTS

We have seen that the original work by Cobb and Douglas was met by a variety of criticisms. However, these were largely overcome by Douglas and his colleagues' subsequent substantial work estimating the Cobb–Douglas production function using cross-sectional data. The estimated output elasticities were invariably close to the observed factor shares, which Douglas and others took as confirming (or strictly speaking not refuting) the assumption that firms were subject to perfect competition and factors were paid their marginal productivities.

In retrospect, these results were too good to be true. Given the complexities of the actual production process, it should have been seen as remarkable that the log of two indices of inputs (total employment and the crude measures of the capital stock) could in cross-section regressions explain over 90 per cent of the variation in the log of output. It was Phelps

---

[15]   Still at this point one may argue that all we are doing is inserting back into the equation the 'Solow residual' and, therefore, we should expect a perfect fit. This argument faces two objections. First, what we are inserting is not the Solow residual itself, but a function of sines and cosines that tracks such a residual better than the linear time trend that is usually introduced. Second, the exercise shows that once this function is found, we recover the identity and, by implication, the elasticities always equal the factor shares.

Brown (1957) who first suggested that these results may be a mere statistical artefact, but his warnings went unheeded for many years. Indeed, two developments led to the aggregate production function becoming an indispensable concept in neoclassical macroeconomics.

First, was Solow's (1956, 1957) two seminal articles: one using the aggregate production function as an integral concept in the theoretical modelling of economic growth; the other using the aggregate production function to show, somewhat counter-intuitively, that technical change (or the TFP growth) accounted for nearly all of productivity growth. This led to the 'growth-accounting' approach, pioneered by Denison (1962, 1967). Second, what were seen as econometric problems in estimating aggregate production functions led to plenty of empirical Kuhnian puzzles. The popularisation of the CES production functions by Arrow et al. in 1961 and the development of the translog production function (Christensen et al., 1973) led to further empirical estimation and also theoretical developments of cost and production functions.

It was not until 1974 that Anwar Shaikh, in a short note, revived interest in the accounting critique, applying it to Solow's (1957) empirical study and leading to an acrimonious rejoinder from Solow (1974). We turn next to this debate and elaborate on it, showing that Solow's methodology is, not surprisingly, as equally flawed as that of Cobb and Douglas.

5. Solow's 'Technical Change and the Aggregate Production Function', and the accounting identity

> The article on technical change was a companion piece [to Solow 1956] in that it showed how the distinction between the effects of capital accumulation and the effects of technical progress . . . can in principle be measured from historical data. . . . A large part of the vast subsequent empirical work on growth and growth accounting owes its origin to this impulse.
>
> (Matthews, 1988, pp. 13–14)

INTRODUCTION[1]

After the initial poor reception that Cobb and Douglas's work received and which was discussed in the last chapter, it was only Douglas with his various colleagues in the 1930s and 1940s who continued to express any interest in the empirical applications of the aggregate production function. It was not until the mid-1950s, with the seminal papers of Solow (1956, 1957) and Swan (1956) that the concept of the aggregate production function became an essential tool in both theoretical and applied analyses of economic growth. (In the 1960s it also became widely used in the short-run analysis of unemployment in the labour market, providing the foundations for the demand for labour function and the aggregate supply side of the neoclassical synthesis AD/AS model.)

Since then there has been a plethora of studies estimating aggregate production functions. The recent interest in endogenous growth theory is also based on the aggregate production function and, paradoxically, has led to a revival of interest in the (augmented) Solow growth model (Mankiw et al., 1992). Likewise, the real business-cycle model has led to a renewed interest in the 'Solow residual'. The neoclassical growth-accounting approach, now over 40 years old, has been used, for example, putatively to determine the proximate sources of growth of the East Asian Tigers, with controversial results (Young, 1992, 1995) and the production function is at the heart of the New Economic Geography,

---

[1]   This draws on McCombie (2000–01, 2001).

albeit within the representative agent framework (Krugman, 1991, 2009).

However, as we showed earlier, there are few, if any, grounds for believing in the existence of the aggregate production function, even as a first approximation. Solow has expressed the view that 'nobody thinks there is such a thing as a 'true' *aggregate* production function' (Solow, 1987, p. 15 emphasis in the original). Nevertheless, aggregate production functions are widely used, albeit with a bad conscience, as Solow put it.

In this chapter we examine Solow's seminal work, with particular reference to his classic (1957) paper on technical change and the aggregate production function. Consequently, the chapter may be seen, in part, as a continuation and extension of the Phelps Brown (1957) and Simon (1979b) critique, elaborated and extended above. Nevertheless, it is more than just an exercise in the history of economic thought as we shall show that the problems surrounding the aggregate production function that are inherent in Solow's (1956, 1957) articles also affect all subsequent neoclassical growth theories.

In the next section we shall discuss what is seen as Solow's (1957) pathbreaking methodological contribution; a brief comment by Hogan (1958); and more extensive comments by Shaikh (1974, 1980) and the supposed rebuttal by Solow (1974). We also briefly revisit the growth-accounting methodology. This is followed by a consideration of Solow's (1987) 'second thoughts' on growth theory where he returns to these issues. These were not really second thoughts at all, as Solow had not, in the intervening period, changed his mind, but still maintained his earlier position that Shaikh's (1974), to our way of thinking, important criticism was 'wrong: not misguided or misleading, but simply wrong' (Solow, 1974, p. 121). Finally we show how, in spite all the theoretical problems, it is possible to obtain a perfect fit to an aggregate production function, although, not surprisingly, we shall show that the estimates tell us nothing about the underlying technology of the economy.

SOLOW'S 'TECHNICAL CHANGE AND THE AGGREGATE PRODUCTION FUNCTION'

The reception of Solow's (1957) paper, 'Technical Change and the Aggregate Production Function' (together with his 1956 companion theoretical paper) could hardly have been more different from that of Cobb and Douglas's (1928) article. Solow's two papers opened up a whole field of research and created a framework of thought about economic growth that is now standard among economists. Even recent developments in endogenous growth theory take as their starting point the Solow growth model.[2] Blinder (1989, pp. 103–4), in his tribute to Solow occasioned by Solow's Nobel prize, commented:

> The 1956 and 1957 papers, in particular, have achieved the status of true classics, meaning that everyone knows what they say, without ever reading them. Despite the fact that the terms 'Solow model' and 'Solow residual' are often used without explicit citation, these two papers continue to be cited more than three decades after their publication and their influence on economic scholarship is profound.

Even after half a century, many economists would still share these sentiments.

Although Solow's (1957) paper may be justifiably regarded as the seminal article in the empirics of economic growth (Matthews, 1988), he adopted a novel estimation procedure that has not been followed since. Solow's main contribution was to link the idea of total, or multifactor, productivity to the aggregate production function. The concept had been used before, but not within the framework of the production function (Griliches, 1996). Solow further devised a method to estimate the contribution of productivity growth to output growth. However, Solow (1974) subsequently admitted that it was based on a tautology (a 'good' tautology according to Solow, but nevertheless a tautology) and how a tautology came to be so influential is an intriguing question.

Solow commenced with the expression for an aggregate production function with Hicks-neutral technical change, namely,

$$V = A(t)f(L, J), \tag{5.1}$$

where V, L and J are output (value added), labour (total hours worked) and capital. $A(t)$ is an index of technology. Writing the production function in intensive form gives $(V/L) = A(t)f(J/L)$. In order to estimate a production function, it was necessary for Solow first to 'deflate' the function to correct for its upward shift over time due to technical progress. In other words, the general form of the production function to be estimated took the form $(V/L)/A(t) = f(J/L)$.

Consequently, Solow had to first construct an index for $A(t)$. The rationale behind this approach may be best seen by considering Figure (5.1). This figure shows the relationship between labour productivity (V/L)

---

    ² Credit also ought to go to the Australian economist Swan (1956) who developed a similar model independently of Solow. Indeed, some economists refer to the Solow–Swan growth model in recognition of Swan's contribution.

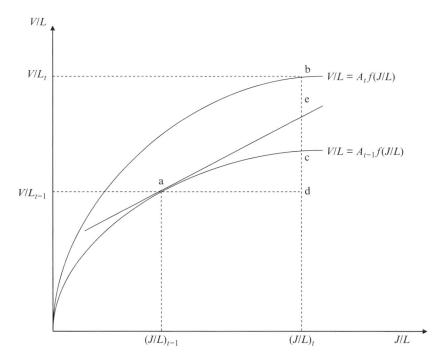

Figure 5.1   The measurement of technical change

and the capital–labour ratio (J/L) given by the production function for two periods, during which time the level of technology has increased from A_{t-1} to A_t.

In terms of Figure 5.1, the level of productivity in the base period, $t-1$, is given by $(V/L)_{t-1}$ (at point a), where the production function is $(V/L) = A_{t-1}f(J/L)$ and A_{t-1} is the base period level of technology which is normalised to unity. Over time, with technical progress, the production function shifts upwards, so that in period t the level of output is given by $(V/L)_t$ (at point b) and the new production function is given by $V/L = A_t f(J/L)$. There are only two observed points, a and b, and Solow 'deflates' $(V/L)_t$ so it becomes $(V/L)_t/A_t$ and lies on the base-year production function at point c. (As we shall see, because of a linear approximation, it is actually point e.) Repeating this for subsequent years gives more observations and allows the base-year production function to be estimated.

The percentage increase in productivity between the two periods, $t-1$ and t, that is given by technical change, $\hat{A}$, is $(b-c)/a$, and that given by the increase in factor inputs is $(c-d)/a$, when each expression is multiplied by 100.

In order to calculate $A(t)$, it was first necessary to calculate $\hat{A}$ for each year. The increase in productivity due to the movement along the initial production function from $(J/L)_{t-1}$ to $(J/L)_t$ is given by:

$$\Delta(V/L)^*_t = A_{t-1}f_{J/L}\Delta(J/L)_t = r_{t-1}\Delta(J/L)_t. \tag{5.2}$$

The superscript * denotes that this is the hypothetical increase in productivity keeping the level of technology constant. It follows that:

$$\frac{\Delta(V/L)^*_t}{(V/L)_{t-1}} = (1 - a_{t-1})\frac{\Delta(J/L)_t}{(J/L)_{t-1}}. \tag{5.3}$$

The marginal productivity theory is invoked and so the output elasticity of capital is taken as being equal to its factor share, $(1 - a_{t-1})$ which equals $r_{t-1}J_{t-1}/V_{t-1}$. Consequently, the rate of profit is evaluated at time $t - 1$, which will introduce a small approximation error. (It implies that the deflated level of output is given by point e rather than point c. For small, such as annual, changes, the differences are small.) Solow (1957, p. 313, Chart 1) takes his reference year as t and evaluates r at this year, rather than at $t - 1$ as in our figure. However, Solow (p. 313) mentions in his text that for reference year $t - 1$, the curve would be approximated by its tangent at point a, that is, by r_{t-1} and so he seems to take $t - 1$ as the reference year.

Consequently, the rate of technical progress over the period $t - 1$ to t is given by:

$$\hat{A} = \frac{\Delta A_t}{A_{t-1}} = \frac{\Delta(V/L)_t}{(V/L)_{t-1}} - \frac{\Delta(V/L)^*_t}{(V/L)_{t-1}} = \frac{\Delta(V/L)_t}{(V/L)_{t-1}} - (1 - a_{t-1})\frac{\Delta(J/L)_t}{(J/L)_{t-1}}. \tag{5.4}$$

Having calculated the yearly growth rates for $A(t)$, the index for each year in the sample is calculated as:

$$A_t = A_{t-1}\left[1 + \frac{(A_t - A_{t-1})}{A_{t-1}}\right]. \tag{5.5}$$

The data used were for the US private non-farm sector from 1909 to 1949. Having calculated the annual growth of $A(t)$ by this method, an index of $A(t)$ was then calculated by setting A_{1909} equal to unity and using these growth rates of $A(t)$ to construct the index for subsequent years. This index was then used to construct $(V/L)/A(t)$.

An alternative, and preferable, method would be to have used exponential growth rates to calculate the growth of technology,

$$\ln \frac{A_t}{A_{t-1}} = \ln \frac{(V/L)_t}{(V/L)_{t-1}} - (1 - \bar{a}) \ln \frac{(J/L)_t}{(J/L)_{t-1}}, \tag{5.6}$$

where $(1 - \bar{a})$ is the average of the values in t and $t - 1$.

Solow uses the phrase 'technical change' as a shorthand expression to cover any kind of shift of the production function: 'Thus slowdowns, speed ups, improvements in the education of the labour force, and all sorts of things will appear as "technical change"' (1957, p. 312). He noted with satisfaction that the trend of $A(t)$ is strongly upwards; 'had it turned out otherwise, I would not now be writing this paper' (p. 316).

Solow (1957) explicitly estimated five different specifications of production functions using the 'deflated' value of productivity as the regressand. These included the linear and log-linear (Cobb–Douglas) specifications and were:

$$(V/L)/A = c + b(J/L) \tag{i}$$

$$(V/L)/A = c + b \ln(J/L) \tag{ii}$$

$$(V/L)/A = c - b/(J/L) \tag{iii}$$

$$\ln[(V/L)/A] = c + b \ln(J/L) \tag{iv}$$

$$\ln[(V/L)/A] = c - b/(J/L). \tag{v}$$

The results obtained by Solow are shown in Table 5.1.

Table 5.1   Results of Solow's regressions

Equation	c	b	r
(i)	0.483	0.091	0.9982
(ii)	0.448	0.239	0.9996
(iii)	0.917	0.618	0.9964
(iv)	0.729	0.353	0.9996
(v)	0.038	0.913	0.9980

Note: r is the correlation coefficient.

Source: Solow (1957, Table 2, p. 319).

Table 5.2   Estimates of the Cobb–Douglas production function using Solow's data

$\ln[(V/L)/A] = c + b\ln(J/L)$

Equation	c	b	$\bar{r}^2$	SER	DW
(a)	−0.568	0.345	0.9998	0.0006	1.86
	(−137.17)	(129.68)			
(b)	−0.605	0.350	0.9995	0.0015	2.19
	(−163.77)	(108.84)			
(c)	−0.791	0.689	0.9936	0.0071	2.07
	(−26.72)	(23.36)			
(d)	−0.561	0.311	0.9691	0.0071	2.06
	(−18.97)	(10.53)			

Notes:
t-values in parentheses. All equations estimated by exact maximum likelihood AR(1) method.
(a)   Cobb–Douglas using capital stock adjusted for capacity utilisation.
(b)   Cobb–Douglas using capital stock unadjusted for capacity utilisation.
(c)   Cobb–Douglas with capital's share taken as the value of labour's share.
(d)   Cobb–Douglas where capital's share is a uniform random variable.

Source: McCombie (2000–01).

Solow was surprised at the closeness of the regression results, with the r^2 in every case exceeding 0.99.[3] 'Considering the amount of a priori doctoring which the raw figures have undergone, the fit is remarkably tight.' Nevertheless, he felt that 'little or nothing hangs on the choice of functional form' (p. 318). 'All five functions, even the linear one, are equally good at representing the general shape of the observed points' (p. 319). Solow found that from an examination of the residuals using the runs test, the linear function was systematically worse than the others and 'the results strongly confirm the visual impression of diminishing returns', (p. 319) in Solow's Chart 4 (p. 317).[4] Table 5.2, equation (a) reports the results of re-estimating the Cobb–Douglas in logarithmic form using the

---

[3]   This is notwithstanding a computational slip that Solow made in calculating $A(t)$ from 1942 to the end of the data series in 1949 (Hogan, 1958). This produced a number of outliers during the period of the Second World War that Solow (1958, p. 411), in his own words, made 'some half-hearted attempts to explain away'. As it turns out, there was nothing to explain away.
[4]   Using Solow's data, we estimated a Box–Cox regression, which corroborated that the Cobb–Douglas function is indeed to be preferred over the linear on statistical grounds (the results are not reported here). Throughout this book, we have used Solow's corrected data.

corrected data. This confirms Solow's original result. We shall return to the other equations in Table 5.2.

A number of small problems were soon pointed out. Levine (1960) noted that Solow omitted an interaction term in his calculation of the discrete growth rates, in equation (5.2). Massell (1962) pointed out that as the period lengthens so the proportion of productivity explained by technical change varies, although this was unlikely to be a problem if the growth rates were calculated over short periods. Moreover, this problem does not arise if exponential growth rates are used and they give results almost identical to those of Solow. Hsing (1992) argued that Solow's method of calculating growth rates invalidated the results of estimating a production function, but see McCombie (1996) for a refutation. But one of the most serious criticisms was the early comment of Hogan (1958) and it is worth considering this in detail as it raises some issues that we shall be concerned with later.

Hogan's (1958) Critique and Solow's Tautology

Apart from pointing out the arithmetical slip that Solow (1957) made in his data, Hogan (1958) raised two further points with respect to Solow's paper. The first concerned the fact that Solow used net rather than gross capital stocks. Although Hogan placed a great deal of emphasis on this difference, it makes very little difference to the results and we shall not discuss it here.

His more important critique, to our way of thinking, was that Solow's procedure of calculating technical change turned his whole method into a tautology. We may see this as follows. The rate of technical progress (remembering that it includes everything that shifts the production function) is calculated as:

$$\hat{A}_t \equiv (\hat{V}_t - \hat{L}_t) - (1 - a_t)(\hat{J}_t - \hat{L}_t). \tag{5.7}$$

Solow, as we have seen, then 'deflated' the growth of productivity, that is, $(\hat{V}_t - \hat{L}_t) - \hat{A}_t$, which by construction must equal:

$$(\hat{V}_t - \hat{L}_t) - \hat{A}_t \equiv (1 - a_t)(\hat{J}_t - \hat{L}_t). \tag{5.8}$$

In Solow's data, the factor shares are roughly constant over time. Let us suppose that they are *exactly* constant. Equation (5.8) can be integrated to give:

$$V/A \equiv c(J/L)^{(1-a)} \tag{5.9}$$

or in logarithmic form as:

$$\ln(V/A) \equiv \ln c + (1-a)\ln(J/L). \qquad (5.10)$$

Equation (5.10) is clearly an identity (but *not* derived from the accounting identity) and therefore there is no point in estimating it as we know that the coefficient on $\ln(J/L)$ must take a value equal to $(1-a)$. Indeed, this is all Solow has achieved in doing, given that the shares have just enough variation to avoid the problem of multicollinearity. The mean of the observed share of capital is 0.344 with a coefficient of variation of 0.05. The estimation of the Cobb–Douglas production function with the corrected data gives an estimate of 0.352 with a t-value of 93.39 and an r^2 as near as unity as makes no difference (it is actually 0.9996).

Solow's (1958a) reply to Hogan is not particularly convincing. He argued that his (Solow's) chain of reasoning is indeed tautological (as Hogan had suggested) as 'how could a chain of exact reasoning be otherwise?'. But Solow makes the distinction between a 'good' and a 'bad' tautology (p.411). If the constraint that $(1-a)$ was a constant was imposed on the data, then this would be a bad tautology, because all the points would by construction lie on an exact Cobb–Douglas. But $(1-a)$ does show some variation, albeit slight. It still yields a tautology 'in the sense that what it yields is that production function, *wiggles and all*, which if shifted neutrally according to the calculated $A(t)$ will pass through the right points with the right outputs and with the right slope. But it seems to me that this is good tautology' (emphasis in the original). Solow (p.412) continues 'although there is a tautologically implied production function embedded in the method, it may still be interesting to see what the function looks like'. But he does concede that he should have 'warned the reader explicitly that the method would automatically produce a perfect Cobb–Douglas fit if the observed shares were constant'.

To show how misleading Solow's procedure can be, we undertook three experiments. In the first one we used his capital stock figures unadjusted for changes in capacity utilisation. (Solow used the unemployment rate as a proxy for the degree of capacity utilisation.) Not surprisingly, the fit in terms of the usual diagnostics is as good as Solow's and the estimated coefficients are virtually identical (Table 5.2, equation (b)).

Second, we assumed that in our economy there were imperfect markets and this resulted in a hypothetical value of labour's share that we took as equal to the observed share of capital in Solow's dataset and vice versa. The results again give an almost perfect fit but with the estimated coefficient taking a value of 0.689 (Table 5.2, equation (c)). While the fit is good, it is not so good as that in equations (a) and (b) in terms of the *t*-values and the standard error of the regression.

Finally, we estimated the Cobb–Douglas, but simulated the share of capital to show a very wide variation around an average value of approximately 0.35. This was done by treating the share as a random variable, being drawn from a uniform distribution between 0.0 and 0.7. The simulated values of capital's share ranged from 0.007 to 0.694 with a sample mean of 0.358. In spite of this wide variation in capital's share, it can be seen that the estimation still gives a very good fit to the data with the estimate of capital's output elasticity very close to the factor share. (Table 5.2, (d)). Lest we be accused of data mining, it should be noted that these results are literally the first ones obtained from the first run of the simulation exercise. In other words, we did not run a multitude of simulations and pick the one with the most favourable results.

Solow's (1958a) rejoinder to Hogan seems to be much of an *ex post* justification. There is little doubt that the immediate impact of Solow's (1957) paper was due to the fact that it was the first to link the concept of technical progress, or the TFP growth, directly to the aggregate production function. This was enhanced by the fact that, implicitly, it seemed to provide empirical support for the existence of an aggregate production function (in terms of the statistical results presented). The fact that correlation coefficients of over 0.99 were found seemed to confirm the existence of a close relationship between inputs and outputs in a simple model, notwithstanding the serious measurement errors that were likely to be present. Indeed, as we noted earlier, Solow himself seemed to be surprised at the goodness of the fit.

But as Hogan (1958, p. 411) pointed out, even if the capital stock figures were randomly generated, we would still get a statistical relationship with as good a fit as Solow obtained. It is not sufficient to counter that 'if the capital stock figures were chosen at random, I'd get a rather odd-looking profile for technical change!' (Solow, 1958a, p. 412, fn. 1). As Solow (1957, p. 316) himself pointed out in his original paper, 'I had very little prior notion of what would be "reasonable" [for a profile of technical change]', so what would he find an odd-looking profile to be? As we have seen, he also fitted several functional forms to the data, but now commented that he should have warned the reader that the best fit would be a Cobb–Douglas, as inspection of the data confirms that factor shares are indeed almost constant. Yet, because of the high collinearity, there is somewhat of a paradox as Solow himself has shown, other functional forms give an almost equally good fit.

Anwar Shaikh (1974) Weighs In

It was not until 17 years after the appearance of Solow's (1957) paper that Shaikh (1974) advanced two serious separate criticisms of Solow's procedure.

The first was an extension and elaboration of the Phelps Brown (1957) and Simon and Levy (1963) criticisms to time-series data. The second concerned the tautological procedure Solow adopted to correct labour productivity for technical change and then to estimate the various specifications of the production function (this extended Hogan's, 1958, earlier critique). We shall next consider the first of these criticisms, before briefly turning to the second.

As we have dealt with this extensively in previous chapters, we can be brief. Shaikh was the first to advance the accounting identity argument with respect to time-series data and he noted that there is an underlying identity of the form:

$$V/L \equiv w + rJ/L, \tag{5.11}$$

and which when differentiated with respect to time and integrated, assuming factor shares are constant, gives the familiar result:

$$V/L \equiv B(J/L)^{(1-a)}, \tag{5.12}$$

where $B = a^{-a}(1 - a)^{-(1-a)}w^a r^{(1-a)}$, or $V \equiv A_0 e^{\lambda t} L^a J^{(1-a)}$ if $a\hat{w} + (1 - a)\hat{r} = \lambda$ is a constant growth rate. It is difficult to overstate the importance of this result. As Shaikh (p. 117) put it: 'I emphasized earlier that the theoretical basis of aggregate production function analysis was extremely weak. It would seem now that its apparent empirical strength is no strength at all, but merely a statistical reflection of an algebraic relationship'.

Shaikh's further criticism was that Solow's procedure bordered on a tautology. This is because if we define $\hat{A}_t \equiv (\hat{V}_t - \hat{L}_t) - \omega(\hat{J}_t - \hat{L}_t)$ where ω is *any* constant and then estimate either $\ln[(V/L)/A] = c + b\ln(J/L)$ or, $[(\hat{V}_t - \hat{L}_t) - \hat{A}_t] \equiv b(\hat{J}_t - \hat{L}_t)$ the estimate of b must equal ω with a perfect fit. This is regardless of the exact values of $\hat{V}$, $\hat{J}$ and $\hat{L}$.

Shaikh demonstrated this by constructing a hypothetical dataset with the property that if V/L was plotted against J/L, the word 'HUMBUG' was clearly discernible by the observations plotted in the scattergram. As the factor shares were those used by Solow and were, as we have seen, roughly constant, when Solow's procedure of deflating V/L by A is followed, it is found that the Humbug production function, not surprisingly, also gives a very good fit to the Cobb–Douglas with a correlation coefficient of 0.9964 and an estimate of capital's share of 0.34. Shaikh (p. 118) finds that 'one has the remarkable conclusion that even the Humbug data can be extremely well represented by a Cobb–Douglas production function having constant returns to scale, neutral technical progress and marginal products equal to factor rewards'.

Solow's (1974) Rejoinder to Shaikh

Shaikh's (1974) criticism was an attempt to drive the final nail into the coffin of the aggregate production function after what at the time had been seen as the success of the Cambridge capital theory controversies. Yet, paradoxically, it may have had precisely the opposite effect because Solow's (1974) rejoinder erroneously rejected the whole argument – it begins with 'Mr Shaikh's article is based on misconception pure and simple'. (See, for example, Heathfield and Wibe (1987, pp. 90–91) who accept that Solow's (1974) comment refutes the critique.)

Solow's (1974) riposte was brief and along the lines of his reply to Hogan (1958). To some, it may be conclusive, but on close examination it is not at all compelling. First, Solow maintained that his 1957 paper was not a *test* of the aggregate production function because it explicitly assumed the marginal productivity conditions: 'Therefore, it is not only not surprising but it is exactly the point that if the observed factor shares were exactly constant, the method would yield an exact Cobb–Douglas and tuck everything else into the shift factor. That is what one would *want* such a method to do' (1974, p. 121, emphasis in the original). Second,

> All this has literally nothing to do with the empirical question of whether the basis of the aggregate production function is strong or weak. When someone claims that aggregate production functions work, he means (a) that they give a good fit to output data *without* the intervention of data deriving from factor shares; and (b) the function so fitted has partial derivatives that closely mimic observed factor prices. (p. 121, emphasis in the original, omitting a footnote)

It is worth emphasising at this point that Solow maintains that it is theoretically possible to test a production function. He then delivered his supposed *coup de grâce*. He estimated the Cobb–Douglas production function by OLS using the Humbug dataset and a linear time trend to proxy for the rate of technical change. The results were (with the notation in this book):

$$\ln(V/L) = -0.14090 + 0.00532t - 0.33071 \ln(J/L)$$
$$(0.52072) \quad (0.01246) \quad (-0.76098)$$

The R^2 was 0.0052 and none of the coefficients was statistically different from zero (standard errors in parentheses). 'If this were the typical outcome with real data, we would not now be having this discussion' (p. 121).

Testing the Aggregate Production Function with 'Real Data'

Consequently, Solow (1974) does consider that production functions are, in principle, testable, so long as there is no use made of the marginal productivity assumption in deriving the specification. The central tenet of this book, of course, disputes this.

In the light of his comments about using 'real data', it is surprising that Solow did not seek to 'test' in like manner the Cobb–Douglas production function using his own data over the period from 1909 to 1949,[5] in other words, to estimate the Cobb–Douglas aggregate production function using a time trend to capture the rate of technical progress. This does not make any direct use of the marginal productivity conditions.

We therefore undertook this exercise, with the coefficients of the logarithm of labour and capital of the aggregate production function both constrained to exhibit constant returns to scale and also unconstrained. The Augmented Dicky–Fuller test suggests that all the logarithms of the variables are I(1). It is possible though to reject the hypothesis of non-cointegration for the various regressions. (In view of the subsequent argument, these issues are very much of secondary importance.) The specifications were, nevertheless, estimated in both logarithmic and in first-difference form by OLS. However, for reasons of space the discussion will be confined to the logarithmic results.

The results of the regression of the conventional Cobb–Douglas are reported in Table 5.3. Equation (a) reports the results where the sum of the coefficients is unconstrained. It can be seen that although the equation passes the usual diagnostic tests (except that there is an indication of serial correlation), the coefficients of $\ln L$ and $\ln J$ differ markedly from their factor shares and, indeed, the coefficient of the capital term is not statistically significant. The fact that this is not due to multicollinearity is confirmed by equation (d) in Table 5.3, where the coefficient of the logarithm of the capital–labour ratio is negative, and also statistically insignificant. Estimating the regressions in terms of exponential growth rates produces virtually identical results. A dummy variable to allow for a structural break from 1933 onwards was not significant in either equation and did not increase the plausibility of the results.

Both equations (a) and (d), consequently, produce highly implausible estimates and if we were estimating a behavioural relationship, would lead us to conclude that the aggregate production function, at least in the form

---

[5]   The capital stock was adjusted by Solow for differences in capacity utilisation using the percentage of the labour force employed.

Table 5.3   *The Cobb–Douglas and the accounting identity: US private non-farm GNP 1909–1949 (estimation using log levels)*

Dep. var.	(a) $\ln V$	(b) $\ln V$	(c) $\ln A$	(d) $\ln(V/L)$	(e) $\ln(V/L)$
Constant	−2.763	0.657	−1.393	−0.435	0.647
	(−4.97)	(29.21)	(−78.00)	(−5.47)	(256.61)
$A(t)$	–	–	–	–	–
t_1	0.016[a]	–	0.011	0.019[a]	–
	(20.81)		(8.32)	(32.17)	
t_2	–	–	0.015	–	–
			(22.79)		
$\ln w$	–	0.653	–	–	0.652
		(247.65)			(318.67)
$\ln r$	–	0.349	–	–	0.349
		(158.42)			(162.49)
$\ln L$	1.167	0.650	–	–	–
	(23.10)	(278.32)			
$\ln J$	0.035	0.349	–	–	–
	(0.064)	(135.20)			
$\ln(J/L)$	–	–	–	−0.081	0.350
				(−1.46)	(156.93)
$\bar{R}^2$	0.992	1.000	0.944	0.971	1.000
DW	1.342	1.765	0.499	0.821	1.756
SER x_1^2	0.031	0.001	0.048	0.037	0.001
HET x_1^2	2.828*	0.006	5.195**	3.121*	0.973
RESET x_1^2	0.048	5.988*	10.727**	0.074	6.409**

Notes:
t-values in parentheses.
** Significant at the 0.05 confidence level; * significant at the 0.10 confidence level.
t_1 1909–33; t_2 1933–49.
[a] denotes $t_1 =$ 1909–49.
The capital stock is adjusted for capacity utilisation using the percentage of the labour force employed.
SER is the Lagrange multiplier test of serial correlation.
HET is a test for heteroscedasticity based on regression of squared residuals on squared fitted values.
RESET is Ramsey's test using the square of fitted values.
Memorandum items:
  Values of α: max = 0.688; min = 0.603; mean = 0.659.
  Exponential growth rate of $A(t)$ is 1.56% per annum.

Source: McCombie (2000–01).

of the Cobb–Douglas was refuted. *We can only speculate whether Solow's (1957) paper would have had such a dramatic impact if these regressions had also been reported.*[6]

In order to provide additional confirmation that these poor results are not a peculiar property of the dataset used (since it included the Great Depression years and the estimates of the capital stock were rudimentary), the regressions were repeated using NBER data for the 1958–91 period for US manufacturing. The results, using the percentage of the labour force employed as an index for capacity utilisation, were also most implausible as the coefficients of both $\ln J$ and $\ln(J/L)$ were negative (and statistically significant). The coefficients were –0.919 (with a t-value equal to –2.45) and –1.934 (–4.31), respectively.

Of course, it could be objected that a more flexible specification using lags or an error-correction mechanism might well rescue the results. This was undertaken and the results including lags in the regressions, estimating an error-correction model, or using an instrumental variable approach are not reported here, in view of the fact that all that is being estimated is a misspecified identity. The question of equilibrium and dis-equilibrium relationships and adjustment mechanisms do not arise in this case. Likewise, there is no point in specifying a simultaneous equation model.

Both these sets of results are not atypical. Phelps Brown (1957) noted that time-series data normally produced bad statistical fits. It is likely that it was for this reason that Douglas, in the 1930s and 1940s, abandoned time-series analysis in favour of cross-industry and regional data. Tatom (1980), using data for 1948–73 for the US private business sector, found a result similar to our postwar regression results. He found that the coefficient of $\ln L$ was significant and took a value of 1.181 while $\ln J$ was statistically significant but *negative*. He cites Lucas (1970) as suggesting that this is a common result.

But given that it has been shown that the production function is merely reflecting an underlying accounting identity, how is it that these poor results are to be explained? The answer is straightforward. The weighted logarithm of the wage and profit rates is approximated by a linear time trend in equa-

---

[6]   Professor Bodkin has drawn our attention to the fact that in collaboration with Klein, some time ago, he had used Solow's data to estimate production functions, including non-linear methods to estimate the CES (Bodkin and Klein, 1967). They likewise found poor fits to the Cobb–Douglas and the CES production functions. However, their analysis was based upon the assumption of the existence of an aggregate production function (and cost-minimising behaviour) and sought to explain the implausible results in terms of single-equation bias, multiplicative versus additive error structures and so on (that is, in a radically different way from the argument put forward in this chapter).

tions (a) and (d). In both cases, the estimates of 'technical change' are statistically significant. In equation (a), the value is 1.6 per cent per annum and in equation (d), 1.9 per cent per annum. However, there is enough cyclical variation in $a \ln w_t + (1 - a) \ln r_t$ (or $\ln A_t$) for the identity to become seriously misspecified, even though, as may be seen from equation (c) in Table 5.4, the linear time trend gives a reasonably good statistical fit to the data. If we indirectly include $\ln A_t$ in the regression by including $\ln w_t$ and $\ln r_t$ (rather than proxying it by a linear time trend) the estimated coefficients are well determined and are almost identical to the relevant factor shares, reflecting their stability over time (equations (b) and (e)). This shows that the poor fits of equations (a) and (d) are *not* due to the fact that factor shares show some small variation over time, but is due to the procyclical fluctuations in the weighted sum of the logarithms of the wage and profit rates. Hence, the results would not be greatly improved by the use of a more flexible functional form such as the CES or translog. Rather, the implausible coefficients are due to using a linear time trend as a proxy for $\ln A(t)$.

Shaikh (1980) Strikes Back

Some years later, Shaikh (1980) reproduced his original argument and added a postscript which directly addressed and refuted Solow's (1974) comments. As it was published in a book, this rejoinder did not get as much recognition as it deserved. Shaikh makes the following telling points.

First, no matter what Solow wrote later, it is apparent from his 1957 paper (and from the 1974 reply to Shaikh) that he *did* consider that he was estimating a behavioural relationship, and not a tautology. If this were not the case, why was he surprised that the goodness of fit was so good, notwithstanding all the measurement problems, and so on?

Second, Solow obtained poor results using Shaikh's (1974) previously calculated Humbug data by imposing a linear time trend in the estimating equation that proved to be a poor proxy for $\ln A(t) = a \ln w_t + (1 - a) \ln r_t$. By experimenting with a variety of complex non-linear time trends, Shaikh (1980) eventually found a very close fit for the Cobb–Douglas relationship with the estimated 'output elasticities' equalling the relevant factor shares.[7]

---

[7] This is the complex form approximating the weighted average of the growth rates of the wage and profit rates that Shaikh (1980) estimated:

$$\hat{A} = a_0 + a_1 t + \Sigma_{i=1}^3 \left[b_i \cos\left(\tfrac{c_i \pi t}{2}\right) + d_i \sin\left(\tfrac{e_i \pi t}{2}\right) \right],$$

where $a_0 = 0.8565$, $a_1 = -3.966 \times 10^{-3}$, $b_1 = -0.0325$, $b_2 = 0.0435$, $b_3 = 0.0206$, $c_1 = 0.4$, $c_2 = 0.6$, $c_3 = 0.6$, $d_1 = 0.035$, $d_2 = -0.032$, $d_3 = -0.0295$, $e_1 = 0.5$, $e_2 = 0.8$, $e_3 = 0.4$.

In fact, the irony is that this procedure is equivalent to Solow's (1957) original estimation procedure. One specification Solow estimated was:

$$\ln(V/L)/A(t) = c + b\ln(J/L)$$

or, equivalently,

$$\ln(V/L) = c + \ln A(t) + b\ln(J/L).$$

The only difference is that Shaikh used a complex (rather than a linear) time trend as a proxy for $\ln A(t)$ rather than $\ln A(t)$ itself. But as Shaikh pointed out, and we have already mentioned, there is nothing in neoclassical production function theory that requires technical change to be a linear function of time, even with a random fluctuation. Moreover, the assumption that technical change is a smooth function of time is *ad hoc* and clearly at variance with the time path of Solow's own index of technical change, $A(t)$.

VARIATION IN FACTOR SHARES AND THE COBB–DOUGLAS 'PRODUCTION FUNCTION'

We have shown in Chapter 1 the restrictive assumptions necessary to aggregate two Cobb–Douglas micro-production functions, should they exist. But the accounting identity shows why the Cobb–Douglas functional form is likely to give a better fit to the data the higher the level of aggregation, contrary to what the aggregation problem would lead us to believe. This will occur if the variation in the factor shares decreases as we sum arithmetically the values of the various industries to give an aggregate relationship.

Following Solow (1958b, p.621), let us assume that the output shares of the industries in total output (namely, $s_i = V_i/V$) are equally variable throughout time and that these shares are of equal size. Labour's shares are assumed to have an equal variance over time. If the output shares fluctuate independently, then it can be simply shown that the variance of the aggregate share of wages (σ^2) will only be $1/s$ times the common sector variance. Thus, in this case, shares will be relatively more stable at the aggregate, as opposed to the individual firm, or sector, level. Hence, the Cobb–Douglas 'production function' will give a better fit, the *higher* the level of aggregation. This is ironically contrary to what the problems of aggregation would normally lead us to expect, as the higher the level of aggregation, the more likely we are to combine very different technologies and micro-production functions.

Table 5.4 Labour's share in private sector GDP; selected indicators, 1978–1996

Sector	s_{ave}	a_{max}	a_{min}	a_{ave}	Variance	Coeff of var.
Agriculture	0.025	0.35	0.26	0.19	0.00207	0.176
Mining and quarrying	0.027	0.40	0.30	0.35	0.00106	0.092
Manufacturing	0.235	0.78	0.65	0.72	0.00124	0.049
Electricity, gas, and water	0.030	0.40	0.31	0.34	0.00050	0.066
Construction	0.054	0.71	0.66	0.68	0.00016	0.019
Wholesale and retail trade	0.171	0.74	0.68	0.72	0.00041	0.028
Transport	0.070	0.66	0.56	0.56	0.00137	0.062
Finance	0.257	0.42	0.34	0.38	0.00058	0.063
Community, social, and personal services	0.115	0.78	0.73	0.76	0.00023	0.020
Total industries	1.000[†]	0.61	0.58	0.60	0.00006	0.013

Notes:
Labour's share is employees' compensation as a proportion of private sector GDP.
Private sector GDP excludes producers of government services.
s_{ave} is the average share of the sector's value added in the total over the period.
a_{max}, a_{min}, and a_{ave} are the maximum, minimum and average labour share.
† Individual shares do not sum to unity because of rounding errors and a statistical discrepancy item in the National Accounts.

Source: OECD National Accounts, Volume II, various years.

Nevertheless, 'predominantly positive correlations among sectors will yield a larger σ^2 and negative correlations a smaller σ^2 (Solow, 1958b, p. 622). Ultimately, the issue is an empirical one. Some early evidence was provided by Solow, who considered the share of employee compensation in income for seven sectors of the US economy (Agriculture; Mining; Construction; Manufacturing; Wholesale and Retail Trade; Transportation; and Communications and Public Utilities). He found that the aggregate variance of these sectors, over selected years between 1929 and 1953, was considerably smaller than the individual variances, with the exception of agriculture. We repeated this exercise for the US for the 1978–96 period and the results (for nine sectors) are reported in Table 5.4.

It can be seen that the variance and the coefficient of variation of labour's share are smaller for total industry than for any of the individual sectors.[8] The aggregate share, in fact, shows very little variation, and hence a Cobb–Douglas 'aggregate production function' will give a very good

---

8 Producers of government services are excluded.

fit to the value data.[9] This is notwithstanding the fact that a number of diverse industries ranging from Agriculture to Community, Social, and Personal Services, and which have completely different technologies, have been aggregated. Consequently, it can be seen why an aggregate Cobb–Douglas production function is likely to give a good empirical fit to the data for total industry, and if the shares show any pronounced change over time, why a more flexible functional form may provide a better fit.[10] But, as we have emphasised, this does not imply that the results can necessarily be interpreted as reflecting the underlying technology.

GROWTH ACCOUNTING REPRISED

Solow's (1957) paper also provided the theoretical foundations of the growth-accounting approach. One of the most celebrated results of this paper was the finding that technical progress accounted for over seven-eighths of the growth of productivity. There was only a very small role for the growth of the capital–labour ratio. Solow (1988), reflecting on this paper some 30 years later, found the result 'startling', as did many others. However, as Solow himself pointed out, he was not the first to arrive at such a result. Fabricant (1954) at the National Bureau of Economic Research a little earlier had calculated that about 90 per cent of the increase in productivity between 1871 and 1951 could only be accounted for by an increase in $A(t)$, or TFP.

There had also been Abramovitz's (1956) careful quantification of the sources of economic growth in the US from 1870. From Table 1 in Abramovitz, the growth of net national product can be calculated as 3.45 per cent per annum over the period 1869/78 to 1944/53. The growth of output per man-hour was 1.93 per cent and TFP was 1.66 per cent. Thus TFP growth accounts for 86 per cent of the growth of productivity over this 75-year period, a figure remarkably close to Solow's finding, and with similar implications. 'This result is surprising in the lopsided importance which it gives to productivity increase, and it should be, in a sense, sobering, if not discouraging, to students of economic growth' (Abramovitz, 1956, p. 11). It was this that led to the growth-accounting approach, pioneered by Denison (1962, 1967), which attempted to whittle down the residual. Solow (1988, p. 314) noted:

---

[9] This is provided that the chosen proxy for technical change closely tracks $a\ln w_t + (1 - a)\ln r_t$.

[10] It was also found that the factor shares for total manufacturing industry were also more stable than that of most of the constituent industries. The results are not reported here.

[Denison's] detailed accounting is an improvement on my first attempt, but it leads roughly to the same conclusion. . . . All I want to point out is that education per worker accounts for 30 percent of the increase in output per worker [for the US from 1929 to 1982] and the advance in knowledge accounts for 64 percent in Denison's figures. Thus, technology remains the dominant engine of growth, with human capital investment in second place.

We have seen above that the growth-accounting approach *assumes* the existence of an aggregate production function and the marginal productivity theory of factor pricing. Notwithstanding this, both Barro (1999) and Hsieh (2002) seem to imply that the growth-accounting approach can be derived simply from differentiating the National Income and Product Accounts (the accounting identity).

Hsieh (2002, p. 502), for example, argues 'it is useful to think about this [growth accounting] as an accounting identity' and reasons as follows:

[W]ith only the condition that output equals factor incomes, we have the result that the primal and dual measures of the Solow residual are equal. No other assumptions are needed for this result: we do not need any assumption about the form of the production function, bias of technological change, or relationship between factor prices and their social marginal products. We do not even need to assume that the data is correct. For example, if the capital stock data is wrong, the primal estimate of the Solow residual will clearly be a biased estimate of aggregate technological change. However, as long as the output and factor price data are consistently wrong, the dual measure of the Solow residual will be exactly equal to the primal measure, and consequently, equally biased.

The two measures of the Solow residual can differ when national output exceeds the payments to capital and labor. (p. 505)

Barro (1999) concurs that 'the dual approach can be derived readily from the equality between output and factor income' (p. 123). Barro and Hsieh agree that (in Barro's words):

It is important to recognize that the derivation of equation (8) [the growth-accounting equation in his paper] uses only the condition $V_t = r_t J_t + w_t L_t$. No assumptions were made about the relations of factor prices to social marginal products or about the form of the production function. (p. 123)[11]

However, it is clear that the growth accounting does require the *existence* of a standard well-behaved production function. Ironically, Barro and Sala-i-Martin (1995 [2003], p. 432) state this explicitly. If all the standard neoclassical assumptions are made, then the dual of the aggregate production function is that the rate of technical progress and, under the usual

---

[11] We have changed the notation to make it compatible with ours.

neoclassical assumptions is given by $a\hat{w}_t + (1-a)\hat{r}_t$. However, a necessary condition for this is that the values of the factor shares equal the aggregate output elasticities (which are assumed to exist). This, in turn, depends on the standard assumptions underlying neoclassical production theory. Moreover, we have shown by simulation analysis above how the 'true' rate of technical progress can differ from the rate implied by the use of value data. Furthermore, even when using value data, the form of the production function and the degree of bias *does* matter, even when accepting all the usual neoclassical assumptions (Nelson, 1973; Felipe and McCombie, 2001b). But we digress.

Solow's (1957) paper, rather than being seen as a test of the aggregate production function, can therefore be interpreted as providing the theoretical foundations for the growth-accounting approach. Solow (1988, p. 313), in reviewing the developments in growth theory to that date, took the view:

> [T]he main result of that [Solow's 1957] exercise was startling. Gross output per hour of work in the US economy doubled between 1909 and 1949; and some seven-eighths of that increase could be attributed to 'technical change in the broadest sense', and only the remaining eighth could be attributed to conventional increases in capital intensity.

However, as we discussed in Chapter 2, once we take account of the identity, we can actually predict this result. All we need to do is simply consider the Kaldorian stylised facts that the rate of profit is roughly constant over time and factor shares show relatively little variation.

It has been shown that the 'technical change' (or TFP growth) is formally defined as $\hat{A}_t \equiv a\hat{w}_t + (1-a)\hat{r}_t$. Given the stylised fact that the rate of return is roughly constant, this may be written as $\hat{A}_t = a\hat{w}_t$. Since factor shares do not vary greatly, it follows that $\hat{w}_t = \hat{V}_t - \hat{L}_t$, and $\hat{A}_t = a(\hat{V}_t - \hat{L}_t)$. Consequently, as a takes a value of about 0.75 for the whole economy, it follows that TFP growth *must* account for about *three-quarters* of the growth of output per worker. In Shaikh's evocative phrase, it is merely due to the 'laws of algebra'. Given that the growth of employment is normally small compared with the growth of output, $\hat{A}_t$ will also explain a similar proportion of output growth.[12] In the light of this, it may

---

[12]   Using Solow's data for the US private non-farm sector over the period from 1909 to 1949, the rate of profit is not, in fact, constant, but grows at 1.04 per cent per annum (from 0.10 to 0.15). However, this does not affect the substance of the argument. The growth of wages is 1.83 per cent and so the weighted growth of wages and the rate of profit is 1.58 per cent. The growth of labour productivity is 1.79 per cent and hence the TFP growth as a proportion of labour productivity may be simply calculated as 1.58/1.79, or 88 per cent. This result is simply due to a little manipulation of the accounting identity. There is no need for an aggregate production function or the marginal productivity theory of factor pricing to hold.

be questioned whether this result is particularly surprising. In fact, it is surprising that anyone should find it 'startling'.

FURTHER THOUGHTS ON SOLOW'S (1987) 'SECOND THOUGHTS ON GROWTH THEORY'[13]

In 1987, Solow returned to the critique that there was no way to disentangle the results of estimating the accounting identity from the production function and dismissed it as simply erroneous. He presented some new arguments which were not made in his 1974 one-page rebuttal of Shaikh. The reason why, according to Solow (1987), this argument is wrong is that the critique may be equally applied to a micro-production function estimated using physical, as opposed to value, data. As, according to Solow, it is transparently wrong to argue that we cannot learn anything of the underlying technology from a relationship between inputs and outputs measured in physical terms, so Shaikh's (1974) argument with respect to the use of value data is equally flawed. However, as we shall see, this contention does not necessarily follow logically. It is possible for Shaikh's critique not to apply to engineering production functions, but still be applicable to the use of value data.

The essence of Solow's argument is as follows. He imagines a production process that converts L and K into Q, all measured in *physical* terms. We can think of Q as corn, L as numbers of employed workers and K as numbers of (identical) machines. (For ease of discussion, any material inputs are ignored. It does not affect the substance of the argument.) To facilitate the exposition, let us assume that there is a true physical production function of the form $Q = CL^{\xi}K^{(1-\xi)}$. The exact form of the production function is not essential to the argument. Following Solow, we initially assume that there is no technical change and so C is a constant. We then assume, again following Solow (1987), that there is a hypothetical clerk, who, when given only these data on Q, L and K, calculates a unique m such that $m = aQ/L$ for an arbitrarily chosen constant a ($0 < a < 1$). The clerk is in a windowless room and knows nothing of the actual production process of the plant. The identity $Q \equiv mL + nK$ is completed by our clerk by calculating the value of n. (It should be noted that n equals $(1 - a)Q/K$.) Consequently, m and n are measured in real terms, say, bushels of corn per worker and bushels of corn per machine. The identity may be differentiated and integrated to derive:

---

[13]   This draws on McCombie (2001).

$$Q \equiv Bm^a n^{(1-a)} L^a K^{(1-a)} \equiv AL^a K^{(1-a)}, \tag{5.13}$$

where $B = a^{-a}(1-a)^{-(1-a)}$. Note that A is not necessarily a constant (the importance of this will become clear below).

An econometrician who knows nothing of these computations, estimates the production function using simply Q, L, and K, that is,

$$\ln Q = c + b_1 \ln L + b_2 \ln K + \varepsilon. \tag{5.14}$$

These estimates must, according to Solow, be picking up a technological relationship. After all, the variables are all *physical* quantities and values nowhere enter the picture. Consequently, the results will be that the estimates of b_1 and b_2 will equal ξ and $(1 - \xi)$, respectively, and not a and $(1 - a)$. Thus, the argument is that Shaikh's critique does not hold for micro-(engineering) production functions and, by implication, is not applicable to aggregate production functions.

What then, according to Solow, is the supposed error in Shaikh's reasoning? Solow answers this question as follows. In equation (5.13), substitute m by $a(Q/L)$ and n by $(1 - a)Q/K$. Solow argues that the following equation is obtained:[14]

$$Q = [Q/L^a K^{(1-a)}][L^a K^{(1-a)}]. \tag{5.15}$$

He continues (1987, pp. 20–21):

> This looks at first like a meaningless identity. But suppose that the true technology, the thing that happens in the factory, is $Q = f(L, K)$. Substituting again on the right-hand side we find:
>
> $$Q = [f(L,K)/L^a K^{(1-a)}][L^a K^{(1-a)}].$$
>
> What Shaikh has discovered, in other words, is that any production function can be written as the product of a Cobb–Douglas and something else; the something else is the production function divided by a Cobb–Douglas.
>
> The 'empirical' meaning of this can be seen in the typical regression equation ... $\{\ln Q = [a \ln m + (1 - a)\ln n] + a \ln L + (1 - a) \ln K\}$. What *does* happen if I regress $\ln Q$ on $\ln L$ and $\ln K$? That depends on whether $\ln A$ is orthogonal to $a \ln L + (1 - a)\ln K$. But $\ln A$ is $\ln Q - [a \ln L + (1 - a)\ln K]$. That is to say, orthogonality will hold precisely when the true production function *is* Cobb–Douglas and will fail whenever it is not. In the latter case, nothing prevents us from doing the regression but the estimated elasticities will not coincide with a and $1 - a$ and the regression will show systematic errors. (Emphasis in the original)[15]

---

[14] Solow omits the multiplicative constant.
[15] The notation has been changed to make it consistent with our notation.

The argument is essentially that the identity reduces to $Q = Q$ (which, in turn, equals $f(L, K)$ and $CL^\xi K^{(1-\xi)}$, and since there are physical data available for Q, L and K, we can estimate the technological parameters of the production function, notwithstanding that we have followed Shaikh's transformation.

It is worth considering further Solow's argument when he discusses the empirical meaning of the regression equation,

$$\ln Q = [a\ln m + (1 - a)\ln n] + a\ln L + (1 - a)\ln K, \qquad (5.16)$$

and asks the question as to what happens if we estimate $\ln Q = c + b_1\ln L + b_2\ln K$. The answer is that the estimates of b_1 and b_2 will equal ξ and $(1 - \xi)$, respectively. In other words, we are correctly estimating the true production function. This can be related to our clerk's accounting procedure as follows. If the clerk coincidentally chooses a to be the same value as ξ, then estimating the identity will give:

$$\ln Q = \ln B' + \xi\ln m + (1 - \xi)\ln n + \xi\ln L + (1 - \xi)\ln K. \quad (5.17)$$

Under these circumstances $\xi\ln m + (1 - \xi)\ln n$ will indeed be orthogonal to $\xi\ln L + (1 - \xi)\ln K$, as the former term is a constant and, in this sense, Solow is correct.[16] For any other value of a, that is, $a \neq \xi$, then $a\ln m + (1 - a)\ln n$ is not orthogonal to $\ln L$ and $\ln K$, but will vary as the last two change over time.

Suppose the clerk tells us (erroneously) that technical change is not constant but is given by $A(t)$ or by a complex time trend that closely approximates $A(t)$. Since we have no independent measure of technical change, *faute de mieux*, we introduce $\ln A$ (where A, it will be recalled, is defined as $m^a n^{(1-a)}$ into the regression given by equation (5.12) 'to let the data decide'. This will lead to a bias in the estimates of the output elasticities, so they become a and $(1 - a)$. (We ignore the inevitable problem of multicollinearity.) In this case, we shall not be estimating the correctly specified production function, but because the construction of $A(t)$ gives an identity, we shall not know from the statistical fit that the production function is misspecified.

Note that it is *not* the case here that orthogonality between $\ln A$ and $\ln K$ and $\ln L$ will hold when the true production function is a Cobb–Douglas. In the situation under discussion, we do have, by assumption, a correctly

---

[16] This may be simply demonstrated. $m = \xi(Q/L)$ and $m^\xi = \xi^\xi(Q/L)^\xi$. Similarly, $n = (1 - \xi)(Q/K)$ and $n^{(1-\xi)} = (1 - \xi)^{(1-\xi)}(Q/K)^{(1-\xi)}$. As $Q = CL^\xi K^{(1-\xi)}$ it can be shown that $m^\xi n^{(1-\xi)} = \xi^\xi(1 - \xi)^{(1-\xi)}C$, which is a constant.

specified underlying Cobb–Douglas production function. The problem as described here is the bias of the estimates of the output elasticities due to the inclusion of $\ln A$ in the regression. Since 'technical change' is unobservable and proxied by a time trend, and Solow concedes that there is no reason why this should be linear, we are, in fact, never in a position of being sure that we are estimating the correctly specified production function.

On Physical and Value Measures of Output and Capital Revisited

Consequently, it is necessary to qualify Solow's argument. However, there is a further crucial point that Solow misses. This is that here we are concerned with output measured in value rather than in physical terms, which we emphasised in Chapter 2.

Imagine that Solow's clerk is now a national accountant. He receives from different firms data on gross output (a value magnitude measured, say, in constant prices), deducts the value of materials and constructs the identity $V_i \equiv w_i L_i + r_i J_i$. He then sums the results to derive industry-wide value-added measures. Thus, $V = \Sigma V_i = w\Sigma L_i + r\Sigma J_i = wL + rJ$, where w is the average wage and r the average rate of profit. J is now a value magnitude expressed in constant prices, but we shall ignore the well-known problems associated with capital aggregation. (This is not material to the argument; we could still regard J as the number of identical machines and r as a monetary value.)

The firms adopt a constant mark-up pricing policy and factor shares in the aggregate are (roughly) constant and given by a and $(1 - a)$. The econometrician now has data on V instead of Q. We can go through the same exercise as Solow undertook and described above (but using value-added V instead of Q) and derive:

$$V = [V/L^a J^{(1-a)}][L^a J^{(1-a)}]. \tag{5.18}$$

Let us now assume that there are no well-defined physical production functions, in the sense that there is a poor statistical relationship between the Q_is and the L_is and K_is for the individual production processes. This may be because production processes are more complex than can be described simply by the relationship between these three variables. However, from the underlying accounting identity, which holds exactly by construct, we have the close approximation (as long as factor shares are relatively constant) that:

$$V = Bw^a r^{(1-a)} L^a J^{(1-a)}. \tag{5.19}$$

To maintain the parallel with Solow's discussion, let us assume that $w^a r^{(1-a)}$ is a constant. This is analogous to assuming no technical change if we had a well-defined production function. If we were to estimate:

$$\ln V = c + b_1 \ln L + b_2 \ln J, \tag{5.20}$$

we would find that the estimated coefficients are the relevant factor shares, a and $(1 - a)$, but these are not the average values of the output elasticities of 'production functions' which, by assumption, do not exist. This contrasts markedly with the use of physical data where the estimates do say something about the technological conditions of production. Equation (5.18) is, indeed, nothing more than a tautology, because the left- and right-hand sides of the equation merely state that $V \equiv V (\equiv wL + rJ \approx AL^a J^{(1-a)})$.[17] If, by chance, we were to have data for another economy that produces exactly the same physical products, but where the mark-up differs so the factor shares were, say, b and $(1 - b)$, then the estimated coefficients of the regression would take these values, solely by virtue of the underlying identity.

Given the significance of this issue, it is worth elaborating further, at the risk of some repetition. There is an important difference between the use of physical output data and constant-price value data in the estimation of putative production functions. The former are independent of factor payments, whereas the latter are not. This may be made clearer as follows. Consider again our 'true' production function (without technical change), namely,

$$Q = CL^\xi K^{(1-\xi)}, \tag{5.21}$$

where Q and K are again physical magnitudes.

Consider the linear relationship:

$$pQ = cL + dK, \tag{5.22}$$

where p is the price of corn (£ per bushel). If there is perfect competition and factors are paid their marginal products, then $w = \xi Q/L = c$ and $r = (1 - \xi) Q/K = d$.

Consequently, the equivalence of labour's share a and the output elasticity with respect to labour (ξ) is a test of the marginal productivity

---

[17] It will be recalled that in the case of the physical production function, it could be argued that this is not a tautology since it reduces to $Q = Q (= f(L, K))$ which is a behavioural relationship that does not involve the accounting identity.

condition (and similarly for capital's output elasticity and factor share) with physical data. Remember that there is no necessary reason for factor shares to equal the relevant output elasticities; it is theoretically possible for labour, for example, to appropriate the whole of the product so that $a = 1 \neq \xi$, in which case $c = Q/L$ and $d = 0$. If the output elasticities do, in fact, equal the factor shares, the direction of causation is from the technical properties of the production function to the values of c and d, via the marginal productivity theory of factor pricing.

However, when we come to the use of value data, in a sense the causation runs the other way. We start with the value-added identity (in constant prices) $V = wL + rJ$ and the assumption that factor shares are constant. The data we have from the national accounts show that labour's share is a and capital's share is $(1 - a)$. The Cobb–Douglas production function can be considered to be a good approximation to the identity (given that factor shares are roughly constant) and the output 'elasticities' *must* take the values a and $(1 - a)$. The causation runs from the accounting identity to the Cobb–Douglas relationship.

Consequently, the equivalence of factor shares and the relevant 'output elasticities' cannot be taken to corroborate the marginal productivity theory of factor prices.[18] Thus, Solow's criticisms do not undermine the critique concerning value data and the accounting identity.

HOW TO ALWAYS OBTAIN A PERFECT FIT TO A 'PRODUCTION FUNCTION'

It can be seen from the above discussion that in order to get a perfect fit to the production function, it is necessary to find a better proxy for the variation over time in the weighted average of the logarithms of the factor returns (or their weighted growth rates). We have seen above that this can be achieved by specifying a complex time trend. Here we follow a different method.

For the moment, let us consider that the estimates of the Cobb–Douglas relationship do imply something meaningful about the underlying production technology of the economy. It was noted above that some production function studies have found poor fits. The explanation often put forward

---

[18] Solow's (1987, p. 17) view is that 'the workability of aggregate production functions and their ability – if they have it – to reproduce the broad distributional facts does reinforce the marginal productivity theory – or better, the supply-and-demand theory – of distribution'. Here he shares the view of Douglas (1976). But Solow is careful not to be dogmatic – 'The implication is far from airtight'.

is that the factor inputs have to be adjusted for changes in their intensity of use over the business cycle. It was for this reason that Solow (1957) adjusted his capital stock data. The argument is that as the economy moves into recession, it departs from its production frontier (an exception to this argument is the real business-cycle theory).

This accounts for the pronounced procyclical nature of productivity growth and the residual. Labour is a quasi-fixed factor of production (Oi, 1962) and during a recession it is not laid off to such an extent as production conditions would warrant. Furthermore, the capital stock is used as a proxy for the flow of capital services and there should also be an adjustment for fluctuations in the latter over the cycle.

Tatom (1980, p. 385) notes that 'one of the more settled facts about the cyclical behaviour of the U.S. economy is that real wages are procyclical, rising during expansions and falling during recessions'. He attributes this to variations in the utilisation of the capital stock. Recent research suggests that the issue is not quite so straightforward as some studies find little movement of real wages over the cycle. But it should be noted that for our purposes, it is sufficient that the combined (weighted) factor returns vary cyclically. An inspection of the data confirms that the weighted growth of factor payments does indeed have a pronounced procyclical component. This is confirmed by using Solow's 1957 dataset and regressing $a_t\hat{w} + (1 - a_t)\hat{r}$ on $\hat{V}$ using OLS. The slope coefficient is 0.466, with a t-statistic of 10.37. The r^2 is 0.739. There is an element of spuriousness in this regression as $a_t\hat{w} + (1 - a_t)\hat{r}$ is by definition a component of $\hat{V}$. However, a similar statistically significant relationship is found between the weighted growth of the factor payments and the weighted growth of the factor inputs, although the statistical fit is somewhat weaker (the slope coefficient is 0.483 and the t-value, 3.80).

It was noted above that Solow (1957) used the unemployment rate to construct an index of capacity utilisation, but we have seen that this did not give plausible results. Consequently, we attempted to construct a better proxy using Solow's (1957) corrected data. The fact that the weighted growth of factor payments varies procyclically was used to construct a measure of the degree of factor input utilisation. The extent to which factor returns deviate from their trend growth rates is assumed to reflect the degree of overfull or less-than-full intensity of factor use. The justification for this is that, in the downturn of the cycle, inputs are used less intensely and so their returns fall relative to the trend. The converse occurs in the upswing. An index of capacity utilisation was calculated as follows. The growth of wages and the rate of profit were regressed on a constant and the residuals were then weighted by the relevant factor shares. This variable was then used to calculate the index $U_1(t)$ in much the same way

Solow estimated $A(t)$, with the exception that 1944 was chosen as the base year and set equal to 100. This was the year of maximum capacity utilisation. (The use of factor shares as weights was not crucial as indices were also computed for labour and capital separately. It made no difference to the regression results discussed below.)

This method of constructing an index of capacity utilisation is similar to a number of other procedures that use available macroeconomic time-series data, such as trend rates of growth of output, the capital–output ratio, employment and the level of unemployment. (See Briscoe et al., 1970 for a discussion of some common methods.)

An inspection of the index U_1 shows that the First World War, and especially, the Second World War, were the periods when the factors were being used most intensively. The greatest degree of underutilisation of resources occurred, not surprisingly, in the depths of the Depression in 1932 and 1933. Thus, the relative values of the index seem to be plausible. The unemployment measure used by Solow (1957) (denoted by U_2) also tracks U_1 closely especially after 1933.[19] As the capacity utilisation index relates to both factors of production, $\ln U_1$ was included as an additional variable in the specification of the production function. (It should be noted that the capital stock was Solow's series, which was not separately adjusted for changes in capacity utilisation.) The results using OLS were as follows (t-values in parentheses):[20]

$$\ln V = -5.259 + 0.015t + 0.993\ln U_1 + 0.656\ln L + 0.346\ln J$$
$$(-133.45)\ (323.31)\ (252.31)\qquad (279.58)\qquad (126.62)$$

$$\bar{R}^2 = 1.000;\ SER\ 0.0007;\ DW = 1.91.$$

Using growth rates gave virtually identical results.

The regression passed the usual diagnostic tests. It can be seen that the factor utilisation variable proved to be highly significant. The results suggest that, holding the level of technology and measured inputs constant, an increase in the utilisation rate of the factor inputs by one-percentage point causes an equiproportionate increase in output. The sum of the output elasticities does not significantly differ from unity. Thus, both these results would seem to suggest that the data give an exceptionally good fit to the Cobb–Douglas production function with constant returns to scale.

---

[19]   Regressing U_2 on U_1 gives a slope coefficient of 0.725 with a t-value of 10.78 and an R^2 of 0.749. On the basis of these results, U_2 could be regarded as a reasonable proxy for U_1.

[20]   Similar results were obtained using the logarithms of the levels.

However, this is erroneous because, even though the procedure that has been adopted may seem to have a sound economic rationale, what has been done in including $\ln U_1$ in the regressions is formally equivalent to including in the regression the deviations of $a \ln w_t + (1 - a) \ln r_t$ (or $\ln A$) around its trend. The end result is that we are again merely estimating the identity with the exception that the trend is capturing the average growth rate of the weighted factor returns (which is 1.5 per cent per annum).

The analysis illustrates an important point. A better statistical fit will always be obtained if a cyclical adjustment is made to the data and this fit will improve the closer the utilisation variable used approaches $\ln U_1$, or $\hat{U}_1$, depending on whether the data are expressed in logarithms of the levels or in growth rates. As this occurs, the estimated 'output elasticities' will approach their respective factor shares, not for any technological reason, but simply because we are more closely approximating the under-lying identity. However, a note of caution should be sounded at this point. Although, as we have noted, there is a reasonably close correspondence between the index of the ratio of employment to the labour force, U_2, and the index of capacity utilisation U_1, the inclusion of $\ln U_2$ as a separate vari-able did not improve the goodness of fit when it was used in the regression equation instead of $\ln U_1$. The coefficient of the capital stock still remained statistically insignificant, which is not surprising given the results of the earlier regressions when the capital stock was adjusted directly using this index. Thus, the procedure adopted above also has the benefit of showing that the estimates prove to be sensitive to the precise values of the factor utilisation index. The exact interpretation of the causes of fluctuations in the Solow residual (and in the weighted index of the real wage and the rate of profit) is of no great concern to the argument. The implication is that once we have proxied for the variation of $A(t)$, by adjusting for factor uti-lisation or including a complex time trend or both, we will always end up with an R^2 of unity and with the putative output elasticities equalling the relevant factor shares. All that is being estimated is an identity.

CONCLUSIONS

In this chapter we have examined Solow's (1957) paper. In retrospect, although perhaps not at the time, the estimations of the various specifica-tions of the 'production relations' conveyed very little new information. Given the tautological way that the index of A was calculated, the resulting regressions were almost bound to give a near perfect fit. The only reason why the statistical fit would not give a perfect fit to Solow's equation (iv) in Table 5.1, the Cobb–Douglas, was if the factor shares were not constant, but even then we have shown that even if the shares show a wide degree of variation we still get a good estimate of the slope coefficient which takes the average value of (capital's) share and an R^2 of over 0.9. The extent of the tautology is seen by the fact that if we use any value of the share (say labour's share rather than capital's share) this value will be reflected in the estimated regression coefficient.

Shaikh (1974) showed most dramatically the limitations of Solow's approach by constructing his artificial Humbug dataset and showing how even this would, following Solow's procedure, give a near perfect fit to the Cobb–Douglas 'production function'. Solow's response that Shaikh's argument was spurious as estimating a Cobb–Douglas with a linear time trend to capture the path of $A(t)$ gave statistically insignificant results was not convincing. (Solow argued that this procedure is actually estimating the parameters of an aggregate production function describing the technology of the US private business sector.) This is because first, Solow's own data perform equally badly and hence, in the light of his own argument, his data refuted the hypothesis that there was an aggregate production function. But more importantly, he ignored the second (and more important) argument of Shaikh that the data would simply reflect the underlying identity. We have seen that Solow's (1987) refutation of this argument is simply not compelling.

The identity also shows that the fact that technical change (or the residual) accounts for such a large proportion of labour productivity is hardly 'startling', but is inevitable given the Kaldorian stylised facts and the accounting identity.

Finally, we showed how, using a not implausible procedure for estimating variations in capacity utilisation, because of the identity, we can always find a perfect statistical fit to a supposed aggregate production function. As we have seen, an alternative way is to use a sufficiently flexible time trend that closely approximates the path of the weighted average of the logarithm wage and the rate of profit.

6. What does total factor productivity actually measure? Further observations on the Solow model

A theory of total factor productivity is needed to understand large international income differences.

(Prescott, 1998, p. 548)

INTRODUCTION[1]

With the revival of interest in both growth theory and growth empirics since the 1980s, a number of economists have returned to the important question of why some countries are richer than others. A crucial development in applied work has been the availability of large databases that allow comparisons across countries to be carried out. While some researchers would claim that the profession has advanced and that it has provided useful answers to this question (Mankiw et al., 1992; Jones, 1998 [2002]), others take the opposite view (Kenny and Williams, 2001; Easterly, 2001).

As we saw in the last chapter, Solow's (1956, 1957) seminal growth model is still generally viewed today as the starting point for almost all analyses of growth, notwithstanding the severe reservations raised in the last chapter. Even models that depart significantly from this model are often best understood through comparison with it. This model, augmented by human capital, is seen by some as providing a satisfactory explanation of disparities in per capita income growth, or at least a useful starting point (Mankiw et al., 1992; Mankiw, 1995, 1997). What does Solow's model say about why some countries are richer than others? The model predicts that countries with high saving/investment rates will tend to have a higher level of income per capita; and countries that have high population growth rates will tend to be poorer. But savings rates and population growth do not affect the steady-state growth rates of per capita output. Therefore, the model does not provide an adequate explanation of the determinants of long-run per capita growth, which are merely captured by the rate of exogenously given technical progress. The approach, however, shows how

---

[1] This chapter draws on Felipe and McCombie (2007c).

an economy's per capita income converges towards its own steady-state value, and in this way it provides an explanation for the observed differences in growth rates across countries. In simple terms, this explanation is that poorer countries tend to grow faster than the richer countries, as they are generally further below their conditional steady-state growth rates.

An important assumption of Solow's growth model is that countries have identical technologies (production functions) (Mankiw, 1995). Some authors have argued, however, that this model cannot account for the large observed variations across countries in total factor productivity (TFP) precisely because it assumes identical technologies (Parente and Prescott, 1994; Durlauf and Johnson, 1995; Jorgenson, 1995; Jones, 1997, 1998 [2002]; Hall and Jones, 1999; Islam, 1999). These authors, therefore, argue for a version of Solow's growth model that incorporates differences in technology levels. Prescott (1998), for example, has argued that a separate, or distinct, theory of TFP differences is needed. In a similar vein, Meier (2001, p. 25), while suggesting a series of research topics for the new generation of development economists, argues that 'Because of the importance of total factor productivity . . . future research will have to increase our understanding of the "unexplained residual factor" in aggregate production functions'.

This chapter addresses the question by taking a step back. It considers some aspects of the neoclassical theory on its own terms before relating the argument once again to the accounting identity. As the conclusion that a theory of TFP is needed in order to explain the observed large income differences across countries has been reached empirically (that is, by calculating TFP), it is shown that the way the estimates of TFP have been computed is not an innocuous issue. In this way we highlight some important, but neglected, issues. In the next section we consider the extent to which the Solow model, and extensions of it, can explain differences between countries in the levels of productivity. (However, we defer a consideration of the Mankiw et al., (1992) model until a later chapter.)

CAN DIFFERENCES IN PRODUCTIVITY BE EXPLAINED BY DISPARITIES IN SAVINGS (INVESTMENT) RATIOS?

The productivity and per capita income of the richest country (the US) is some 30 to 35 times that of the poorest country (Pritchett, 1997). The first question we shall review is the extent to which such differences in productivity in the neoclassical model can be explained by differences in the rate of savings (which we shall assume equals the investment–output ratio) over a long period. In other words, can the fact that the more-advanced countries have generally had higher savings rates in the past than the poorer countries explain why some countries are rich and others poor?

The conclusion of a number of economists (Romer, 1994; Prescott, 1998) is that within the Solow model differences in these ratios (and hence in the capital–output ratios) can explain very little of the disparities in per capita income. To show this, let us assume that the economy may be described by the Cobb–Douglas aggregate production function $Y = [A(t)L]^{\alpha}K^{(1-\alpha)}$, where Y, L and K are output, employment and the capital stock. (In this chapter, for ease of comparison, we adopt the notation of the studies that we are discussing and, in particular, use Y for output and K for capital, the context making it clear whether they refer to a value or a physical measure.)

The parameters α and $(1 - \alpha)$ are the output elasticities of labour and capital, and $A(t)$ is the level of technology. The value of the capital stock is constructed by the perpetual inventory method:

$$K_t = \sum_{v=0}^{v=m} (1 - \delta)^v I_{t-v},$$ (6.1)

where m is the age of the oldest vintage still in use, δ is the rate of depreciation and I is gross investment.

Let us assume that, over the period under consideration, the investment–output is constant and so investment grows at a rate equal to the growth of output, denoted by $\hat{Y}$. In these circumstances, equation (6.1) may be written as:

$$K_t = \sum_{v=0}^{v=m} (1 - \delta)^v (1 - \hat{Y})^v I_t.$$ (6.2)

If the time period is sufficiently large, then equation (6.2) may be written as the approximation $K_t = I/(\hat{Y} + \delta)$ (ignoring the interaction term $\delta \hat{Y}$) and the capital–output ratio as $K_t/Y_t = s/(\hat{Y} + \delta)$, where s is the investment (savings)–output ratio. As we have assumed that the growth of output over the period of the calculation of the capital stocks (which, because of the depreciation factor could be as short as 30 years) has been constant as has been the average propensity to save, the capital–output ratio could also be regarded as the steady-state level. The Cobb–Douglas production function for a particular country, $Y_i = (AL_i)^{\alpha}(K_i)^{(1-\alpha)}$, may be written in intensive form as:

$$\frac{Y_t}{L_t} = A_t \left(\frac{K_t}{Y_t}\right)^{(1-\alpha)/\alpha}.$$ (6.3)

Table 6.1   Steady-state investment–output ratios, capital–output ratios, relative productivities and rates of return

Investment–output ratio	Capital–output ratio	Relative productivity		Rate of return	
		(i)	(ii)	(i)	(ii)
(a) 5%	0.625	0.63	0.55	40%	48%
(b) 10%	1.25	0.79	0.74	20%	24%
(c) 20%	2.50	1.00	1.00	10%	12%
(d) 30%	3.75	1.14	1.19	7%	8%
(e) 40%	5.00	1.26	1.35	5%	6%
Ratio of (e) to (a)	8	2.00	2.45	0.125	0.125

Note: (i) assumes $(1 - \alpha) = 0.25$ and (ii) assumes $(1 - \alpha) = 0.30$. The steady-state rate of return is calculated as $(1-\alpha)(n + g + \delta)/s$, where $(1 - \alpha)$ is capital's share; n is the growth rate of population; g is the rate of technical progress; s is the investment–output ratio.

Source: After Prescott (1998).

It can be seen that the productivity is positively related to the capital–output ratio. Table 6.1 reports the savings ratios and the calculated associated 'steady-state' capital–output ratio. Following Prescott (1998), it is assumed that output growth $(\hat{Y})$ is 0.03 and the depreciation rate (δ) is 0.05. In order to see the extent to which variations in the capital–output ratio can explain differences in productivity, we take the US with a savings ratio of 20 per cent as the reference country. Assuming that other countries have the same level of technology (A^{α}), and a value for $(1 - \alpha)$ as either 0.25 or 0.30, the table also reports the difference in productivity due to differences in the capital–output ratio.

From Table 6.1 it can be seen that when $(1 - \alpha) = 0.25$, the capital–output ratio of a country with a 40 per cent investment–output ratio (that is, eight times that of a country investing only 5 per cent of its output) has only twice the level of productivity (or per capita income). This is several orders of magnitude less than that observed in reality. Increasing the output elasticity of capital to 0.30 does not alter the conclusions.

The table also reports the steady-state rates of return associated with each capital–output ratio, and it can be seen that those associated with a small investment–output ratio are implausibly high. Thus, not only can differences in the investment or savings ratio explain very little of the disparities in productivity, but they also involve some very implausible rates of return.

Romer (1994) makes the same point but in a slightly different way.

He considers two countries, say, the US and the Philippines, which are growing at the same rate, and where all parameters, except the savings rate and productivity, are the same. As the level of productivity of the Philippines is only 10 per cent that of the US, the latter, if the output elasticity of capital is 0.40, would have to have a savings ratio that was $0.1^{-1.5}$ or about 30 times that of the Philippines. If elasticity is 0.25, the figure increases to 1,000 times. In reality, the US savings ratio is not all that different from that of the Philippines.

Consequently, under the assumptions of Solow's model, differences in savings and investment can account for only a small difference in relative productivity levels. The explanation must lie elsewhere.

HUMAN CAPITAL TO THE RESCUE?

One response to the issue at hand has been that employment is not the appropriate proxy to measure the flow of labour services, but rather that this should be augmented by the quality of the labour input, which varies across countries. In this way, Mankiw et al., (1992), using regression analysis, allowed the data to determine the values of the elasticities of the production function in the context of an extended Solow model that included a measure of human capital (H). They concluded, under the assumption that technology is the same in all countries, that exogenous differences in saving and education cause the observed differences in levels of income. The production function consistent with their results is $Y = AK^{1/3}H^{1/3}L^{1/3}$. In this formulation the elasticity of physical capital is not different from its share in income. There are also no externalities to the accumulation of physical capital. These results, however, have been seriously questioned by the literature for lacking robustness.

Jones (1998) assumed that human capital can be estimated as $H = e^{\psi u}L$, where u is the number of years of schooling and η is the Mincerian rate of return to an extra year of schooling. This is taken empirically to be 0.10, and so an increase in one year's schooling increases the effective labour input by 10 per cent. We have reservations with this formulation: one year of schooling in an advanced country surely increases human capital by more than one year of schooling in a less developed country. It is not just a question of the number of years spent in school, but the quality of that education (Easterly, 2001, ch. 4). Nevertheless, in this framework, given that the greatest difference between countries in terms of years of schooling is of the order of 10 years, it means that education could only account for a factor of 2 in the differences between the richest and poorest countries.

Prescott (1998, p. 541), following Lucas (1988), used an explicit equation for the production of human capital. For various values of the parameter of the human capital production sector, Prescott uses US data to calibrate a model and finds that either the implied values of time are so implausibly large or else the implied rates of return to education are so high in the poorest countries that he is led to 'reject this model as a theory of international income differences' (p. 543).

Consequently, if differences in investment ratios and human capital cannot explain much of the international differences in the levels of productivity, the answer in the neoclassical approach must lie, by definition, in disparities in TFP. (However, in Appendix 6A, we show how, depending on the assumptions made, the growth-accounting approach can explain either virtually none or nearly all of the residual.)

SOLOW'S MODEL AND THE RELATIONSHIP BETWEEN ACTUAL AND STEADY-STATE LEVELS OF PRODUCTIVITY

Jones (1998 [2002]), in his well-known textbook on economic growth,[2] and drawing on Jones (1997), putatively tested the Solow model, augmented by human capital, by calculating the steady-state levels of labour productivity of a number of countries relative to that of the US, (y_i^*/y_{US}^*), where the subscript i denotes the ith country and the superscript * denotes the steady-state value. These values were then compared with the actual, or observed, relative values of labour productivity (y_i/y_{US}). When the two ratios were found to be sufficiently close, then Jones inferred that the steady-state augmented Solow growth model provided a good explanation of economic growth.

Assuming first a constant level of technology between firms but including differences in human capital, he found that the relationship between $\ln(y_i^*/y_{US}^*)$ and $\ln(y_i/y_{US})$ gave a slope of less than unity, but he nevertheless concluded that 'the neoclassical model still describes the distribution of per capita income across countries fairly well' (Jones, 1998, p. 53). The relationship found by Jones is given by Figure 6.1.

He then made allowances for differences in technology, savings as a

---

[2]   It is perhaps unusual to concentrate on a textbook. However, as Kuhn (1962 [1970]) pointed out, textbooks are crucial in the propagation of a paradigm, and are important as they are seen as presenting generally agreed upon and uncontroversial views. Moreover, often textbooks set the agenda for future research problems or 'puzzles'. Moreover, Jones's analysis draws on Jones (1997).

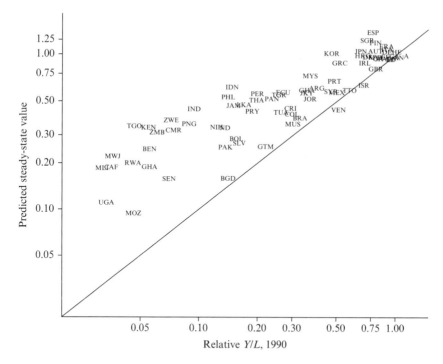

Note: A log scale is used on both axes.

Source: Jones (1998, Figure 3.1, p. 52).

Figure 6.1   The 'fit' of the neoclassical growth model, 1990

share of output, and human capital and the correspondence between the actual and steady-state relative productivity levels greatly improved and was very close: 'The model broadly predicts which countries will be rich and which will be poor' (p. 54) (See Figure 6.2). He concluded that now 'the Solow framework is extremely successful in helping us to understand the wide variation in the wealth of nations' (p. 56).

However, in the second edition of the book, Jones (1998 [2002]) omits this last piece of analysis between the actual and steady-state levels of productivity. After noting that the predictive correspondence between the relative steady-state and the actual levels of productivity is poor, he again allows for differences in technology. But the analysis showing the much improved fit between the two variables $\ln(y_i^*/y_{US}^*)$ and $\ln(y_i/y_{US})$ is dropped, and instead the Cobb–Douglas production function $Y_t = (A_t L_t)^\alpha K_t^{(1-\alpha)}$ is used to show the range of values of A necessary to fit

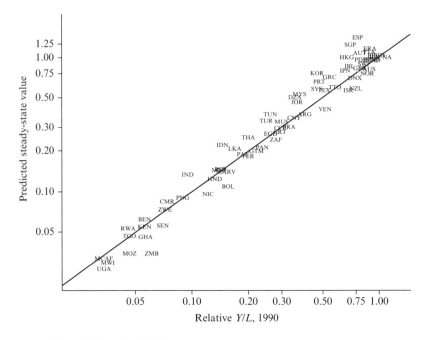

Note: A log scale is used on both axes.

Source: Jones (1998, Figure 3.2, p. 54).

Figure 6.2   The 'fit' incorporating technological differences

the model to the data. He examines the relationship between relative *A*s and the actual (and not the steady-state) relative levels of productivity and finds that there is a reasonably close relationship. 'Rich countries generally have high levels of *A* and poor countries generally have low levels' (Jones, 1998 [2002], p. 61). This analysis is also found in Jones (1998) (see Table 6.2), where the estimates for *A*, the actual and the steady-state values of the relative productivity levels are all reported (Table 3.1, p. 55). It is shown there that the actual and the steady-state relative levels of productivity are very close. The table is subsequently omitted from the second edition.

How is it that Jones gets these very close fits which he claims supports the Solow model? We shall show that it is because there is no independent measure of *A* and the way it is calculated makes it inevitable that the relative observed and steady-state levels of productivity will closely correspond. Jones's (1998) argument is as follows.

Table 6.2 *Data and predictions for the neoclassical model*

	y/y_{US}		s_K	u	n	A/A_{US}
	Actual	Steady state				
US	1.00	1.00	0.210	11.8	0.009	1.00
West Germany	0.80	0.83	0.245	8.5	0.003	1.02
Japan	0.61	0.71	0.338	8.5	0.006	0.76
France	0.82	0.85	0.252	6.5	0.005	1.28
UK	0.73	0.76	0.171	8.7	0.002	1.10
Argentina	0.36	0.30	0.146	6.7	0.014	0.61
India	0.09	0.10	0.144	3.0	0.021	0.30
Zimbabwe	0.07	0.06	0.131	2.6	0.034	0.20
Uganda	0.03	0.02	0.018	1.9	0.024	0.25
Hong Kong	0.62	0.77	0.195	7.5	0.012	1.25
Taiwan	0.50	0.64	0.237	7.0	0.013	0.99
South Korea	0.43	0.59	0.299	7.8	0.012	0.74

Note: y/y_{US} is the level of productivity relative to the US; s_K is the share of investment in GDP, n is the growth of population (both averages 1980–90); u is the average number of years of schooling in 1985, and A/A_{US} is the level of TFP relative to that of the US. A/A_{US} includes the contribution of human capital.

Source: Jones (1998, Table 3.1 p. 55).

(i) The Level of Technology is Assumed to be Constant across Countries

The production function for country i, expressed in intensive form, is given by:

$$y_i = (A_i' h_i)^\alpha k_i^{(1-\alpha)} = (A_i' e^{\psi u_i})^\alpha k_i^{(1-\alpha)}, \tag{6.4}$$

where y, h and k are output per worker, capital per worker and a measure of human capital per capita, proxied by u, the average years of schooling. η is a constant. (A' denotes the level of technology when human capital is explicitly included in the production function, A when it is omitted.) The parameters α and $(1 - \alpha)$ are once again the output elasticities of labour and capital. The time subscript has been dropped for notational convenience.

Jones derives the steady-state level of productivity from equation (6.4) by assuming that $\hat{Y} = \hat{K}$ and that the rate of technical progress is the same for all countries (that is, $g_i = g$). The steady-state level of productivity is given by:

$$y_i^* = \left(\frac{s_{K_i}}{n_i + g + \delta}\right)^{(1-\alpha)/\alpha} A_i' h_i, \tag{6.5}$$

where s_K is the share of physical investment in output, n is the growth of employment,[3] and δ is the rate of depreciation.

Equation (6.5) is used to calculate the ratio of the steady-state levels of productivity of various countries to that of the US:

$$\frac{y_i^*}{y_{US}^*} = \frac{\left(\dfrac{s_{K_i}'}{n_i + g}\right)^{(1-\alpha)/\alpha}}{\left(\dfrac{s_{K_{US}}'}{n_{US} + g}\right)^{(1-\alpha)/\alpha}} \frac{A_i'}{A_{US}'} \frac{h_i}{h_{US}}. \tag{6.6}$$

For expositional convenience, we define s_K' as the share of *net*, rather than *gross*, investment in output and so δ is not now an explicit argument of the equation.

Jones first assumes that the level of technology does not vary across countries, but allows h_i to vary. Under these circumstances, $A_i'/A_{US}' = 1$. A comparison of $\ln(y_i^*/y_{US}^*)$ with $\ln(y_i/y_{US})$ provides a moderately close fit, but with the slope noticeably less than unity as may be seen again from Figure 6.1. (See also Jones, 1998, Figure 3.1, p. 52.)

(ii)   Technology Differs Between Countries

Jones next relaxes the assumption that the level of technology is constant. As Jones (1998, p. 51) put it: 'differences in technology presumably explain to a great extent why some countries are richer than others'.[4] A_i' is defined as:

$$A_i' \equiv \left(\frac{y_i}{k_i}\right)^{(1-\alpha)/\alpha}\left(\frac{y_i}{h_i}\right). \tag{6.7}$$

The value of A' that is calculated from equation (6.7) is substituted into equation (6.6) to derive a value for (y_i^*/y_{US}^*). A visual comparison of $\ln(y_i^*/y_{US}^*)$ with $\ln(y_i/y_{US})$ now shows a closer fit with a slope of about unity. (See Figure 6.2 and Table 6.1 and Jones, 1998, Figure 3.2, p. 54.)

However, much of this good fit is merely a result of the method Jones adopts to calculate A_i'. To see this, let us first assume for expositional ease that the production function excludes human capital. It also demonstrates the tautological nature of the procedure, as we shall show that we get an equally good fit regardless of whether or not we explicitly include h. At the

---

[3]   Alternatively denoted by $\hat{L}$.
[4]   Jones (1998 [2002], p. 58) tones it down and the sentence becomes 'differences in technology presumably help to explain why some countries are richer than others.'

risk of getting ahead of ourselves, this is because the way A is calculated (as opposed to A') implicitly includes h.

Equation (6.7), in these circumstances, is written as:

$$A_i \equiv \left(\frac{y_i}{k_i}\right)^{(1-\alpha)/\alpha} y_i. \tag{6.8}$$

As we are excluding human capital, equation (6.6) may be written as:

$$\frac{y_i^*}{y_{US}^*} = \frac{\left(\dfrac{s_{K_i}'}{n_i + g}\right)^{(1-\alpha)/\alpha}}{\left(\dfrac{s_{K_{US}}'}{n_{US} + g}\right)^{(1-\alpha)/\alpha}} \frac{A_i}{A_{US}}. \tag{6.9}$$

Using equation (6.8) to substitute for A_i and A_{US} gives:

$$\frac{y_i^*}{y_{US}^*} = \frac{\left(\dfrac{s_{K_i}'}{n_i + g}\right)^{(1-\alpha)/\alpha}}{\left(\dfrac{s_{US}'}{n_{US} + g}\right)^{(1-\alpha)/\alpha}} \frac{\left(\dfrac{Y_i}{K_i}\right)^{(1-\alpha)/\alpha}}{\left(\dfrac{Y_{US}}{K_{US}}\right)^{(1-\alpha)/\alpha}} \frac{y_i}{y_{US}}, \tag{6.10}$$

where, it will be recalled, g is the rate of technical progress or $\hat{A}$.

Consider the expression $s_{K_i}'/(n_i + g)$. The net investment ratio can be written as

$$s_{K_i}' \equiv I_i'/Y_i \equiv \Delta K_i/Y_i \equiv \hat{K}_i(K_i/Y_i),$$

where I_i' is net investment.

Hence:

$$\left(\frac{s_{K_i}'}{n_i + g}\right)\left(\frac{Y_i}{K_i}\right) = \left(\frac{\hat{K}_i}{n_i + g}\right). \tag{6.11}$$

Equation (6.10) may therefore be expressed as:

$$\frac{y_i^*}{y_{US}^*} = \frac{\left(\dfrac{\hat{K}_i}{n_i + g}\right)^{(1-\alpha)/\alpha}}{\left(\dfrac{\hat{K}_{US}}{n_{US} + g}\right)^{(1-\alpha)/\alpha}} \frac{y_i}{y_{US}}, \tag{6.12}$$

or in logarithmic form as:

$$\ln\left(\frac{y_i^*}{y_{US}^*}\right) = \frac{1-\alpha}{\alpha}\ln\left(\frac{x_i}{x_{US}}\right) + 1.0\ln\left(\frac{y_i}{y_{US}}\right), \qquad (6.13)$$

where $x_i = \hat{K}_i/(n_i + g)$.

Consequently, if we were to regress $\ln(y_i^*/y_{US}^*)$ on $\ln(y_i/y_{US})$, we can see immediately that there will be a close statistical fit as (y_i/y_{US}) is, by definition, a component of (y_i^*/y_{US}^*), given the stylised fact that the capital–output ratio does not greatly vary between countries.[5] Moreover, if $\ln(x_i/x_{US})$ is orthogonal to $\ln(y_i/y_{US})$, then the coefficient of the latter must be equal to unity. In fact, plotting $\ln(y_i^*/y_{US}^*)$ against $\ln(y_i/y_{US})$ gives a slope that is less than unity, suggesting that $\ln(x_i/x_{US})$ is negatively correlated with $\ln(y_i/y_{US})$.

(iii) Introducing Human Capital

Ironically, if we now introduce human capital we get exactly the *same* relationship between the relative steady-state and the actual productivities. If we substitute equation (6.7) into equation (6.6), we obtain equation (6.10) again. This is because $A_i \equiv A_i' h_i$ or $A_i' \equiv A_i/h_i$. Due to the way A and A' are calculated, including a measure of human capital, no matter how it is calculated would not improve the goodness of fit. Or to put it another way, excluding human capital using Jones's procedure will not worsen the explanatory power of the model.

(iv) Allowing the Rate of Technical Progress to Vary

By introducing a more general (neoclassical) assumption, namely that the rate of technical progress is not constant across countries, we can improve the relationship by making it even more tautological. Assuming a well-behaved (aggregate) cost function and perfectly competitive markets, it can be shown that, using the aggregate marginal productivity conditions and Euler's theorem, the rate of technical progress is given by the dual (Chambers, 1988, ch. 6) as, for a Cobb–Douglas technology, $g_i = \hat{w}_i + [(1-a)/a]\hat{r}_i$ where a and $(1-a)$ are the factor shares of labour and capital. This is the standard result from the growth-accounting approach.

---

[5]   This is a condition for steady-state growth in the neoclassical growth model, but is also one of Kaldor's (1961) stylised facts, which do not depend upon the existence of the neoclassical aggregate production function.

The underlying assumption is that if countries have different technologies, part of the differences in the growth rates of productivity will be accounted for by disparities in the rate of technical progress, as the benefits of the latest technology diffuse from the more to the less advanced countries.

Jones (1998), however, makes the assumption that the levels of technology differ among the countries; yet rather surprisingly, he assumes that all countries have the same common rate of technical progress (so that $g_i = g$). He justifies this as follows:

> If g varies across countries then the 'income gap' between countries eventually becomes infinite. This may not seem plausible if growth is driven entirely by technology. . . . It may be more plausible to think that technological transfer will keep even the poorest countries from falling too far behind, and one way to interpret this statement is that the growth rates of technology g are the same across countries. (p. 51)

A couple of observations are in order here.

First, Jones's model departs from the traditional augmented Solow model (for example, Mankiw et al., 1992), where all countries are assumed to have the same rate of technological progress because they all have access to the *same* level of technology. However, most diffusion of technology models which assume differences in the levels of technology predict that, because of the technological catching-up phenomenon, the countries with the lower levels of technology will experience faster temporary productivity growth. This is because they achieve a faster rate of technical progress as they benefit from the inter-country transfer of technology (Fagerberg, 1987).[6] We should thus expect the rate of technical progress (or TFP growth) to vary between countries with their level of technology. This is precisely what the growth-accounting studies suggest for most countries – the rate of technical progress or the growth of TFP does vary between countries.[7] It would be purely coincidental, and implausible, to expect the rate of technical progress in these circumstances to remain constant across

---

[6]   In fact, the relationship is likely to be more complex than this. Gomulka (1971) has suggested that there is likely to be a hat-shaped relationship between the growth of productivity and the level of productivity (a proxy for the level of technology). Very underdeveloped countries are unlikely to have the social and human capital and infrastructure to take advantage of the diffusion of technology from the advanced countries. As development occurs, so the absorptive capability for adopting new technology increases with the result that productivity growth rates increase, until after a point a greater level of development leads to a decrease in productivity growth as the scope for catch-up decreases.

[7]   Indeed, this is confirmed by Jones in his growth-accounting exercise, reported in Jones (1998, ch. 2).

countries. Thus, the usual assumptions made are either that all countries have access to the same level of technology and the rate of technological progress is constant across countries, or that countries differ in their level of technology, and because of this, the rate of technical progress differs between countries. The combined assumption of differing levels of technology and constant rates of technical change does not seem plausible.

Second, the relative income gap will be constant if g is the same for all countries, but this fails to explain the reasons for the initial disparities in technology. But even if the relative per capita income gap remains constant, the absolute differences in per capita income will widen.

If we adopt the more general assumption that the rate of technical progress varies between countries, as we have already noted, neoclassical theory shows that the rate of technical progress is equal to the dual, that is, $g_i = \hat{w}_i + [(1 - a)/a]\hat{r}_i$. It is straightforward to see that in these circumstances the whole exercise reduces to nothing more than a tautology. Recall equation (6.12):

$$\frac{y_i^*}{y_{US}^*} = \frac{\left(\dfrac{\hat{K}_i}{n_i + g_i}\right)^{(1-\alpha)/\alpha}}{\left(\dfrac{\hat{K}_{US}}{n_{US} + g_{US}}\right)^{(1-\alpha)/\alpha}} \frac{y_i}{y_{US}}.$$

This may be written as:

$$\frac{y_i^*}{y_{US}^*} = \left(\frac{x_i'}{x_{US}'}\right)^{(1-\alpha)/\alpha} \frac{y_i}{y_{US}}. \tag{6.14}$$

Given that $\hat{Y}_i = \hat{K}_i$, it follows that $\hat{K}_i = n_i + g_i$ and hence $x_i' = x_{US}' = 1$.[8] Consequently, $\ln(y_i^*/y_{US}^*)$ *must* necessarily equal $\ln(y_i/y_{US})$. Hence, plotting $\ln(y_i^*/y_{US}^*)$ against $\ln(y_i/y_{US})$ would result in all the observations lying on the 45-degree line. But this does not convey any information beyond the growth of output must be equal to the growth of capital.

To the extent that g is assumed to be a constant in that it does not vary between countries, this will slightly weaken the fit between $\ln(y_i^*/y_{US}^*)$ and $\ln(y_i/y_{US})$, but we have seen above why the slope coefficient will be close to unity.

In Jones (1998 [2002]), as we have mentioned, greater emphasis is placed on the relationship between the relative levels of technology (A_i/A_{US}) and

---

[8] This may be seen from the following equation: $\hat{Y}_i = a\hat{w}_i + (1 - a)\hat{r}_i + an + (1 - a)\hat{K} = ag_i + an + (1 - a)\hat{K}$. If $\hat{Y}_i$ equals $\hat{K}_i$ then $\hat{K}_i = n_i + g_i = \hat{Y}_i$.

the observed relative levels of productivity. There is no discussion of the steady-state values. The relationship is given by:

$$\frac{A_i'}{A_{US}'} \equiv \frac{\left(\dfrac{Y_i}{K_i}\right)^{(1-\alpha)/\alpha} \dfrac{y_i}{h_i}}{\left(\dfrac{Y_{US}}{K_{US}}\right)^{(1-\alpha)/\alpha} \dfrac{y_{US}}{h_{US}}},$$

(6.15)

or, assuming that the capital–output ratios are constant, by:

$$\frac{A_i'}{A_{US}'} = \frac{h_{US}}{h_i} \frac{y_i}{y_{US}}.$$

(6.16)

Thus:

$$\ln\left(\frac{A_i'}{A_{US}'}\right) = \ln\left(\frac{h_{US}}{h_i}\right) + \ln\left(\frac{y_i}{y_{US}}\right).$$

(6.17)

It should be emphasised that equation (6.16) is also true by construction and therefore cannot be used to *test* the Solow model. If a different proxy for h is used, the calculated value of A' will alter to preserve the equation. It is analogous to the growth-accounting approach, as Jones (1998 [2002]) admits, although in terms of relative levels. As such, while it can give quantitative estimates of the various components given the usual neoclassical assumptions, it cannot give any idea of whether the components of equation (6.15) (that is, A and h) are causally significant in the growth process.

THE ACCOUNTING IDENTITY ONCE AGAIN

The reason why introducing differences in technology will nearly always ensure that there will be a very close correspondence between y and the steady-state value y^* is, not surprisingly, also due to the accounting identity. (It should be emphasised that the tautological procedure discussed above does not rely on the accounting identity, but is very similar to Solow's procedure discussed in the last chapter.)

The accounting identity may be written in intensive form (retaining the current notation for convenience) as:

$$y_i \equiv w_i + r_i k_i \equiv w_i + r_i (K_i / Y_i) y_i \equiv w_i + (1 - a_i) y_i.$$

(6.18)

The ratio of the level of productivity of country i to that of the US is given by:

$$\frac{y_i}{y_{US}} \equiv \frac{w_i}{w_{US}}. \tag{6.19}$$

This is based on the stylised fact that the factor shares do not greatly differ between countries. The equivalent analysis may be undertaken with the Cobb–Douglas approximation of the identity:

$$y_i = A_i \left(\frac{K_i}{Y_i}\right)^{(1-a)/a} \equiv B^{1/a} w_i (1-a)^{(1-a)/a}, \tag{6.20}$$

as $A_i \equiv B^{1/a} w_i \, r_i^{\,(1-a)/a}$ and $(r_i K_i / Y_i)^{(1-a)/a} = (1-a)^{(1-a)/a}$. (Note that in this chapter $A_i^a \equiv B w_i^a r_i^{(1-a)}$ rather than $A_i \equiv B w_i^a r_i^{(1-a)}$. This is merely a change in notation and makes no difference to the analysis.) Taking the ratio of the productivity of country i and the US gives us equation (6.19).

Now let us assume that there is a well-defined Cobb–Douglas aggregate production function and all the usual neoclassical assumptions are assumed, including that there are constant returns to scale and factors are paid their marginal products. The production function can be written as:

$$y_i = A_i \left(\frac{K_i}{Y_i}\right)^{(1-\alpha)/\alpha} = A_i \left(\frac{K_i}{Y_i}\right)^{(1-a)/a}. \tag{6.21}$$

In the steady state we have:

$$\frac{y_i^*}{y_{US}^*} = \frac{A_i}{A_{US}}. \tag{6.22}$$

But from the usual neoclassical assumptions and optimisation conditions the dual of the aggregate production gives, $A_i = A_0 w_i r_i^{(1-a)/a}$. Consequently, given factor shares are constant, a constant capital–output ratio implies that the rate of profit is constant across countries using the stylised fact that r and (K/Y) do not show much variation between countries or:

$$\frac{y_i^*}{y_{US}^*} = \frac{w_i}{w_{US}} = \frac{y_i}{y_{US}}. \tag{6.23}$$

Thus, if we allow 'total factor productivity' to vary between countries because the wage rate differs, and that the capital–output ratio also does not greatly vary, we can see that the so-called 'steady-state' ratio of productivity, y_i^*/y_{US}^*, *must* closely approximate the observed ratio, y_i/y_{US}. If we do not allow for differences in $w_i r_i^{(1-a)/a}$ between countries, then the relationship between the two ratios will be very weak. If we use a proxy for human capital such as the one derived from average schooling, then this is likely to be correlated with the real wage and so produce a better fit between the two variables. This analysis from the accounting identity essentially explains the results of Jones.

But it can be seen that this follows through from the accounting identity, even when no aggregate production exists. All we require is the Kaldorian stylised factor of constant capital–output ratio.

But as we have emphasised throughout this book, a constant capital–output ratio does not rely on the existence of an aggregate production function, never mind it being at its steady state. Because of the heterogeneity of physical output and capital goods, there is no such thing as an aggregate physical capital–output ratio. Simon (1986, pp. 172–83, Appendix A, 'A Constant Long-run K/Y Ratio is a Meaningless Observation') provides a discussion as to why the *constant-price* monetary value of the capital–output ratio will always tend to be approximately constant regardless of what is happening to the various individual *physical* capital–output ratios.

STEEDMAN'S CRITIQUE OF 'MEASURING' KNOWLEDGE

In an important note, Steedman (2003) has questioned what is actually meant by A in the neoclassical framework. In the neoclassical endogenous growth theory it has become fashionable to discuss A as the 'stock of knowledge' or number of 'ideas' and we could similarly give this interpretation to A in the Solow model.

For example, rather than treating $\hat{A}$ as exogenous, in endogenous growth theory, it has been modelled, *inter alia*, as the output of an R&D sector comprising a production function for ideas. One typical specification is $dA/dt = \psi L_A A^\phi$ where L_A are the number of workers in the R&D sector and ψ and ϕ (< 1) are constants. But, as Steedman points out, this approach requires a *cardinal* measure of a single stock of knowledge. While, with the exception of Aghion and Howitt (1998, pp. 435–48),[9] this assumption is made implicitly, rather than explicitly. It is often assumed

---

[9]   Aghion and Howitt appreciate the problem, but having looked it squarely in the face pass it by.

that the stock of knowledge has decreasing or increasing marginal product or that a production function with A as one of its arguments has constant or increasing returns. If knowledge can only be measured *ordinally*, then the use of A in this fashion has no meaning.[10] Steedman cites with approval Metcalfe (2001, p. 580): 'The weights (prices) with which an idea in carbon chemistry, say, is to be combined with an idea in the production of insurance services. It is not obvious what the weights are, and they certainly are not to be found in market prices.'

To take one example cited by Steedman (2003, p. 131, emphasis in the original),

> Barro and Sala-i-Martin (1995) consider a production for firm i:
>
> $$Y_i = F(K_i, A_iL_i)$$
>
> 'where L_i and K_i are the conventional inputs, and A_i is the index of knowledge available to the firm' (p. 146; by p. 147, A_i has become the firm's 'stock of knowledge'). We are told that 'a steady state exists when A_i grows at a constant rate' (p. 146). And what can that *mean* when A_i is an 'index' or a 'stock of knowledge'? Nothing; unless A_i has a cardinal measure and, once again, we are told nothing of how such a measure may be found or constructed.

Thus, it is clear that conceptually it will be difficult, if not impossible, to measure A cardinally. Of course, we know from the identity that the A is a function of the wage and profit rate. But this is of no help for neoclassical production theory as A should theoretically be capable of being measured *independently* of factor prices. We have seen that the production function is theoretically an engineering concept. To assume that A cannot be constructed independently of the accounting identity means that, independently of our critique, the whole concept becomes incoherent even from a neoclassical point of view. Or to follow Solow (1957) in measuring A as a cardinal index derived from the residual involves a high degree of circularity. There is still no way of independently testing whether the Solow index reflects the stock of knowledge given all the assumptions underlying its construction.

CONCLUDING COMMENTS: IS A THEORY OF TOTAL FACTOR PRODUCTIVITY REALLY NEEDED?

A number of authors during the last decade have advocated models that account for differences in TFP across countries in order to explain differ-

---

[10]   The same criticism also applies to H, the stock of human capital.

ences in income per capita. Prescott (1998), for example, presents evidence that TFP differs across countries and time in industries for reasons other than differences in the stock of technical knowledge. These findings lead the author to conclude 'Needed: A Theory of Total Factor Productivity'. This theory must account for differences in TFP growth that arise for reasons other than growth in technology.

However, this chapter has shown that the procedure used to estimate TFP is tautological. Thus, asking whether a theory of TFP is needed begs the question. In our opinion, and for the reasons set out in this chapter, the concepts of TFP and the aggregate production function serve more to obfuscate than to illuminate the important problem of 'why growth rates differ'.

Given the above conclusions, we are sceptical that this literature is advancing knowledge in the fields of economic growth and development in a particularly useful way. What neoclassical economics terms TFP is, *tautologically*, a function of the wage and profit rates. Therefore, what this literature has discovered is that in order to explain the observed large income differences across countries, one needs a theory of this weighted average. Although neoclassical theory reaches this result through the so-called 'dual measure' of TFP, we have shown that it follows simply from the income accounting identity, and thus it is not testable because it cannot be refuted. As the well-behaved aggregate production function does not exist, then it is not possible to calculate separately the contribution to economic growth of technical change (or TFP growth) and the growth of each factor input. This is equally true of both econometric techniques and the growth-accounting methodology (the endogenous growth theory also relies on the concept of the aggregate production function and takes us no further forward in understanding the determinants of growth).

Acknowledgement of this obvious point might help in deciding if a theory of TFP is needed in order to explain income differences across countries. The critique does not deny that authors like Parente and Prescott (1994), for example, may be on the right track when they argue that one important reason why many developing countries do not perform well is that they erect barriers in order to protect industry insiders from outside competition, but which prevent the efficient use of available technologies. However, arguing that the erection of these barriers *causes* differences in the aggregate-level TFP, which then *cause* differences in international income levels is an altogether different proposition.

APPENDIX 6A   HOW THE GROWTH OF HUMAN CAPITAL CAN EXPLAIN EITHER NONE OR ALL OF THE GROWTH OF TOTAL FACTOR PRODUCTIVITY

Solow (1957) appreciated that the growth of TFP represents '*any kind of shift* in the production function' (p. 312, emphasis in the original) and not just the rate of technical change. One factor that has been put forward as a possible explanation of TFP growth is the growth of human capital or the skills in the workforce. Ideally, the labour input is the flow of homogeneous labour services and a skilled worker can produce more of these than an unskilled worker. However, ever since Denison's (1967) detailed growth-accounting approach, the growth of human capital within this framework appears to explain very little of the residual (Lee and Hong, 2012). This appendix explains why this must logically be the case, and suggests by modifying the approach, particularly one of the restrictive assumptions, that it can explain *all* of the residual.

The standard neoclassical approach to human capital is to assume that the total labour input is expressed in efficiency units (L^*). To simplify the exposition, let us assume that the labour force consists of two categories, skilled workers (L_2) and unskilled workers (L_1). The 'adjusted' labour force is given by:

$$L^* = \Sigma \eta_i L_i \qquad (i = 1, 2), \qquad (6A.1)$$

where η is a measure of the efficiency of labour. This may be rewritten as:

$$H = \sum (\eta_i L_i)/L, \qquad (6A.2)$$

where H is a measure of the average human capital per worker and $HL = L^*$.

Growth accounting, drawing on neoclassical human capital theory, assumes that η_i can be proxied by the *relative* wage rate, that is, $\eta_2 = w_2/w_1$ and $\eta_1 = w_1/w_1 = 1$ (see O'Mahony and De Boer, 2002, pp. 59–60).

The Cobb–Douglas production function is specified as:

$$Q = A_0 e^{\lambda' t}(HL)^\alpha K^{(1-\alpha)} \qquad (6A.3)$$

compared with the specification in the absence of human capital:

$$Q = A_0 e^{\lambda t} L^\alpha K^{(1-\alpha)}. \qquad (6A.4)$$

Hence, from equations (6A.3) and (6A.4) (omitting time subscripts):

$$\lambda = \lambda' + \alpha \hat{H} \text{ or } \lambda' = \lambda - \alpha \hat{H}. \tag{6A.5}$$

In other words, the rate of growth of TFP is dichotomised into the 'unexplained' rate of technical progress and the growth of human capital per worker. Consequently, the more the growth of human capital explains, the smaller will be λ', the residual.

The contribution of the growth of the labour input, adjusted for the rate of change of human capital, to output growth, is:

$$\alpha(\hat{H} + \hat{L}) = \alpha \hat{L}^* = \alpha[\theta(\hat{w}_2 - \hat{w}_1) + \theta \hat{L}_2 + (1 - \theta)\hat{L}_1], \tag{6A.6}$$

where:

$$\theta = \left(\frac{(w_2/w_1)/L_2}{(w_2/w_1)L_2 + L_1} \right) = \left(\frac{w_2 L_2}{w_2 L_2 + w_1 L_1} \right).$$

Consequently, θ is the share of the total compensation of the skilled workers in the total wage bill. Surprisingly, as we have noted above, the growth of human capital generally explains relatively little of the residual in the growth-accounting approach. However, it is easy to see why this is the case from a consideration of the accounting identity. First, the growth of employment is approximately given by:

$$\hat{L} \approx \theta \hat{L}_2 + (1 - \theta) \hat{L}_1. \tag{6A.7}$$

This will occur if $\hat{L}_2 \approx \hat{L}_1$ or $\theta \approx [L_2/(L_2 + L_1)]$ or both.

Consequently, from the accounting identity:

$$\lambda' \equiv \lambda - a[\theta(\hat{w}_2 - \hat{w}_1)] \equiv a\hat{w} + (1 - \alpha)\hat{r} - a[\theta(\hat{w}_2 - \hat{w}_1)], \tag{6A.8}$$

where $\hat{w}$ is the growth of the average wage rate.

It can be seen that for human capital to make any contribution to reducing the residual requires an increasing wage differential and even then the contribution is likely to be small as $a < 1$ and $\theta < 1$ so $a\theta$ is likely to be relatively small. Moreover, empirically it is likely that the growth of the wage of the unskilled workers will more or less keep pace with that of the skilled workers. If this is the case, then the contribution of the growth of human capital, as measured here, to output growth, will be very small. Even if the quality of schooling and training is increasing over time, the contribution of the growth of human capital will be negative if there are economic and/or political forces (such as minimum wage legislation) that lead to a reduction in real wage rate disparities. This, perhaps more than anything, points to the implausibility of this approach.

Another assumption is that it is the wage rate of totally unskilled workers with *no* formal education or instruction that remains constant over time. Let us denote this wage by $\tilde{w}$. However, over time, even the workers in group 1 acquire more expertise and learning and become more efficient, so that $\eta_1 = w_1/\tilde{w}$ and $\hat{\eta}_1 = \hat{w}_1$. Likewise, $\eta_2 = w_2/\tilde{w}$ and $\hat{\eta}_2 = \hat{w}_2$.

Consequently, expressing $(HL)^\alpha \equiv (\sum (w_i/\tilde{w}) L_i)^\alpha$ in growth rates gives:

$$\alpha(\hat{H}+\hat{L}) = \alpha\left\{\left[\frac{(w_2/\tilde{w})L_2}{(w_2/\tilde{w})L_2 + (w_1/\tilde{w})L_1}\right](\hat{w}_2 + \hat{L}_2)\right.$$

$$\left. + \left[\frac{(w_1/\tilde{w})L_1}{(w_2/\tilde{w})L_2 + (w_1/\tilde{w})L_1}\right](\hat{w}_1 + \hat{L}_1)\right\} \tag{6A.9}$$

$$= \alpha[\theta'(\hat{w}_2 + \hat{L}_2) + (1 - \theta')(\hat{w}_1 + \hat{L}_1)] = \alpha(\hat{w} + \hat{L}). \tag{6A.10}$$

Hence, using value data, we have from the 'production function':

$$\hat{V} = \lambda + \alpha\hat{L} + (1 - \alpha)\hat{J} = \lambda' + a\hat{w} + a\hat{L} + (1 - a)\hat{J}. \tag{6A.11}$$

From the identity we have:

$$\hat{V} = a\hat{w} + (1 - a)\hat{r} + a\hat{L} + (1 - a)\hat{J},$$

and given that $(1 - a)\hat{r}$ is negligible, the growth of value added may be expressed as:

$$\hat{V} = a\hat{w} + a\hat{L} + (1 - a)\hat{J}. \tag{6A.12}$$

From a comparison of equations (6A.11) and (6A.12) we can see that the growth of 'human capital' has now explained *all* of the TFP growth. We do not, of course, necessarily advocate adopting the assumptions of either of these approaches. Our argument merely shows the arbitrariness of the neoclassical explanation of the residual.

7.   Why are some countries richer than others? A sceptical view of Mankiw–Romer–Weil's test of the neoclassical growth model

> I have always found the high R^2 reassuring when I teach the Solow growth model. Surely, a low R^2 in this regression would have shaken my faith that this model has much to teach us about international differences in income.
>
> (Mankiw, 1997, p. 104)

INTRODUCTION[1]

Previously, we raised some serious problems concerning the foundations of the aggregate production function and with Solow's growth model. But his model became established as the foundation of modern growth theory,[2] to the extent that it appears, with subsequent developments in growth theory, in nearly every modern macroeconomics textbook (for example, Mankiw, 2010). Yet, during the 1980s there was growing dissatisfaction with the predictions of the model. Given the assumption that all countries (or regions) have access to the same level of technology, the model predicts that the steady-state rate of growth of productivity will be equal to the (common) rate of technical progress. Any differences in growth rates can only be transitory, the result of countries not all being at their steady-state capital–labour ratio. The productivity growth rate of those countries where their actual capital–labour ratio is below the steady-state value will temporarily exceed the rate of technical progress. If the countries all invest the same proportion of their GDP then there should be an inverse correlation between the growth of labour productivity and the initial (log) level of productivity. There is evidence that such 'beta absolute

---

[1]   This chapter is a condensed version of Felipe and McCombie (2005b).

[2]   However, Solow's (1956) model was primarily a theoretical attempt to remove the unsatisfactory situation where the natural rate of growth differed from the warranted. The former is the maximum possible growth of output given by the supply side and the latter is the equilibrium situation where desired investment equals desired savings, in a closed economy. The Solow model accomplishes this by allowing the capital–output ratio to vary. (See Thirlwall, 2002, ch. 1.)

convergence' can be found at the regional level of the US and Japan (Barro and Sala-i-Martin, 1995 [2003]). However, for the world as a whole there is no evidence of such convergence. Consequently, the literature split into two approaches.

The first approach was to abandon the assumption that all countries had the same growth of technology that was a pure public good and occurred exogenously like manna from heaven. Thus were born the endogenous and semi-endogenous growth models.

The second approach, with which we are concerned in this chapter, was pioneered in a well-known paper by Mankiw et al. (1992) (hereafter MRW) who revived and extended the canonical Solow (1956) growth model.[3] This became the first effort in what Klenow and Rodriguez-Clare (1997) have referred to as a 'neoclassical revival'. In MRW's words: 'This paper takes Robert Solow seriously' (p. 407). By this, MRW meant that Solow's growth model had been misinterpreted in the literature since the 1980s. MRW showed how, in their opinion, the model should be correctly specified and its predictions tested, and they emphasised that it predicted conditional, rather than absolute, beta convergence. In other words, the estimations of convergence should take into account that countries invested different proportions of their output in physical and human capital. Once this was done, the evidence did suggest that there was world-wide convergence.

In this chapter we discuss the problems posed by the accounting identity for the way that MRW, and the subsequent papers evaluating the latter, have tested the predictions of Solow's growth model. We further show that MRW's initial regression equation is, not surprisingly, a particular case of this identity, subject to two empirically implausible assumptions. These are that differences in the level of technology, resource endowments and institutions can be modelled as a constant plus a random error term, and that each country has the same rate of technical progress. The argument in this chapter explains why the coefficients in the estimated equation must take a given value and sign, irrespective of whether the neoclassical assumptions concerning the existence of a worldwide aggregate produc-

---

[3]   However, in reference to the international cross-section regressions programme initiated in the early 1990s, Solow (1994, p. 51) has indicated the following: 'I had better admit that I do not find this a confidence-inspiring project. It seems altogether too vulnerable to bias from omitted variables, to reverse causation, and above all to the recurrent suspicion that the experiences of very different national economies are not to be explained as if they represented different "points" on some well-defined surface. . . . I am thinking especially of Mankiw, Romer and Weil (1992) and Islam (1992)'. Islam (1992) was finally published as Islam (1995). Solow (2001) indicates that he thought of 'growth theory as the search for a dynamic model that could explain the evolution of one economy over time' (p. 283).

tion function hold. It also shows why, if the assumptions underlying Solow's augmented growth model are granted and the model is specified correctly, because of the identity, it should yield a very high statistical fit, potentially with an R^2 equal to unity.

At this juncture, it is important to emphasise a point that has been consistently and surprisingly misunderstood by, for example, Temple (2006, 2010) and raised in Chapters 2 and 12 where we discuss his misperceptions. In the course of our argument, we show that given the stylised facts that the capital–output ratio does not greatly vary between countries and over time and that factor shares are constant, the accounting identity alone will ensure that MRW's model gives a very good fit to the data. It is not an *exact* fit as we shall show below, and indeed we shall demonstrate, how from a consideration of the identity, a perfect statistical fit can, in fact, be obtained. However, the accounting identity critique does not stand or fall by these two stylised facts, *pace* Temple. If they do not hold, the identity tells us immediately that the MRW model will give a poor fit to the data, before a single regression is run. This is because MRW derive their initial estimating equation from a Cobb–Douglas production function with the assumption of a constant capital–output ratio. The identity shows that this will give a good fit to the data only if factor shares are constant and total factor productivity (which is determined by the wage and profit rate), is allowed to vary between countries. We return to this point below.

SOLOW'S GROWTH MODEL AND THE MRW SPECIFICATION

The elaboration of Solow's growth model by MRW is well known and so it needs only to be briefly rehearsed here. They started from the standard aggregate Cobb–Douglas production function with constant returns to scale:

$$Y_t = (A_t L_t)^\alpha K_t^{(1-\alpha)}, \tag{7.1}$$

where in MRW's notation (as they implicitly assume the theoretical legitimacy of a single-sector aggregate production function) Y is output, K is the capital stock, L is the labour input, and α and $(1 - \alpha)$ are labour's and capital's output elasticities $(0 < \alpha < 1)$. A is a measure of the common level of technology. They assumed constant exponential growth rates for labour n (denoted by $\hat{L}$ in other chapters), that is, $L_t = L_0 e^{nt}$; and technology g, that is, $A_t = A_0 e^{gt}$ (denoted by λ in other chapters, apart from Chapter 6). Consequently, the number of effective units of labour $A_t L_t$

grows at rate $(n + g)$. MRW also assumed, following Solow (1956), that a constant fraction of output, s, is saved over time (although this fraction differs across countries), and depreciation is a constant fraction of the capital stock, namely δK.

With these assumptions, it is straightforward to derive the steady-state value of the capital per effective unit of labour ratio (K/AL), which upon substitution into the production function yields the steady-state productivity:

$$\ln y = \ln A_0 + gt + \frac{1 - \alpha}{\alpha}\ln s - \frac{1 - \alpha}{\alpha}\ln(n + g + \delta), \qquad (7.2)$$

where y denotes labour productivity (Y/L). The model predicts that countries with higher savings and investment rates will tend to be richer (in per capita *levels*). These countries accumulate more capital per worker, and consequently have more output per worker; and countries that have high population growth rates will tend to be poorer. The model also predicts the magnitudes of the coefficients of these two variables. But savings rates and population growth do not affect the steady-state *growth rates* of per capita output. This is determined by the rate of technical progress.

At this point, MRW introduced a couple of crucial assumptions. First, they assumed $(g + \delta)$ to be constant across countries (neither variable is country specific) and set it equal to 0.05. Second, they postulated that the term A_0 reflects not just the initial level of technology (which is the same for all countries), but resource endowments, climate, institutions and so on. On this basis, they argued that it may differ across countries, and assumed that $\ln A_0 = b_0 + \varepsilon$, where b_0 is a constant, and ε is a country-specific shock. Furthermore, they made the identifying assumption that the shock is independent of the savings and population growth rates.

Therefore, equation (7.2), using cross-country data, becomes:

$$\ln y = b_0 + \frac{1 - \alpha}{\alpha}\ln s - \frac{1 - \alpha}{\alpha}\ln(n + 0.05) + \varepsilon. \qquad (7.3)$$

In this context, Islam (1999) commented:

> The problem . . . lies in the estimation of A_0. It is difficult to find any particular variable that can effectively proxy for it. It is for this reason that many researchers wanted to ignore the presence of the A_0 term . . . and relegated it to the disturbance term. This, however, creates an omitted variable bias for the regression results. (Islam, 1999, p. 503)

This assumes that the variable being proxied by the constant is correlated with the regressors.

Equation (7.3) provides the framework for testing Solow's model as a joint hypothesis as it specifies the signs and magnitudes of the coefficients (together with the identifying assumption). Assuming that countries are at their steady-state growth rates, this equation can be used to test how differing savings rates and labour force growth rates can explain the differences in current productivity across countries. This is the essential point of the MRW paper. The argument is that for purposes of explaining cross-country variations in income levels, economists can retain the old Solovian framework and the assumption that the term A_0 is the same across countries. This contrasts with other attempts at understanding differences in income per capita, in particular the one advocated by Jorgenson (1995), in whose view the assumption of identical technologies across countries implicit in the neoclassical growth model may not hold. Prescott (1998) has also noted that savings rate differences are not that important; what matters is total factor productivity (TFP) growth, which leads him to conclude that a theory of TFP is needed (see Chapter 6). Parente and Prescott (1994) argue that the development miracle of South Korea is the result of reductions in technology adoption barriers, while the absence of such a miracle in the Philippines is because there were no such reductions.

Mankiw (1995, p. 281) defended the assumption that different countries have approximately the same production function. He argued that the assumption that developing and developed countries share a common production function is not as preposterous as some writers have indicated, and is a compelling one. In his view this assumption only means that if different countries had the same inputs, they would produce the same output.

Equation (7.3) was estimated by MRW using OLS with data for 1960–85 for three samples, the first one including 98 countries, the second one 75 countries, and the third one containing only the 22 OECD countries. MRW (1992, p. 411) acknowledged that the specification estimated could lead to inconsistent estimates, since s and n are potentially endogenous and influenced by the level of income.

The estimation results were mixed. Although the results for the first two samples were quite acceptable, with, in both cases, an $\bar{R}^2$ of 0.59 and an implied elasticity of capital $1 - \alpha = 0.6$, the results for the OECD countries were rather poor, with the estimate of the coefficient of $\ln (n + 0.05)$ insignificant (although with the correct negative sign) and a very low $\bar{R}^2$, namely 0.01 ($\bar{R}^2 = 0.06$ in the regression with the coefficients of $\ln(s)$ and $\ln(n + 0.05)$ restricted to take on the same value).

The results of our replication, using OLS, of MRW's estimation of the augmented Solow model using data for the OECD countries over the 1960–85 period with the assumption of a constant technology and a constant rate of technical progress gives a poor fit similar to their results:[4]

$$\ln y = 8.776 + 0.586 \ln s - 0.605 \ln (n + 0.005) \quad \bar{R}^2 = 0.025 \ \ SER = 0.375$$
$$\quad (3.51) \quad (1.36) \quad \quad (-0.71)$$

where y is real GDP per person of working age in 1985; s is the investment–output ratio (average for 1960–85); and n is the average rate of growth of the working–age population (average 1960–85).

The implied output elasticity of capital obtained from the two regression coefficients are 0.369 (2.16) and 0.377 (1.15) (t-values are in parentheses) which is nearer capital's share than the value obtained by MRW. Nevertheless, overall these results are broadly consistent with those of MRW and they are rather poor.

These results led MRW to propose an augmented Solow model in which they included human capital. The model improved the explanatory power of all three samples, but still the $\bar{R}^2$ for the OECD countries was a disappointing 0.24 (0.28 in the restricted regression). The authors concluded, under the assumption that technology is the same in all countries, that exogenous differences in saving and education cause the observed differences in levels of income. The production function consistent with their results is $Y = A K^{1/3} H^{1/3} L^{1/3}$, where H denotes human capital. In this formulation the elasticity of physical capital is not different from its share in income.

MRW concluded that Solow's model accounted for more than half of the cross-country variation in income per capita, except in one of the subsamples, namely that of the OECD economies. MRW claimed that 'saving and population growth affect income in the directions that Solow predicted. Moreover, more than half of the cross-country variation in income per capita can be explained by these two variables alone' (p. 407). They continued: 'Overall, the findings reported in this paper cast doubt on the recent trend among economists to dismiss the Solow growth model in favor of endogenous-growth models that assume constant or increasing returns to capital' (p. 409). Their results showed that each factor receives its social return, and that there are no externalities to the accumulation of physical capital.

A number of papers subsequently re-evaluated MRW's work. At the risk of oversimplifying, discussions of MRW's original work have split

---

[4]   In this chapter we confine ourselves to only a number of the key regression results contained in Felipe and McCombie (2005b). The numbers in parentheses are t-values.

into (i) those that propose further augmentations of the MRW regression, (ii) those that concentrate on the discussion of econometric issues, and (iii) those critical of the literature and who propose important methodological changes. (See the discussion in Felipe and McCombie, 2005b, pp. 365–7 for further details and also in the next section.)

RELAXING THE ASSUMPTION OF A COMMON TECHNOLOGY ACROSS COUNTRIES WITHIN THE NEOCLASSICAL FRAMEWORK

In this section, a solution is proposed for improving upon the poor results obtained by MRW for the OECD countries. This consists in relaxing the assumption of a common rate of technical progress introduced by MRW. Attention is restricted to the OECD sample, which it will be recalled is the one that yielded the most disappointing results in MRW's paper.

We have noted above that Jorgenson (1995), Prescott (1998) and Parente and Prescott (1994), *inter alios*, consider that differences in the level and growth of TFP are important explanatory factors.

Easterly and Levine (2001) extend the MRW model explicitly to allow for differences in TFP. They accomplish this by using all-inclusive dummies that permit ln$A$ to differ between regions (East Asia, South Asia, Sub-Saharan Africa, and so on) oil-producing and non-oil-producing countries and OECD and non-OECD countries. The dummies are all highly significant, with t-values often over 40. Hence, they conclude that 'most of the cross-country variation in growth rates per capita is due to differences in TFP growth and not to transitional dynamics between steady states' (p. 191). It should be noted that they did *not* allow the rate of exogenous technical progress to differ between regions and so on.

This approach can be improved upon as, under the usual neoclassical assumptions, the rate of technical progress may be determined from the dual of the production function, and is likely to differ among countries. Consequently, these are calculated and included in the regression. Contrary to Islam (1999), quoted above, standard neoclassical production theory suggests that this is a suitable proxy for technical progress. Under the usual neoclassical assumptions, the dual rate of technical progress is given by:

$$g_t = \frac{\alpha \hat{w}_t + (1 - \alpha)\hat{r}_t}{\alpha}, \tag{7.4}$$

which implies that $A_t^\alpha = B_0 w_t^\alpha r_t^{1-\alpha}$, where α is labour's output elasticity, $\hat{w}_t$ is the growth rate of the wage rate, and $\hat{r}_t$ is the growth rate of the profit rate. Under the assumption of perfect competition and that factors are paid their marginal products, $\alpha = a$, where a is labour's share in output. MRW's model (without human capital) can then be estimated as:

$$\ln y = c + 1.0 \ln w + \frac{1-\alpha}{\alpha} \ln r + \frac{1-\alpha}{\alpha} \ln s - \frac{1-\alpha}{\alpha} \ln\left[n + 0.02 \right.$$

$$\left. + \frac{\alpha\hat{w} + (1-\alpha)\hat{r}}{\alpha} \right] + \varepsilon, \tag{7.5}$$

where:

y is real GDP per person of working age in 1985;
s is the investment–output ratio (average for 1960–85);
w is the average of the wage rates in 1963 and 1985;
n is the average rate of growth of the working-age population (average 1960–85);
r is the average of the profit rates in 1963 and 1985 (total profits divided by the capital stock);
$\hat{w}$ is the exponential annual growth rate of the wage rate for 1963–85;
$\hat{r}$ is the exponential annual growth of the profit rate for 1963–85; and
δ is the rate of depreciation and equals 0.02.

In constructing $[\alpha\hat{w} + (1-\alpha)\hat{r}]/\alpha$ we use the average factor shares for 1963–85 as the weights $(1-\alpha)$ and α.

Allowing both the level and the rate of technical progress to vary between the OECD countries greatly improves the regression results:

$$\ln y = c + 1.001\ln w + 0.833\ln r + 0.794\ln s - 0.673\ln(n + \delta + g) \quad \bar{R}^2 = 0.823$$
$$\qquad\quad (12.52) \qquad (2.80) \qquad (3.02) \qquad (-4.78) \qquad\qquad SER = 0.155.$$

These results show a substantial improvement in the goodness of fit compared with MRW's results. Solow's growth model *does* now seem to work for the OECD countries, contrary to MRW's findings. It is notable that the estimate of $\ln w$ is statistically not different from unity, and that we can also recover the capital share from the regression estimates. The implied share of capital from the regression coefficients now ranges from 0.422 (*t*-value, 5.13) to 0.402 (*t*-value, 7.99). Restricting the coefficients to take the same value where appropriate does not significantly affect the results.

At first sight it might seem that Solow's growth model in its steady-state form allowing technology to vary is the most satisfactory explanation of 'why some countries are richer than others'. It could be further argued that these results strongly justify MRW's faith in Solow's model. Countries are rich (poor) because they have high (low) investment rates, low (high) population growth rates, and high (low) levels of technology. See Jones (1998, p. 53) for a similar view.

Paradoxically, these results are rather suspicious. This is because they are too good to be true given all the theoretical problems associated with the concept of the aggregate production function, as discussed earlier. Furthermore, it is surprising that only three variables (technology, employment and capital), notwithstanding their likely serious measurement problems, so comprehensively explain the variation in per capita income. And Srinivasan (1994, 1995) has argued that the data in the Summers and Heston (1991) database, the one used by most authors (including MRW), are of very poor quality as much of the data for the developing countries are constructed by extrapolation and interpolation.

In the next section, it is shown why the data must, indeed, always give a near perfect fit to the 'model'. This raises serious problems for the previous interpretations of Solow's model. In this sense, we believe that our arguments go beyond those of, for example, Brock and Durlauf (2001) in their criticisms of the empirical growth literature. They confined their criticisms to the fact that it is difficult to know what variables to include in the analysis; the problem that the failure to refute a theory does not imply the falsity of another one; the unrealistic assumption of parameter homogeneity across countries; and the lack of attention to endogeneity problems.

TOO GOOD TO BE TRUE? THE TYRANNY OF THE ACCOUNTING IDENTITY

In this section it is shown that the results in the last section can be regarded as merely a statistical artefact. This is because the above results are totally determined by the national income accounting identity that relates value added to the sum of the wage bill plus total profits together with a couple of stylised facts. The argument will be familiar from the earlier chapters. From the accounting identity, and if factor shares are constant, we obtain the, by now, familiar result that the identity can be expressed as:

$$V_t \equiv B_0 w_t^a r_t^{1-a} L_t^a J_t^{1-a} \equiv B(t) L_t^a J_t^{1-a}, \qquad (7.6)$$

where $B(t) \equiv B_0 w_t^a r_t^{1-a}$ and V and J again denote constant-price values.

The growth of the capital stock is defined as:

$$\frac{\Delta J_t}{J_t} \equiv \hat{J}_t \equiv \frac{I_t}{J_t} - \delta \equiv \frac{sV_t}{J_t} - \delta, \tag{7.7}$$

where, again, I is gross investment, δ is the constant rate of depreciation and s is the investment–output ratio.

It is assumed that the capital–output ratio does not change over time, so that $\hat{V}_t = \hat{J}_t$. While this is a condition for steady-state growth in the neoclassical schema, it is also one of Kaldor's (1961) stylised facts, unrelated to neoclassical theory. However, while this is the case for the dataset used here, over a longer period there is evidence of a secular increase in the capital–output ratio (Maddison, 1995). The latter, together with constant factor shares, implies a fall in the rate of profit. But this does not affect the more general argument.

Using only the accounting identity (7.6), the definition of the growth of the capital stock, equation (7.8); the stylised fact that factor shares are constant, $a_t = a$ and $1 - a_t = 1 - a$; and the stylised fact that there is no growth in the capital–output ratio, $\hat{V}_t = \hat{J}_t$; then an equation for labour productivity may be straightforwardly derived as:

$$\ln y = c + 1.0\ln w + \frac{1-a}{a}\ln r + \frac{1-a}{a}\ln s - \frac{1-a}{a}\ln\left[n+\delta+\frac{a\hat{w}+(1-a)\hat{r}}{a}\right]. \tag{7.8}$$

The variable y is now defined as value added per capita (that is, V/L). It should be noted that these stylised facts also imply that $\hat{r} = 0$.

The question that arises at this point is 'how is equation (7.8) to be interpreted?'. It is obvious that equation (7.8) is identical to equation (7.5). Equation (7.5) was derived from the Cobb–Douglas production function and could be considered to be a generalisation of the MRW model, as, using neoclassical duality theory, it allowed for technical progress and technology to vary between countries.

But, and here is the important point, equation (7.8) which is identical to equation (7.5), was derived without any recourse to neoclassical production theory. All we did was to transform the income accounting identity into another identity, under two stylised facts, namely, constant factor shares, and a constant growth of the capital–output ratio. *What is important to note is that equation (7.8) and the two stylised facts are equally compatible with the absence of a well-behaved aggregate production function. There is no requirement that factors be paid their marginal products, and no assumptions need be made about the state of competition, or that growth is steady state.*

Indeed, if the assumptions are roughly correct, econometric estimation of equation (7.8) must yield a near perfect fit, and simply because of the underlying identity, we should expect the estimates of the profit rate, savings rate and that of the sum of the growth rate of the labour force plus depreciation plus 'technical progress' to give a ballpark figure for $(1 - a)/a$ of 2/3 and for $(1 - a)$ of 0.4. The estimate of the coefficient of the logarithm of the wage rate should equal unity.

In fact, it turns out that matters are a little more complicated than this. The following terms of the right-hand side of equation (7.8) may be expressed as:

$$c = -\frac{1-a}{a}\ln(1-a) - \ln a,\qquad(7.9)$$

$$\frac{1-a}{a}\ln r = \frac{1-a}{a}\ln\left[(1-a)\frac{V}{J}\right],\qquad(7.10)$$

$$\frac{1-a}{a}\ln s = \frac{1-a}{a}\ln(\hat{J}+\delta)\frac{J}{V},\qquad(7.11)$$

$$\frac{1-a}{a}\ln\left[n+\delta+\frac{a\hat{w}+(1-a)\hat{r}}{a}\right] = \frac{1-a}{a}\ln(\hat{J}+\delta).\qquad(7.12)$$

Substituting these equations into equation (7.8) gives:

$$\ln y = -\ln a + 1.0\ln w.\qquad(7.13)$$

Equation (7.13) has been derived on the assumption that factor shares are constant across countries and there is no growth in the capital–output ratio.[5] The fact that equation (7.8) gives a good fit to our data is due to the fact that, ironically, there is enough variation in the factor shares and in the growth of the capital–output ratio to prevent perfect multicollinearity and this helps to give reasonably precise estimates of the coefficients of all the terms.

But can all this be interpreted to be a test, in the sense of providing verification (strictly speaking, non-refutation) of Solow's model? The answer is clearly 'no' because, as we have noted, the estimates are compatible with the assumption of no well-defined aggregate production function. Moreover, an R^2 of unity would be suspicious. All the argument

---

[5]   Note that we could undertake the analysis for each country separately which would mean that while factor shares are assumed to be constant over time, they could differ between countries. In these circumstances, equation (7.13) would give a poor fit using cross-country data.

implies is that if factor shares are roughly constant and the capital–output ratio does not grow, equation (7.8) will always yield a high fit (with data for any sample of countries) and with the corresponding parameters well determined. Moreover, equation (7.13) must also hold, by definition, solely if factor shares are constant as $wL/V \equiv a$. Thus, although we have used the assumption that there is no growth in the capital–output ratio to derive equation (7.8), equation (7.13) does not require this assumption.

Furthermore, if implausibly $g_t = \hat{w}_t + [(1 - a)\hat{r}_t]/a$ and $A_t^a = B_0 w_t^a r_t^{1-a}$ are constant across countries, then equation (7.8) becomes MRW's equation given by (7.3), and it will similarly give highly significant and plausible estimates.

These two stylised facts used are quite general. The hypothesis of a constant capital–output ratio is, as noted earlier, one of Kaldor's (1961) stylised facts. It is a very general proposition. In fact, Kaldor would not have been pleased to discover that this stylised fact is interpreted in terms of an aggregate production function, a notion that for many years he heavily criticised. Suppose, for example, that oligopolistic firms adopt a constant mark-up pricing policy with any underlying technology at the plant level and set prices to achieve a certain target rate of return, which may vary between firms. If the average rate of return does not greatly vary over the period being considered, then the growth of the capital–output ratio will be roughly constant. This does not depend upon the economy being in steady state in the neoclassical sense of the term.

Regarding the assumption of constant shares, another of Kaldor's stylised facts, it could be asked whether it implies an aggregate Cobb–Douglas production function. It is standard to argue that the reason why factor shares appear to be more or less constant is that the underlying technology of the economy is an aggregate Cobb–Douglas production function (Mankiw, 1995, p. 288). The answer, however, is that this is not necessarily the case. This was one of Fisher's (1971b) conclusions in his seminal simulations.

The fact that when the necessary assumptions are exactly fulfilled, equation (7.8) reduces to equation (7.13), even more graphically illustrates the argument. As we have noted, the fact that shares are constant over time and across countries does not, *per se*, imply that there is an underlying aggregate production function or that it is a Cobb–Douglas. Thus, while the neoclassical model under the assumption of constant factor shares (together with differences in the rate of technical progress and in the wage rate and possibly the profit rate) gives rise to equations (7.8) and (7.13), the finding that the statistical estimates are close to their expected values cannot be taken as a test of the Solovian hypothesis. In other words: that

Solow's model is *consistent* with some stylised facts of growth does not necessarily make it a good model: 'Consistency alone is a poor merit: a model that says nothing about anything is consistent with everything, yet that does not make it a good model' (Valdés, 1999, p. 60).

The conclusion is that if the two assumptions used above are empirically correct, the national income accounts imply that an equation like (7.8) exists, and we will *always* find that there is a positive relationship between the savings rate and income per capita, and a negative relationship between population growth and income per capita. Moreover, as we have noted, if shares are exactly constant, equation (7.13) will give a good statistical fit, even though the stylised fact of a constant growth in the capital–output ratio is not met.

One may be tempted to argue that the problem is similar to that of observational equivalence, in this case between equations (7.13), (7.8) and (7.5). Observational equivalence refers to the situation where two different *models* give rise to the same predictions or have identical reduced forms. Here, however, we do not have two alternative theories that generate the same distribution of observations. There is Solow's theory, but the other explanation is just an identity. Therefore, this is not an identification problem in the strict sense. Placing a priori restrictions on Solow's model will never identify an identity.

The important question is whether MRW's approach can in any way be interpreted as a test of Solow's model. The answer is, again, no. If the estimated coefficients are identical to those predicted by equation (7.8), it could be because the model satisfies all the Solovian assumptions; but the estimated coefficients are equally compatible with none of Solow's assumptions being valid. The data cannot discriminate between the two explanations and all one can say is that the assumptions of constant shares and a constant capital–output ratio have not been refuted.

The case perhaps more difficult to gauge is the one when there is not a perfect fit to the data, like in MRW (and virtually all applications). In fact, with data taken from the national accounts we shall never obtain a perfect fit. The reason is simply that neither factor shares nor the capital–output ratio are exactly constant. Does this then imply a rejection of Solow's model? We suggest that it does not. All this means is that either factor shares or the capital–output ratio are not constant. The first can be taken under a neoclassical interpretation as a rejection that the underlying production function is a Cobb–Douglas. However, we can always find a better approximation to the identity (and which will resemble another production function) that allows factor shares to vary, and this could be (erroneously) interpreted as a production function, for example, a CES, or a translog 'production function'. The second does refute the proposition that growth is in steady state, but the results convey no more information than a direct test of whether the capital–output ratio is constant.

Moreover, given our arguments, the statistical estimation of equation (7.8) is not needed. One simply has to check whether or not the two assumptions above are empirically correct. For most countries, the assumption that factor shares are constant is correct in the sense that factor shares vary very slowly and within a narrow range. This is true of our dataset. So, it all comes down to confirming whether or not the capital–output ratio is constant. Here again we observe a similar pattern: capital–output ratios increased over time in all countries but the standard deviations in both initial and terminal years were small and identical in both periods. We conclude that, overall, equation (7.8) has to work well in terms of the goodness of fit and must yield estimates close to the hypothesised results. The variation in factor shares is not small enough for equation (7.13) to be preferred to equation (7.8).

A related important issue is that estimation of equation (7.8) does not require instrumental variable methods, as MRW (1992, p.411) suggest, because the equation is fundamentally an identity. The error term here, if any, derives from an incorrect approximation to the income accounting identity. There is no endogeneity problem in the standard sense of the term. Certainly, the wage rate, the profit rate, employment and capital are endogenous variables, but nobody would argue that estimation of equation (7.6), an identity, requires instrumental variables, since there is no error term (see Felipe et al., 2008). If equation (7.8) is a perfect approximation to equation (7.6), the argument remains the same. It is true, however, that if equation (7.8) is not a perfect approximation to equation (7.6), the estimation method will matter. It may be possible that instrumental variable estimation could yield, under these circumstances, estimates closer to the theoretical values. But this is a minor issue once the whole argument is appreciated.

What is the result of further augmenting Solow's model in the sense of including additional variables, such as human capital? If the variables used in these regressions are statistically significant, it must be because they serve as a proxy for the weighted average of the log of the wage and profit rates. Consequently, they reduce, to some extent, the degree of omitted variable bias. Knowles and Owen (1995) and Nonneman and Vanhoudt (1996) extended MRW's model by introducing health capital and the average annual ratio of gross domestic expenditure on research and development to nominal GDP, respectively. The correlations between the logarithm of this variable and the logarithms of wages and profit rates are 0.811 and −0.768, respectively. It is not surprising that the addition of this variable to the MRW specification improved the fit of the model as they found a 'good' proxy for $B(t)$, although the savings rate, the proxy for human capital, and the growth rate of employment plus technology and depreciation, were statistically insignificant. This is because Nonneman and Vanhoudt used $\ln(n + 0.05)$, and thus the log of the weighted average of the growth of the wage and profit rates was poorly approximated (this is also true of the modification of Knowles and Owen).

Islam (1995), on the other hand, used panel estimation and heterogeneous intercepts. The use of individual country dummies also helps to approximate better the identity. Temple (1999) correctly pointed out that the MRW specification lacks robustness. The problem, however, is not that the model is flawed because its goodness of fit varies substantially with the sample of countries. Even the specification given by equation (7.8), derived directly from the identity, may conceivably not give a close fit. It all depends on whether or not the assumptions used (namely, that constant factor shares, TFP (or A), and the capital–output ratio are constant across countries), are approximately correct. It would be possible to find a sample of countries where these do not hold and thus there would be a poor fit to the identity. This would not, however, affect the theoretical argument concerning the problems posed by the underlying identity for the interpretation of the parameters of the model.

Paul Romer (2001) has strong reservations (from a methodological point of view) about this research programme. In essence, Romer argues that what this programme has done is to advocate a narrow methodology based on model testing and on using strong theoretical priors with a view to restricting attention to a very small subset of all possible models:

> [It shows] that one of the models from within this narrow set fits the data and, if possible, show[s] that there are other models that do not. Having tested and rejected some models so that the exercise looks like it has some statistical power, accept the model that fits the data as a 'good model'. (p. 226)

Romer is correct in his assessment that MRW never considered alternative models. For example, the finding of a negative coefficient for the initial income variable is interpreted, in the context of the neoclassical model, as evidence of diminishing returns to capital. But, as Romer argues, this finding could also be interpreted as implying that the technology of the country that starts at a lower level of development is lower and it grows faster as better technology diffuses there. Romer claims that MRW's approach does not advance science and refers to it as a dead end.

We close this section by quoting Solow (1994) in reference to this research programme:

The temptation of wishful thinking hovers over the interpretation of these cross-section studies. It should be countered by cheerful skepticism. The introduction of a wide range of explanatory variables has the advantage of offering partial shelter from the bias due to omitted variables. But this protection is paid for. As the range of explanation broadens, it becomes harder and harder to believe in an underlying structural, reversible relation that amounts to more than a sly way of saying that Japan grew rapidly and the United Kingdom slowly during this period. (p. 51)

THE CONVERGENCE REGRESSION AND THE SPEED OF CONVERGENCE

The steady-state growth rate of per capita output in the standard Solow growth model is independent of the savings ratio and population growth rates. Therefore, the model does not provide explanations of the differences in the long-run per capita growth. The model, however, has some important implications about transitional dynamics. This transition shows how an economy's per capita income converges towards its own steady-state value, and thus it provides an explanation for the observed differences in growth rates across countries. In simple terms, this explanation is that poor countries tend to grow faster than rich countries. The neoclassical growth model predicts that an economy that begins with a stock of capital per worker below its steady-state value will experience faster growth in per capita output along the transition path than a country that has already reached its steady-state per capita output.

It is necessary to consider the implications of the arguments in the previous section for the estimates of the speed of convergence given by the MRW specification. One of the main points MRW stressed in their paper was that Solow's growth model predicts conditional, not absolute, convergence. The speed of convergence, denoted by ξ, measures how quickly a deviation from the steady-state growth rate is corrected over time. In other words, it indicates the percentage of the deviation from steady state that is eliminated each year. When MRW tested the conditional convergence hypothesis, they found that indeed it occurs, but the rate implied by Solow's model is much faster than the rate that the convergence regressions indicate. A number of studies, including MRW's, have found evidence of conditional convergence at a rate of about 2 per cent per year. That is, each country moves 2 per cent closer to its own steady state each year (Mankiw, 1995, p. 285). This implies that the economy moves halfway to steady state in about 35 years. On the other hand, it can be shown that the speed of convergence according to Solow's model equals $\xi = (n + \delta + g)\alpha$ (Barro and Sala-i-Martin, 1995, pp. 36–8; Mankiw, 1995, p. 285). Using the averages in our dataset (we assume $\delta = 0.02$), ξ equals $(0.01 + 0.02 + 0.021)*0.768$, or 3.91 per cent per year, almost twice the rate of the estimate of most other studies.

The convergence regression is derived by taking an approximation around the steady state (Mankiw, 1995). Empirically, ξ is estimated through a regression of the difference in income per capita between the final and initial periods on the same regressors as previously used (that is, savings rate and the sum of the growth rate of employment, depreciation rate and technology), plus the log-level of income per capita in the initial period. The coefficient of the initial income variable (τ) is a function of the speed of convergence, namely, $\tau = -(1 - e^{-\xi T})$ (MRW, 1992, p. 423). In the neoclassical model, this equation is:

$$(\ln y_t - \ln y_0) = gT + (1 - e^{-\xi T})\ln A_0 + (1 - e^{-\xi T})\frac{1 - \alpha}{\alpha}\ln s$$
$$- (1 - e^{-\xi T})\frac{1 - \alpha}{\alpha}\ln(n + 0.05) + \tau \ln y_0 + \varepsilon, \quad (7.14)$$

where y_t and y_0 are the levels of income per worker in 1985 and 1960, respectively, and the expression $gT + (1 - e^{-\xi T})\ln A_0$ is assumed to be constant across countries. Here T is the length of the period under consideration.

Estimation results of equation (7.14) are reported below:

$$\ln y_t - \ln y_0 = 2.646 + 0.447\ln s - 0.649\ln(n+0.05) - 0.352\ln y_0 \quad R^2 = 0.666$$
$$(2.40) \quad (2.75) \quad (-2.04) \quad (-5.86) \quad SER = 0.141.$$

The implied shares of capital from the regression coefficients are 0.559 (t-value of 5.83) and 0.648 (5.56).

The results are close to those of MRW (Table IV), with a very similar speed of convergence, slightly below 2 per cent a year. The speed of convergence is derived from the last coefficient, that is, $\tau = -(1 - e^{-\xi T})$. Once ξ is determined, the implied capital share is obtained from the other coefficients. Note that the traditional MRW is misspecified to the extent that ξ is a function of n, population growth (p. 422) which varies between countries. Hence ξ also varies. In our reformulation ξ also varies to the extent that g now varies. However, we merely follow the traditional approach here.

What do our arguments imply for the convergence regression and the speed of convergence? In terms of equation (7.8) above, this specification can be derived by subtracting the logarithm of income per capita in the initial period from both sides of the equation. This yields:

$$(\ln y_t - \ln y_0) = c + 1.0 \ln w + \frac{1-a}{a} \ln r + \frac{1-a}{a} \ln s - \frac{1-a}{a} \ln \left[n + \delta \right.$$

$$\left. + \frac{a\hat{w} + (1-a)\hat{r}}{a} \right] + \tau \ln y_0. \tag{7.15}$$

Equation (7.15) indicates that the parameter of $\ln y_0$ has to be $\tau = -1$ (that is, the estimate obtained is minus unity). Our argument indicates that since equation (7.15) is essentially an identity with the assumptions of a constant growth rate of the capital–output ratio, subtraction of $\ln y_0$ on both sides implies that the estimate of $\ln y_0$ will be minus one.

The results of estimating equation (7.15) are:

$$(\ln y_t - \ln y_0) = 1.121 \ln w + 0.814 \ln r + 0.829 \ln s - 0.799 \ln (n + 0.02 + g) - 1.154 \ln y_0$$
$$ (5.58) \qquad (2.67) \qquad (3.03) \qquad (-3.21) \qquad\qquad (-4.62)$$

$$\overline{R}^2 = 0.580 \quad SER = 0.158.$$

The implied share of capital ranges from 0.444 (t-value equals 5.78) to 0.453 (5.54).

These results provide a very different picture of the convergence discussion. The findings for τ are as predicted, and the rest of the parameters continue being well determined in terms of size and sign (and the restrictions on the parameters are not rejected).

If this equation were to be interpreted as being the neoclassical growth model, the results imply that $\tau = -(1 - e^{-\xi T}) = -1$, or $\xi = \infty$ (under the null hypothesis that $\tau = -1$). Equation (7.15) is based on the assumption of a constant growth of the capital–output ratio. However, two points are in order here. First, empirically, the growth of the capital–output ratio is not exactly constant in the dataset – the statistical fit is not perfect. Second, under the neoclassical assumption, theoretically the estimate of ξ should be a constant and equal to $\xi = (n + \delta + g)\alpha$ regardless of how near the economies are to their steady-state growth rate. If all the economies are growing at their steady-state growth rate, then the speed of convergence is not infinite but undefined as:

$$\hat{y}_t = g + \alpha(\delta + n + g)(\ln y_t^* - \ln y_t), \tag{7.16}$$

where the superscript * denotes the steady-level of per capita income and in the steady-state $\ln y_t = \ln y_t^*$. But, as we have seen, with differences in technical progress allowed for and a roughly constant growth in the capital–output ratio, the identity will always give this result. The only reason why the conventional estimates are greater than minus unity is due to the assumption imposed on the model of a rate of technical change and level of technology that do not vary between countries. It should be emphasised that if there is no well-behaved aggregate production function and all we are estimating is an identity, then there is no reason why τ should be a measure of the speed of convergence.

CONCLUSIONS: WHAT REMAINS OF SOLOW'S GROWTH MODEL?

Why are some countries richer than others? Is the neoclassical growth model, based on an aggregate production function, a useful theory of economic growth? This chapter has evaluated whether the predictions of Solow's growth model – namely, that the higher the rate of saving, the richer the country; and the higher the rate of population growth, the poorer the country – can be tested and potentially refuted in the framework of MRW.

We have shown that a form identical to that used by MRW can be derived by simply transforming the income accounting identity that relates output to the sum of the total wage bill plus total profits. To do this only requires the assumptions that factor shares and the capital–output ratio are constant. This has allowed us to question whether Solow's growth model can be tested in the sense of allowing its refutation.

It has been argued that the key to understanding the results discussed in the literature lies in the assumption of a common level of technology and rate of technical progress across countries. Although this assumption has been discussed in the literature, the important point has been overlooked that all that is being estimated is an approximation to an accounting identity. From this point of view, the assumption of a common rate of technological progress amounts to treating the weighted average of the logarithm of the wage and profit rates that appears in the accounting identity as a constant across countries. The form derived from the accounting identity explicitly incorporating differences in growth of the weighted average of the wage and profit rates and using only two assumptions (constant shares and a constant capital–output ratio) is so close to the identity itself that it explains most of the variation in income per capita in the OECD countries. Moreover, if shares are sufficiently constant, this is sufficient to give a relationship that will explain the variation across countries in the level of productivity.

MRW's original regression, on the other hand, explained only 1 per cent. It has been argued that MRW's equation imposes on the identity the empirically incorrect assumptions that the weighted average of the wage and profit rates and the weighted average of the growth rates of the wage and profit rates are constant across countries. The fact that this gives a less-than-perfect statistical fit may give the impression that a behavioural regression, rather than an identity, is actually being estimated. Once these two assumptions are relaxed the identity, or a good approximation to it, guarantees a good statistical fit, where the implicit values of the output elasticities are very close to the respective factor shares. The estimate of the coefficient of the savings rate must be positive and that of the sum of employment and technology growth rates must be negative. All this is solely the result of the accounting identity.

The conditional convergence equation discussed in the literature is also affected by our arguments. It has been shown that once the weighted average of the wage and profit rates is properly introduced, the 'identity' predicts that the speed of convergence, under neoclassical assumptions, must be infinite or alternatively interpreted as undefined.

The conclusion that has to be drawn is that the predictions of Solow's growth model cannot be refuted econometrically, at least in MRW's framework. In view of the above findings, it is difficult to end on an optimistic note. This neoclassical framework does not, in our opinion, help answer the central question of why some countries are richer than others. The implications of our discussion, therefore, go far beyond a mere critique or a proposal for improvement in the estimation and testing of the neoclassical growth model. The problem discussed is far more fundamental than that of the necessity for a further augmentation of Solow's model, or the use of more appropriate econometric techniques.

From the policy perspective (Rashid 2000; Kenny and Williams, 2001), the argument implies that we cannot measure the impact of standard growth policies, for example, the effect of an increase in the savings rate on income per capita. However, these arguments should not be taken as implying that a country's income level is not, in some sense, related to savings and investment, population growth and technology, any more than that the production of an individual commodity is not related to the volume of inputs used, just because an aggregate production function cannot theoretically exist.

The arguments in the chapter should not be misconstrued either as a claim that any regression explaining income per capita is futile because, one way or another, the right-hand-side variables (for example, countries' latitude) are proxying the right-hand-side variables of the income accounting identity. The same applies to the convergence literature, that is, studying whether historically countries have tended to converge is an important issue (the notion of sigma convergence is not affected by our arguments). And a regression of growth rates on initial income (and perhaps other variables) certainly says something. But care is needed in the interpretation of the coefficients. The technology gap approach, for example, posits that the rate of productivity growth of a country is inversely related to the technological level of the country. Important factors in this paradigm are the catch-up process and the country's ability to mobilise resources for transforming social, institutional and economic structures. (See Fagerberg, 1987.)

What has to be inferred is that the neoclassical growth model, as formulated in Solow's and MRW's specifications and derived from an aggregate production function, is not the appropriate place to start any discussion about growth, development and convergence. And the argument casts doubt on whether the growth rates of the labour and capital input, each weighted by its factor share, can be regarded as the 'contribution' of the factor inputs to the growth of output in a causal sense.

8. Some problems with the neoclassical dual-sector growth model

INTRODUCTION[1]

In a seminal article, 'On Exports and Economic Growth', Feder (1982) attempted to develop a two-sector model of economic growth. He extended the neoclassical production function approach explicitly to allow for a dual economy (namely, exports and the 'rest of the economy') in the less developed countries (LDCs). This approach was later extended by others to include additional sectors, including defence and government services and the model was also applied to the advanced countries (ACs). Here we extend and develop an argument first noted by Sheehey (1990). It is shown that these models are deeply flawed and cannot support the interpretation placed upon them. It will come as no surprise that the problem of identities crops up again.

Feder started from the observation that there is often a close correlation between the growth of GDP and exports, which he interpreted as the latter causing the former. One explanation of this relationship is that it represents the effect of the balance-of-payments constraint working through the Hicks super-multiplier (McCombie and Thirlwall, 1994).

However, Feder proposed a supply-side, rather than a demand-oriented, explanation, and one which is quite independent of the existence of a balance-of-payments constraint. His approach dichotomises the economy into the export sector and the rest of the economy. The basic premise is that the LDCs are essentially in disequilibrium, with the marginal products of capital and labour being higher in the export sector than elsewhere in the economy. This is because it is held that the export sector is more advanced and commercialised than the rest of the economy and so factor inputs are used there more efficiently. Consequently, as the export sector expands and factors are transferred to it from the rest of the economy, so there will be a gain in both output and total factor productivity (TFP). The loss in production in the rest of the economy as a unit of a factor of production is withdrawn from this sector is more than offset by the gain in output obtained by using this resource in the

---

[1] This draws on McCombie (1999).

export sector. Moreover, the export sector itself will also raise productivity in the rest of the economy by providing a gateway for modernising techniques and attitudes that will raise the level of efficiency outside the export sector.

Consequently, the growth of the export sector exerts a positive externality on the rest of the economy. It is an externality as the effect is not reflected in market prices. Feder specified a model (discussed below) to test these effects and estimated this using cross-country data for a number of LDCs. On the basis of these regression results, Feder (1982, p. 71) reaches the important conclusion:

> [T]he success of economies which adopt export-oriented policies is due, at least partially, to the fact that such policies bring the economy closer to an optimal allocation of resources. The estimates show that there are, on average, substantial differences in marginal factor productivities between export and non-export sectors.

It was quickly realised that this methodology could be adapted putatively to test the role of other key sectors in the economic growth process. Most notably, Ram (1986) published an influential study that considered the impact of the growth of government expenditure, rather than exports, on economic growth of both the ACs and the LDCs. While he extended the approach to include time-series regression analysis, the basic framework remained that of Feder.

Ram's study attracted a great deal of attention because the conclusions he drew from the regression results were at variance with the orthodox view of the detrimental impact of government expenditure on economic growth. The conventional wisdom is that government goods and services are inherently inefficiently produced and 'crowd out' private sector investment and that high tax rates reduce incentives and distort the price mechanism, thereby further reducing the growth rate. Therefore, at first glance, it was perhaps surprising that Ram should find that the growth of government expenditure had a positive externality effect on the growth of GDP and, furthermore, the marginal factor productivities were higher in the government, as opposed to the private, sector:[2]

---

[2]   Landau (1983), for example, found that the larger the share of government expenditure in GDP, the lower the growth rate of GDP per capita. Thus, an *increase* in the share of government expenditure *reduces* the rate of growth of GDP. As we shall see, the reason for these different statistical results is that Landau uses the ratio of government expenditure to output as a regressor whereas Ram uses some function of the growth of government expenditure. Consequently, the conclusion drawn depends crucially upon whether shares or growth rates are used.

> The main result [of the study] is that it is difficult not to conclude that govern-
> ment size has a positive effect on economic performance and growth, and the
> conclusion appears to apply in a vast majority of settings considered. Even
> more interesting seems to be the nearly equally pervasive indication of a
> positive externality effect of government size on the rest of the economy. (Ram,
> 1986, p. 202)

While this approach has not been without its critics (for example, Carr, 1989; Rao, 1989), it has given rise to a number of other studies along similar methodological lines (Biswas and Ram, 1985; Ram, 1987; Grossman, 1988, 1990; Kohli and Singh, 1989; and Alexander, 1990, 1994). However, as noted above, it will be shown that the whole approach is misconceived and cannot shed any light whatsoever on the issue of the importance of the determinants of economic growth. The reason for this is the presence of two underlying accounting identities on which these models are implicitly based.

FEDER'S MODEL

It is useful to begin by outlining Feder's model. In the simplest version, the economy is divided into two sectors and the output of each sector is denoted by V_1 and V_2. Production in the latter sector is assumed to have an externality effect on the output of the former, for the reasons set out above. It is assumed that each sector may be represented by a well-behaved production function of the form:

$$V_1 = F(L_1, J_1, V_2) \tag{8.1}$$

and

$$V_2 = G(L_2, J_2,). \tag{8.2}$$

For expositional ease, technical change is ignored for the moment. The model can also be specified so V_1 has an externality effect on V_2. As we have noted, in the two pioneering studies, the sectors were taken as either non-exports and exports (Feder, 1982) or the private sector and government services (expenditure) (Ram, 1986). Ram merely applies Feder's model using government expenditure in place of exports. Of course, if both exports and government services are thought to play an important role in economic growth, there is nothing to stop a three-sector model from being specified where, for example, V_3 has an externality effect on V_2 and both have an externality effect on V_1:

$$V_1 = F'(L_1, J_1, V_2, V_3), \qquad (8.3)$$

$$V_2 = G'(L_2, J_2, V_3), \qquad (8.4)$$

$$V_3 = H'(L_3, J_3). \qquad (8.5)$$

Alexander (1994) extends the Feder model in this fashion, using equations (8.3) to (8.5), where V_1, V_2 and V_3 are the rest of the economy, exports and government services. The model can be generalised to include any number of sectors (subject only to having sufficient degrees of freedom). A sector that has also been commonly included is defence (see Biswas and Ram, 1985; Alexander, 1990). However, one can think of a number of other sectors, such as manufacturing, as suitable candidates. Apart from the externality effect, we have noted that the effect of differing marginal productivities between the various sectors may also have a positive effect on growth if the sectors with the highest productivity growth rates are the fastest-growing sectors. Confining our attention to the two-sector model (equations (8.1) and (8.2)), Feder (and Ram) assume that the marginal productivities of capital and labour differ between sectors by the same amount (although there is no a priori reason to believe that this is necessarily the case), that is,

$$G_J = (1 + \chi)F_J, \qquad (8.6)$$

$$G_L = (1 + \chi)F_L, \qquad (8.7)$$

where $\chi > 0$. Consequently, the marginal productivities of labour and capital in the second sector (which, it will be recalled, is either exports or government services) each exceed those of the rest of the economy by the same proportion. This is a limitation of the analysis, especially when cross-country data are used, because it implies that this proportion is the same for every country, no matter what its level of development. Feder, consequently, regards the estimate of χ, derived from the reduced form of the model (discussed below) merely as some average value for the LDCs. Equations (8.6) and (8.7) suggest that if $\chi > 0$, there is a misallocation of resources with too little capital and labour being devoted to exports. A problem immediately arose because data limitations meant that it was not possible to estimate specific functional forms for equations (8.1) and (8.2) separately. There were no statistics available for capital and labour at the required sectoral levels.

Nevertheless, Feder circumvented this difficulty by specifying a reduced-form equation for the model that requires data only on output, employment and capital (investment) for the whole economy and output data for the other sectors. To achieve this, equations (8.1) and (8.2) are differentiated with respect to time. Using the identities $\dot{V} \equiv \dot{V}_1 + \dot{V}_2$ (where $\dot{V} = dV/dt$, and so on), $\dot{J} \equiv \dot{J}_1 + \dot{J}_2$ and $\dot{L} \equiv \dot{L}_1 + \dot{L}_2$, together with the assumption that there is a linear relationship between the marginal productivity in a given sector and the average output per worker in the economy, $F_{L_1} = \alpha V_1/L_1$, the following equation is obtained for the growth of total output:

$$\hat{V} = \alpha\hat{L} + F_{J_1}\frac{I}{V} + \left[\frac{\chi}{1+\chi} + F_{V_2}\right]\left(\frac{V_2}{V}\right)\hat{V}_2, \tag{8.8}$$

where $\hat{V}$ is the growth of V, and so on, I/V is the gross investment ratio; F_{J_1} is $\partial F/\partial J_1$, the marginal product of capital in sector one and F_{V_2} is $\partial F/\partial V_2$. Sector one, in Feder's model, is the rest of the economy (non-export sector) and sector two is the export sector.

It is still not possible to obtain separate estimates of χ and F_{V_2} from equation (8.8). Feder consequently derives an alternative specification that enables this to be accomplished by assuming that exports (V_2) affect the production of the rest of the economy with a constant elasticity, γ, that is to say, $V_1 = V_2^\gamma f(L_1, J_1)$. In this case, the growth of total output is given by:

$$\hat{V} = \alpha\hat{L} + F_{J_1}\frac{I}{V} + \left[\frac{\chi}{(1+\chi)} - \gamma\right]\left(\frac{V_2}{V}\right)\hat{V}_2 + \gamma\hat{V}_2, \tag{8.9}$$

Thus, from equation (8.9) it is possible to derive estimates of the marginal productivities differential (χ) and the externality elasticity (γ). While Feder considers this to be a plausible specification, further consideration suggests that this is not in fact the case, since it suggests that exports are a *sine qua non* for non-export production. If $V_2 = 0$ it follows that $V_1 = 0$. While the externality effect may be important for increasing the level of output in the rest of the economy, it is not realistic to postulate that *no* production could take place in a closed economy. Moreover, none of the reasons cited above, which Feder suggests are responsible for the externality, implies that export production is indispensable for production in the rest of the economy. A further problem is the possibility of severe multicollinearity between $\hat{V}_2(V_2/V)$ (or, equivalently, $\dot{V}_2/V$) and $\hat{V}_2$. If V_2 is a constant fraction of V, then there will be perfect multicollinearity and it will not be possible to obtain precise estimates of the coefficients of $\hat{V}_2$ (V_2/V) and $\hat{V}_2$ and hence of χ and γ.

While the share of exports in total output is not exactly the same for all countries, the possibility of problems posed by multicollinearity nevertheless remains. Finally, Feder points out that if $\chi/(1+\chi) = \gamma$ (which would be a remarkable coincidence), the model reduces to:[3]

$$\hat{V} = \alpha\hat{L} + F_{J_1}\left(\frac{I}{V}\right) + \gamma\hat{V}_2. \tag{8.10}$$

To summarise, there are three specifications of the model which can be estimated, namely:

$$\hat{V} = b_0 + b_1\hat{L} + b_2\left(\frac{I}{V}\right) + b_3\left(\frac{V_2}{V}\right)\hat{V}_2, \tag{8.11}$$

$$\hat{V} = b_0 + b_1\hat{L} + b_2\left(\frac{I}{V}\right) + b_4\hat{V}_2, \tag{8.12}$$

$$\hat{V} = b_0 + b_1\hat{L} + b_2\left(\frac{I}{V}\right) + b_3\left(\frac{V_2}{V}\right)\hat{V}_2 + b_5\hat{V}_2, \tag{8.13}$$

where b_0 is a constant and supposedly captures the rate of exogenous technical progress.

In Table 8.1, we reproduce a selection of the more important results from Feder's and Ram's studies, together with some results from a comment on Ram by Rao (1989). However, before discussing these results, it is necessary to mention briefly some criticisms common to all of the studies. First, there is the poor quality of the data which inevitably have large measurement errors, especially for the LDCs. Capital input, for example, is proxied by the gross investment–output ratio. Under normal neoclassical assumptions, there should be a deduction for scrapping (if we assume a 'one hoss shay') or for depreciation (if we assume economic loss and physical wear and tear occurs over the life of the asset).

The use of the gross investment–output ratio as the correct measure of the growth of capital input has been advocated by Scott (1989), but this is a very controversial proposition.[4] None of the studies provides an explicit

---

[3]   This is similar to a number of models where exports are hypothesised to exert an externality effect directly on *total* output. In other words, the aggregate production function takes the form $V = f(L, J, X)$, rather than $V_1 = F(L_1, J_1, X)$ where X is exports. (See, for example, Sheehey (1990, p. 112) and the references that are cited there.) There is a problem of equifinality here as it is not possible to distinguish between the two models. (See also Ram, 1986, footnote 5, p. 193.)

[4]   Scott (1989) argues that depreciation of capital equipment is largely due to obsolescence, rather than physical wear and tear. This obsolescence is a price effect due to the increase in the relative price of labour over time. However, since the effect of the latter is

*Table 8.1   Selected regression results from Feder (1982), Ram (1986)
and Rao (1989). Dependent variable, growth of output ($\hat{V}$)*

(A) Study: Feder (1982, Tables 1 and 3), Semi-industrialised Countries, 1964–73

Constant		$\hat{L}$	I/V	$(X/V)\hat{X}$	$\hat{X}$	$\bar{R}^2$	n
(a)	−0.010	0.739	0.284	–	–	0.370	31
	(−0.55)	(1.99)	(4.31)				
(b)	0.002	0.747	0.178	0.422	–	0.689	31
	(0.18)	(2.86)	(3.54)	(5.45)			
(c)	0.006	0.696	0.124	0.305	0.131	0.809	31
	(0.60)	(3.40)	(3.01)	(4.57)	(4.24)		

(B) Studies: Ram (1986), All Less Developed Countries and Advanced Countries, 1960–70 and Rao (1989), Less Developed Countries and Advanced Countries Separately, 1960–70

Constant		$\hat{L}$	I/V	$(G/V)\hat{G}$	$\hat{G}$	$\bar{R}^2$	n
Ram (1986)							
(d)	n.a.	0.517	0.118	1.286	–	0.33	115
		(2.49)	(4.96)	(4.63)			
(e)	n.a.	0.551	0.114	–	0.226	0.34	115
		(2.69)	(4.79)		(4.77)		
(f)	n.a.	0.504	0.114	0.672	0.139	0.35	115
		(2.45)	(4.81)	(1.59)	(1.92)		
Rao (1989)							
Less developed countries							
(g)	n.a.	0.398	0.127	1.284	–	0.368	94
		(1.63)	(4.35)	(4.31)			
Advanced countries							
(h)	n.a	−0.110	0.213	−0.489	–	0.199	21
		(−0.14)	(1.99)	(−0.20)			

Notes:
Figures in parentheses are the *t*-statistics.
G and $\hat{G}$ are the level and growth rate of government expenditure.
n is the number of observations.

Sources: Feder (1982, Table 1, p. 65; Table 3, p. 68); Ram (1986, Table 1, p. 196); Rao (1989, Table 1, p. 275).

---

not taken into account through an allowance for the corresponding appreciation in human capital, obsolescence should *not* be deducted from the capital measure. Scott argues that if this procedure is followed and gross investment is used, the residual in economic growth disappears.

justification for the use of the gross investment ratio along these lines, and presumably it is used simply *faute de mieux*. Second, the growth of total population is used as a proxy for the growth of labour input and it is unnecessary to emphasise just how crude this procedure is, especially for the LDCs where disguised unemployment is likely to be widespread and to differ markedly between countries.

Equation (a) in Table 8.1 (where for ease of exposition we shall use the notation X for V_2, that is, exports) reports the results of what Feder terms the conventional (one-sector) neoclassical model. The coefficient of I/V (the marginal productivity of capital in the non-export sector) is statistically significant although somewhat higher than would be expected from the results of other production function studies. The output elasticity with respect to labour is about three-quarters, which is in accord with other studies (and approximately equal to labour's share, although the standard error is rather large).

Feder (1982, p. 65) considers that the results of equation (b) 'lend strong support to the hypothesis that marginal factor productivities in the export sector are higher than in the non-export sector, as the coefficient of $[(X/V)\hat{X}]$ is positive and significantly different from zero'. Equation (c) shows that the externality parameter (the coefficient of $\hat{X}$) is statistically significant and the estimate of χ (the productivity differential) is approximately equal to 0.75, 'implying that there is a substantial productivity differential between exports and non-exports in addition to the differential due to externalities' (p. 67). (Feder also reports the results of a limited sample excluding those LDCs that are only marginally semi-industrialised. It makes little difference to the results.)

Ram (1986) likewise considers that his regression results provide support for the importance of government expenditure (denoted by G) as a stimulus to overall economic growth. He provides results for 1960–70 and 1970–80, using statistics from the well-known Summers and Heston (1984) dataset for over a hundred countries. For reasons of space, we only report results for 1960–70 (which do not differ greatly from those of the later period). It may be seen from Table 8.1, equations (d) and (e), that the coefficients of both $(G/V)\hat{G}$ and $\hat{G}$ are statistically significant when included separately in the regressions. However, when both regressors are included simultaneously (equation (f)), both are statistically insignificant at the 5 per cent confidence level, although the coefficient of $\hat{G}$ is significant at the 10 per cent confidence level. The insignificance of the coefficient on (G/V) $\hat{G}$ leads Ram to consider that $\chi/(1+\chi)$ equals γ, and to prefer equation (e) in Table 8.1, although as Rao (1989) points out this result is almost certainly due to strong multicollinearity between the two variables.

Rao also shows that while Ram reports results for the LDCs and the

ACs pooled as well as for the LDCs only, he omits results for the ACs considered separately. Rao replicates the study, finding that the regression results for the latter are considerably poorer than those for the LDCs. For example, for equation (h) in Table 8.1, the conventional F-test diagnostic (not reported here) is not statistically significant even at the 10 per cent confidence level. Ram's (1989, p. 282) rejoinder to this criticism is simply that the 'estimates for the ACs have no relevance to the main issue' which, may, of course, lead us to wonder why he considered them in the first place. On the basis of both cross-sectional and time-series regression results for individual countries, Ram concludes that the results generally provide strong support for the contention that the growth of government expenditure has a positive effect on the growth of output. Moreover, he considers that this procedure uses a 'reasonably defensible theoretical framework' (Ram, 1986, p. 202). We now address this highly questionable assertion.

EXTERNALITIES AND THE SECTORAL OUTPUT IDENTITY

Ram's view is debatable because there are *two* identities underlying the various specifications given by equations (8.11) to (8.13) which preclude giving the regression results any economic or behavioural interpretation along the lines of Feder and Ram. The specifications are merely hybrids of two underlying identities, subject to omitted variable bias. (For this reason, the various misspecification and causality tests, together with the other usual statistical diagnostics that Ram and Rao report, are not discussed.) The first problem is posed by the accounting identity discussed in earlier chapters that underlies the production function, namely, with the usual notation, $V \equiv wL + rJ$. As we have seen, under the assumptions that factor shares are constant and the weighted growth of the wage rate and the rate of profit is also relatively constant (or the growth of the rate of profit is zero and the growth of the wage rate is constant), this will be closely approximated by $V = A_0 e^{\lambda t} L^a J^{(1-a)}$ where $\lambda \equiv a\hat{w} + (1 - a)\hat{r}$. The identity may also be written in growth rate form as:

$$\hat{V} \equiv \lambda + a\hat{L} + r \dot{J}/V, \tag{8.14}$$

with the usual notation, and where, as we have noted, the net accumulation of capital, $\dot{J} = dJ/dt$, is proxied in empirical work by I, gross investment. It should be noted, however, that $a\hat{w} + (1-a)\hat{r}$, the weighted sum of the growth of real wages and the rate of profit, is likely to vary across countries and so the intercept obtained by estimating the Cobb–Douglas relationship in growth-rate form using cross-country data should be regarded as reflecting some average value.

The other identity underlying the regression analysis may be written as:

$$\hat{V} \equiv \Sigma \omega_i \hat{V}_i, \tag{8.15}$$

where ω_i is the share of V_i in total output, V, that is, $\omega_i = V_i/V$.

In the case of only two sectors, this may be expressed as:

$$\hat{V} \equiv \left(\frac{V_1}{V}\right)\hat{V}_1 + \left(\frac{V_2}{V}\right)\hat{V}_2, \tag{8.16}$$

where V_1 is the 'rest of the economy' and V_2 is, say, either exports or government expenditure depending upon the sector of interest.

Recall equations (8.11) to (8.13) where we considered the case where there was only one sector with a supposed externality effect and/or a productivity differential compared with the rest of the economy. It can be seen that the equations are essentially a hybrid of these two identities, namely, equations (8.14) and (8.16).

It can be seen from the identity given by equation (8.14) that b_1 in equations (8.11) to (8.13) will be approximately equal to a (labour's share in output) and take some value between 0.50 and 0.75. The estimate of b_2 will be approximately equal to r which is normally likely to be between 0.1 and 0.2. If the fit is not exact so there is not perfect multicollinearity, then from identity given by equation (8.16) it can be seen that the coefficient of $(V_2/V)\hat{V}_2$ (that is, b_3), when not biased by the omission of $\hat{V}_1$, will be approximately equal to unity; and the coefficient of $\hat{V}_2$ (that is, b_4) in equation (8.12), when unbiased, will be approximately equal to V_2/V. We have seen that the argument can be generalised to any number of sectors.[5]

There are two important qualifications to the preceding argument that all we are doing is estimating a hybrid of two identities, neither of which diminishes its importance. The first qualification is that when the specifications are estimated using cross-country data the individual shares ω_i are likely to vary between countries, thus reducing the goodness of fit in equation (8.12) as the estimated coefficient b_4 will merely reflect the (possibly biased) average share. Indeed, we need each identity *not* to hold exactly

---

[5]   The position is a little more complicated in equation (8.13), but we would expect $b_3(V_2/V) + b_5$, when unbiased, to be approximately equal to V_2/V.

for the estimates of the individual coefficients to reflect the parameters of the two underlying identities. If one identity holds precisely, then the coefficients of the other identity are likely to be statistically insignificant and/or the equation will be subject to severe multicollinearity.

There is also the question of unbiasedness, which brings us to the second point. The rest of the economy (appropriately defined, depending upon the other regressors) does not appear in any of the specifications given by equations (8.11) to (8.13). Thus, unless the growth of the rest of the economy is orthogonal to the other regressors, the latter will suffer from omitted variable bias.

Let us consider, for example, equation (8.11), where V_2 is some as yet unspecified sector. We can determine the approximate degree of bias as follows from equation (8.16). The auxiliary regression of the weighted growth of the 'rest of the economy' V_1 on that of V_2 is given by:[6]

$$\left(\frac{V_1}{V}\right)\hat{V}_1 = c_0 + c_1\left(\frac{V_2}{V}\right)\hat{V}_2. \tag{8.17}$$

The 'biased' estimated of b_3 in equation (8.11) due to the omission of $(V_1/V)\hat{V}_1$ is $b_3 = c_1 + b'_3$ where $b'_3 = 1.0$. If there is no close relationship between $(V_1/V)\hat{V}_1$ and $(V_2/V)\hat{V}_2$ then we should expect a highly significant estimate of b_3 with a value of around unity.

Next consider again equation (8.12), namely, $\hat{V} = b_0 + b_1\hat{L} + b_2 (I/V) + b_4\hat{V}_2$. If the auxiliary regression between the growth of the rest of the economy (V_1) and that of the sector under consideration (V_2) is given by:

$$\hat{V}_1 = d_0 + d_1\hat{V}_2, \tag{8.18}$$

the biased estimate of the share of V_2 in GDP will be given by $b_4 = (V_1/V)d_1 + b'_4$ where b'_4 is the true value, which will be approximately equal to V_2/V. We can gain some idea of the likely degree of bias. Consider, for example, the land- and resource-based industries, namely, agriculture and mining. For the ACs, it is likely that the growth of these is largely independent of the growth of GDP. Hence, the relationship between their growth rates and the growth of the rest of the economy is likely to be orthogonal. If this is the case, the estimated coefficients (b_4)

---

[6]   For expositional convenience, we have omitted the other regressors ($\hat{L}$ and I/V) that should be included in the auxiliary regression.

are likely to take the average values of their sectoral shares (10 and 2 per cent respectively, for the ACs).

On the other hand, consider a sector such as commerce. It is likely that in this case the growth rate will be highly correlated with the growth of the rest of the economy. In other words, a fast-growing economy is likely to have a fast-growing demand for commercial services, while the converse is also likely to be true. If, for example, the growth of commerce is the same rate as the growth of the rest of the economy for our sample of countries, then the coefficient b_4 will be equal to unity. Under the Feder/Ram interpretation, this would indicate a substantial externality/productivity differential effect. The irony is that as we add more and more sectors to the model, we know a priori that the value of the estimated coefficient will converge to the value of its sectoral share. This is because the share of the rest of the economy (ω_z) becomes progressively smaller, the more sectors we add. In other words, the more sectors that are included, the smaller ω_z will be and, *ceteris paribus*, the less the degree of omitted variable bias resulting from not including $\hat{V}_1$ in the identity. Indeed, the more sectors that are included, the more the coefficients will approximate the (positive) value of the sectoral shares and the greater the temptation, following Feder and Ram, to ascribe this to a positive externality effect.

The auxiliary regressions, equations (8.17) and (8.18) do convey some additional information, apart from that already known from the identity; namely, the relationship between the weighted or unweighted growth rates of the two separate components of GDP. But this may be merely coincidental or may be due to differences in the growth of demand (through differing income elasticities). It does not necessarily have anything to do with differences in sectoral productivities or externalities, *pace* Feder and Ram.

As we have noted, some of these arguments were first broached by Sheehey (1990) for the two-sector model, who finds that the growth rates, over the 1960–70 period, of the following sectors and GDP for 36 countries have a significant Spearman rank correlation coefficient: exports (0.482); government consumption (0.328); private consumption (0.724); investment (0.374); agriculture (0.502); manufacturing (0.616); construction (0.407); electricity, gas and water (0.456); and services (0.447). Consequently, the strong empirical link between export or government expenditure growth and GDP growth is found in other sectors. Sheehey also casts doubt on the neoclassical interpretation of the regression results, although he overlooks the existence of the accounting identity, as he still refers to the Feder model as consisting of 'production function regressions'.

Table 8.2   Regressions with two sectors, advanced countries, 1950–70

Estimating equation: $\hat{V} = b_0 + b_1\hat{L} + b_2(I/V) + b_4\hat{V}_i$

Sector i	b_4	(t-value)	$\bar{R}^2$	Av. share
Agriculture	0.129	(1.43)	0.239	0.09
Mining	0.058	(0.20)	0.224	0.02
Manufacturing	0.536	(14.62)	0.889	0.33
Construction	0.267	(5.65)	0.544	0.07
Public Utilities	0.078	(1.43)	0.239	0.02
Transportation	0.352	(3.09)	0.370	0.08
Commerce	0.511	(6.95)	0.661	0.13
Other services	0.605	(3.01)	0.604	0.23

Notes:
The estimates of b_0, b_1, b_2 are omitted for reasons of space.
Av. share is the average share for the 12 advanced countries of the sector in GDP

Source: Cripps and Tarling (1973).

Table 8.2 reports a similar exercise using data for the 12 ACs, where only one sector is assumed to have an externality effect, as in equation (8.11).[7] It can be seen that all of the estimated coefficients are positive (although agriculture, mining and public utilities are statistically insignificant), but do not differ greatly from their share values. Manufacturing, construction, transportation, commerce and other services greatly exceed their share values. The reason for this is not hard to find. We are using cross-country data and so there is likely to be a strong positive correlation between the rest of the economy and the sector under consideration, to the extent that the fast-growing countries (such as Japan) tend to have fast growth in all their sectors whereas the laggards (such as the UK) tend to grow slowly across the board. Thus, omitting the growth of the rest of the economy will bias upwards the estimated coefficient of the remaining sector. However, as we have noted above, the statistically significant and large regression coefficients cannot be taken as independent evidence of the existence of externalities and/or differences in marginal productivities.

---

[7]   We use the period from 1950 to 1970, which is not important as we are making a general point, as this period gives the greatest variation in the growth rates of the industrialised countries.

Table 8.3   *Percentage shares of government expenditure, exports and the rest of the economy, advanced countries*

Country	Year	Government expenditure	Exports	Rest of the economy
Japan	1961	14.5	6.3	79.2
West Germany	1961	16.9	18.1	65.0
Italy	1959	15.3	9.3	75.4
France	1960	15.2	7.8	73.0
Netherlands	1960	15.2	34.8	50.0
Denmark	1962	20.3	23.3	56.4
Austria	1961	18.9	20.5	60.6
Canada	1966	18.9	21.2	60.0
Norway	1960	14.4	33.4	52.2
Belgium	1964	15.4	33.1	51.5
US	1966	20.3	6.0	73.7
UK	1960	21.7	19.4	58.9
Unweighted average		17.3	19.8	63.0

Sources: OECD National Accounts (various years).

The Three-sector Model

Let us consider next the three-sector model where the sectors are the 'rest of the economy' (Z), government output and exports.

Equation (8.16) may be now expressed as:

$$\hat{V} \equiv \left(\frac{Z}{V}\right)\hat{Z} + \left(\frac{G}{V}\right)\hat{G} + \left(\frac{X}{V}\right)\hat{X} \tag{8.19}$$

or

$$\hat{V} \equiv \omega_Z \hat{Z} + \omega_G \hat{G} + \omega_X \hat{X}, \tag{8.20}$$

where Z, G, and X denote the 'rest of the economy', government services and exports.[8]

In the case of a relatively homogeneous group of countries, such as the ACs, the degree of relative variation in the share of government expenditure is likely to be small. (See Table 8.3 for the ACs. The years chosen are

---

[8]   We assume that no government services are exported.

simply the boom years near the middle of the Golden Age of economic growth, although other years present much the same picture.) However, the share of exports shows much greater inter-country variation. The problem of the variation in shares does not, of course, affect the coefficient of $(V_2/V)\,\hat{V}_2$ in equation (8.11) which, when unbiased, will be unity for every country.

Table 8.4 reports some illustrative regressions for 12 advanced countries over the 1950–70 period. The period was chosen merely because it was the Golden Age (although, strictly speaking, this ended in 1973), when there was a great deal of variation in growth rates between the advanced countries. However, since we are demonstrating a theoretical argument, the exact period (and the choice of countries) does not greatly matter.

Let us consider first the specification:

$$\hat{V} = b_0 + b_1\hat{L} + b_2\frac{I}{V} + b_6\left(\frac{Z}{V}\right)\hat{Z} + b_7\left(\frac{G}{V}\right)\hat{G} + b_8\left(\frac{X}{V}\right)\hat{X}, \quad (8.21)$$

where $(Z/V)\hat{Z}$ is usually omitted and as sometimes are either the weighted growth of government services or the weighted growth of exports. The argument concerning the degree of bias follows through, although now the auxiliary equations will differ depending upon the included and excluded variables.

Equation (i) in Table 8.4(A) shows that, not surprisingly, the estimates of the 'production function' are reasonably close to what would be expected a priori from the accounting identity, although the fit is not particularly good. When the two combined identities are estimated (equation (j)), the coefficients of the 'production function' do not prove robust, but the coefficients of the three sectors take their expected values of unity. When either $(G/V)\hat{G}$ or $(X/V)\hat{X}$ is omitted, the coefficients on the remaining sectors remain statistically significant with values often not significantly different from unity. However, it is interesting to note that when $(Z/V)\hat{Z}$ is omitted, the coefficients of both $(G/V)\hat{G}$ and $(X/V)\hat{X}$ become statistically insignificant (equation (m)). This is because there is substantial omitted variable bias as evidenced by the 'auxiliary' regression, equation (n), although it is difficult to give an economic explanation for this relationship. It is best regarded as a statistical artefact.[9] Certainly, equation (m) cannot be taken as a refutation of the hypothesis of the

---

[9]   This result is not robust and the exclusion of, for example, Japan (with a small export share but fast growth rates of exports and the remainder of the economy) significantly affects the regression estimates.

Table 8.4   *Regression results: advanced countries, pooled data, 1950–70.*
Dependent variable, growth of output ($\hat{V}$)

(A)	(i)	(j)	(k)	(l)	(m)	(n)[a]
Constant	−0.282	0.026	0.282	−0.298	−0.204	−0.230
	(−0.22)	(1.03)	(0.49)	(−1.20)	(−0.15)	(−0.17)
$\hat{L}$	0.871	−0.001	0.077	0.172	0.838	0.838
	(3.25)	(−0.14)	(0.53)	(3.02)	(2.79)	(2.78)
I/V	0.174	−0.002	0.079	0.038	0.198	0.200
	(3.70)	(−1.72)	(3.09)	(3.48)	(3.47)	(3.50)
$\omega_Z \hat{Z}$	–	1.001	0.746	0.957	–	–
		(313.60)	(12.76)	(30.93)		
$\omega_G \hat{G}$	–	1.002	0.846	–	−0.335	−1.238
		(137.00)	(2.18)		(−1.09)	(−1.43)
$\omega_X \hat{X}$	–	1.040	–	0.966	−0.198	−1.336
		(60.26)		(13.31)	(−0.23)	(−4.36)
$\overline{R}^2$	0.317	1.000	0.867	0.974	0.304	0.433
SER	1.544	0.030	0.681	0.301	1.559	1.557

(B)	(o)	(p)	(q)	(r)	(s)	(t)[b]
Constant	–	−0.501	−0.086	−1.022	−0.807	−0.621
		(−1.17)	(−0.14)	(−2.10)	(−0.76)	(−0.31)
$\hat{L}$	–	0.050	0.034	0.204	0.636	1.188
		(0.50)	(0.23)	(1.82)	(2.79)	(2.79)
I/V	–	0.048	0.079	0.097	0.083	0.071
		(2.42)	(2.72)	(5.24)	(1.69)	(0.78)
$\hat{Z}$	0.504	0.493	0.580	0.483	–	–
	(14.90)	(13.91)	(11.99)	(11.44)		
$\hat{G}$	0.300	0.202	0.174	–	0.156	−0.094
	(8.55)	(4.09)	(2.40)		(1.27)	(−0.41)
$\hat{X}$	0.205	0.168	–	0.159	0.300	0.266
	(9.82)	(6.64)		(5.28)	(5.11)	(2.44)
$\overline{R}^2$	0.991*	0.932	0.932	0.904	0.581	0.246
SER	0.517	0.486	0.486	0.580	1.210	2.254

Notes:
[a] Dependent variable is $\omega_Z \hat{Z}$; [b] dependent variable is $\hat{Z}$.
Figures in parentheses are the *t*-statistics.
The countries are Austria, Belgium, Canada, Denmark, France, Germany, Italy, Japan,
Netherlands, Norway, US and UK.
* denotes that the R^2 does not have its conventional meaning as there is no constant in the
regression.

Sources: OECD National Accounts (various years).

importance of these sectors in economic growth, any more than statistically significant coefficients can be taken as providing support.

The extended model based on equation (8.12) is given by:

$$\hat{V} = b_0 + b_1\hat{L} + b_2(I/V) + b_7\hat{Z} + b_8\hat{G} + b_9\hat{X}, \qquad (8.22)$$

again usually with $\hat{Z}$ and possibly either $\hat{G}$ or $\hat{X}$ omitted. Notwithstanding the variation in export shares, it may be seen from Table 8.4(B) equation (o) that the regression of $\hat{V} = \omega_Z\hat{Z} + \omega_G\hat{G} + \omega_X\hat{X}$ gives a good fit, although the estimate of the average share of the rest of the economy is on the low side at 50 per cent, whereas that of government expenditure is somewhat high at 30 per cent. The reason for these discrepancies is likely to be the incidence of multicollinearity and it is noteworthy that the sum of the three coefficients is 1.09, which is not significantly different from unity. Estimating the two identities combined (equation (p)) shows that while the coefficients of the production function are again not robust, those of the three sectors are reasonably so. Equations (q), (r) and (s) report the results when one of the sectors is omitted.

It can be seen that although $\hat{Z}$, $\hat{G}$ and $\hat{X}$ are not quite orthogonal, when one variable is dropped from the regression, the coefficients of the remaining two variables are not far removed from their average sector shares, and are therefore positive and statistically significant (with the exception of $\hat{G}$ in equation (s)). Consequently, if we were unaware of the underlying identities, there would be a temptation to assume for any pair of sectors that they exerted a positive externality (with the exception noted above). But, of course, this argument would hold for *all* combinations of pairs of sectors because of the underlying identity. Table 8.4 clearly illustrates that all that is being captured are the sector shares, although subjected to omitted-variable bias. The specification given by equation (8.13) complicates the story somewhat since it includes both $\hat{V}_i$ and $(V_i/V)\hat{V}_i$ and we shall not pursue this case for reasons of space. Nevertheless, it can easily be seen that the identities still preclude any unambiguous economic interpretation of the regression results.

CONCLUSIONS

To summarise, we have examined a methodology that has sought to determine statistically the importance of certain key sectors (especially exports and government services) for the growth of the whole economy. But because of the underlying identities, it has been shown that it is not possible to substantiate the inferences that Feder and Ram have drawn.

The estimates would have been the same even if all the sectors had the same marginal productivities and there were no externality effects at all. It has been argued by Kaldor (1966), Cornwall (1977) and McCombie and Thirlwall (1994), *inter alios*, that a rapid growth of manufacturing will induce fast growth in the rest of the economy. If we were to repeat the above approach using manufacturing in conjunction with, or instead of, government expenditure and exports, we would find significant coefficients that support this hypothesis – but the exercise would be meaningless. Of course, it should be emphasised that the preceding critique does not mean that exports, government expenditures or manufacturing are not of great importance in the growth process. The point is simply that the Feder approach can shed no light on the issue.

9. Is capital special? The role of the growth of capital and its externality effect in economic growth

> Our methodology is a neo-classical one (inspired in the main by Jorgenson et al., 1987) so we are conscious that it will not command universal assent. But we hope that even those who are impatient with growth accounting will find something of value here. After all, to calculate MFP [multi-factor productivity] growth, one must first calculate outputs and inputs, so those who reject our methodology can put our estimates to their own preferred use.
>
> (Oulton and O'Mahony, 1994, p. 3)

INTRODUCTION[1]

One of the weaknesses of the Solow growth model is the fact that it treats the rate of technical change as exogenous and as a public good. The endogenous growth models, as their name suggests, attempted to provide an explanation of the rate of technical progress while remaining within the neoclassical framework, including the use of the aggregate production function. The earliest form of the endogenous growth theory emphasised the particular role of capital accumulation in the growth process. One of the first new growth models, the so-called 'linear-in-K' model or $Q = \Lambda K$ model (where Λ is a constant) assumed that the externalities associated with capital accumulation were so strong that the aggregate output elasticity of K (sometimes interpreted as broad capital) was unity.[2] While this assumption is now generally accepted as being too heroic, it is still hypothesised that capital is special, in that its aggregate output elasticity is greater than its factor share. This is because capital accumulation induces technical change.

The simplest explanation is to assume that firm i has a Cobb–Douglas production function where $Q_{it} = (A_0 e^{\lambda t} L_{it})^\alpha K_{it}^{(1-\alpha)}$ and the output elasticities equal the factor shares, $\alpha = a$ and $(1 - \alpha) = (1 - a)$ where a is

---

[1] This chapter draws on Felipe and McCombie (2009a).
[2] This model is often termed the 'AK model'. We use the expression 'ΛK' to emphasise the fact that Λ is a constant, in contrast to the inclusion of $A(t)$, which is often assumed to grow over time, in the production function.

labour's factor share. The rate of technical change is partly determined at the industry level by the growth of the aggregate capital–labour ratio, for example, through a learning-by-doing process (Arrow, 1962):

$$\lambda = \psi(\hat{K}_t - \hat{L}_t). \tag{9.1}$$

Ignoring aggregation problems and aggregating across firms we obtain

$$(Q/L)_t = A_0^\alpha (K/L)_t^{(1-\alpha+\psi\alpha)}, \tag{9.2}$$

where the output elasticity of capital $(1 - \alpha + \psi\alpha)$ exceeds the capital share $(1 - a)$. Hence, capital plays a more important contribution to the growth of output than its factor share would suggest, given that it has an important externality effect.

The linear-in-K model assumes that $1 - \alpha + \alpha\psi = 1$ which means that there are constant returns to capital (broadly defined) and this is sufficient for capital accumulation to determine the steady-state rate of growth without the need to postulate any exogenous technical change. In other words, the production function is given by

$$Q_t = A_0^\alpha K_t = \Lambda K_t. \tag{9.3}$$

In this chapter we consider Valdés's (1999) and Romer's (1987) tests of the endogenous growth model. Admittedly, both tests are of the 'back-of-the-envelope' variety rather than sophisticated econometric analyses, but notwithstanding (or, perhaps, because of) this, they clearly show the role of the accounting identity in deriving the results.

Valdés considers the linear-in-K model and examines the extent to which data from the US is compatible with it. 'How good are these results?' he asks (1999, p.108); 'They are very accurate indeed'. And 'the "linear-in-K" version of the New (that is, *endogenous*) Theory of Growth is useful' (p.126, emphasis in the original). Given the accounting identity, the results could not be otherwise. (It should be emphasised that, notwithstanding this, Valdés does appreciate the problem of observational equivalence and cites the reservations of Solow (1997)).

Romer (1987) examines the extent to which, in the absence of technical change, the output elasticity of capital exceeds its factor share. While the production functions he examines do not give particularly robust results, he does find that generally capital's output elasticity is about 0.7. We explain why.

We finally turn to two tests of Oulton and O'Mahony (1994) who also test the extent to which 'capital is special'. But contrary to Romer, they find that capital's output elasticity is very close to its factor share and conclude that there is nothing special about the contribution of capital. We again show why this must be the case and reconcile their results with those of Romer.

VALDÉS'S TEST OF THE *AK* MODEL

We first consider Valdés's (1999, pp. 104–7) argument that the linear-in-K, or *AK*, model of Rebelo (1991) gives a very good fit to the data. This case is instructive because, as we have seen, the linear-in-K model is based on different assumptions from those of the augmented Solow model (notably the existence of constant returns to capital alone). It is also interesting to consider this example because, while Solow's growth model identifies technological progress (where the growth of TFP is assumed to provide an estimate of it) with anything that raises factor efficiency, the endogenous growth models, by endogenising technological progress, suggest specific mechanisms for how the growth of total factor productivity ($T\hat{F}P$) occurs within the framework of the model. Technical progress in the standard Solow growth model is exogenous, which implies that it is generated outside the economic realm of the private sector. For example, Romer (1990), the pioneer of the endogenous growth literature, has, however, identified technological progress with increases in the stock of knowledge, determined by economic factors such as resources devoted to R&D. Another possibility is provided by the so-called Schumpeterian endogenous growth models built on the idea that each innovation affects one intermediate sector at a time, and involves winners and losers (Aghion and Howitt, 1998). What all these models have in common is that they provide specific explanations for how $T\hat{F}P$ is determined.

However, we shall see that the reason why the linear-in-K model putatively gives a good fit to the data is, again, that it just reflects the underlying accounting identity. Valdés considers the so-called 'Arrow–Romer' model, given by equations (9.1) to (9.3).

In our notation, as we are using value data,

$$V_t = \Lambda J_t. \tag{9.4}$$

The steady-state growth of productivity (assuming that the rate of depreciation, δ, is constant) is given by:

$$\hat{V}_t - \hat{L}_t = \hat{J}_t - \hat{L}_t = s_J \Lambda - (n + \delta), \tag{9.5}$$

where $n = \hat{L}$ is the growth of the labour input, s_J is the investment ratio, and the growth of output and capital is given by:

$$\hat{V}_t = \hat{J}_t = s_J \Lambda - \delta. \tag{9.6}$$

For the US over the period from 1950 to approximately 1990, Valdés (p. 108) suggests that the following values are plausible:

- The capital–output ratio (J/V) is 2.5, which suggests that $\Lambda = V/J = 0.4$.
- The rate of depreciation is taken as a constant and is given by $\delta = 0.04$.
- Population growth (strictly speaking it should be employment growth, $\hat{L}$) is $n = 0.015$.
- The gross investment ratio (s_J) is 0.187.

It follows from equation (9.5) that:

$$\hat{V}_t - \hat{L}_t = s_J \Lambda - (n + \delta) = 1.98 \text{ per cent per annum}$$

and from equation (9.6) that:

$$\hat{V}_t = s_J \Lambda - \delta = 3.48 \text{ per cent per annum.}[3]$$

As noted above, Valdés (p. 108) asks, and answers, the question 'How good are these results? They are very accurate indeed'. In other words, the predicted growth rates of productivity and output given by the linear-in-K model for the US are almost identical to the actual outcomes over the postwar period.

However, we can show that given the stylised facts that the growth of capital and output are equal and factor shares are constant, the data could not fail to give an accurate prediction. We start with the familiar accounting identity expressed in growth-rate form:

$$\hat{V}_t \equiv a_t \hat{w}_t + (1 - a_t)\hat{r}_t + a_t \hat{L}_t + (1 - a_t)\hat{J}_t. \tag{9.7}$$

If factor shares are constant, $\hat{w}_t = \hat{V}_t - \hat{L}_t$, and, given the stylised fact that $\hat{V}_t = \hat{J}_t$, it follows that $\hat{r}_t = \hat{V}_t - \hat{J}_t = 0$. Consequently, substituting for $\hat{w}$ and $\hat{r}$, the accounting identity becomes simply:

---

[3]   Valdés mistakenly reports 3.25 per cent per annum.

$$\hat{V}_t = \hat{J}_t, \tag{9.8}$$

or, integrating

$$V_t = \Lambda J_t, \tag{9.9}$$

where Λ is the constant of integration.

Thus, the accounting identity with constant factor shares can be transformed into a form that resembles a Cobb–Douglas production function, or given the stylised fact of a constant capital–output ratio, into the linear-in-K model.[4]

Consequently, as

$$s_J\Lambda - \delta \equiv (I_t/V_t)(V_t/J_t) - \delta \equiv (I_t/J_t) - \delta \equiv \hat{J}_t,$$

(where I, it will be recalled, is gross investment) it follows that *if* the growth of output ($\hat{V}$) is equal to the growth of the capital stock, then the definition $\hat{J}_t \equiv s_J\Lambda - \delta$ must also be equal to $\hat{V}$, irrespective of whether the underlying production function is a Cobb–Douglas or linear-in-K; or, more importantly for our purposes, even though an aggregate production function does not exist. Hence, equation (9.5) must give a growth rate of 1.98 per cent per annum and equation (9.6), 3.48 per cent per annum.

Thus, the fact that the growth of productivity and the growth of output are closely approximated by equations (9.5) and (9.6) merely reflects the stylised fact that the growth of output equals the growth of the capital stock. It implies nothing about whether the linear-in-K model outperforms the Solow model or, indeed, whether or not there exists an aggregate production function at all. At the expense of labouring the obvious, consider the identity in growth-rate form. Assuming factor shares and the rate of return are constant (or, equivalently, from the latter, $\hat{V}_t = \hat{J}_t$), we have shown how it may be used to derive the relationship $V_t \equiv \Lambda J_t$, and this is equivalent to deriving it from the Cobb–Douglas. Thus, the data are equally compatible with the conventional neoclassical model or the linear-in-K model. As Romer (1994, p. 10) commented in another context, 'if you are committed to the neoclassical model, the . . . data cannot be made to make you recant. They do not compel you to give up the convenience of a model in which markets are perfect'.

---

[4] It should be obvious that the whole process is tautological. The stylised fact (assumption) that $\hat{V}_t = \hat{J}_t$ itself implies that $V_t = \Lambda J_t$ (where Λ is the constant of integration), the linear-in-K model!

ROMER'S EVIDENCE

Romer (1987) proposed two models with a view to dropping 'the notion of technical change altogether and working with a production function that can be described as a stationary function of measurable inputs' (p. 164). The key feature of these models is that they have production functions with an elasticity of capital of unity.[5] In the first model Romer hypothesised that output (Q, in his notation) is determined through the production function by the inputs of capital (K) and labour (L) and the stock of human knowledge (E), that is, $Q = F(K, L, e)\Omega(E)$, where e is knowledge available only to a firm, whereas E represents the amount of generally available knowledge. If it is assumed that E increases at the same rate as e which in turn increases at the same rate as K, and that F is a Cobb–Douglas production function, then total output can be expressed as $Q_t = AL_t^\alpha K_t^{(1-\alpha+\psi)}$ (Romer's equation (9.5)) where ψ reflects the capital-related externalities. It is hypothesised that $1 - \alpha + \psi = 1$ in order to generate unceasing growth, so that there are constant returns to capital with overall increasing returns. The fact that increasing returns are external to the firm ensures that a competitive equilibrium is preserved.

An alternative to the previous model is to assume, following Adam Smith (1776) and Allyn Young (1928), that the greater the degree of specialisation, or division of labour, the greater, *ceteris paribus*, the level of output. To capture the degree of specialisation, output is specified as a function of the number of specialised capital inputs (rather than just the aggregate volume of the capital stock) as well as of labour. It is assumed that there is a fixed cost in producing the specialised capital goods, otherwise there would simply be an infinite number of them. Romer's production function is $Q_t = AL_t^\alpha K_t$ (Romer's equation (11), although in different notation).

What empirical evidence did Romer provide? First, Romer fitted four Cobb–Douglas production functions to decennial data for the US for the 1890s to the 1970s (Table 1, p. 183, in Romer's paper). These were regressions in growth-rate form. In the first two, Romer did not include the effect of exogenous technical change (that is, no constant term). In both cases the coefficient of capital was close to one and significant, but the coefficients of labour, measured separately as hours worked and the labour force, were insignificant. In the third and fourth regressions,

---

[5] Recall that when the Cobb–Douglas production function was first introduced in the late 1920s, the argument for its validity was that, empirically, the elasticities were close to the factor shares in the national accounts. Lucas (1970) and Fisher (1971b) considered whether an aggregate production function was plausible in these same terms.

Romer included the constant term (technical progress). Then, when he used hours worked to proxy employment, the coefficient (output elasticity) of capital was statistically insignificant, and that of hours worked was significant and large (0.76). When he used the labour force, on the other hand, the coefficient of capital was again large and significant (0.87), but that of the labour force was −0.64, although not statistically significantly different from zero.

Subsequently, Romer used annual data for 1950–84 for Cobb–Douglas production functions in level form (log of output on log of inputs), also with and without technical change (Table 2, p. 185, in Romer's paper). Again, when the time trend (that is, technical progress) was omitted from the regression, the coefficient of capital was very close to one, and that of labour was insignificant. When the trend was allowed, the coefficient of capital became negative. After examining all the regressions in the table, Romer quite rightly concluded that 'it should not be surprising that production function regressions using annual data yield estimates that are ambiguous' (Romer, 1987, p. 186). All in all, the support for Romer's model is pretty weak, as small changes in specification cause important changes in the estimates.

Finally, Romer used longer time periods (1770–1870 to 1950–79) using growth-rate data from Maddison (1982) for the G7 countries. Regression (18) in Romer's paper (p. 193) shows a coefficient on capital of 0.87, not statistically significantly different from one; while the coefficient on the growth rate of hours was statistically insignificant. This was when an intercept was included.

Let us confine ourselves to the general conclusions of Romer and see how the accounting identity can explain them. He argues that 'the tentative conclusion that I draw from this exercise is that the appropriate growth accounting equation is [$\hat{V}_t = \alpha \hat{L}_t + \beta \hat{J}_t$], with values of [$\beta$] likely to fall in the range 0.7 to 1.0 and the values of [α] likely to fall in the range 0.1 to 0.5' (p. 198). As α was considerably below labour's observed share in national income, Romer was forced to provide an *ex post* justification, namely, that there must be a significant negative externality associated with labour (p. 166). Romer accounts for this by suggesting that the rate of labour-saving innovations could be a function of the growth of real wages, and that a faster growth of labour, by depressing the growth of real wages, could lead to a slower rate of innovations. Thus, the effect of an increase in the labour supply has a positive effect in allowing more output to be produced but a negative effect in slowing the rate of innovation.

If we accept the stylised fact that there is no secular growth of the rate of profit and factor shares are roughly constant, then the identity can be written in value terms as:

$$\hat{V}_t \equiv a\hat{w}_t + a\hat{L}_t + (1 - a)\hat{J}_t,$$

which, using the values of factor shares for labour and capital as 0.7 and 0.3, can be written as:

$$\hat{V}_t \equiv 0.7\hat{w}_t + 0.7\hat{L}_t + 0.3\hat{J}_t \tag{9.10}$$

or

$$\hat{V}_t \equiv 0.7(\hat{V}_t - \hat{L}_t) + 0.7\hat{L}_t + 0.3\,\hat{J}_t. \tag{9.11}$$

Romer uses the stylised fact that $\hat{V}_t = \hat{J}_t$. Consequently the identity becomes:

$$\hat{V}_t \equiv 0.7(\hat{J}_t - \hat{L}_t) + 0.7\hat{L}_t + 0.3\,\hat{J}_t. \tag{9.12}$$

What happens if we omit the first term on the left-hand side of equation (9.12) as does Romer? We can see that equation (9.12) can be rewritten as:

$$\hat{V}_t \equiv 0\hat{L}_t + 1.0\hat{J}_t \equiv \hat{J}_t, \tag{9.13}$$

with the coefficients of $\hat{L}$ and $\hat{J}$ taking the orders of magnitude found by Romer. This merely reflects the bias in the estimation of the accounting identity and tells nothing about the contribution that capital and labour make to economic growth in a technological sense determined by an underlying aggregate production function.

OULTON AND O'MAHONY'S TWO TESTS[6]

Oulton and O'Mahony (1994) also tested if the contribution of capital to output growth was special to the extent that its contribution exceeded that of its factor share, as some versions of endogenous growth theory suggest. To do this, they used cross-industry UK manufacturing data expressed in growth rates for over 120 industries at the three-digit Minimum Lists Heading (MLH) and considered the 1954–86 period, broken down into eight subperiods. They used gross output, rather than value added. However, we shall show that the best statistical fit could not fail to find *no* externality effect, which is indeed the result that Oulton and O'Mahony

---

[6]   This draws on Felipe and McCombie (2009a).

find, because of once again the presence of the accounting identity. In this, they came to the opposite conclusion of Romer.

The First Test

Oulton and O'Mahony start with the definition of TFP growth ($T\hat{F}P$) (which they term 'multi-factor productivity growth') 'actually being measured' as:

$$T\hat{F}P_{it} = \hat{Y}_{it} - (\theta_{Lit}\hat{L}_{it} + \theta_{Jit}\hat{J}_{it} + \theta_{Mit}\hat{M}_{it}), \qquad (9.14)$$

where θs are the factor shares, $\hat{Y}$ and $\hat{J}$ denote the growth of gross output (not value added) and the capital stock both measured in constant price monetary values, $\hat{L}$ is the growth of the labour input and $\hat{M}$ is the growth of materials. The factor shares must sum to unity by definition, that is, $1 \equiv \theta_{Lit} + \theta_{Jit} + \theta_{Mit}$. Oulton and O'Mahony assume that the 'true' rate of TFP growth is given by:

$$T\hat{F}P^* = \hat{Y}_{it} - (\theta^*_{Lit}\hat{L}_{it} + \theta^*_{Jit}\hat{J}_{it} + \theta^*_{Mit}\hat{M}_{it}), \qquad (9.15)$$

where the θ^*s are the 'true' output elasticities, which need not be equal to the factor shares.

In other words, Oulton and O'Mahony assume that each industry has a well-behaved aggregate production function of the general form $Y_{it} = f(J_{it}, L_{it}, M_{it}, A_{it})$. Expressing this in growth rates gives:

$$\hat{Y}_{it} = \hat{A}_{it} + \theta^*_{Lit}\hat{L}_{it} + \theta^*_{Jit}\hat{J}_{it} + \theta^*_{Mit}\hat{M}_{it}. \qquad (9.16)$$

If there is perfect competition, constant returns to scale and factors are paid their marginal products, then the output elasticities will equal the observed factor shares, that is, $\theta^* = \theta$. In these circumstances, the growth of TFP equals:

$$T\hat{F}P_{it} = \hat{A}_{it} = \theta_{Lit}\hat{w}_{it} + \theta_{Jit}\hat{r}_{it} + \theta_{Mit}\hat{m}_{it}.$$

In other words, the rate of technical progress (or T$\hat{F}$P) is equal to the sum of the growth of real factor prices, each weighted by its factor share. ($\hat{m}_{it}$ is the growth of the real (relative) price of materials.)

Subtracting equation (9.14) from equation (9.15) and rearranging gives:

$$T\hat{F}P_{it} \equiv T\hat{F}P^*_{it} + (\theta^*_{Lit} - \theta_{Lit})\hat{L}_{it} + (\theta^*_{Jit} - \theta_{Jit})\hat{J}_{it} + (\theta^*_{Mit} - \theta_{Mit})\hat{M}_{it}. \qquad (9.17)$$

As $T\hat{F}P_{it}^*$ is unobservable, Oulton and O'Mahony argue that, as it differs across industries, it can be proxied by a simple equation:

$$T\hat{F}P_{it}^* = \eta_i + \chi_t + \varepsilon_{it}, \tag{9.18}$$

where η_i varies across industries, but is constant over time, χ_t is constant across industries but varies over time and, hence, can be omitted if only one time period is considered, and ε_{it} is a random error term. η_i is assumed to be absorbed in the error term and the constant term is $E(\eta_i) + \chi_t$. This implicitly assumes that ε_{it} is not correlated with the regressors. The equation estimated is, therefore:

$$T\hat{F}P_{it} = c_i + b_1\hat{L}_{it} + b_2\hat{J}_{it} + b_3\hat{M}_{it} + \varepsilon_{it}. \tag{9.19}$$

Oulton and O'Mahony estimated equation (9.19) using UK industry data at the three-digit MLH. They ran the regressions for 10 separate subsamples over the 1954–86 period and found that estimated coefficients b_1, b_2, and b_3 were nearly always statistically insignificant. Therefore, they concluded that the θ^*s do not significantly differ from the θs. Consequently, 'these results therefore provide no support for the view that the role of capital has been understated' (Oulton and O'Mahony, 1994, p. 162).

But how is equation (9.19) to be interpreted? Recall that we are using constant-price monetary data and therefore the following accounting identity must always hold:

$$\hat{Y}_{it} \equiv (\theta_{Lit}\hat{w}_{it} + \theta_{Jit}\hat{r}_{it} + \theta_{Mit}\hat{m}_{it}) + (\theta_{Lit}\hat{L}_{it} + \theta_{Jit}\hat{J}_{it} + \theta_{Mit}\hat{M}_{it}) \tag{9.20}$$

or,

$$T\hat{F}P_{it} \equiv (\theta_{Lit}\hat{w}_{it} + \theta_{Jit}\hat{r}_{it} + \theta_{Mit}\hat{m}_{it}) \equiv \hat{Y}_{it} - (\theta_{Lit}\hat{L}_{it} + \theta_{Jit}\hat{J}_{it} + \theta_{Mit}\hat{M}_{it}). \tag{9.21}$$

In other words, empirically equations (9.20) and (9.21) hold exactly, irrespective of the true underlying industry aggregate production functions, if, in fact, they exist. Consequently, by simply manipulating the identity we obtain:

$$T\hat{F}P_{it} \equiv (\theta_{Lit}\hat{w}_{it} + \theta_{Jit}\hat{r}_{it} + \theta_{Mit}\hat{m}_{it}) + (\theta_{Lit} - \theta_{Lit})\hat{L}_{it} + (\theta_{Jit} - \theta_{Jit})\hat{J}_{it} + (\theta_{Mit} - \theta_{Mit})\hat{M}_{it}$$

$$= T\hat{F}P_{it} + (\theta_{Lit} - \theta_{Lit})\hat{L}_{it} + (\theta_{Jit} - \theta_{Jit})\hat{J}_{it} + (\theta_{Mit} - \theta_{Mit})\hat{M}_{it}. \tag{9.22}$$

Note that all the variables are the observed variables. Consequently, if *TFP* (or the observed weighted growth of the factor prices) is uncorrelated with the growth of the factor inputs, and there is no a priori reason why we should expect the contrary (Salter, 1966), and we were to estimate equation (9.19) we should expect to find that the estimated coefficients b_1, b_2 and b_3 are equal to zero.

All this shows is that TFP_{it} (or the weighted growth of factor prices) is orthogonal to the regressors. Alternatively, we can simply regard equation (9.19) as an auxiliary regression between the regressors in the identity given by equation (9.20). It should be emphasised that all this has nothing to do with an aggregate production function, which, as we have emphasised, in all probability does not theoretically exist.

These observations are confirmed by the results in Table 9.1. Oulton and O'Mahony report the results for 10 subperiods between 1954 and 1986. As we are merely dealing with an identity, we should not expect the results to differ greatly between the separate periods and so we have pooled the data.

Equation (i) in Table 9.1 is nothing more than the estimation of the full identity given by equation (9.20). The coefficient of $\hat{Y}_{it}$ should be approximately unity and the coefficients of the other regressors are the (negative) average values of the factor shares. It can be seen that the estimated coefficients are close to the shares, but are not exactly the same given the variability of the shares between industries and over time. But the point is

Table 9.1   *Estimating various specifications of the identity; dependent variable TFP (equations (i) and (ii)) and output growth (Ŷ) (equation (iii)), pooled subperiods, 1954–1986*

	$T\hat{F}P$		$\hat{Y}$
	(i)	(ii)[a]	(iii)[a]
$\hat{Y}$	0.817 (55.12)	–	–
$\hat{J}$	–0.095 (–6.53)	–0.015 (–0.33)	0.153 (3.13)
$\hat{L}$	–0.202 (–20.85)	0.061 (1.95)	0.311 (9.27)
$\hat{M}$	–0.493 (–37.49)	–0.040 (–1.82)	0.558 (23.70)
R^2	0.751	0.145	0.790

Note: *t*-statistics in parentheses. Regressions (ii) and (iii) include a constant term. [a] Fixed-effects estimation, time and industry dummies. Percentage shares of inputs in gross output (figures in parentheses are the standard deviations); capital, 14.1 (5.5); labour, 25.9 (8.2) and intermediate inputs, 60.0 (8.5).

Source: Data from Oulton and O'Mahony (1994).

that this is *not* a test of a behavioural hypothesis, but merely illustrates the above argument which is a question of logic.[7]

Equation (ii), which Oulton and O'Mahony use to test the externality hypothesis, replaces $\hat{Y}$ by a constant. All that the results show is that the growth rate of the weighted factor prices is orthogonal to the growth of the factor inputs or, equivalently, that the growth of output is correlated with the growth of the factor inputs. The last is explicitly tested by regressing $\hat{Y}$ on $\hat{J}$, $\hat{L}$ and $\hat{M}$, that is,

$$\hat{Y}_{it} = c_i + b_4 \hat{J}_{it} + b_5 \hat{L}_{it} + b_6 \hat{M}_{it} + \mu_{it}, \tag{9.23}$$

and the results are reported as equation (iii). Because $\hat{L}$, $\hat{J}$ and $\hat{M}$ are large components of $\hat{Y}$, it is not surprising the R^2 is so high (0.79). It is also not surprising that the estimate coefficients are very close to the average values of the relevant factor shares (0.153 and 0.141 for capital; 0.311 and 0.259 for labour; and 0.559 and 0.600 for materials).

The conclusion is that this test can shed no light on the degree of returns to scale, as the identity guarantees that the estimates of the putative output elasticities will always equal the factor shares. If $T\hat{F}P$ and the variables $\hat{J}$, $\hat{L}$ and $\hat{M}$ were correlated, the estimates of the factor shares would be biased and their sum may be statistically significantly different from unity. There might be an economic explanation for this, but it would have nothing to do with an aggregate production function. What is determining the goodness of fit, and the (biased) estimates of the coefficients (the factor shares), is still the identity, albeit misspecified by the omission of $T\hat{F}P$.

The Second Test

Oulton and O'Mahony also proposed a second test, which is equally problematical. They estimated the equation:

$$(\hat{Y}_{it} - \hat{L}_{it}) = T\hat{F}P^*_{it} + \theta^*_{Jit}(\hat{J}_{it} - \hat{L}_{it}) + \theta^*_{Mit}(\hat{M}_{it} - \hat{L}_{it}) + (\theta^*_{Lit} + \theta^*_{Jit} + \theta^*_{Mit} - 1)$$
$$\hat{L}_{it} + \zeta_{it}, \tag{9.24}$$

using panel-data methods. This would allow $T\hat{F}P^*_{it}$ to be modelled by fixed effects and time-period dummies. Oulton and O'Mahony argue:

> If the theory underlying the calculation of TFP growth rates is correct, we would expect that the estimated coefficients on $\hat{J}_{it} - \hat{L}_{it}$ and $\hat{M}_{it} - \hat{L}_{it}$ in a panel

---

[7]   The regression was run for each period separately and we found, not surprisingly, very similar results.

regression would be approximately equal to the sample average of the value shares for capital and intermediate input respectively and that the coefficient of $\hat{L}_{it}$ would be equal to zero, since the value shares sum to one. On the other hand, if standard theory understates the role of capital and if increasing returns exist, then the sum of the elasticities exceeds one (that is $\theta^*_{Lit} + \theta^*_{Jit} + \theta^*_{Mit} > 1$), and coefficient on $\hat{L}_{it}$ is positive. Also, the coefficient on capital should be significantly larger than capital's share. (1994, p. 163. The notation has been changed to make it consistent with the rest of the text)

They find that the regression results 'all reject the hypothesis of a special role for capital' (p. 165). 'The coefficient on $\hat{L}_{it}$ is never statistically significant and the coefficients on $\hat{J}_{it}$ and $\hat{M}_{it}$ are very close to their average shares.'

The fallacy of this interpretation may be straightforwardly shown as the problem is that the data could give no other result. Definitionally, the following identity holds:

$$(\hat{Y}_{it} - \hat{L}_{it}) \equiv (\theta_{Lit}\hat{w}_{it} + \theta_{Jit}\hat{r}_{it} + \theta_{Mit}\hat{m}_{it}) + \theta_{Jit}(\hat{J}_{it} - \hat{L}_{it}) + \theta_{Mit}(\hat{M}_{it} - \hat{L}_{it}) + 0\hat{L}_{it}. \tag{9.25}$$

It is likely that the sum of the weighted factor prices, that is, $(\theta_{Lit}\hat{w}_{it} + \theta_{Jit}\hat{r}_{it} + \theta_{Mit}\hat{m}_{it})$, varies between industries (and possibly over time) and so all the fixed effects captured in equation (9.24) is this variation in the identity.

Given the previous results it is not surprising that Oulton and O'Mahony find the estimates of the coefficients of $(\hat{J} - \hat{L})$ and $(\hat{M} - \hat{L})$ not to be significantly different from the average factor shares and the coefficient on $\hat{L}$ was not significantly different from zero. These results are precisely what we would expect from the identity if the fixed effects were accurately capturing the variation across industries and time in the weighted growth of factor prices in the identity. In fact, estimating this regression is superfluous given the previous results. All that is being captured is the underlying identity and the results cannot be used to infer that capital is not special as do Oulton and O'Mahony and, following them, Crafts and Toniolo (1996).

This is illustrated in Table 9.2. Equation (i) reports the full identity, where it can be seen that the coefficient of $T\hat{F}P$ is slightly smaller than the predicted 1.00. Nevertheless, the estimated shares of capital (0.145) and of intermediate inputs (0.597) are very close to the average values over the 10 subperiods (0.15 and 0.59, respectively). The coefficient of the growth of the employment is not statistically significant, which is in accord with equation (9.25).

Equation (ii) omits $T\hat{F}P$ and estimates the panel data using fixed effects

Table 9.2 Estimating various specifications of the identity: dependent variable ($\hat{Y} - \hat{L}$), pooled data 1954–1986

	(i)	(ii)[a]
$T\hat{F}P$	0.913 (55.12)	–
$(\hat{J} - \hat{L})$	0.145 (9.68)	0.153 (4.80)
$\hat{L}$	–0.001 (–0.05)	0.022 (0.52)
$(\hat{M} - \hat{L})$	0.597 (56.53)	0.558 (23.70)
R^2	0.925	0.503

Note: *t*-statistics in parentheses. Equation (ii) includes a constant. [a] Fixed-effects estimation, time and industry dummies.

Source: Data from Oulton and O'Mahony (1994).

and industry dummies. As we know from the above results that $T\hat{F}P$ is almost orthogonal with the growth of factor inputs, dropping it from the regression does not greatly bias the coefficients of the included variables. This is confirmed by equation (ii), although the growth of the labour input is now statistically significant. This is simply a respecification of equation (9.23), where the regressand is now $\hat{Y} - \hat{L}$ and the coefficients of $\hat{J}$ and $\hat{M}$ should be exactly the same as in Table 9.1 equation (ii), and that on $\hat{L}$ should be equal to zero, which is the case. This regression conveys no new information in addition to that implicit in equation (9.23). Similarly, both regressions tell us nothing about the underlying technological conditions of production.

CONCLUSIONS

This chapter has revisited the estimation of aggregate production functions in the context of the literature on increasing returns and externalities associated with the early endogenous growth models. It has been shown, once again, that because the data used to test these models are constant-price values and not physical quantities, the income accounting identity compels regressions to yield estimates of the parameters interpreted as the output elasticities that must be close to the factor shares. When this does not happen, it is simply the result of a serious misspecification of the weighted average of the growth rates of the factor prices. This does not mean that increasing returns do not exist. Rather, it means that the method used is inappropriate because the data that researchers use are in terms of constant-price value terms and, therefore, consistent with the identity.

10. Problems posed by the accounting identity for the estimation of the degree of market power and the mark-up

INTRODUCTION

In addition to the assumption that a production function exists, neoclassical economic theory often makes the assumption that markets in capitalist economies behave as if they are perfectly competitive with factors of production paid their marginal products. This is notwithstanding the highly oligopolistic nature of the industrial structure in most countries. Consequently, it is an important empirical question as to whether or not this is the case, although it is not an easy proposition to test.

In a series of articles, Hall (1986, 1987, 1988a, 1988b, 1990) has proposed what some see as an innovative method to estimate whether firms set prices above or equal to marginal costs, and hence whether or not they exhibit market power. The method consists in comparing movements in output and inputs, through the production function. An extension of this approach also estimates the degree of returns to scale. Although several alternative procedures to Hall's method have been subsequently proposed, and it has been re-evaluated, it nevertheless represents the standard departure point for many analyses of market power.

The purpose of this chapter is to provide an assessment of the methodological foundations of this approach, and to demonstrate an important limitation. The problem with Hall's method is that the parameter that is theoretically derived as the mark-up, and estimated as such, cannot be unambiguously interpreted in this manner. Hall interprets the fact that there is a significant mark-up on marginal cost as implying the presence of market power and hence that markets are not perfectively competitive. The difficulty arises from the fact that the method used to obtain an equation for the mark-up is based upon a transformation of the aggregate production function. Not surprisingly, it is shown that the equation used to estimate the mark-up can be derived simply as an algebraic transformation of the accounting identity that defines the measure of output in terms of the total compensation of the factors of production. As we have repeatedly shown in earlier chapters, this has no behavioural implications.

The estimates do not necessarily reflect either the underlying technology of the economy or the state of competition. The fact that often the supposed mark-up takes a value that is greater than unity, especially when value-added data are used, is due merely to omitted variables bias and cannot necessarily be taken to indicate the existence of market power. The same argument also explains why the use of gross output leads to values of this parameter that are significantly smaller than when value-added data are used. Hall's model, it has been argued, also has important implications for understanding the causes of business cycles. We also question this interpretation.

HALL'S METHOD OF ESTIMATING THE MARK-UP

Hall, and the studies that have broadly followed his approach, have all assumed that a form derived from a production function may be used to estimate the degree of market power. However, the accounting identity critique suggests that the empirical models that this literature has generated do not produce estimates of the true degree of market power. In order to see why, we start with a consideration of the theoretical foundations of Hall's approach. He starts by postulating a production function $Q = Af(L, K)$ where A denotes Hicks-neutral technical change.

The rationale of his approach is that in the presence of market power where marginal cost (which we shall denote by x) is less than price (p), the competitive share of labour (a_c) will be less than the observed share in revenue (a), and the latter will not equal the output elasticity of labour.

Hall proceeds as follows. Holding the capital stock constant, the marginal cost x may be expressed as:

$$x = \frac{w\Delta L}{\Delta Q}.$$
(10.1)

It follows that:

$$\frac{\Delta Q}{Q} = \frac{wL}{xQ} \cdot \frac{\Delta L}{L}.$$
(10.2)

This may be written as

$$\hat{Q}_t - \hat{K}_t = \frac{wL}{xQ}(\hat{L}_t - \hat{K}_t),$$
(10.3)

where wL/xQ is the output elasticity of labour. As Hall (1988, p. 925) put it, 'again, the factor share measures the elasticity of output with respect to input, independent of the form of technology'.

If there is perfect competition, and $p = x$, then the observed share of labour in revenue, *a*, equals the output elasticity of labour. If they differ, then the following holds:

$$(p/x)(wL/pQ) = \mu a = wL/xQ, \tag{10.4}$$

where μ is the mark-up, that is, price over marginal cost, and the observed share of labour in revenue is smaller than both its share under perfect competition and its output elasticity. Introducing technological change, equation (10.3) may be written as:

$$\hat{Q}_t - \hat{K}_t = \lambda_t + \mu[a_t(\hat{L}_t - \hat{K}_t)], \tag{10.5}$$

which provides one specification from which the size of the mark-up, μ, may be estimated. Gross output, instead of value added, has also been used. A finding that the mark-up exceeds unity, therefore, is sufficient to reject the joint hypotheses that firms operate under constant returns to scale and that factor markets are perfectly competitive.

A BRIEF SURVEY OF THE LITERATURE[1]

The discussion here is confined to the key articles and a summary of the findings is presented in Table 10.1. In his seminal studies, Hall (1988a, 1990) used US industry data at the one-digit and two-digit SIC levels. He applied instrumental variable (IV) estimation, as in the presence of market power the Solow residual is correlated with $a_t(\hat{L}_t - \hat{J}_t)$. The instruments used were variables that affect demand but that should be uncorrelated with technical change. They were the growth rate of the price of oil, the growth rate of military expenditures, and a dummy variable for whether the President was a Democrat or a Republican.[2]

However, for empirical purposes, Hall did not estimate equation (10.5). Instead, he provided the inverse estimate of the instrumental variable regression, that is, $a_t(\hat{L}_t - \hat{J}_t) = c + b_1(\hat{V}_t - \hat{J}_t)$. The estimate of the reciprocal $\mu = 1/b_1$ maps all mark-ups greater than unity into the interval from zero to one. The rationale for estimating the inverse regression is that

[1] Bresnahan (1989) provides a survey of empirical studies on the estimation of market power. He concludes that industry case studies for some concentrated industries tend to indicate the existence of substantial market power. The main difference between this literature and that pioneered by Hall is that the former uses case studies, and the mark-up is calculated by estimating the slope of the demand curve.

[2] Abbott et al. (1998) and Eden and Griliches (1993) raise questions about the validity of Hall's instruments.

Table 10.1 Estimates of the mark-up: summary of findings and methods

	Size of the mark-up	Output measure	Estimation method
Hall (1986)	Large	Value Added	IV
Hall (1987)	Large	Value Added	IV
Domowitz et al. (1988)	Small	Gross Output	IV
Hall (1988a, 1990)	Large	Value Added	IV (Inverse regression)
Waldman (1991)	Not applicable	Data construction and instrumental problems	Not applicable
Norrbin (1993)	Small	Gross Output	IV
Basu (1996)	Small	Gross Output	SUR

Notes: The classification of the mark-ups as 'large' or 'small' refers to how much they depart from $\mu = 1$, and is relative to Hall's findings. Hall (1986) used as an instrument the growth rate of real GNP. Hall (1987) used five sets of instruments: (i) oil, oil lagged, and three military variables; (ii) three military variables; (iii) oil, military variables, and political dummy; (iv) military variables and political dummy; (v) rate of growth of real GNP. Hall (1988a &b, 1990) used military expenditures, oil price (both in growth rates), and a political party dummy. Domowitz et al. (1988) ran the regressions with two sets of instruments: one was output, and the other one was military expenditures and the import price. Norrbin (1993) used the same three instruments as Hall (1988a). Basu (1996) did not directly estimate the mark-up. He inferred this result from the rest of his work. Since he estimated approximately constant returns to scale, and in practice we do not observe large pure profits, it must be the case that mark-ups of price over marginal cost must also be small. He used Seemingly Unrelated Regression (SUR) estimation.

when overhead labour is substantial and the degree of labour hoarding is high, the growth of labour is only likely to be weakly correlated with the instruments, even though the growth of output is highly correlated (Hall, 1988a, p.934). Under these circumstances, the estimated mark-up and its variance are large.[3]

The regressions yielded, in general, relatively high and statistically significant estimates of μ, suggesting either that firms fail to maximise profits, or that they possess substantial market power. Therefore, the results were taken to refute the oft-made assumptions of constant returns to scale and perfectly competitive markets.[4]

---

[3] The direct instrumental variable estimator is $\hat{\mu} = \frac{Cov(\dot{V}_t, \hat{Z}_t)}{Cov(\dot{L}_t, \hat{Z}_t)}$, where $\hat{Z}_t$ are the instruments. Under the circumstances described in the text, the denominator becomes an artificially small number and the numerator a high number.

[4] Hall did not include lags in his regressions, or test the order of integration of the data. As this does not affect our critique, we have followed Hall's procedure for comparability.

Waldman (1991) noted that exceptionally high mark-ups were found by Hall (1988a) in some non-manufacturing industries. Waldman argued that this was caused by the procedures used by the Bureau of Economic Analysis (BEA) to estimate real value added in non-manufacturing industries (the data used by Hall). He argued, in particular, that the deflation method adopted, whether it was double deflation, direct deflation, extrapolation, or some mixture of these methods, was crucial in order to explain Hall's results for the non-manufacturing industries. The essence of the problem lies in the procedures used by the BEA to estimate real value added in non-manufacturing industries. The defects in the deflation method used by the BEA for those industries biased upward Hall's estimates of the mark-ups. For the industries where the BEA used direct deflation, or extrapolation, real value added was underestimated during years of upward oil price shocks. In those cases where the BEA used double deflation, the estimates of value added have no immediate bias. Waldman, nevertheless, concluded that his critique did not invalidate Hall's overall method of estimating the mark-up, as it was only concerned with the measurement of the data.

Domowitz et al. (1988) and Norrbin (1993) also adopted Hall's method, but introducing intermediate inputs in the analysis.[5] Their findings were different. Although Domowitz et al. (1988) also rejected the null hypothesis that price equals marginal cost in US manufacturing, their estimates were much lower than Hall's. Norrbin, on the other hand, estimated relatively small mark-ups that were insignificantly different from unity. Both argued that Hall's estimates were subject to a bias from the use of value added rather than gross output, which they argued was a preferable measure of output for estimating the mark-up. Norrbin, following Hall, derived a similar expression to provide an estimate of the mark-up, but obtained it from the gross output production function $Y_t = A'F(L_t, J_t, M_t)$, where Y_t and M_t denote gross output and intermediate materials, respectively, and λ' is the Hicks-neutral rate of technical progress. The equation is:

$$(\hat{Y}_t - \hat{J}_t) = \lambda' + \mu(\theta_{Lt}(\hat{L}_t - \hat{J}_t) + \theta_{Mt}(\hat{M}_t - \hat{J}_t)) + u_t, \qquad (10.6)$$

where $(\hat{Y}_t - \hat{J}_t)$ denotes the growth of the gross output–capital ratio, $(\hat{M}_t - \hat{J}_t)$ is the growth of the intermediate materials–capital ratio, λ' is the

---

[5] Domowitz et al. (1988) used a slightly different procedure. Instead of estimating $\mu = p/x$ (where p is the price and x is the marginal cost), they estimated the mark-up as $(p - x)/p$. This led to an estimating equation slightly different from Hall's. They regressed the Solow residual on the growth of the output–capital ratio.

constant rate of technical progress and u_t is the error term. The shares of labour and intermediate materials in gross output are $\theta_{Lt} = w_t L_t / Y_t$ and $\theta_{Mt} = m_t M_t / Y_t$, respectively. w, L, Y, m and M are the wage rate, employment, gross output, the price of intermediate material inputs (strictly, the price deflator) and intermediate material inputs, respectively.

Norrbin's main results are: (i) that no significant correlations existed between the instruments and the Solow residual, that is, the latter is orthogonal to the instruments selected by Hall; and (ii) in contrast to Hall's estimates of large mark-ups, the mark-ups were relatively small and insignificant (that is, the estimates of μ were approximately equal to one).

HALL'S ESTIMATION PROCEDURE AND THE ACCOUNTING IDENTITY

In this section, we show from knowledge of the accounting identity that we can virtually predict, before running a single regression, that Hall's procedure will reject the null hypothesis and thus conclude that there is market power. As we have seen, the production function may be written in growth rate form as equation (10.5). Assuming a constant rate of technical change, Hall estimates, *inter alia*, the following equation:

$$\hat{V}_t - \hat{J}_t = c + b_1[a_t(\hat{L}_t - \hat{J}_t)], \tag{10.7}$$

where, of necessity, $\hat{V}$ and $\hat{J}$ are the growth rates of value added and the constant-price value of the capital stock. Hall finds that the estimate of b_1 substantially exceeds unity and hence concludes that this shows the presence of considerable market power.

However, as we have repeatedly observed, the move from the theoretical use of homogeneous output and capital to the actual use of value measures is not innocuous. We know that there is an underlying accounting identity, namely,

$$\hat{V}_t \equiv a_t \hat{w}_t + (1 - a_t)\hat{r}_t + a_t \hat{L}_t + (1 - a_t)\hat{J}_t, \tag{10.8}$$

where the shares are the observed shares and $\hat{r}$ is the growth rate of *ex post* rate of profit (that is, it also includes monopoly profits).

Consequently, the identity may be written as:

$$(\hat{V}_t - \hat{J}_t) \equiv a_t \hat{w}_t + (1 - a_t)\hat{r}_t + \mu[a_t(\hat{L}_t - \hat{J}_t)], \tag{10.9}$$

where $\mu = 1$ by definition.

In a nutshell, Hall finds that $\mu > 1$ because he estimates:

$$(\hat{V}_t - \hat{J}_t) = c + \mu[a_t(\hat{L}_t - \hat{J}_t)]. \tag{10.10}$$

In other words, he assumes that the Solow residual, or the rate of technical progress, is a constant with a random error term. But, from the identity, λ is the expression $a_t\hat{w} + (1 - a_t)\hat{r}$ and far from being constant over time and subject to a random error, it empirically fluctuates procyclically around a constant trend. While there has been much debate about whether the wage rate fluctuates procyclically (the general consensus is that it does slightly), the rate of profit shows a much greater degree of procyclical variation. Thus proxying it by a constant plus a random error in this way causes, in effect, an omitted variable bias, which affects the estimate of μ. It can be straightforwardly shown that μ is biased upwards and hence gives the misleading result of the existence of market power. To see this, consider the auxiliary regression given by:

$$a_t\hat{w}_t + (1 - a_t)\hat{r}_t = c + b_2[a_t(\hat{L}_t - \hat{J}_t)], \tag{10.11}$$

and so the biased slope coefficient of equation (10.11) is equal to the true value, 1 plus the slope coefficient from the auxiliary regression b_2, that is, the estimate of $b_1 = 1 + b_2$. As empirically the weighted growth of the factor payments is positively related to $(\hat{L}_t - \hat{J}_t)$ (and this is discussed further below), so the mark-up will be biased upwards and exceed unity, giving the erroneous impression that this implies the existence of market power.

The IV approach does not completely overcome this problem, and moreover, as we are dealing with an identity the questions of exogeneity, endogeneity and simultaneity do not arise. Moreover, the instruments are often weakly correlated with the regressors and so the estimated coefficients become less precisely estimated (their standard errors increase).

It should be emphasised that our reasoning does not say that market power does not in fact exist, it is just that this method cannot test this hypothesis.

Hall (1988a) also approaches the problem from another angle. Suppose, he argues, that there is no market power. Then the Solow residual is given by (using production function notation):

$$(\hat{Q}_t - \hat{K}_t) - a_{ct}(\hat{L}_t - \hat{K}_t) = \lambda + e_t, \tag{10.12}$$

where again it is assumed that λ is constant and e_t is a random error term. The competitive share, a_c, is equal to the observed share, a. With market power, the Solow residual is given by:

$$(\hat{Q}_t - \hat{K}_t) - a_{ct}(\hat{L}_t - \hat{K}_t) = \lambda - (\mu - 1)a_{ct}(\hat{L}_t - \hat{K}_t) + u_t, \qquad (10.13)$$

where u_t is the error term.

Assume that there is an IV that is correlated with output and input growth, but not with shifts in productivity, that is, not with the right-hand side of equation (10.13) when there is no market power. If there is market power, Hall suggests that the instrument will now be correlated with the residual, because of the presence of $(\mu - 1)a_{ct}(\hat{L}_t - \hat{K}_t)$ on the right-hand side of equation (10.13). Hall suggested military spending, the world oil price and the political party of the US President as possible instruments. Generally, he finds that the instruments are correlated with the Solow residual and that 'the evidence favors a certain amount of market power as against the hypothesis of pure competition' (Hall, 1988a, p. 938).

However, using value data, the identity is given by:

$$(\hat{V}_t - \hat{J}_t) - a_t(\hat{L}_t - \hat{J}_t) \equiv a_t\hat{w}_t + (1 - a_t)\hat{r}_t. \qquad (10.14)$$

Moreover, we know that empirically the weighted growth of the real wage rate and the rate of profit varies procyclically. Thus, any IV that is correlated with the left-hand side of equation (10.13) must necessarily be correlated with the right-hand side, and no inference about the existence market power, or otherwise, should be drawn from this result.

AN EMPIRICAL ILLUSTRATION

In this section we illustrate the problems with Hall's analysis by re-estimating his model but now taking explicit consideration of the identity and the degree of bias. We use the NBER dataset for manufacturing which covers the period from 1958 to 1991 and we use both value-added and gross-output data. We followed Hall in estimating, for both value added:

$$(\hat{V}_t - \hat{J}_t) = \lambda + \mu[a_t(\hat{L}_t - \hat{J}_t)] \qquad (10.15)$$

and the inverse specification, namely:

$$a_t(\hat{L}_t - \hat{J}_t) = -\lambda/\mu + (1/\mu)(\hat{V}_t - \hat{J}_t). \qquad (10.16)$$

The equivalent specifications for gross output are:

$$(\hat{Y}_t - \hat{J}_t) = \lambda' + \mu[\theta_{Lt}(\hat{L}_t - \hat{J}_t) + \theta_{Mt}(\hat{M}_t - \hat{J}_t)] \qquad (10.17)$$

Table 10.2   Value added and gross output mark-ups

	Value added			Gross Output		
	OLS	IV	Inverse IV[a]	OLS	(IV)	Inverse IV[a]
Equation number	(10.15)	(10.15)	(10.16)	(10.17)	(10.17)	(10.18)
λ or (λ')	0.038	0.030	0.090	0.009	0.008	−0.009
	(6.42)	(1.65)	(1.05)	(7.23)	(5.37)	(−5.72)
μ	3.573	2.747	8.992	1.425	1.346	1.380
	(10.54)	(1.62)	(1.05)	(37.53)	(9.00)	(9.52)
$\overline{R}^2, \overline{GR}^2$	0.775	−0.010	−0.017	0.978	0.034	0.042

Notes: [a] The reported coefficients λ or (λ') and μ are derived from the inverse regression coefficients equations (10.16) and (10.18). R^2 is for OLS regressions, $\overline{GR}^2$ is the generalised R^2 for IV regressions. *t*-statistics are in parentheses.

Source: Felipe and McCombie (2002, p. 197, Table 2).

and

$$\theta_{Lt}(\hat{L}_t - \hat{J}_t) + \theta_{Mt}(\hat{M}_t - \hat{J}_t) = -\lambda'/\mu + (1/\mu)(\hat{Y}_t - \hat{J}_t). \qquad (10.18)$$

Table 10.2 reports the results (omitting the usual statistical diagnostics which are reported in Felipe and McCombie, 2002). If we were to take these results at face value, they would indicate the presence of substantial market power. The mark-up of prices over marginal cost, using value added, is between 3.6 and 2.8 (we ignore the statistically insignificant estimate from the IV estimate of the inverse relationship) using value-added data. The values for the mark-up using gross output are smaller, but nevertheless statistically significant, and range from 1.3 to 1.4.

However, we cannot take these results at face value. The problem is that, from the previous discussion, we know that all we are estimating is a misspecified accounting identity and the estimate of μ is simply the value of unity which is biased by the omission of the weighted growth of the factor inputs, or, rather, by assuming that their effects are captured in the constant term.

We confirmed this directly by estimating the auxiliary regressions for the OLS procedure, that is to say, regressing the growth of each of the factor prices weighted by their factor shares separately on the regressors. That is to say, we regressed $a_t\hat{w}_t$ and $(1 - a_t)\hat{r}_t$ each on $a_t(\hat{L}_t - \hat{V}_t)$ (Table 10.3, equations (i) and (ii)) and similarly $\theta_{Lt}\hat{w}_t$, $\theta_{Jt}\hat{r}_t$ and $\theta_{Mt}\hat{m}_t$ separately on $\theta_{Lt}(\hat{L}_t - \hat{J}_t) + \theta_{Mt}(\hat{M}_t - \hat{J}_t)$ (Table 10.3, equations (iii), (iv)

Table 10.3 OLS auxiliary regressions

Equation	Regressand	Regressor	Constant	Slope Coefficient	$\bar{R}^2$
Value added					
(i)	$a_t \hat{w}_t$	$a_t(\hat{L}_t - \hat{J}_t)$	0.008 (4.06)	0.251 (2.05)	0.091
(ii)	$(1-a_t)\hat{r}_t$	$a_t(\hat{L}_t - \hat{J}_t)$	0.029 (6.64)	2.327 (9.12)	0.720
Gross output					
(iii)	$\theta_{Lt}\hat{w}_t$	$\theta_{Lt}(\hat{L}_t - \hat{J}_t) + \theta_{Mt}(\hat{M}_t - \hat{J}_t)$	0.003 (4.61)	0.078 (3.69)	0.283
(iv)	$\theta_{Jt}\hat{r}_t$	$\theta_{Lt}(\hat{L}_t - \hat{J}_t) + \theta_{Mt}(\hat{M}_t - \hat{J}_t)$	0.005 (4.72)	0.387 (11.78)	0.811
(v)	$\theta_{Mt}\hat{m}_t$	$\theta_{Lt}(\hat{L}_t - \hat{J}_t) + \theta_{Mt}(\hat{M}_t - \hat{J}_t)$	0.001 (0.87)	−0.042 (−1.47)	0.035

Note: t-statistics are in parentheses.

Source: See Table 2.

and (v)) to determine the degree of bias obtained by omitting them from equations (10.15) and (10.17). $\hat{m}_t$ is the growth of the price of material inputs (or rather the growth of their deflator).

The implicit mark-up (or the degree of omitted variable bias) obtained from the auxiliary regressions is one plus the sum of the slope coefficients. In other words, for value added $\mu = 1 + 0.251 + 2.327 = 3.578$ which compares with the direct estimate of 3.573. The difference is due to rounding error. For gross output it is $1 + 0.078 + 0.387 - 0.42 = 1.423$ (compared with the direct estimate of 1.425).

We are now in a position to make two comments on Hall's results. First, the reasonably good statistical fit, notwithstanding all the serious aggregation problems, if we interpret the regressions as reflecting a production function, is due to the underlying accounting identity. Second, if the full identity were estimated, we know that the mark-up should be unity. The fact that it is not, is due to Hall's assumption that the rate of technical change is a constant with a random error term. We know, however, that this (that is, the rate of technical change) is merely the weighted growth of the factor prices, which shows a strong procyclical bias. Therefore, modelling it as a constant plus a random error is a misspecification. The growth of the prices of materials shows little variation over the cycle (it has a statistically insignificant slope coefficient in the auxiliary regression, reported in Table 10.3). Consequently, the procyclical fluctuations in the weighted growth of factor returns when using the growth of gross output are also smaller. It is for this reason alone that the mark-up found by other researchers using gross output is much smaller than value-added data.

There is a further problem with this procedure. If we estimate equations

10.15 to 10.18 in unrestricted form, we find the implied estimates of the output elasticities highly implausible with the coefficient of, for example, capital taking the wrong sign using value added and being implausibly small using gross output (see Felipe and McCombie, 2002, p. 203).

The same problem, not surprisingly, affects Hall's (1988a) own results. If we take labour's share of 0.5 as the value that produces the upper limit for the estimate of capital's output elasticity, only one of his estimates for the seven one-digit SIC industries (services) gives a positive value for capital's output elasticity, and even here it is an implausible 0.07.[6] (See Hall, 1988a, Table 4, p. 940.) Consequently, even if one accepts all the usual neoclassical assumptions, this alone should raise questions as to whether the correct specification of the production function is being estimated and whether the results are reliable.

THE SOLOW RESIDUAL, INCREASING RETURNS TO SCALE, AND REVENUE AND COST SHARES

Hall (1988a, p. 922) states that 'the test developed in this paper rests on the assumption of constant returns to scale. That is, the hypothesis being tested is the joint hypothesis of competition and constant returns to scale'. Ignoring for the moment the implausible estimates obtained for the output elasticity of capital, a significant mark-up is found which rejects the null hypothesis of perfectly competitive markets. Consequently, it is not clear why Hall estimates the value of the mark-up by a method that *assumes* constant returns to scale. There seems to be an internal contradiction in this procedure.

It is noticeable that Hall's (1988b, 1990) later work extends his analysis to allow for the possibility of increasing returns to scale. The degree of returns to scale is given by Hall as

$$v = (\partial F/\partial L)\,(L/Q) + (\partial F/\partial K)\,(K/Q) = \alpha + \beta.$$

As $\mu\bar{a}$ is taken to be labour's output elasticity when value-added data are used, it follows that $\beta = v - \mu\bar{a}$, where β is the output elasticity of capital. It is a straightforward matter to show that, using revenue shares, the specification allowing for increasing returns to scale becomes:

---

[6]   In the case of nondurables, we can be more specific as from Hall (1988a, Table 1) the average labour share is 0.72. This, together with an estimated value of the mark-up ratio of 3.096 gives capital's output elasticity of −1.23.

$$(\hat{V}_t - \hat{J}_t) = \lambda + \mu a_t (\hat{L}_t - \hat{J}_t) + (v - 1)\hat{J}_t. \tag{10.19}$$

Equation (10.19) is identical to Hall's (1990) equation (5.26).

This equation was estimated using our dataset. Because of the significant autocorrelation, the exact AR(1) ML method was used. The results for value added were:

$$(\hat{V}_t - \hat{J}_t) = 0.079 + 3.529(\hat{L}_t - \hat{J}_t) - 1.675\hat{J}_t \quad \bar{R}^2 = 0.837, \, DW = 1.99$$
$$\phantom{(\hat{V}_t - \hat{J}_t) = }(5.07) \quad (13.13) (-3.39)$$

This gives an implausible value of the degree of returns to scale of -0.675 (with a t-value of -1.36). Using the IV approach does not improve the results:

$$(\hat{V}_t - \hat{J}_t) = 0.080 + 4.574(\hat{L}_t - \hat{J}_t) - 1.274\hat{J}_t \quad \overline{GR}^2 = -0.024.$$
$$\phantom{(\hat{V}_t - \hat{J}_t) = }(1.92) \quad (2.02) (-1.27)$$

The fit is poor and the estimate of v is -2.274 (and the t-value equals -2.44).

Hall (1988b, 1990) used cost, rather than revenue factor shares in his regression analysis. The advantage is that no assumption about the state of competition is needed when the cost shares are used. The cost share of labour is calculated as $a_{ct} = w_t L_t / (w_t L_t + r_{ct} J_t)$, where r_c is the shadow or competitive rate of profit, calculated under a number of what can best be described as heroic assumptions, but which will not be considered here.

Hall's methodology using cost shares is similar to that using revenue shares, but with some important differences. First, when cost shares are used and there are constant returns to scale, there should be no correlation between the residual and exogenously determined movements in output and input growth. On the other hand, with increasing returns to scale, the Solow residual will be positively correlated when output growth increases, even though there has been no shift in the production function. Hall's estimating equation now becomes:

$$\hat{V}_t = \lambda + v[a_{ct}\hat{L}_t + (1 - a_{ct})\hat{J}_t]. \tag{10.20}$$

The focus of interest is on the degree of returns to scale. A direct estimate of the mark-up may be calculated as the ratio of labour's revenue to cost share, $a/a_c = \mu = p/x$. Hall (1988a, Table 1 and 1988b, Table 1) reports data for the nondurable goods industry. Using these data, we calculated that the mark-up for this industry is on average 1.10, which is significantly less than the value of 2.06 obtained from the regression analysis using revenue shares as weights. Hall (1988b, p. 4) now concludes: 'As a practical matter, it makes almost no difference whether cost or revenue shares appear in the productivity measure, because pure profit is sufficiently small that cost and revenue are the same'. This is somewhat at variance with the results of his previous approach, namely the estimates of the mark-up obtained from the regression analysis discussed above, to the extent that the latter implied substantial market power. However, Hall (1988b, 1990) finds significant estimates of increasing returns to scale at both the one- and the two-digit SIC levels.

We confirmed this for the nondurable goods industries, using Hall's data for 1953–80. When the inverse IV regression

$$[a_{ct}\hat{L}_{t} + (1 - a_{ct})\hat{J}_{t}] = -\lambda/v + (1/v)\,\hat{V}_{t}$$

is estimated, it is found that the estimate of v is 3.731 (with a t-value of 2.10), which is close to Hall's estimate of 3.107.[7] Regressing the growth of output directly on the weighted growth of the factor inputs using the IV method gives a smaller, but still substantial, value of increasing returns to scale of 2.658 (t-value: 2.74).

However, the reason for these results is similar to the one we have discussed above, namely that all that is being estimated is a misspecified identity. As the cost and revenue shares are very close in value, the accounting identity is given by (approximately):

$$\hat{V}_{t} = a_{c}\hat{w}_{t} + (1 - a_{c})\hat{r}_{t} + a_{c}\hat{L}_{t} + (1 - a_{c})\hat{J}_{t} \qquad (10.21)$$

or, alternatively,

$$\hat{V}_{t} = \lambda_{t} + v[a_{c}\hat{L}_{t} + (1 - a_{c})\hat{J}_{t}], \qquad (10.22)$$

where $v = 1.0$. The fact that empirically v exceeds unity is because once again λ_{t} is proxied erroneously by a constant. However, the argument is a little more complex than this, as we have seen above.

To recapitulate: in the neoclassical analysis, even though in the presence of market power the appropriate values of the output elasticities are the cost shares, the measure of the 'volume' of output is still constant-price value added. This is measured as $V \equiv wL + r_{c}J + \Pi$, where Π is total monopoly profits. This last term may be written as $r_{nc}J$ where r_{nc} is the monopoly or noncompetitive component of the rate of return derived from the accounting identity. Consequently, total profits may be written

---

[7]   The reason for the difference is that we only used the two instruments for which Hall reports the data, namely the rate of growth of oil prices and military expenditure.

as $rJ = r_c J + r_{nc} J$. Thus, it could be legitimately argued that monopoly profits should be excluded from the definition of the 'volume' of output (that is, value added should be calculated using marginal costs rather than market prices) so that the residual does not include the rate of change in monopoly profits. The latter, of course, has nothing to do with the rate of technical change. Hence, if this procedure is followed and the adjusted value added is given by $V_c = wL + r_c J$, the arguments above concerning the identity follow through exactly.

Finally, even if we were to assume an underlying aggregate production function together with the standard neoclassical assumptions, Hall's specification of equation (10.20) conceals the evidence of a serious misspecification error, similar to that found above with the use of revenue shares. When equation (10.19) is estimated by IV in the unrestricted form of

$$\hat{V}_t = \lambda + v(a_{ct}\hat{L}_t) + v[(1 - a_{ct})\hat{J}_t]$$

the following results are obtained, which include a negative output elasticity for capital:

$$\hat{V}_t = 0.083 + 1.950(a_{ct}\hat{L}_t) - 8.389[(1-a_{ct})\hat{J}_t].$$
$$\quad\;\; (2.61) \quad (2.58) \qquad\qquad (-1.82)$$

Using OLS gives comparable results:

$$\hat{V}_t = 0.051 + 1.410(a_{ct}\hat{L}_t) - 3.203[(1 - a_{ct})\hat{J}_t] \quad \bar{R}^2 = 0.726, \; DW = 1.531.$$
$$\quad\;\; (2.61) \quad (8.26) \qquad\quad (-2.64)$$

Thus, even granted the usual neoclassical assumptions, no reliance can be placed on Hall's results as correctly measuring the degree of returns to scale or that a correctly specified production function is being estimated.

CABALLERO AND LYONS'S (1989) EXTENSION OF HALL'S PROCEDURE

Caballero and Lyons (1989, 1992) extended Hall's work by introducing an externality effect in production. The difficulty of estimating the size of this is related to that discussed in chapter 9. They postulated that each individual industry i, was subject to an externality effect (as suggested by Young (1928)) which could be proxied by the growth of either total manufacturing input or output. Equation (10.20) is then estimated as:

$$\hat{V}_{it} = \lambda + v \left[a_{ct} \hat{L}_{it} + (1 - a_{ct}) \hat{J}_{it} \right] + \psi \hat{V}_t + u_t, \tag{10.23}$$

where now $\hat{V}_{it}$ is the growth rate of value added for a manufacturing branch (for example, food, chemicals), and $\hat{V}_t$ is the growth rate of value added of the overall manufacturing sector. The parameter ψ provides an estimate of the externalities of total manufacturing (that is, aggregate activity).[8] Caballero and Lyons found values of v lower than those with equation (10.20) when individual industries are used, and ψ positive and statistically significant. To the extent that λ_{it} and $\hat{V}_t$ are correlated, this, however, is to be expected as equation (10.23) is an approximation to the identity, where λ_{it} has been proxied by $\hat{V}_t$.

Empirical evidence is provided in Table 10.4. Three specifications were estimated by OLS for total manufacturing, and for four manufacturing branches, food (SIC 20), textiles (SIC 22), chemicals (SIC 28), and fabricated metals (SIC 34), for the US.

Equation (i) in the table is the accounting identity which serves as the reference equation. λ_{it} is given by $a_{cit} \hat{w}_{it} + (1 - a_{cit}) \hat{r}_{it}$. As expected, the coefficients of both the weighted growth of the factor prices and of factor inputs are unity. Equation (ii) is Hall's specification equation (10.20) discussed above. As can be seen, omitting the procyclical weighted growth of the wage and profit rate biases the coefficient on $[(a_{cit} \hat{L}_{it}) + (1 - a_{cit}) \hat{J}_{it}]$ upwards. Equation (iii) includes the growth of total manufacturing in equation (ii) which is an 'irrelevant independent variable'. As it has a strong procyclical component, it is correlated with the excluded weighted growth of the wage rate and the rate of profit as well as the weighted growth of the factor inputs. Consequently, this explains its positive coefficient; it provides no evidence as to whether or not there are externalities in manufacturing.[9]

---

[8]   Caballero and Lyons assumed that the share of each industry in value added is equal to the share of its inputs. Then,

$$\hat{V}_t = [\lambda/(1 - \psi)] + [v/(1 - \psi)] [a_{ct} \hat{L}_t + (1 - a_{ct}) \hat{J}_t] + \varepsilon_t,$$

where ε is the error term. Consequently, the estimated coefficient of $[a_{ct} \hat{L}_t + (1 - a_{ct}) \hat{J}_t]$ is, under this interpretation, a hybrid of the influence of returns to scale and the externality effect that Caballero and Lyons are unable to unravel. They argued that the finding that the coefficient of $[a_{ct} \hat{L}_t + (1 - a_{ct}) \hat{J}_t]$ exceeds unity in this specification cannot be taken as implying returns to scale, *per se*. From the results using pooled industry data and the growth of aggregate inputs as the proxy for the externality effect, the estimate of ψ is statistically significant and positive and the preferred estimation method shows the degree of returns to scale close to unity.

[9]   It is worth noting that in all the studies discussed here, v is estimated as the coefficient of the weighted growth of the inputs. None of the studies estimates this coefficient separately as the coefficients of $a_{ct} \hat{L}_t$ and of $(1 - a_{ct}) \hat{J}_t$, and then tests whether the two

Table 10.4   US manufacturing industry production functions, externalities and the identity (OLS estimates)

Equation (i) (The identity) $\hat{V}_{it} \equiv c_1\lambda_{it} + b_1\,[(a_{cit}\,\hat{L}_{it}) + (1 - a_{cit})\hat{J}_{it}]$

Industry	c_1	b_1	R^2
MNF	1.02 (72.47)	0.97 (62.72)	0.998
SIC20	1.00 (147.02)	1.04 (65.23)	0.999
SIC22	1.00 (99.38)	1.00 (58.75)	0.998
SIC28	1.00 (406.79)	1.01 (220.80)	0.999
SIC34	0.98 (108.09)	0.99 (87.71)	0.999

Equation (ii) (Hall's specification) $\hat{V}_{it} = c + b_1\,[(a_{cit}\,\hat{L}_{it}) + (1 - a_{cit})\hat{J}_{it}]$

Industry	c	b_1	R^2
MNF	0.01 (0.65)	1.46 (5.67)	0.640
SIC20	0.05 (0.44)	1.37 (1.59)	0.117
SIC22	0.02 (1.66)	1.40 (4.00)	0.457
SIC28	0.03 (0.78)	0.33 (0.30)	0.005
SIC34	−0.03 (−2.11)	1.99 (6.85)	0.710

Equation (iii) (C&L's specification) $\hat{V}_{it} = c + b_1\,[(a_{cit}\hat{L}_{it}) + (1 - a_{cit})]\hat{J}_{it} + b_2\hat{V}_t$

Industry	c	b_1	b_2	R^2
SIC20	0.003 (0.36)	1.31 (1.33)	0.17 (1.49)	0.210
SIC22	0.006 (0.67)	0.26 (0.51)	0.65 (2.73)	0.610
SIC28	0.03 (2.12)	−0.48 (−0.30)	1.04 (12.03)	0.890
SIC34	−0.01 (−2.31)	0.57 (2.64)	0.95 (8.31)	0.940

Notes: MNF, total manufacturing; SIC20, food; SIC22, textiles; SIC28, chemicals; SIC34, fabricated metals; C&L is Caballero and Lyons.

Sources: Total manufacturing: OECD database; industries: NBER, manufacturing database. Felipe (2001), Table 4, pp. 417–18.

estimates are equal. This is surprising, given the statistically insignificant coefficient of the growth of the capital stock that occurs in many estimations of production functions. We were able to remedy this shortcoming for durable goods using Hall's (1988b) data for 1953–80. Using $[a_{ct}\hat{L}_t + (1 - a_{ct})\hat{J}_t]$ as a regressor gives a statistically significant value of v of 2.652 (t-value = 2.80). However, estimating $\hat{V}_t = c + b_3(a_{ct}\,\hat{L}_t) + b_4(1 - a_{ct})\hat{J}_t = u_t$ gives estimates of b_1 of 1.921 (t-value, 3.11) and of b_2 of −1.739 (t-value, −1.46) (the method of estimation was IV using the growth of oil prices and military expenditure as instruments). In other words, the results suggest that a faster growth of capital actually lowers the growth of output. These results would suggest that, even if it is accepted that a production function is being estimated, there is a serious specification error which renders the estimates of v extremely problematical.

THE USE OF GROSS OUTPUT

As noted above, it has been argued that a possible reason behind Hall's and Caballero and Lyons's high estimates of the degree of returns to scale (when no externality is included in the regression) could be that they used value added as opposed to gross output. Indeed, Basu and Fernald (1995, 1997) concluded that the use of gross output in Hall's framework leads to the finding of constant returns to scale. This section shows why the use of gross output leads in general to estimates of the degree of returns to scale around unity. The reason is also embedded in the identity, and therefore such a finding cannot be interpreted as evidence of constant returns to scale. To see this, we write the income identity for gross output in real terms as:

$$Y_t \equiv w_t L_t + r_t J_t + m_t M_t. \tag{10.24}$$

Expressing this in growth rates gives:

$$\hat{Y}_t \equiv \theta_{Lt} \hat{w}_t + \theta_{Jt} \hat{r}_t + \theta_{Mt} \hat{m}_t + \theta_{Lt} \hat{L}_t + \theta_{Jt} \hat{J}_t + \theta_{Mt} \hat{M}_t. \tag{10.25}$$

The following equation is estimated to obtain an estimate of supposedly increasing returns to scale given by the estimate of v:

$$\hat{Y}_t = \lambda' + v(\theta_{Lt} \hat{L}_t + \theta_{Jt} \hat{J}_t + \theta_{Mt} \hat{M}_t) + u_t. \tag{10.26}$$

The reason why the estimate of v in equation (10.26) will tend to be lower than that in equation (10.23), and nearer unity is that the degree of bias, induced by proxying the weighted growth of the wage and profit rate by a constant, is lower. The share of intermediate materials in total costs is much larger than those of labour and capital so that θ_L and θ_J are much smaller than their corresponding shares in value added. Furthermore, the growth of materials ($\hat{M}_t$) shows a much larger cyclical fluctuation than the growth of either labour or capital, and it is highly correlated with the growth of output. Therefore, the inclusion of the weighted growth of materials engenders greater fluctuation in the total sum of the weighted inputs and reduces the degree of bias caused by the omitted variables.

Finally, when Basu and Fernald (1995) added the proxy for externalities to regression (10.25) they found no evidence of positive output spillovers across industries (that is, an insignificant coefficient). The reason is that aggregate output, the proxy for externalities has a much lower coefficient when regressed on the term $(\theta_{Lt} \hat{w}_t + \theta_{Jt} \hat{r}_t + \theta_{Mt} \hat{m}_t)$. And the reason why this estimate is much smaller than in the case of value added is that the weighted average of the growth rates of the factor prices shows a smaller fluctuation because the relative price of materials shows relatively little cyclical variation and it forms a large share of the weighted growth of the factor inputs. It must be stressed that these arguments have been derived without any reference to a production function.

CONCLUSIONS

This chapter has shown that some recent attempts to estimate econometrically the degree of market power and the degree of returns to scale are problematical. The method pioneered by Hall is based on a comparison of rates of change of output and inputs based on the usual neoclassical assumptions and the existence of a well-behaved production function. However, there is a problem in that there is also a relationship between the growth of output in value terms and that of inputs (together with factor prices) given by the underlying accounting identity. Because of this, it has been shown that the estimate of the putative mark-up is also the same as unity plus the size of the omitted variable bias inherent in estimating the (misspecified) identity.

It turns out that the fact that the estimate of the coefficient of the growth of the labour–capital ratio, weighted by its revenue share, differs from unity is simply due to the fact that the weighted growth of factor prices varies procyclically. This is also the reason why estimates of the supposed degree of returns to scale find such large magnitudes. There are a number of reasons why this procyclical fluctuation may occur (for example, cyclical variation in capacity utilisation rates) that have nothing to do with the degree of competition. There is no way to identify Hall's model (as there are not two behavioural equations) and to show unambiguously that what he and others have estimated is the value of the mark-up. Indeed, as has been noted above, for reasons of parsimony or Occam's razor, the data are more likely to be reflecting only the identity. Whatever view is taken, Hall's procedure does not measure the mark-up. We have also shown that any estimates that are supposedly of the degree of returns to scale are also merely due to the misspecification of the accounting identity.

11. Are estimates of labour demand functions mere statistical artefacts?

The estimated elasticities that seem to confirm the central prediction of the theory of labor demand are not entirely an artefact produced by aggregating data. . . . The Cobb–Douglas function is not a very severe departure from reality in describing production relations.

(Hamermesh, 1986, pp. 454 and 467)[1]

INTRODUCTION[2]

One of the most enduring controversies in macroeconomics is the question as to whether or not unemployment can be largely attributed to the real wage being too high. The question has been interpreted as essentially an empirical issue. The neoclassical approach suggests that, in the long run, capital–labour substitution and wage flexibility guarantee full employment, and, hence, using the neoclassical production function one can derive estimates of the elasticity of employment with respect to the real wage.

Indeed, the motivation for Paul Douglas originally to begin his seminal estimations of the aggregate production function was the spectacle of lecturers in the 1920s drawing labour demand schedules on the blackboard without any idea of the steepness of their (downward) slopes (Douglas, 1948). Since the mid-1960s, there have been numerous studies that have attempted to resolve this issue by drawing on neoclassical production theory and explicitly, or implicitly, estimating the elasticity of the demand for labour with respect to the real wage. While a variety of different data sources, estimation techniques, and specifications (the modelling of the dynamic adjustments and so on) have been used, all the studies, in effect, estimate a labour demand function derived from an aggregate production function, although, as we shall see below, the marginal revenue product of labour function has also been used.

The factor supply functions are not normally modelled, as they are assumed to be perfectly elastic for the individual firm. Hamermesh (1993)

---

[1] Cited by Lavoie (2008).
[2] This draws on Felipe and McCombie (2009b). See also Felipe and McCombie (2007a).

has provided a useful survey of the literature and although the estimates of the elasticity vary often quite considerably between studies, they are nearly always statistically significant and negative: 'If one were to choose a point estimate for this parameter [the elasticity of labour demand, holding output constant], 0.30 would not be far wrong' (p. 92). This is roughly the same figure that Douglas (1934) found and is consistent with the Cobb–Douglas production function where labour's share is 0.7. As Hamermesh (1993, p. 92, omitting a footnote) further remarks, 'the immense literature that estimates the constant-output demand elasticity for labour in the aggregate has truly led us "to arrive where we started and know the place for the first time"'[3].

These results, taken as a whole, have been seen by some as confirming the neoclassical view that an increase in the real wage, *ceteris paribus*, will increase unemployment by lowering the demand for labour.[4] As Lewis and MacDonald (2002, p. 18) put it: 'The elasticity of demand for labour at the aggregate level is an important parameter for macroeconomic analysis. In particular, policy issues concerning the impact of wage falls on employment hinge on the size of this parameter'.

However, we shall show that any policy implications may be very misleading, such as the putative adverse effect on employment of the introduction, or increase, of the minimum wage. The contention of this chapter is that the empirical evidence does not necessarily support the policy conclusions that have been drawn from the various labour demand studies. The problem is that the labour demand function is derived from an aggregate production function. The previous chapters have established that the use of value data (either value added or gross output) poses intractable problems for the interpretation of any statistical estimates derived from the aggregate production function.

Nevertheless, Michl (1987, p. 361), for example, has argued that 'the methodology of estimating employment equations does not founder on the shoals of algebraic tautology, which diminish the estimates of some estimates of aggregate production functions, as noted by Shaikh (1974)'. We find it difficult to understand this argument and in this chapter, we show that this is not the case. Because of an underlying accounting identity, it is possible to obtain a negative value of the elasticity of labour

---

[3] The quotation is from T.S. Eliot's poem, 'Little Gidding'.

[4] Some Keynesians, while accepting the marginal productivity theory of factor pricing, would dispute this line of reasoning. They argue that while there is an inverse relationship between the wage rate and the level of employment (because of diminishing returns), the causation is not that of the neoclassicals. It is the level of demand that determines the demand for labour which in turn determines the real wage. (See, for example, Davidson, 1983; Thirlwall, 1993.) We shall not pursue this argument here.

demand with respect to the wage rate, even though there may be no relationship involved. Indeed, it is very difficult to obtain anything other than a statistically significant negative 'elasticity'. All that is being estimated is an approximation of an identity, which is, of course, true by definition.

We commence by briefly setting out the four neoclassical labour demand and marginal revenue functions that have been used to estimate the elasticity of employment with respect to the real wage. We next consider the underlying accounting identity that defines value added, namely that value added is equal to the average wage rate multiplied by the numbers employed plus the rate of profit multiplied by the capital stock. We show that if factor shares are constant (although our argument does not depend upon this assumption), the logarithm of employment is positively related to the logarithm of output (value added) and negatively related to the logarithm of the real wage rate, the rate of profit and the capital stock. It is shown that it is this underlying identity that generates the negative relationship between the logarithms of employment and the real wage rate. We demonstrate that the regression equations commonly used to estimate the elasticity of demand for labour are simply a misspecification of the identity (such as through the omission of variables or proxying them by a time trend). Moreover, we further show that if we specify them correctly from a neoclassical point of view by allowing 'technical progress' to be proxied by a non-linear time trend, rather than as a linear time trend as is usually the case, then, as a result, two of the specifications are *exact* identities under the usual neoclassical assumptions.[5] A consequence is that all these estimated regressions have no policy implications.

We further consider the study by Anyadike-Danes and Godley (1989), which also questions the putative labour demand function. Using a simulation analysis, they show that the logarithm of the real wage rate is statistically significantly inversely related to the logarithm of employment, even when it is known by construction that employment is not a function of the real wage. We show that this seemingly perverse result is more generally due to the underlying accounting identity and the arguments that we advance.

Lavoie (2000) has shown that the non-accelerating inflation rate model of Layard et al. (1991), like the labour demand function, also merely reflects the underlying accounting identity. Hence, no policy conclusions can be drawn from it. We discuss Lavoie's argument in Appendix 11A.

---

[5]   This is because under the usual neoclassical assumptions, the rate of technical progress is given by the growth of the real factor prices weighted by their factor shares. This means that the specifications become exact identities.

THE NEOCLASSICAL THEORY OF THE DEMAND FOR LABOUR

The neoclassical theory underlying the estimation of labour demand functions is now standard. Nevertheless, given the controversy that surrounds certain aspects of the theory (Rowthorn, 1999; Dowrick and Wells, 2004; Lewis and MacDonald, 2004), it is useful briefly to rehearse it here.

A well-behaved aggregate production function, $Q = A(t)f(L,K)$, is assumed; perfect competition prevails and factors are paid their marginal products so that from the marginal productivity conditions, $w^n/p = w = f_L$ and $\rho^n/p = \rho = f_K$. Q is the volume of homogeneous output, $A(t)$ is the shift factor, where $A(t) = A_0 e^{\lambda t}$ and λ is the exogenous constant rate of technical change. K is the physical capital stock and L the level of employment. p is the price of output. The variables w^n and ρ^n are the nominal wage rate and the rental price of capital, while w and ρ are their values in real (product) terms.

Two different assumptions are made in deriving estimates of two separate types of the elasticity of the demand for labour. One holds output constant, while the other holds capital constant.

Holding Output Constant

The first assumption is to hold output constant, but to allow the capital–labour ratio to vary as the relative price of the factor inputs changes. Solving the system of equations given by the production function and the two first-order conditions yields a value of the elasticity of demand for labour, namely, $\eta_{LL/Q} = -(1 - a)\sigma$, where $(1 - a)$ is capital's share in total output (and equals capital's output elasticity $(1 - \alpha)$) and σ is the elasticity of substitution. $a\ (= \alpha)$ is labour's share. In the case of a Cobb–Douglas, $\eta_{LL/Q} = -(1 - a) \approx -0.30$ given that capital's share of output is approximately 30 per cent. More generally, estimates of the elasticity of substitution are generally found to be between 0.5 and unity. Consequently, we should expect $\eta_{LL/Q}$ to lie between -0.15 and -0.30. This, of course, assumes the existence of an aggregate production function together with an aggregate elasticity of substitution. We shall have more to say on this below. The cross-elasticity of demand for labour is given by $\eta_{LK/Q} = (1 - a)\sigma$ and in the case of the Cobb–Douglas this takes a value of approximately 0.30 (Hamermesh, 1993, p. 24).[6]

---

[6] However, an increase in the money wage may increase the price of output relative to that of other goods and services. Assuming a demand equation for output as $Q = cp^{-\eta}$, where $\eta \geqslant 0$ is the absolute value of the elasticity of product demand and c is a constant,

For the Cobb–Douglas production function, the elasticity of demand for labour is given by:

$$\ln L = -\ln A_0 + (1 - \alpha) \ln [\alpha/(1 - \alpha)] + \ln Q - (1 - \alpha) \ln w$$
$$+ (1 - \alpha) \ln \rho - \lambda t, \qquad (11.1)$$

where the estimate of the coefficient of $\ln w$ is the elasticity of demand of labour, as noted above.

Alternatively, the marginal revenue product of labour curve may be derived from the first-order conditions by differentiating the Cobb–Douglas production function with respect to labour and equating it to the wage rate (w). In logarithmic form this is:

$$\ln L = \ln \alpha + \ln Q - \ln w. \qquad (11.2)$$

The coefficient of $\ln w$ (that is, -1) is not the elasticity of the demand for labour curve, which is equal to $-(1 - \alpha)$ and may be derived from the estimate of the intercept.

In fact, equation (11.2) is not usually estimated, *per se*, but rather it is a restricted case of the more general CES function, within which it is nested. In the case of this production function, the marginal revenue product of labour curve is given by:

$$\ln L = -(1 - \sigma) \ln A_0 + \sigma \ln \delta - \sigma \ln w + \ln Q - (1 - \sigma)\lambda t. \quad (11.3)$$

It is important to note again that the coefficient of $\ln w$ is not the elasticity of demand for labour, which, as we noted above, is $\eta_{LLQ} = -(1 - a)\sigma$. Equation (11.3) is the specification used by Lewis and MacDonald (2002). It can be seen that as σ tends to unity and δ, the distribution parameter of the CES, tends to α, so equation (11.3) will tend to $\ln L = \ln \alpha + \ln Q - \ln w$, which is the Cobb–Douglas specification. It can also be seen that an increase in the real wage, *ceteris paribus*, will result in a decline in employment, which is the crucial result.

---

the wage elasticity of the demand for labour becomes $\eta_{LLQ} = -(1 - a)\sigma - a\eta$. As precise estimates of the price elasticity of demand for output are difficult to obtain, the demand side is normally ignored in the literature, which is equivalent to assuming that the demand for the industry's output is either completely price inelastic or supply constrained.

Another implicit assumption is that the elasticity of supply of capital goods and structures is infinite. If it is not, the expression for the wage elasticity becomes more complicated with the elasticity of supply of the capital stock being one of its arguments. Again, it is normally assumed that this is infinite, in which case the elasticity of demand for labour is again equal to $-(1 - a)\sigma$ or alternatively to $-(1 - a)\sigma - a\eta$.

Holding the Capital Stock Constant

An alternative assumption, perhaps more suitable for short-run analysis, is to keep the capital stock constant, in which case output varies, but not because of exogenous changes in demand. If the capital stock remains constant, then as employment falls with a rise in the real wage, so output will decrease. Thus, in the CES case, the wage elasticity is given by $\eta_{LL/K} = -\sigma/(1 - a)$ (Rowthorn, 1999), and the expected range of values of $\eta_{LL/K}$ is -1.67 to -3.33 for a value of capital's share of 0.30 and the elasticity of substitution ranging between 0.5 and unity. Thus, the fall in employment is considerably greater when the capital stock cannot alter, compared with when output is constant, which is to be expected.

In the case of the Cobb–Douglas production function, $\eta_{LL/K}$ can be obtained from the first-order condition for labour $(\partial Q/\partial L) = \alpha A(t)[(K/L)^{(1-\alpha)}] = w$, which in logarithmic form becomes:

$$\ln L = \frac{1}{(1 - \alpha)}\ln\alpha + \frac{1}{(1 - \alpha)}\ln A_0 + \frac{1}{(1 - \alpha)}\lambda t - \frac{1}{(1 - \alpha)}\ln w + \ln K, \quad (11.4)$$

where $\eta_{LL/K}$ is the elasticity of demand for labour and this is equal to $-1/(1 - \alpha)$ or the negative of the inverse of capital's share (Rowthorn, 1999). This is the equation used by Layard et al. (1991), who estimated equation (11.4) adding lags. Rowthorn criticises Layard et al. on the grounds that the expected absolute elasticity of demand for labour (keeping capital constant) should be around 3, but Layard et al.'s estimates suggest that it is an order of magnitude smaller in the case of many countries, and is often less than unity (Rowthorn, 1999, table 1, p.416). The aim of Rowthorn's paper is to show that investment does have some positive effect on employment, *pace* Layard et al., who demonstrate that, using a Cobb–Douglas production function, there is no impact. Rowthorn argues that this result depends upon the elasticity of substitution being unity, whereas he argues that Layard et al.'s own estimates show that the elasticity must be substantially below unity.

The problem is that in many of the labour demand studies the distinction between the different specifications of the real wage elasticities (and hence their different a priori values) is not made. Indeed, it is often not made explicit whether or not the coefficient of ln*w* should be interpreted as an elasticity of demand. But, for our purposes, this is not an issue – what matters is that all specifications predict a negative coefficient on the logarithm of the real wage.

To summarise, we have two different specifications of the labour demand curve, namely, equations (11.1) and (11.4) and two for the marginal revenue specification, equations (11.2) and (11.3).

MORE PARSIMONIOUS INTERPRETATION

Expressing the value-added accounting identity in growth rates, $\hat{V} \equiv a\hat{w} + (1 - a)\hat{r} + a\hat{L} + (1 - a)\hat{J}$ and then integrating this equation gives at any instance of time:

$$V \equiv Bw^a r^{(1-a)} L^a J^{(1-a)}, \tag{11.5}$$

where B is the constant of integration and equals $a^{-a}(1-a)^{-(1-a)}$, where a and $(1 - a)$ are again the shares of labour and capital in total output. If factor shares are constant, this can be estimated using time-series data.

Equation (11.5) may be written in logarithmic form as:

$$\ln L \equiv -\frac{1}{a}\ln B + \frac{1}{a}\ln V - \ln w - \frac{(1 - a)}{a}\ln r - \frac{(1 - a)}{a}\ln J, \tag{11.6}$$

which underlies all the neoclassical demand for labour functions.

It should be noted that the neoclassical procedure is to use the rental price of capital, rather than the *ex post* rate of profit, in the identity (see, for example, Clark and Freeman, 1980; Hsieh, 2002). However, as was discussed in Chapter 2, this does not affect the argument: we just have a slightly different specification of the identity. How does the rental price of capital relate to the accounting identity, equation (11.5)? It is easy to see that equation (11.5), which does not make any assumption about the state of competition, can be written as:

$$V \equiv wL + rJ \equiv wL + r_c J + r_{nc} J, \tag{11.7}$$

where r_c and r_{nc} are the competitive and the non-competitive components of the rate of profit, and consequently $r \equiv r_c + r_{nc}$. The rental price of capital, as noted above, is calculated under neoclassical assumptions and is analogous to the competitive rate of profit.[7] If all markets are competitive, $r_{nc} = 0$ and value added is given by:

---

[7]   The matter is complicated by the fact that the rental price of capital is calculated using the rate of depreciation and the degree of revaluation or the capital gain or loss (see Jorgensen and Griliches, 1967). Under this approach, the real capital stock is calculated by the UK Office of National Statistics, the OECD, and the US Bureau of Labor Statistics (BLS), using the nominal values of the rental price of capital to determine the asset shares in profits with which to weight the various assets (OECD, 2001; see Lau and Vaze, 2002; BLS, 2006). The BLS also adjusts for the rate of corporate taxation in its calculations, and so the rental price of capital can be either gross or net of company taxation. Hsieh (2002) uses the accounting identity within the neoclassical growth-accounting framework. He utilises the

$$V \equiv wL + r_c J. \tag{11.8}$$

What about the case where there are abnormal profits and $r_{nc} \neq 0$? In neoclassical production theory, V is used as a proxy for output, but as the latter is a physical measure, it should not include any abnormal profits (as these are a distributional component). The correct identity under neoclassical assumptions when there are abnormal profits should be:[8]

$$V_c \equiv V - r_{nc} J \equiv wL + r_c J. \tag{11.9}$$

It should be noted that the identity is preserved and consequently, the arguments discussed above follow through when the usual neoclassical assumptions are made, but in terms of the identity given by equation (11.9).

We have couched the argument in terms of equation (11.5) in order to stress that the problem of the identity does not require the assumption of perfectly competitive markets. For strict equivalence with the neoclassical approach, the *ex post* rate of profit is equivalent to the rental price of capital only if all markets are competitive. (It will be recalled that theoretically the rate of profit is a pure number which when multiplied by the *value* of the capital stock gives total profits. The rental price of capital is theoretically a price which when measured by the *number of units* of capital gives total profits.)[9]

---

rental price gross of corporate taxes because of data limitations, but considers the rental price of capital adjusted for taxation to be the preferable measure of the cost of capital to be used in identity. (Clark and Freeman (1980) also use the rental price of capital net of tax.) To the extent that corporation tax does not differ over the years, the net and gross measures should be closely correlated. Nevertheless, as value data are still being used, the accounting identity must still be used (we have termed this the 'virtual identity'). As we show in the text, the *ex post* estimate of the competitive rate of profit will be closely correlated with the competitive rental price of capital.

[8]   A serious problem is that there is no way of testing whether the rental price of capital (which is calculated using a number of restrictive assumptions and suffers from serious aggregation problems) correctly measures the competitive rate of profit. It can be compared with the *ex post* rate of profit but it is impossible to determine whether any difference is due to the state of competition or to errors inherent in calculating the rental price of capital.

In a perceptive comment, Jorgenson and Griliches (1967, p.257, fn 2, emphasis in the original) note: 'The answer to Mrs. Robinson's ... rhetorical question, 'what units is capital measured in?' is dual to the measurement of the price of capital services. Given either an appropriate measure of the flow of capital services or a measure of its price, the other measure may be obtained from the value of income from capital. Since this procedure is valid only if the necessary conditions for producer equilibrium are satisfied, the resulting quantity may not be employed to *test* the marginal theory of distribution, as Mrs Robinson and others have pointed out'. However, what they have overlooked is that this holds regardless of whether or not the conditions for producer equilibrium exist, as we show in the text.

[9]   It could also be argued that it is not clear that large oligopolistic firms necessarily base

Summing up so far, we could have started our argument with equation (11.9), using the (competitive) rental price of capital, and then derive an equation equivalent to equation (11.7), but on the left-hand side we would have had V_c instead of V and on the right-hand side we would have had ρ instead of r.

ESTIMATING THE 'LABOUR DEMAND' FUNCTION OR THE ACCOUNTING IDENTITY?

As shown above, we have four equations that are commonly estimated, namely,

$$\ln L = -\ln A_0 + (1 - \alpha)\ln[\alpha/(1 - \alpha)] + \ln V - (1 - \alpha)\ln w$$
$$+ (1 - \alpha)\ln r - \lambda t, \tag{11.1}$$

$$\ln L = \ln \alpha + \ln V - \ln w, \tag{11.2}$$

$$\ln L = -(1 - \sigma)\ln A_0 + \sigma \ln \delta + \ln V - \sigma \ln w - (1 - \sigma)\lambda t, \tag{11.3}$$

$$\ln L = [1/(1 - \alpha)]\ln A_0 + [1/(1 - \alpha)] \ln \alpha + \ln J - [1/(1 - \alpha)]\ln w$$
$$+ [1/(1 - \alpha)]\lambda t. \tag{11.4}$$

Q, as noted above, is proxied by value added in constant prices, V. K is proxied by the value of the capital stock measured in constant prices, J, and, for the moment, r is the *ex post* rate of return and defined as $r \equiv (V - wL)/J$. Initially we use the rate of profit, rather than the rental price of capital, to emphasise that the argument is not dependent upon any assumptions about the state of competition.

Clark and Freeman (1980), in their classic study, used equation (11.1), although they used the rental price of capital instead of the rate of profit, while Lewis and MacDonald (2002) used equation (11.3), and both studies assume that all markets are competitive. We shall return to these studies below.

---

their investment and labour-hiring decisions on the rental price of capital, which is derived from an untested optimising microeconomic model. The rate of profit of a firm, which closely correlates with its internal funds from which most investment is financed, may actually be of greater importance (as, indeed, is the state of expectations about future demand). Thus, the labour demand function is correctly specified using r, the *ex post* rate of profit. However, it must be emphasised that the argument we are making in this chapter does not rely on this assumption. Moreover, equations (11.2), (11.3) and (11.4) do not use the rental price of capital.

Let us consider these four specifications and analyse the conditions under which they become formally equivalent to the identity. The latter, it will be recalled, is given by equation (11.6). For purposes of the empirical analysis, we shall retain the use of α when discussing the neoclassical interpretation and a when considering the identity.

If we were to estimate the identity, we should expect the estimates to be:

$$\ln L \equiv c + 1.33 \ln V - 1.0 \ln w - 0.33 \ln r - 0.33 \ln J, \qquad (11.10)$$

provided that labour's share, a, is about 0.75. c is a (generic) constant.

It should be re-emphasised that as this equation is an identity (as long as factor shares are constant), it is compatible with *any* state of competition and whether or not an aggregate production function exists.

At first sight, as we noted above, it might seem that the identities, given by equations (11.6) and (11.10) are incompatible with equation (11.1), even if we substitute a linear time trend for $\ln J$ as a proxy for it in equation (11.6). This is because although they contain the same variables, the parameters are different. The coefficients of $\ln V$ and $\ln r$ in equation (11.1) are 1.0 and $(1 - \alpha)$ respectively, but in the amended equation (11.6), they are $1/a$ and $-(1 - a)/a$ (recalling that, because of the identity, α equals a). However, these discrepancies can be simply reconciled.

Let us start with the identity given by equation (11.6). First, we know that $\ln J \equiv \ln(1 - a) + \ln V - \ln r$ and substituting this into the identity, equation (11.6), gives $\ln L \equiv \ln a + \ln V - \ln w$, which is formally equivalent to equation (11.2). Second, it follows from the identity (and the usual neoclassical assumptions)[10] that:

$$\ln A(t) \equiv \ln A_0 + \lambda(t)t \equiv \ln B + a \ln w + (1 - a) \ln r, \qquad (11.11)$$

where $\lambda(t)$ is not necessarily constant and is likely to be a non-linear function of time with a pronounced cyclical component. It follows that if we equate $-\ln A_0 - \lambda(t)t + \ln B + a \ln w + (1 - a) \ln r = 0$ to $\ln L - \ln a - \ln V + \ln w = 0$, that is, to equation (11.2), and rearrange the terms, we get:

$$\ln L \equiv (\ln B - \ln A_0 + \ln a) - \lambda(t)t + \ln V - (1 - a) \ln w + (1 - a) \ln r, \qquad (11.12)$$

where $\ln B + \ln a = (1 - a) \ln[a/(1 - a)]$.

---

[10] Under the usual neoclassical assumptions the dual of TFP growth, when factor shares are constant, is given by $\lambda(t) \equiv a\hat{w} + (1 - a)\hat{r}$ and also $\ln A(t) = \ln B + a \ln w + (1 - a) \ln r$.

Equation (11.12) is none other than equation (11.1), once it is appreciated that $\ln A(t)$ is given by equation (11.11). The only difference is that the neoclassical specification derived from the aggregate production function often imposes a *linear* time trend, λt, although there is no theoretical reason for doing this – indeed, quite the opposite (Solow, 1957). *In other words, when equation (11.1), the putative labour demand equation, is correctly specified with a non-linear time trend, it is nothing more than the full identity.* It should be noted that in this analysis we have *not* had to proxy $\ln J$ by a time trend in the identity. We have merely used the identity together with the definition of capital's share and the definition of $A(t)$ to derive the correctly specified (in neoclassical terms) labour demand function. It is correctly specified in that we take the general definition of $A(t)$ rather than arbitrarily assuming that it is proxied by a linear time trend. Equation (11.4) is only equal to the misspecified identity when it is constrained to have a linear time trend.

The sign of $\ln r$ in equation (11.12) is now positive (compared with equation (11.6) where it is negative). The former accords with neoclassical production theory in that a rise in the price of capital, *ceteris paribus*, should increase the demand for labour through the factor substitution effect. However, it can now be seen that it is merely a result that *must* always occur because of the identity. It is interesting to note that Clark and Freeman (1980) find the estimate of the coefficient of the logarithm of the price of capital to be positive, even though they use a linear time trend.

In practice, $\ln A(t)$ has a distinct procyclical fluctuation, as we shall see, which means that equation (11.1) may not give a perfect fit to the data, even though factor shares are constant. This may give the misleading impression that we are actually estimating a behavioural equation rather than a (misspecified) identity. It is, however, always possible to derive a non-linear time trend, often including sines and cosines, to give a perfect fit to $\ln A(t)$. It also demonstrates that in terms of the neoclassical model, a linear time trend is a poor proxy for the rate of technical progress, if all the usual neoclassical assumptions are met.

If we similarly assume that equation (11.4) has a non-linear time trend, then under the usual neoclassical assumptions, it may easily be shown that it is an exact identity. Substituting $\ln B + a\ln w + (1 - a)\ln r \equiv \ln A(t)$ and $\ln J \equiv \ln(1 - a) + \ln V - \ln r$ into equation (11.4) gives the identity $\ln L \equiv \ln a + \ln V - \ln w$.

Thus, we have the irony that if we specify the labour demand functions, equations (11.1) and (11.4), correctly from a neoclassical point of view so that technical change is allowed to vary non-linearly, their estimation will always give a perfect fit as they are merely tracking a identity. However, if technical change is constrained to be a linear function of time, then the labour demand functions are merely tracking a misspecified identity. Equation (11.2) is definitionally true and equation (11.3) is simply this identity with a time trend and hence the negative coefficient of ln*w* will be driven by the identity.

EMPIRICAL RESULTS

In order to estimate the labour demand functions, we used data for manufacturing over the 1960–93 period from the NBER Manufacturing Industry Database, supplemented by data from the OECD database.[11]

It is useful to comment on some characteristics of the statistics. The wage rate is strongly trended upwards. Fitting a time trend to ln*w* and estimating it by the Exact AR(1) Newton–Raphson iterative method gives a growth rate of 2.04 per cent per annum (with a *t*-value of 15.40). However, this conceals a cyclical component – the fastest growth of the wage rate in a particular year was 6.50 per cent and the slowest was a decline of 5.38 per cent. The rate of profit showed no well-defined trend, with a statistically insignificant trend growth rate of 0.59 per cent per annum. But the cyclical fluctuations were even more violent than for real wages; the annual growth rates ranged between 45 and −23.68 per cent per annum. Consequently, while a linear time trend gives a statistically significant fit to the weighted growth of the wage rate and the rate of profit, it does not capture the cyclical fluctuation and is thus, *ex post*, not a very good proxy. The trend-weighted growth of the wage and profit rates is 1.53 per cent per annum, with a *t*-value of 2.27.

We first confirmed empirically the expected results for the coefficients of the identity expressed as equation (11.6). As we are dealing with an identity, the problem of the endogeneity or otherwise of the regressors does not arise. This also applies to the order of integration of the various variables, which is very much a secondary issue. Consequently, we do not report the usual battery of diagnostic statistics, except for the $\bar{R}^2$, the standard error of the regression (SER), and the Durbin–Watson diagnostic (DW).

The results of estimating the full identity are reported in Table 11.1, equation (i).[12] From a consideration of the data, the shares of labour,

---

[11] As we are illustrating a theoretical point, the exact period of the dataset used is not particularly important.

[12] As we are not dealing with behavioural equations, the exact specifications in terms of lags and so on in the empirical results are determined by the goodness of fit.

Table 11.1   The 'labour demand function' for US manufacturing; 1960–1993 (dependent variable: lnL)

	(i)[a]	(ii)[b]	(iii)[b]	(iv)[c]	(v)[f]	(vi)[f]
Constant	−0.626	−1.250	−4.045	−1.310	−0.107	1.549
	(−2.32)	(−6.76)	(−13.23)	(−0.77)	(−0.07)	(0.89)
ln V	1.338	1.297	1.271	1.008	0.965	0.948
	(90.60)	(85.47)	(75.29)	(10.89)	(11.03)	(11.13)
ln w	−0.996	−0.960	−0.910	–	−1.013	−0.699
	(−48.27)	(−51.13)	(−35.14)		(−8.40)	(−3.30)
ln r	−0.349	−0.325	−0.307	–	–	–
	(−26.91)	(−42.88)	(−40.13)			
ln(w/r)	–	–	–	−0.129	–	–
				(−4.29)		
ln J	−0.348	−0.249	–	–	–	–
	(−47.70)	(−12.41)				
t	–	−0.003	−0.012	−1.332[d]	–	−0.007
		(−5.57)	(−17.39)	(−9.48)		(−1.80)
$\bar{R}^2$	0.999	0.999	0.998	0.999	0.935	0.940
SER	0.002	0.002	0.003	0.002	0.016	0.015
DW	1.498	2.445	1.936	0.299[e]	1.916	1.812

Notes:
Average share of labour = 0.729.
[a] Exact AR(1) Newton–Raphson iterative method.
[b] Exact AR(2) Newton–Raphson iterative method.
[c] OLS, long-run elasticities; one-year lags of ln$L$, ln$V$, and ln$A^*(t)$ (or $a$ln$w$ + $(1 − a)$ln$r$).
[d] Coefficient of ln$A^*(t)$ (or $a$ln$w$ + $(1 − a)$ln$r$), which is substituted for the linear time trend.
[e] Durbin's h-test.
[f] Long-run elasticities; one-year lag of ln$V$ and ln$w$. Exact AR(1) Newton–Raphson iterative method.

Sources: NBER Manufacturing Database; OECD database.

a, are reasonably stable over the long run with a mean of 0.729 and a standard deviation of 0.024. Consequently, it is not surprising that the estimated coefficients are well determined and are close to their expected values, namely 1.338 compared with the theoretical value of 1.371 for ln$V$, −0.996 (−1.000) for ln$w$, −0.349 (−0.372) for ln$r$ and −0.348 (−0.372) for ln$J$.

Equation (ii) reports the results of estimating the identity including the linear time trend, denoted by t, which at this stage can simply be regarded as an irrelevant included variable, and, consequently, its expected coefficient is zero. However, it can be seen that the coefficient is actually statistically significant. We know that this must be purely coincidental, or perhaps occurs because factor shares are not exactly constant and we are consequently estimating the 'wrong' functional form. The other coefficients in the regression are only marginally affected by its inclusion.

Equation (iii) in Table 11.1 drops the capital stock variable and replaces it with a time trend and the close correspondence of this specification, which has no causal implications, and the labour demand function, equation (11.4), is readily apparent, apart from the difference in the theoretical values of the coefficients of $\ln V$, $\ln w$ and $\ln r$ (including the sign on the last). The only other difference between this 'labour demand function' and the full identity is that the labour demand function excludes the logarithm of the capital stock and includes a time trend (putatively to capture the growth of TFP). When $\ln J$ is simply dropped from the identity, that is, from equation (i), and replaced by a time trend in equation (iii), it is found that when the AR(2) Newton–Raphson iterative method is used to correct for the autocorrelation, the estimates of the remaining coefficients are scarcely different from those obtained using the full identity.

Consequently, we can see that the negative coefficient of $\ln w$ in the 'labour demand function' is being driven solely by the underlying accounting identity.

However, as shown above, we can get a perfect correspondence between equation (11.1) and the identity. In equation (iv), the linear time trend was replaced by $\ln A^*(t) \equiv a\ln w + (1 - a) \ln r$, which, as we have seen, is what both the neoclassical approach (if all its assumptions are fulfilled) and the identity suggest should be the case. (Equation (iv) and equation (11.1) are now theoretically identical, provided that a flexible time trend is incorporated in the latter.) Because of multicollinearity, we constrained the coefficients of $\ln w$ and $-\ln r$ to be the same. Hence, we estimated equation (11.1) as:

$$\ln L = -\ln B - \ln A^*(t) + (1-\alpha) \ln [\alpha/(1- \alpha)] + \ln V - (1 - \alpha) \ln (w/r),$$
$$(11.13)$$

where $\ln A^*(t)= a \ln w + (1 - a) \ln r$.

Equation (iv) reports the OLS long-run estimates when the equation is estimated using one-period lags of $\ln L$, $\ln V$ and $\ln A^*(t)$. The estimated coefficient of $\ln V$ is 1.008 as opposed to its theoretical value of 1.000, the coefficient of $\ln(w/r)$ is -0.129 compared with -0.271, and of $\ln A^*(t)$ is -1.332 compared with -1.000. There is thus a little difference between the estimated values of the coefficients and those that are to be expected from the identity. The disparities are not large and are due to the cyclical fluctuation in the factor shares. What is important is that the statistically significant negative coefficient of $\ln(w/r)$ is due to the identity.

These results are similar to those of Clark and Freeman (1980), although they used the rental price of capital instead of the rate of profit and gross output instead of value added. They also obtained a larger absolute value for the coefficient of $\ln(w/r)$. As we noted above, they used a linear time trend, which suggests that this was, in fact, a good proxy for the weighted growth of the wage and profit rates.

We also confirmed empirically that using the rental price of capital, as opposed to the rate of profit, did not make any difference to the results reported above. We used the manufacturing capital input estimates (calculated using the implicit rental capital prices, net of taxes, in the aggregation of the assets) calculated by the BLS and we assumed that all the usual neoclassical assumptions were met.

The data for manufacturing used by the BLS for calculating estimates of TFP covered the 1948–2005 period. Estimating the complete identity by the Exact AR(2) Newton–Raphson Iterative Method gave a very good fit:

$$\ln L = -0.930 + 1.490 \ln V - 0.986 \ln w - 0.500 \ln \rho - 0.498 \ln J$$
$$(-66.94) \ (155.32) \qquad (-191.58) \quad (-89.07) \qquad (-61.67)$$

$$\bar{R}^2 = 0.9999, \text{SER} = 0.0008, \text{DW} = 2.045.$$

The average share of labour is 0.664 (with a range from 0.702 to 0.625) and that of capital is 0.336 (with a range of 0.375 to 0.298). Consequently, the estimated coefficients are very close to the expected values from the identity which are 1.50; -1.00; -0.500 and -0.500, respectively.

We also re-estimated equation (11.13), that is, the correctly specified neoclassical labour demand function using the rental price of capital, by the exact AR(1) Method and we got similar results to those using the *ex post* rate of profit, namely:

$$\ln L = -0.641 - 1.069 \ln A^*(t) + 0.939 \ln V^* - 0.169 \ln (w/\rho)$$
$$(-5.05) \ (-18.37) \qquad (33.24) \qquad (-10.0)$$

$$\bar{R}^2 = 0.9993, \text{SER} = 0.0007, \text{DW} = 1.747,$$

where in this equation $\ln A^*(t) = a\ln w + (1 - a)\ln\rho$. The estimated coefficients are close to those of the identity except that the coefficient of $\ln(w/\rho)$ is about half the expected value of -0.336.

When we replaced $\ln A^*(t)$ with a linear time trend, the value of the coefficient of $\ln V$ was 1.043 (t-value of 5.87). But the coefficient of $\ln(w/\rho)$, while −0.125, was statistically insignificant (t value of −1.48) (the full results are not reported here for reasons of space). When we estimated the regression with the coefficients of ln$w$ and ln$p$ unconstrained, we found that both were statistically significant but both were also negative. This is what the identity would lead us to expect but it was not what Clark and Freeman found. They found the coefficient on ln$p$ statistically significant and positive.

The question arises as to whether or not the introduction of lags (based here purely on the criterion of statistical significance) undermines the interpretation of the results as solely reflecting the identity. We know that the identity ln$a \equiv$ ln$w +$ ln$L -$ ln$V$ holds if ln$a$ is exactly constant. However, while over the period as a whole, ln$a$ is roughly constant, it nevertheless displays a strong lagged component as evidenced by the following OLS regression:

$$\ln a = -0.064 + 0.805 \ln a_{-1}$$
$$(-1.77) \quad (7.09)$$

$$\bar{R}^2 = 0.607, \text{SER} = 0.020, \text{Durbin } h-test = 0.917,$$

where ln$a$ is regressed on its value lagged one year. The long-run estimate of the coefficient is −0.328. This gives an estimate of labour's share of 0.720.[13]

Consequently, when the lagged values of ln$V$, ln$w$ and ln$L$ are included in the above regression instead of the lagged value of ln$a$, it is a foregone conclusion that they must be statistically significant. As the intercept in the regressions is a function of the factor share(s), it is not surprising that, in some cases, the goodness of fit is improved by the inclusion of the lagged variables. But it should be emphasised that this does not alter the interpretation that the estimated coefficients are simply reflecting the parameters of the identity.

We next estimated equation (11.2), namely ln$L = c + b_1$ln$V + b_2$ln$w$, which could be viewed as an alternative specification of the labour demand function where the expected values of the coefficients b_1 and b_2 are 1 and −1 and the results are reported as equation (v) in Table 11.1. Given that factor shares are approximately constant, this equation is again an identity, and so the coefficients *must* take these values. From a neoclassical point of view, equation (11.2) has the advantage that it avoids the possible misspecification inherent in proxying technical change by a linear (or even

---

[13] Simply regressing ln$a$ on a constant gives a coefficient of −0.318 with a t-value of −57.21. This gives a value of labour's share of 0.728.

non-linear) time trend. It has the disadvantage that the coefficient of $\ln w$ cannot now be interpreted as the elasticity of employment with respect to the real wage rate, but this can be calculated from the estimate of the intercept. It can be seen that the coefficient of $\ln V$ is 0.965 (with a t-value of 7.74) and $\ln w$ is -1.013 (-8.40) both of which are close to their expected values. (These are the long-run estimates when a one-period lag of $\ln L$ is included.) However, the estimate of the intercept is poorly determined and is statistically insignificant.

The advantage of equation (11.3), $\ln L = -(1 - \sigma)\ln A_0 + \sigma\ln\delta + \ln V - \sigma\ln w - (1 - \sigma)\lambda t$, is that it also avoids the need to calculate the rental price of capital and the capital stock, and can be derived from the more flexible CES production function. This is the functional form estimated by Lewis and MacDonald (2002) using quarterly Australian data. (As noted above, it is a marginal product revenue curve and not, strictly speaking, a labour demand curve. The elasticity can, however, be calculated from the estimated parameters.) In this case, as L is definitionally related to V and w, we can see that the estimates will still reflect those of the identity, albeit biased by the omission of $\ln r$ and $\ln J$ as they are not adequately proxied by the time trend. The results are reported in Table 11.1 equation (vi), and it can be seen that the omission of $\ln r$ and $\ln J$ causes the goodness of fit to fall and the estimate of $\ln w$ is biased upwards, taking a value of -0.699 instead of -1.

Finally, we turn to the labour demand function when capital is kept constant, equation (11.1). The statistical fit is not particularly good, with the coefficient of $\ln w$ taking the wrong sign:

$$\ln L = 8.632 + 0.723 \ln J + 0.447 \ln w - 0.032t$$
$$(2.27) \quad (2.97) \quad\quad (1.61) \quad\quad\quad (-3.80)$$
$$\overline{R}^2 = 0.759, \text{SER} = 0.032, \text{DW} = 1.961.$$

(The estimation method is the Exact AR(2) Newton–Raphson iterative method.) The reason is relatively straightforward. $\ln J$ shows very little variation while the two omitted variables, $\ln r$ and $\ln V$ show considerable variability and this causes the poor statistical fit and the substantial degree of bias on the coefficients, especially of $\ln w$.

We also have the problem that, at first glance, this specification seems to be incompatible with the identity. However, it will be recalled from equation (11.8) that $\ln B + a\ln w + (1 - a)\ln r = \ln A(t) = \ln A_0 + \lambda(t)t$. If we use this equation to substitute for $\ln A_0 + \lambda t$ in equation (11.13) (that is, assuming that $\lambda = \lambda(t)$) and also use the relationship $\ln a = \ln w + \ln L - \ln V$, we derive the identity given by equation (11.6). (It will be recalled that $a = \alpha$.)

THE WAGE ELASTICITY AND ERROR-CORRECTION MODELS

In this section we shall, for simplicity, confine ourselves to the marginal revenue product curve defined by equation (11.3) and used by Lewis and MacDonald (2002).

If we were dealing with a behavioural equation, then the question of whether the estimation of this specification gives rise to a spurious regression would be relevant. Consequently, assuming for the moment that it is a behavioural equation, we followed the procedure of Lewis and MacDonald and estimated equation (11.3) within an Autoregressive Distributed Lag (ARDL) model following the approach of Pesaran and Shin (1999) and Pesaran et al. (2001). The advantage of this approach is that it can be applied to models that contain a mixture of I(0) and I(1) variables and hence avoids the pre-testing problems involved with the standard cointegration analysis.

The error-correction version of equation (11.3) is:

$$\Delta \ln L = c + \chi_0 t + \chi_1 \Delta \ln L_{t-1} + \chi_2 \Delta \ln V_{t-1} + \chi_3 \Delta \ln w_{t-1} + \varsigma_1 \ln L_{t-1}$$
$$+ \varsigma_2 \ln V_{t-1} + \varsigma_3 \ln w_{t-1} + u_t. \tag{11.14}$$

The first test is the null hypothesis $H_0: \varsigma_1 = \varsigma_2 = \varsigma_3 = 0$. Using the critical bounds test devised by Pesaran et al. (2001), the obtained F-value of 18.17 exceeds the upper bound of the non-standard F-value of 5.76 and so the null hypothesis of there being no long-run relationship between $\ln L$, $\ln w$ and $\ln V$ is rejected. Estimating equation (11.3) by an ARDL approach gives the long-run relationship as:

$$\ln L = 8.948 - 0.009t + 1.636 \ln V - 1.380 \ln w$$
$$(2.87) \quad (-2.22) \quad (3.96) \quad (-2.22)$$

and the error-correction term from the specification including the lags – not reported here – is significant and is -0.280 with a t-value of -2.83. (As we are concerned with the long-run relationship, we do not report the specification with the lags.) However, the t-values of the long-run estimates are rather low and the estimated coefficient of $\ln w$ is rather small (-1.380), as opposed to the expected value of -1.000 implicit in the identity. The coefficients are also somewhat different from those reported in Table 11.1, equation (vi). This is due to the different estimation method.[14] However, the key point remains:

---

[14] The long-term estimates of Lewis and MacDonald (2002) using Australian quarterly data for the whole economy over the 1961–98 period are:

$\ln L$, $\ln V$ and $\ln w$ are definitionally related and even though the estimated values may diverge, to some extent, from those of the identity, they are still statistical artefacts. The error-correction term is not the result of disequilibrium in the economic sense, but simply because the introduction of lagged values improves the goodness of fit of the (misspecified) identity.

THE CRITIQUE BY ANYADIKE-DANES AND GODLEY

A similar critique to the one discussed above (although with one or two key differences) has been put forward in an important, but somewhat neglected, paper by Anyadike-Danes and Godley (ADG) (1989). Using a mark-up pricing model and an employment equation where real wages are not an argument, they show by simulation analysis that if the real wage is (erroneously) included in the regressions of the employment demand functions, its coefficient will still be negative and highly significant.

ADG specify four alternative models, but we shall consider only one of them here, namely their Model 2. In this model, the authors postulate that there is a 'true' underlying employment function of the form:

$$\Delta \ln L = \phi[(C_1 + \ln Q - \ln S) - \ln L_{-1}]. \tag{11.15}$$

The variable $\ln S$ is the logarithm of the trend (and not the actual) rate of growth of productivity and there is a first-order partial adjustment process denoted by ϕ, which, in constructing the simulation data, is taken to be 0.3. Q denotes output in physical terms and C_i ($i = 1, 2, 3$ and 4) denotes a constant, namely, combinations of different parameters. In the long run, the growth of labour is determined by the growth of output and the exogenous trend growth of productivity. Prices are determined by current and lagged normal unit costs and the pricing equation is given by:

$$\ln p = C_2 + \mu(\ln w^n - \ln S) + (1 - \mu)(\ln w^n_{-1} - \ln S_{-1}), \tag{11.16}$$

where μ describes the speed of adjustment. (Empirically, μ takes a value of about 0.75.) Combining equations (11.15) and (11.16), we obtain the hybrid function:

$\ln L = -0.0981 - 0.0031t + 1.058 \ln Q - 0.446 \ln w$
$\qquad (-0.26) \quad\;\; (-8.31) \quad (17.05) \qquad (-6.20)$

$$\ln L = C_3 - \varphi(\ln w^n - \ln p) - \varphi\left(\frac{1 - \mu}{\mu}\right)(\ln w^n_{-1} - \ln p_{-1}) + \varphi \ln Q$$

$$+ \varphi\left(\frac{\mu}{1 - \mu}\right)(p - p_{-1}) + \left[\frac{\mu}{(1 - \mu)}\right]\ln S_{-1} + (1 - \varphi)\ln L_{-1}. \quad (11.17)$$

If the mark-up is just on current labour costs (that is, $\mu = 1$), equation (11.17) reduces to:

$$\ln L = C_3 - \phi \ln w + \phi \ln Q + (1 - \phi)\ln L_{-1}, \quad (11.18)$$

where $w = w^n - p$, so the long-run coefficients of $\ln w$ and $\ln Q$ are again -1 and 1.

If we were to test the neoclassical model by estimating equation (11.18), we would find the real wage term negative and highly significant, even though we know by construct that the real wage term has *no* role in determining the level of employment in a causal sense (it does not appear in the 'true' employment function).

ADG find that in estimating equation (11.18), the coefficients of all the independent variables are statistically significant and the long-run estimates of the coefficients of $\ln Q$ and $\ln w$ are 0.935 and -0.968, respectively.

ADG compare the performance of their model with the statistical estimations of employment, or labour demand, function by Bean et al. (1986) which takes the form:

$$\Delta \ln L = c + b_3 t + b_4 t^2 + b_5(\ln L_{-1} - \ln J) + b_6 \ln w + b_7 \Delta \ln L_{-1} + b_8 D, \quad (11.19)$$

where D represents real demand. This is constructed, as ADG point out, by first regressing the (logarithm of) output relative to capital stock on current and lagged fiscal and monetary policy variables (similarly scaled) together with a lagged dependent variable. ADG proxy $\ln J$ by a log linear trend that rises by 1 per cent per annum more than the trend of $\ln Q$ and a random fluctuation is then added to this trend. ADG's Model 2 simply assumes that $D = \ln V - \ln J$.

Bean et al.'s results for three countries, together with ADG's Model 2 as a comparison, are reported in Table 11.2. The constant and time trend are not reported. It can be seen that the data are not able to discriminate between the two markedly different competing hypotheses, one that theoretically accords a causal role to real wages in determining the level of employment and the other that does not.

Table 11.2 Estimates of the Bean, Layard and Nickel (1986), Anyadike-Danes and Godley (1989a) and related models (dependent variable ΔlnL)

	Bean et al.'s estimates			ADG's Model2	Authors' estimates			Expected values from the identity
	UK	France	Germany		Equation (i)	Equation (ii)	Equation (iii)	
$\ln L_{-1}-\ln J$	−0.63	−0.28	−0.64	−0.32	−1.03	−0.86	−0.66	−1.00
	(−4.8)	(−3.5)	(−2.1)	(−23.2)	(−64.4)	(−9.0)	(−14.1)	
$\ln w$	−0.40	−0.17	−0.53	−0.23	−1.05	−0.45	−0.12	−1.00
	(−2.0)	(−3.4)	(−3.5)	(−10.0)	(−49.7)	(−3.5)	(−1.9)	
$\Delta\ln L_{-1}$	0.45	0.22	0.51	−0.01	−0.01	0.16	−0.07	0.00
	(2.3)	(1.0)	(1.8)	(−0.4)	(−0.9)	(1.9)	(−1.4)	
D	0.50	0.14	0.46	–	–	–	–	–
	(7.1)	(1.3)	(1.4)					
$\ln V - \ln J\,(=D)$	–	–	–	0.31	1.39	0.57	–	1.37
				(26.8)	(68.8)	(10.6)		
$\ln CAP$	–	–	–	–	–	–	0.85	–
							(21.6)	
$\ln r$	–	–	–	–	−0.38	–	–	−0.37
					(−41.7)			
t	n.r	n.r	n.r	n.r.	–	−0.01	−0.02	–
						(−4.8)	(−13.0)	

Note: n.r. denotes not reported. Bean et al. (1986) use a linear and quadratic time trend. The 'expected values' in the last column are those of the full identity given by equation (11.21). Figures in parentheses are *t*-values.

Sources: Bean et al. (1986); Anyadike-Danes and Godley (1989, p. 183); and authors' estimates.

Our approach reinforces this conclusion. It will be recalled that the identity is given by equation (11.6), which subtracting $\ln L_{-1}$ on both sides and rearranging it yields:

$$\Delta \ln L \equiv -\frac{1}{a}\ln B - (\ln L_{-1} - \ln J) - \ln w + 0\Delta \ln L_{-1} + \frac{1}{a}(\ln V - \ln J) + \frac{(1-a)}{a}\ln r. \tag{11.20}$$

For US manufacturing over the 1960–93 period, it will be recalled that labour's share, a, takes an average value of 0.73. Hence, the identity can be written as:

$$\Delta \ln L \equiv C_4 - (\ln L_{-1} - \ln J) - \ln w + 0\Delta \ln L_{-1} + 1.37(\ln V - \ln J) + 0.37\ln r, \tag{11.21}$$

where $\ln V - \ln J = D$. The variable $\Delta \ln L_{-1}$ has an expected coefficient of zero, as it should not be included in the identity. The results of estimating equation (11.21) are reported in Table 11.2, equation (i), where it can be seen that the shares are sufficiently constant to give a good statistical fit. As expected, the coefficient of $\Delta \ln L_{-1}$ is statistically insignificant.

The identity is, of course, compatible with *any* underlying technology including one where the real wage has no role in determining the level of employment. Indeed, given the wide variety of industries, probably there is not a well-defined relationship between aggregate employment and aggregate output, even if both could be aggregated. However, from the identity, we see once again why there is likely to be a statistically significant relationship. In the Bean et al. formulation, the growth of the rate of profit does not appear, so this was dropped from the identity and, following Bean et al., a time trend was included instead. (It was found that a linear time trend gave the best fit and so, unlike in Bean et al., a quadratic time trend was not included.) The results are reported in Table 11.2 as equation (ii). It is interesting to note that the coefficient of $\Delta \ln L_{-1}$ is now positive and statistically significant. It is positive in all three estimations by Bean et al. (but not in ADG's Model 2, where it was statistically insignificant).[15]

As we have noted, the variable $(\ln V - \ln J)$ may be interpreted as a proxy for Bean et al.'s measure of demand, and the coefficient of this variable falls to 0.57 in Table 11.2, equation (ii), which is not far off Bean et al.'s estimates of the coefficient of D, especially for the UK and Germany. It should be emphasised that the differences in the values of the coefficients from those of the full identity are just due to omitted variable bias and the

---

[15]   It is positive and statistically significant in their Model 1, which we have not discussed.

inclusion of irrelevant variables. To this extent they may be regarded as purely coincidental – there is certainly nothing in production theory that suggests that the biases ought to be of either the sign or the order of magnitude that they take.

Finally, we replaced $(\ln V - \ln J)$ by $\ln CAP$, which is the logarithm of a capacity utilisation variable.[16] It can be seen that it is a good, but not perfect, proxy for $\ln V - \ln J$ and as a result the estimates of the coefficients change somewhat. But the negative coefficient of $\ln w$ is still statistically significant although its absolute value is low.

ADG compare their simulation results with further empirical estimates from other studies of the side relations derived from the neoclassical production function, and we have done likewise. The results are not reported here, but the statistically significant negative coefficient of real wages, not surprisingly, is also found in these other neoclassical studies.

CONCLUSIONS

This chapter has shown that the test of the neoclassical hypothesis that employment and the wage rate are inversely related, that is, the estimation of the labour demand function and the marginal revenue product curve, faces insoluble problems. This is due to the fact that empirical applications use value data as opposed to physical quantities. Since value data and employment are linked through an accounting identity, we show that estimation of the labour demand function and the marginal revenue product curve with these data will always yield a negative relationship between the level of employment and the real wage.

In fact, the data must normally give a good statistical fit to either the neoclassical labour or the capital demand functions even when, because of the multitude of firms with very different production functions, there might not be any well-defined aggregate production function or factor demand functions at all. Moreover, the negative coefficient on the wage term in the labour demand equations (and the marginal revenue product curve) is determined solely by the underlying identity. However, we have also shown with our data that, even when the factor shares are roughly constant, some of the specifications do not give near perfect statistical fits. This may give rise to the mistaken belief that a behavioural equation is being estimated.

---

[16]   We are grateful to Anwar Shaikh for providing us with his capacity utilisation estimates.

We have taken the simplest labour and capital demand functions because these most clearly demonstrate the problems involved. But the problems posed carry through to more complicated factor demand functions. This has been shown by reconsidering the argument of Anyadike-Danes and Godley (1989) and we have confirmed the importance of their arguments, which are similar, although not identical, to the ones outlined in this chapter.

It is clear that no reliance can be placed on estimates of the wage elasticities in formulating economic policy. Arguments that an increase in the real wage rate will necessarily lead to a fall in the level of employment cannot be inferred from the statistical estimates of the elasticity of employment with respect to the real wage. To base policy solely on this evidence may have unforeseen and unwanted consequences.

APPENDIX 11A: THE NAIRU AND THE LAWS OF ALGEBRA

Lavoie (2000, 2008) has shown that a variant of a NAIRU model of Layard et al. (1991) (LNJ) by Cotis et al. (1998) (CRS) can be easily derived as a series of simple transformations of the variables that define the income side of the National Income and Product Accounts (NIPA). Hence, its econometric estimation has no policy implications whatsoever. This appendix presents a summary of Lavoie's arguments, published originally in French. LNJ argued that their model allowed them to explain the path of the rate of *equilibrium unemployment*, or NAIRU. They argued that 60 per cent of the increase in unemployment in France was due to increases in real interest rates and the rest was due to increases in the social security payments and other benefits. The results seem to be very persuasive because the path of the equilibrium unemployment rate seems to match the evolution of observed unemployment. Lavoie (2000) argues that there seem to be a number of studies on the NAIRU highlighting the role of tax rates, as opposed to other traditional variables, such as the rate of unionisation or the different measures of the costs of severance payment or of the generosity of social programmes. The model estimated consists of the following three equations:

$$\ln w = a_1 U + a_2 \ln wedge + \gamma t \tag{11A.1}$$

$$\ln w = b_1 U + b_2 (\ln V - \ln N) + b_3 t \tag{11A.2}$$

$$\ln w = \gamma t - \frac{(1 - a)}{a} \ln i, \tag{11A.3}$$

where (11A.1) is a behavioural equation that defines the workers' target salary. w is the real wage rate; U is the rate of unemployment; *wedge* is the tax wedge, that is, the difference between workers' take-home pay and the costs of employing them, including income taxes and social security contributions; and t is a time trend. Equation (11A.2) represents the short-term labour demand curve. V denotes real output and N is the level of economically active population. Finally, equation (11A.3) represents the long-term labour demand curve. i denotes the real interest rate. The variable γ is a measure of labour productivity growth, and $(1 - a)/a$ is the ratio of the capital share to the labour share in output.

The intersection of equations (11A.1) and (11A.2) determines the *medium-term* equilibrium unemployment rate; while the intersection of equations (11A.1) and (11A.3) determines the *long-term* equilibrium unemployment rate, which in LNJ's model depends only on the tax wedge (*wedge*), and on the real interest rate (plus a constant). These two relationships allow the authors to assert that the high long-term equilibrium unemployment rate is mainly due to the high real interest rates and due also partially to the high social security payments and other benefits.

CRS argue that theory implies that $b_1 = b_2 = 1$ in equation (11A.2). The only econometric result from this equation is $b_3 = -0.002$ (with quarterly data). The authors verify that in equation (11A.1), $a_1 < 0$ while $a_2 > 0$ and is around unity. This means that when the unemployment rate decreases, workers negotiate real salaries above what would be justifiable given the increases in productivity and also that increases in social security taxes and other benefits lead to increases in negotiated real salaries.

According to CRS, equation (11A.2) indicates that for a given increase in *full employment productivity*, an increase in the real salary entails an increase in the unemployment rate, as a result of the maximisation behaviour of firms.

However, Lavoie has argued that these equations can easily be derived from the income side of the NIPA, and thus their econometric estimation does not imply anything in terms of testing a theory and policy implications. The NIPA allows the derivation of equations (11A.2) and (11A.3) in a few steps. Starting from the accounting identity, expressing in growth rates and rearranging gives:

$$\hat{w}_t \equiv (\hat{V}_t - \hat{L}_t) + \frac{(1-a)}{a}(\hat{V}_t - \hat{J}_t) - \frac{(1-a)}{a}\hat{r}_t. \qquad (11A.4)$$

Note that $U = (N - L)/L = (N/L) - 1$ implies that $(1 + U) = N/L$ and $\ln(1 + U) = \ln(N/L)$. From the approximation $\ln(1 + U) \approx U$, it follows that:

$$U \approx \ln\left(\frac{N}{L}\right) = \ln(N) - \ln(L). \qquad (11A.5)$$

Taking the derivative with respect to time, the last expression becomes $dU/dt = \dot{U}_t = \hat{N}_t - \hat{L}_t$ and implies that $\hat{L}_t \approx \hat{N}_t - \dot{U}_t$. Substituting this expression for $\hat{L}$ into (11A.4) yields:

$$\hat{w}_t \approx (\hat{V}_t - \hat{N}_t) + \dot{U}_t + \frac{a}{(1-a)}(\hat{V}_t - \hat{J}_t - \hat{r}_t). \qquad (11A.6)$$

Integrating yields:

$$\ln w \approx (\ln V - \ln N) + U + \frac{(1-a)}{a}ht, \qquad (11A.7)$$

where h = $(\hat{V}_t - \hat{J}_t - \hat{r}_t)$ It is obvious that equations (11A.2) and (11A.7) are the same, for all practical purposes. It is not surprising that econometric estimations lead to $b_1 = b_2 = 1$ and no wonder either that economists have succeeded at verifying empirically, based on equations such as (11A.2) (or (11A.7), that excessive increases in real salaries lead to increases in the unemployment rate. However, since this result is derived from an accounting identity, it does not have such an interpretation.

Let us now derive equation (11A.3). Returning to (11A.5), note that it can be written as:

$$\hat{w}_t = \frac{1}{a}\{\hat{V}_t - [a\hat{L}_t + (1-a)\hat{J}_t]\} - \frac{(1-a)}{a}\hat{r}_t \qquad (11A.8)$$

or,

$$\hat{w}_t = \frac{\lambda}{a} - \frac{(1-a)}{a}\hat{r}_t, \qquad (11A.9)$$

where $\lambda = \hat{V}_t - [a\hat{L}_t + (1-a)\hat{J}_t]$. Integrating yields:

$$\ln w = \frac{\lambda}{a}t - \frac{(1-a)}{a}\ln r, \qquad (11A.10)$$

which can be approximated as:

$$\ln w = \gamma t - \frac{(1-a)}{a}\ln i, \qquad (11A.11)$$

where $\gamma = \lambda/a$ and i is the interest rate. Note that if $\hat{V}_t = \hat{J}_t$ then γ equals the growth of labour productivity. It can be seen that equation (11A.11) and (11A.3) are the same. But again, since (11A.11) is an accounting identity, its estimation does not have any economic implications. Finally, Lavoie argues that the only behavioural equation in the system is (11A.1), even though he argues that the results are not convincing, but for reasons unrelated to those summarised above.

12. Why have criticisms of the aggregate production function generally been ignored? On further misunderstandings and misinterpretations of the implications of the accounting identity

How is it possible to have a controversy over a purely logical point?
(Joan Robinson, 1975, p. 32)

INTRODUCTION

As we have seen in previous chapters, there are two serious problems with the aggregate production function – so serious that the whole concept is deeply flawed. First, there is the 'aggregation problem', broadly defined to include the Cambridge capital theory controversies. Second, there is the problem that, because of the underlying accounting identity in value terms, empirical estimation of the production function using value data can neither provide a refutation of its existence nor can the estimated coefficients necessarily be interpreted as technological parameters. Yet while both these shortcomings have been known for decades, as we noted in the introduction and in previous chapters, they are either barely mentioned or totally ignored in the literature where aggregate production functions are discussed.[1] In this chapter we attempt to answer the question, 'why'? (See McCombie, 1998b for a methodological assessment.)

We have seen the difficulties that aggregation poses for the aggregate production function and which date from the 1940s (May, 1946, 1947; Nataf, 1948). Subsequent work includes Joan Robinson (1953–54), Solow (1955–56) and the research of Fisher (1969, 1992). Nor has there been an absence of warnings to the profession. Walters (1963a, p. 11), in a classic study of production and cost functions, many years ago, came to the following conclusion:

---

[1] An exception is Temple's (2006, 2010) detailed critique of our work, which is not compelling. See Felipe and McCombie (2010b, 2012). This debate is summarised below.

> After surveying the problems of aggregation one may easily doubt whether there is much point in employing such a concept as an aggregate production function. The variety of competitive and technological conditions we find in modern economies suggest that we cannot approximate the basic requirements of sensible aggregation except, perhaps, over firms in the same industry or for narrow sections of the economy.

More recent work on the aggregation problem has not altered this conclusion: 'Such results show that the analytic use of such aggregates as "capital", "output", "labour" or "investment" as though the production side of the economy could be treated as a single firm is without sound foundation' (Fisher, 1987, p. 55). While the conditions of successful aggregation are matters of logic or formal proof, whether or not the problems are sufficiently serious to warrant the abandonment of the use of the aggregate production function is a subjective matter. As Fisher continued in the above quotation, the aggregation problem 'has not discouraged macroeconomists from continuing to work in such terms'.

Indeed, Blaug (1974), who can scarcely be viewed as sympathetic to the Cambridge, UK, view of the interpretation, or importance, of the Cambridge capital theory controversies, nevertheless considers that the aggregation problem effectively destroys the rationale of the aggregate production function: 'Even if capital were physically homogeneous, aggregation of labour and indeed aggregation of output would still require stringent and patently unrealistic conditions at the economy-level'. Moreover,

> '[T]he concept of the economically meaningful aggregate production function requires much stronger and much less plausible conditions than the concept of an aggregate consumption function. And yet, undisturbed by Walter's conclusions or Fisher's findings, economists have gone on happily in increasing numbers estimating aggregate production functions of even more complexity, barely halting to justify their procedures or to explain the economic significance of their results'. (p. 17)

A good early example of this persistence with the aggregate production function despite its enduring problems is Walters (1963b) who, in the same year as publishing his survey cited above, also published the results of estimating an aggregate production function using US time-series data. Walters admits that 'the theoretical foundations of the aggregate production function give one grounds for doubting whether the concept is at all useful'. Nevertheless, he justified this exercise on the grounds that 'there is no doubt that it is useful to rationalize data along these lines', (p. 425), without providing any convincing explanation as to why this should be the case.

The traditional defence to these problems is that whether or not the theoretical problems raised are serious is essentially an empirical one. The fact that aggregate production functions can give good fits to the data with plausible estimates gave confidence in the use of the aggregate production function. Reswitching was likened to the 'Giffen good paradox' in demand theory and of equal empirical insignificance (Stiglitz, 1974).

As Solow (1975, p. 277) put it, the neoclassical position 'is only a crude simplification for the purpose of applying the theory to real numbers, and so has to be judged pragmatically and not by standards of rigorous analysis'. Ferguson on numerous occasions reiterated the view that the aggregate production function should be seen as a 'parable', an approximation that nevertheless gives valuable insights into the production and the distribution of factor rewards:

> But to empirically-minded economists, such as Douglas or Solow, the parable has meant something more. In particular, it offers a set of hypotheses that can be subject to statistical examination and evaluation. Assume the existence of an aggregate production function, such as Cobb–Douglas or CES, that meets the requirements of the Clark parable. In such circumstances, do the conventionally defined aggregates furnished by the OBE [Office of Business Economics] and other government statistical agencies tend to confirm or reject the inferences of the neoclassical parable? Without documentation, which is readily available, I will assert that the answer is 'Confirm'. (Ferguson, 1972, p. 174)

The empirical evidence has also been interpreted as confirming the simple, not to say simplistic, neoclassical aggregate marginal productivity theory of distribution (Douglas, 1976).

Nevertheless, Ferguson was far more circumspect in 1963 before he had nailed his colours to the mast by publishing the *Neoclassical Theory of Production and Distribution* (1969). For example, he wrote:

> On the empirical level, we face something of a dilemma. . . . There are fairly substantial grounds for questioning the correspondence between observable magnitudes and the theoretical constructs in which we are interested . . . Many economists have obtained excellent results by fitting the Cobb–Douglas function to aggregative and semi-aggregative data. . . . . . Suppose we find a specific form for the function $Y = f(K, L)$, such that the first partial derivative with respect to L, when multiplied by L and divided by Y, yields acceptable approximations of the relative share of the product going to labor. Steeped as most of us are in neoclassical theory, it is tempting to infer that $f(K,L)$ is a production function. *Yet we should probably not do so.* (Ferguson, 1963, p. 312, emphasis added)

See Carter (2011a) for a comprehensive assessment of Ferguson's views on these matters.

THE INSTRUMENTAL DEFENCE OF THE AGGREGATE PRODUCTION FUNCTION

The common defence of the use of unrealistic assumptions in economics is Friedman's (1953) methodological stance that a 'theory is to be judged by its predictive power of the class of phenomena which it is intended to "explain" . . . the only relevant test of the *validity* of a hypothesis is comparison of its predictions with experience' (pp. 8–9, emphasis in the original). The realism of its assumptions is irrelevant. The only problem is 'whether they are sufficiently good approximations for the purpose at hand. And this question can only be answered by seeing whether a theory works, which means whether it yields sufficiently accurate predictions' (p. 15). While Friedman's methodological stance has been heavily criticised (Samuelson, 1963; Kincaid, 1996, pp. 227–8), his approach is one that is still widely accepted by economists.

As far as the aggregate production function is concerned, as we noted in the Introduction, Wan (1971, p. 71) views the aggregate production function as an empirical law in its own right, which is capable of statistical refutation. The instrumental defence is also implicit in Solow's remark to Fisher, that 'had Douglas found labor's share to be 25 per cent and capital's 75 per cent instead of the other way around, we would not now be discussing aggregate production functions' (cited by Fisher, 1971b, p. 305). Ferguson (1969, p. xvii) explicitly made this instrumental defence with respect to the criticism about the measurement of capital as a single index in Cambridge capital theory controversies. 'Its validity is unquestionable, *but its importance is an empirical or an econometric matter* that depends upon the amount of substitution there is in the system. Until the econometricians have the answer for us, placing reliance upon [aggregate] neoclassical economic theory is a matter of faith. I personally have faith' (emphasis added).

The justification as to why the Cobb and Douglas (1928) article should be regarded as one of the 20 most influential articles in the last hundred years published in the *American Economic Review* was stated as follows: "Cobb and Douglas explored the elementary properties and implications of the functional form, and pointed to the approximate constancy of the relative shares of labor and capital in total income as the *validating empirical fact*' (Arrow et al., 2011, p. 2, emphasis added). Hoover (2012, p. 326) also adopts an instrumental position in his intermediate macroeconomic textbook.[2] He briefly notes the aggregation problems which 'are well beyond the scope of this book'. So instead,

---

[2]   As Kuhn (1962 [1970]) points out, textbooks are crucial in that they are generally taken

> [O]ur strategy will be to start with a conjecture that the economy can be described by a particular production function [the Cobb-Douglas], one that shares important properties with microeconomic production functions. We will then test our conjecture empirically. *If it seems to describe the data well, we shall be satisfied that it provides a useful approximation.* (Emphasis added)

What is this test? It is simply the approximate constancy of shares. The fact that the data bear out this assumption 'provides a good reason to take the Cobb–Douglas production function as a reasonable approximation of aggregate supply in the U.S. economy' (p. 330).

But as we have repeatedly demonstrated in the earlier chapters, this methodological stance is untenable because of the existence of the underlying accounting identity. However, it is not the existence of the identity, *per se*, that poses the problem, but the identity together with the fact that constant-price monetary values have to be used for output and capital, instead of physical measures, together with the accounting identity. While we have considerably extended and elaborated the argument in this book, as we have noted before, the problem has been known for some time, even though its full implications may not have been fully appreciated. Simon (1979a, p. 497), for example, as we mentioned in the Prologue, thought it important enough to mention in his Nobel Prize Lecture:

> Fitted Cobb–Douglas functions are homogeneous, generally of degree close to unity with a labor exponent of about the right magnitude. These findings, however, cannot be taken as strong evidence for the classical theory, for the identical results can readily be produced by fitting a Cobb–Douglas function to the data that were in fact generated by a linear accounting identity (value of goods equals labor cost plus capital cost (see E.H. Phelps-Brown [1957]). The same apples to the SMAC production function. (See Richard Cyert and Simon [1971])

Simon's (1979b) article provides his definitive statement of the problem. Moreover, as Carter (2011b) has shown, Simon entered into correspondence with Solow about precisely this issue in the early 1970s, who was, consequently, made aware of the problem. Fisher also warned Solow of the implications of the aggregation problems for the aggregate production function at about the same time.

Nevertheless, Blaug (1974, 1992), for example, who has provided a succinct critique of the aggregate production function which he describes as 'measurement without theory', mentions neither Phelps Brown (1957) nor

---

by students as being uncontroversial and they delineate the legitimate methods and assumptions for 'puzzle solving' within the paradigm.

Shaikh (1974). Furthermore, he does not address the putative defence of the aggregate production function, namely, that the results of the empirical estimations of the production function suggest that the problem is not serious.

WHY HAS THE ACCOUNTING CRITIQUE BEEN OVERLOOKED?

The accounting identity critique is one of logic (a matter of 'the laws of arithmetic', as Shaikh (1974) memorably put it) rather than of subjective interpretation. Has it been ignored because the criticism is logically wrong or simply because the way it has been put forward has not been persuasive? We examined some of these questions in the Introduction and elaborate the argument in the remainder of the chapter.

The fact that the critique has been largely overlooked stems, to some extent, from the fact that the early discussions of the Phelps Brown critique did not take its implication to its logical conclusion, namely that it is not possible to *test* the existence of the aggregate production function using value data. Let us take a few examples. As we have noted, in Walters's (1963a) early, but influential, study surveying production and cost functions, the Phelps Brown criticism is there, but buried in a short paragraph on page 37 of Walter's article:

> The early commentators pointed out that the data may be explained by what Bronfenbrenner called the interfirm function $pQ = wL + \rho K$. Evidence has been adduced by Phelps Brown [1957] to show that the scatter of observations of Australia in 1909 can be explained in terms of this simple linear relationship. Thus, in fitting a Cobb Douglas function (with $\alpha + \beta = 1$), we merely measure the share of wages in the value added. The result does not provide a test of the marginal productivity law.[3]

This would seem to be pretty conclusive, but in the very next paragraph, Walters goes on to argue:

> The inter-industry results give, I think, the most unsatisfactory estimates of the production function. But aggregate industry data have been used with considerable success in *interstate* [or *international*] studies of the SMAC [or the CES, as it is now more commonly known] function. The authors used observations of the same industry in different countries to estimate the parameters. Given that the industry has the same production function in each country, the different

---

[3]   The notation has been changed to make it consistent with that in this chapter.

ratios of factor prices will generate observations which should trace out the production function. (Emphasis in the original)

It is difficult to reconcile these two arguments of Walters (1963a). True, inter-industry estimations of putative production functions are likely to be suspect for other reasons, such as we do not really expect each different industry to have the same 'production function' parameters. There may also be little variation in factor prices because of competition, so, under neoclassical assumptions, all the data will be simply observations for one particular capital–labour ratio. But the Phelps Brown critique, although originally addressed to Douglas's cross-industry study, applies, of course, equally to estimates for the same industry but using interregional or inter-national data. Hildebrand and Liu (1965), for example, is an early study that uses regional data to estimate production functions for the same industry.

It may be that Walters implicitly assumes that for the accounting iden-tity to pose a problem, wages and the rate of profit must be constant so that $V = b_1 L + b_2 J$ gives a good statistical fit. This is violated in the data used by Arrow et al. (1961) and so perhaps Walters assumes that there is now no problem. But, as we have shown, this assumption of the constancy of the wage rate and the rate of profit is not necessary for the critique. See Felipe and McCombie (2001a) for a discussion of Arrow et al. (1961) in light of the accounting identity.

Intriligator's (1978, p.272) more recent textbook treatment of the issue displays a similar ambivalence. After discussing Simon and Levy's (1963) interpretation of the Phelps Brown critique, he concludes: 'assum-ing only small variations in output and inputs, the form of the produc-tion function and the equality of the values of output and income imply that the production function exhibits approximately constant returns to scale and that factor shares are approximately the elasticities'. But again, there is no mention that this undermines the very possibility of testing the production function. Instead, Intriligator goes on to discuss other specifications of production functions, including those estimated by time-series data.

A possibility is that he considers that the critique only applies to the Cobb–Douglas production function or the use of cross-section data or both. This mistake is made by Temple (2006, 2010) and is discussed below.

Wallis (1979, p.62) also accepts that 'the equation as estimated by Douglas and his co-workers is a close approximation to this [accounting] identity in the data and there is very little point in attempting to redis-cover it. If all revenue is paid to either capital or labour, it is difficult [or, rather, impossible] to distinguish between this accounting identity and the estimated equation'. Again, we infer that Wallis considers that this is only a problem if wages and the rate of profit are constant.

We also noted in Chapter 2 that the critique has occasionally been rediscovered. It is interesting to note that Simon (1979b) was unaware of Shaikh's (1974) extension of the critique to time-series data, although Simon himself considered this aspect in his article. Samuelson (1979), for example, in reviewing Douglas's academic contribution on the latter's death, became yet another to discover, to his evident surprise, that the Emperor had no clothes. While he shows that cross-sectional Cobb–Douglas production functions may merely reflect the underlying identity, he strangely does not extend the critique to time-series data. He does note, however, even though the data may give a good fit to the data, 'we cannot rule out the possibility that some other model could generate the same observations' (p. 936).

Fisher's (1971b) simulations showed that a good fit would be given to the aggregate Cobb–Douglas production function and the wage equation, even though aggregation problems suggest intuitively that this should not occur. But importantly the causation was that the stable factor shares were responsible for the good fit to the Cobb–Douglas and not that the aggregate Cobb–Douglas gave rise to the constant factor shares. This result went largely unnoticed (except for the few critics of the aggregate production function, notably Shaikh, 1974, and, especially, 1980), although it was published in one of the leading neoclassical journals, the *Review of Economics and Statistics*.

A follow-up paper written jointly with Solow and Kearl using micro CES production functions came to a similar result (Fisher, et al., 1977). The aggregated simulated data gave plausible estimates (although not always) of the value of the 'aggregate elasticity of substitution', which in the simulations did not exist. The implications were summarised by Fisher et al. as 'the aggregative data themselves do not tell you *very clearly* whether the estimated parameters are likely to have average meaning or not' (p. 319, emphasis added). However, the concluding paragraph of the paper considerably dilutes the force of this statement.

> For many problems, aggregate production functions are simply too useful to pass up, especially as they can work, as our experiment shows. Our parting advice is to handle them the way the old garbage man tells the young garbage man to handle wrapped in plastic bags of unknown provenance: 'Gingerly, Hector, gingerly'. (p. 319)

This conclusion is difficult to reconcile with the article's insistence of the non-existence of the aggregate production function. Reassuringly for the neoclassical economist, it implies that we can continue to use aggregate production functions. But the imperative to handle the results 'gingerly', while a nice metaphor, gives no practical guidance at all; it's business as usual; carry on estimating aggregate production functions. Moreover, the insertion of the emphasised words 'very clearly' just after 'do not tell you' in the above citation further weakens the force of the conclusions.

But what is meant by the statement that aggregate production functions 'work'? It is not that they have good *explanatory*, as opposed to *predictive*, power. The whole thrust of the two papers is to show that they have predictive power without there being a true underlying aggregate production function. As Fisher et al. (p. 312) say: 'the elasticity of substitution in these production functions is an "estimate" of nothing; there is no "true" aggregate parameter to which it corresponds'.[4] Prediction is *not* the same thing as explanation.

SHAIKH'S HUMBUG PRODUCTION FUNCTION AND SOLOW'S REPLY REVISITED

Undoubtedly a key paper in the development of the accounting identity argument was that of Shaikh (1974). While we discussed the critique in a previous chapter, it is useful to briefly recapitulate the argument here and consider why it was not persuasive. Solow's (1974) reply provides a good example of how the use of rhetoric can serve to obfuscate rather than illuminate an argument. Shaikh's title grabs the attention: 'Laws of Production and Laws of Algebra: The Humbug Production Function'. In the article he links his subsequent discussion to the Cambridge capital theory controversies, illustrating immediately the potential importance of his argument. As we have seen, Shaikh made two major points.

First, he set out the accounting critique in clear terms and applied it, for the first time, to time-series data – recall that Phelps Brown had merely discussed cross-sectional data. If the data display constant factor shares, the 'production function' must be a Cobb–Douglas. Second, he turned his attention to the procedure Solow (1957) followed, which is nothing but a tautology, but for different reasons. In order to estimate a production function, Solow first purged the data of shifts in technology by creating an index $A(t)$ essentially using the identity $\hat{A}_t \equiv (\hat{V}_t - \hat{L}_t) - (1 - a_t)(\hat{J}_t - \hat{L}_t)$ and

---

[4]   Reflecting on these two papers some time later, Fisher (2005, p. 491, fn 2) remarked that the accounting identity explains the results of his 1971 simulations. It also 'explains the puzzles of some of those experiments that, while finding the same phenomenon [that the aggregate production function works well], no similar organizing principle occurred when experimenting with CES functions'.

then $\hat{A}$ is used to calculate the index $A(t)$. But as Shaikh points out, so long as factor shares are roughly constant (which they are in Solow's data) the estimation of the Cobb–Douglas using V_t/A_t or $\ln V_t/A_t$) the independent variable must give a perfect fit due to the way $A(t)$ was calculated. This actually has nothing to do with the accounting identity but just the laws of algebra.

To drive home the point that with constant shares *any* underlying data for V, J and L and Solow's procedure of deflating V by $A(t)$ will give an excellent fit to the Cobb-Douglas, Shaikh constructs an artificial dataset where the scatterplot of the observations of V/L against J/L traces out the word 'HUMBUG'. Capital's share was the same as in Solow's actual data. Not surprisingly, following Solow's procedure, Shaikh obtains a very good fit to the Cobb–Douglas and where the estimate of the slope of the regression equals the average value of capital's share. The format of his note in the *Review of Economics and Statistics* mimics the paper of Solow (1957) published in the same journal, with analogous figures and the dataset out in an appendix for the Humbug data in a similar way to Solow's statistics. It should have been convincing.

Solow's one-page rejoinder begins with the unequivocal 'Mr Shaikh's article is based on misconception pure and simple' (1974, p. 121). This putative error by Shaikh was that Solow, according to Solow, had never intended to *test* the aggregate production function. The 1957 paper 'merely shows how one goes about interpreting given time series if one starts by *assuming* that they were generated by a production function and that capital-marginal product relations apply' (p. 121, emphasis in the original). Most readers would probably end their reading at that point. Given the standing of Solow, and that Shaikh's paper was, after all, only a note, there could not be much to the comment. Solow's supposed *coup de grâce* was to estimate a Cobb–Douglas production function without imposing the marginal productivity conditions using the Humbug data (that is, Solow estimates $\ln(V/L) = c + at + b\ln(J/L)$) and finds no significant statistical relationship. Hence, the 'humbug seems to be on the other foot'. The inescapable conclusion is that Shaikh's note is trivial and hardly worth taking seriously. Consider the following expressions and phrases taken from Solow's rejoinder: 'misconception pure and simple'; 'even simpler'; 'hardly a deep thought'; the 'cute humbug'; 'bowl you over at first'; 'but when you think about it for a minute'; and any 'educated mind'.

Shaikh's compelling reply (1980) came in the form of an appendix to an elaboration of his original article in a book and as such, it is not surprising that it went largely unnoticed. Turner (1989, p. 196) cites Joan Robinson as noting that Shaikh, in writing his 1974 paper, was not allowed the usual right to reply.[5] It is always useful to have the 'last word' as Solow did in this case.

Yet, it raised some serious questions. If Solow claimed that all along he was not testing a production function and if shares are exactly constant then it would then yield an exact Cobb–Douglas, how come he thought the 'fit is remarkably tight' (1957, p. 317)? How could it be otherwise? Why did he estimate five different specifications of the production function, including the accounting identity which, although it assumes that the wage rate is constant (it is captured by the intercept) and also r, also gives a very close statistical fit? The very close statistical fits give the reader the impression that the aggregate production function provided a very good representation to the data, rather than that it had been merely assumed. As for the poor statistical result using the Humbug data, this is due to the imposition of the assumption that the rate of technical change is constant. But there is nothing in neoclassical production theory that requires this. Moreover, in Solow's (1957, p. 314, Chart 2) own data, the rate of technical change takes a saw-tooth path. Shaikh showed that a more complex time trend, including sines and cosines, that captured the path of this so-called 'technical change' would both rescue the identity and give a very close fit to the data.

We also started from Solow's (1974) comment that 'when someone claims that aggregate production functions work, he means (a) that they give a good fit to input–output data *without* the intervention of data deriving from factor shares; and (b) that the function so fitted has partial derivatives that closely mimic observed factor prices' (omitting a footnote). We showed in Chapter 5 using Solow's data, and repeating the exercise that Solow had done with Shaikh's data, that there was no statistically significant relationship and the estimated 'output' elasticities bore no correspondence to the factor shares. In other words, Solow would have been forced to conclude, by his own criterion, that there was no empirical basis for the aggregate production function. This raises the interesting questions that we mentioned in Chapter 5: in these circumstances, would Solow have submitted the paper for publication and, if so, would it have been accepted? If this hypothetical paper had been published instead of the original, would the intellectual history of the aggregate production function have been very different?

As we have also seen, Solow (1987) returned to these issues, arguing that Shaikh's argument could be applied to physical data, and as these could always be used to estimate a production function, it followed that

---

[5]   Shaikh has confirmed this (personal communication, 17 November 2011).

the use of value data could likewise be used, which is a *non sequitur*. He also argued that substituting the equations $r = (1 - a)(V/J)$ and $w = a(V/L)$ into the identity in the form $V = a^{-a}(1 - a)^{(1-a)}w^a r^{(1-a)}L^a J^{(1-a)}$ gives $V = [V/L^a J^{(1-a)}]/L^a J^{(1-a)}$, where V on the right-hand side of the equation equals $f(L,J)$: 'What Shaikh has discovered, in other words, is that any production function can be written as a product of a Cobb–Douglas and something else; and that something else is the production function divided by the Cobb–Douglas' (p. 20). But this is a classic case of circular reasoning as far as value data are concerned because it *assumes* that $V = f(L, J)$ is a production function that can be estimated using value data. The fact that it cannot is at the heart of the critique.

THE ACCOUNTING IDENTITY WORKS 'FULL-TIME', NOT 'PART-TIME': ON TEMPLE'S MISUNDERSTANDINGS AND MISINTERPRETATIONS OF THE CRITIQUE

Temple (2006, 2010) is an exception in that he has explicitly considered the accounting critique in some detail, to which we replied (Felipe and McCombie, 2010b, 2012). His contribution is important on two counts. First, he is one of the few economists working in growth theory and with neoclassical production functions who seems to be aware of the critique. Indeed, he has some sympathy for the implications of the argument: 'Overall the critique has some force. It deserves to be more widely known among researchers estimating production relationships using time series or panel data, including researchers who never doubted the existence of a well-behaved underlying relationship' (Temple, 2006, p. 307).

Nevertheless, in both his papers, he misunderstands some key arguments. In Temple (2010), which is his reply to Felipe and McCombie (2010b), he largely ignores the counter-arguments made there, and merely repeats some of his earlier criticisms. Ironically, his arguments that supposedly limit the applications of the critique merely serve to show its robustness and explain why, if others likewise hold erroneous views, it has not had the impact it warrants.

In his 2010 article, he concludes that we make substantially more of the criticism of production functions estimated using value data (at any level of aggregation) than it deserves. Hence, he labels it 'the part-time tyranny of the identity'. While he concedes that there are some areas of agreement and that the argument deserves to be better known, he contends that we have gone too far and exaggerated the scope and implications of the argument.

As we shall see, however, there is nothing in Temple's criticism that should lead to any downplaying of the argument. This is that the use of value data (as opposed to physical quantities) in the estimation of *any* specification of an aggregate production function, whether or not it is a Cobb–Douglas, precludes the researcher from interpreting the regression results as the technological parameters (for example, the factor output elasticities or the elasticity of substitution). However, Temple, surprisingly, erroneously persists in maintaining that the critique *only* relates to the Cobb–Douglas. We also show that it is true for any level of aggregation using value data. The aggregate production function is, in fact, unlikely to exist, not least because of serious aggregation problems and variations in X-efficiency and so on. The only certainty is that the regression results and the values of the estimated parameters are determined by the accounting identity. The tyranny of the identity works 'full-time'.

Temple, nevertheless, agrees with us on two points. The first one is that the aggregation problem should receive more attention in the literature than it does, although he argues that there are other approaches that are not so reliant on aggregation, for example, the use of multi-sector models, reduced-form regressions, and methods inferring productivity levels from bilateral trade data (Temple, 2010, p. 686). We do not deal with this view in detail here, but limit ourselves primarily to the problems posed by the accounting identity for the aggregate production function, as it is the latter that is widely used in macroeconomics.

As we have noted above, both the Cambridge capital controversies and the more general aggregation literature suggest:

> Even under constant returns, the conditions for aggregation are so very stringent as to make the existence of aggregate production functions in real economies a non-event. This is true not only for the existence of a capital stock but also for such constructs as aggregate labor or even aggregate output. . . . One cannot escape the force of these results by arguing that aggregate production functions are only approximations. (Fisher, 2005, p. 490)

Indeed, Temple (2005, p. 438) himself gives the simple example that two Cobb–Douglas production functions with different exponents cannot be aggregated to give a single Cobb–Douglas production function. Nevertheless, ironically, this does not stop Temple (2005) from assuming that the production functions of agriculture and non-agriculture are each represented by an aggregate Cobb–Douglas, and that factors are paid their aggregate marginal products, as if aggregation problems did not matter for these individual sectors.

Surprisingly, later in his comment, he declares himself 'agnostic' on this aggregation issue (Temple, 2010, p. 689), although no compelling reasons are given for this. It is not clear why aggregation problems disappear and a true production function can be estimated if 'we have no prior reason to believe that output and inputs are badly measured' (p. 689), especially when it is agreed that the accounting identity critique has nothing to do with measurement errors.

The second area where there is agreement is that an applied researcher may appear to obtain meaningful results from estimating a production relationship, even when the researcher is making assumptions that do not hold in the data. As we cited in Chapter 2, Temple comments:

> One important instance arises when factors are not paid their marginal products. In that case, although researchers often interpret their results as if the estimated parameters can be used to derive output elasticities, the identity *suggests* that the estimates may be more closely related to the factor shares. (p. 686, emphasis added)

This would seem to go a long way to conceding our position and poses difficulties for understanding the rationale for his criticisms. We would indeed agree with this statement, except that the identity *shows*, not *suggests*, that the estimated coefficients will take values that are equal to the factor shares, even when no well-defined aggregate production function exists.[6] An implication of Temple's statement cited above is that given that the researcher has access only to constant-price value data, it can never be known whether or not the researcher is correctly estimating the parameters of a production function, or, indeed, whether or not the latter exists. This is precisely our critique.

Yet, at times in his reply, Temple (2010) takes the opposite view, and argues erroneously that if factor shares vary to an unspecified extent and the researcher can correctly specify 'total factor productivity', all will be well. The aggregate production function can then be estimated and the values of the coefficients will correctly reflect the aggregate technological parameters of the economy, albeit with the necessity of finding the most appropriate statistical estimating technique.

In the rest of this chapter, we briefly point to the problems with Temple's (2006, 2010) arguments. Broadly speaking, there are two issues that should be emphasised. First, Temple erroneously continues to imply that the critique holds only if certain *ad hoc*, or what he terms 'auxiliary',

---

[6]   Where this does not prove to be the case, it is because the mathematical transformation of the identity to give a specific functional form (that is, what the neoclassical economist calls the 'aggregate production function') does not accurately mirror the identity. In other words, this is when the statistical fit of the transformation is less than perfect. We elaborate on the reasons for this below.

assumptions are made; typically the 'stylised facts' that factor shares are constant and the weighted growth of the wage rate and the rate of profit are constant. To this he incorrectly adds, in the case of our critique of Mankiw et al.'s (1992) growth model that we have, of necessity, to assume also a constant capital–output ratio for the criticism to hold. (In fact, we also show that the identity will give a very poor statistical fit using international data if the assumption of a constant level and growth of the real wage is imposed.)

At times, as we noted above, Temple seems to assume that the critique applies only to the case of the Cobb–Douglas and so, presumably, once there is some variability in factor shares, he implies that we can actually be confident we are estimating a 'true' aggregate production function. He nowhere answers the question posed by Felipe and McCombie (2010b) as to how much variability in factor shares is required to suddenly remove the problems posed by the accounting identity and aggregation problems.

Second, we show below that his argument at times reduces to *petitio principii*, or circular reasoning. Temple often *assumes* that the aggregate production function exists, and uses this assumption to supposedly counter the argument that the relationship between output and inputs in value terms does not necessarily reflect a technological production relationship.

1. The Accounting Identity Critique Does Not Depend on Constant Factor Shares

Temple maintains the opposite and argues that the problems posed by the identity hold *only* with the assumption of constant factor shares and a constant weighted growth of the wage rate and the rate of profit. He claims that it is necessary to use these arbitrary, or *ad hoc*, assumptions for the criticisms of accounting identity to hold. Thus, although the Cobb–Douglas is widely used, theoretically there is nothing to stop a 'true' production function being estimated provided that there is enough variability in the factor shares.

Temple (2006, pp. 306–7, omitting footnotes) explicitly makes this argument as follows:

> Some interpretations of this result become overenthusiastic and suggest that a Cobb–Douglas technology will always fit the data well, simply because of an identity. This should make us pause: for example, if the underlying technology were translog, could we really expect a Cobb–Douglas to fit the data well? Given sufficient variation in the input ratios, movements in factor shares would immediately reveal that Cobb–Douglas is not the right specification. The argument that Cobb–Douglas results are spurious uses not only the value added

identity, but also some additional structure: namely constant factor shares and the constancy of the weighted average of the wage and profit rate growth rates.

The need for this extra structure points to the heart of the problem in estimating production relationships. Estimation must usually treat the level or growth rate of technology (TFP) as unobservable and it is this omitted variable that poses the fundamental difficulty. If the data were generated by a translog, and the researcher had identified a good proxy for TFP,[7] a suitably specified regression would accurately recover the parameters of that translog production function, and reject the Cobb–Douglas specification given sufficient variation in the data. It is the inability to control for the TFP term that causes problems and this means that the 'statistical' and 'economic' critiques are closer together than is usually acknowledged.[8]

He repeats this claim in (2010) as may be most clearly seen from the following statement:

All of their [Felipe and McCombie's] arguments share a common structure which is to manipulate the value added identity, add some auxiliary assumptions, and then show – under these maintained assumptions – that the data will appear to have been generated by a production relationship of a certain type, typically, *but not always*, Cobb–Douglas, even when no such relationship exists.

Here is their main claim stated explicitly: 'Can a researcher using value data ever establish whether or not the coefficients reflect a production function, or are they simply predetermined by the value added accounting identity? Our answer is that unequivocally the results are always determined by the identity'. *Yet, the very next sentence in their paper assumes that the weighted average of growth of factor prices and factor shares are all constant.* These assumptions are needed to show how the identity leads to estimates that appear to support a Cobb–Douglas production function. Since these assumptions will not always be met, it is clear that the value added identity does not always lead to a spurious Cobb–Douglas result. (Temple, 2010, pp. 687–8, emphasis added)

Temple's argument, consequently, is that we assert (correctly in our opinion) that the results are 'always determined by the identity', even when these 'auxiliary assumptions' are not met. But Temple disputes this and argues that if a good proxy for total factor productivity (TFP) can be found:

---

[7]   This problem is more serious than may be gathered from Temple. The Diamond–McFadden impossibility theorem has shown that with labour- and capital-augmenting technical change growing at different rates over time, it is not possible to identify the technological parameters of the aggregate production function, even when the latter exists (Diamond et al., 1978).

[8]   The statistical critique refers to econometric and specification problems concerning the accounting identity. The 'economic' critique refers to what is generally known as 'the accounting identity' problem.

there is no reason why a researcher should not discriminate between, say, a trans-log and a Cobb-Douglas specification. Say that the data have been generated by a stable production relationship, and the researcher specifies this relationship correctly, including controls for productivity differences such as TFP. In that case, the researcher is estimating a model that corresponds to the data generating process. There is no reason for the estimates to be biased, or for the parameters to be unidentified. In contrast, and for the same reason – the equivalence between the form of the estimated model and the data generating process – the dynamic version of the value added identity cannot do better than this. It will certainly do worse, when the auxiliary assumptions introduced by Felipe and McCombie are not a good approximation to the data. (p. 688, omitting a footnote)

The circular reasoning of Temple is readily apparent here. He assumes that a 'stable production function exists' (that is, the data is generated by an aggregate production function). This can be estimated provided that TFP can be correctly specified, another concept dependent on the aggregate production function. Of course, if one adopts this *petitio principii* then the problem is merely one of determining the best specification and estimation techniques, which has been the subject of the numerous articles that have estimated the production function.

And it is simply wrong to assert that the critique applies just to the Cobb–Douglas production function as we have demonstrated in Chapter 2 and elsewhere (see Felipe and McCombie, 2001a, 2001b, 2005a; see also Simon, 1979b).

However, as the 'dynamic value added identity' is an identity, then a better way of putting it is that the estimate of any specification of an 'aggregate production function' can do no better than this identity (which of course gives a perfect fit to the data), rather than *vice versa* as Temple argues in the quotation cited above. And if factor shares vary, then, of course, the functional form that gives the best fit to the identity will not be the Cobb–Douglas. But this ignores (rather than refutes) the critique that what is driving the results is the identity as the estimates are not of a behavioural equation. We spelt this out in Felipe and McCombie (2010b) immediately prior to our argument in the above citation and this was ignored by Temple in his selective quotation from us.

Consequently, the argument follows through *whether or not* factor shares and the weighted growth of the wage rate and the rate of profit are constant. In practice, as we have repeatedly noted, researchers will attempt to find an explicit functional form that will give a good fit to the data generated by the identity in growth-rate form. Thus we have:

$$V_t \equiv w_t L_t + r_t J_t \Rightarrow \hat{V}_t \equiv a_t \hat{w}_t + (1 - a_t)\hat{r}_t + a_t \hat{L}_t + (1 - a_t)\hat{J}_t \Rightarrow$$

$$\hat{V}_t \equiv \lambda_t + a_t \hat{L}_t + (1 - a_t)\hat{J}_t \equiv \hat{V}_t + \lambda_t + \alpha_t \hat{L}_t + \beta_t \hat{J}_t \Rightarrow V_t = f(L_t, J_t, t)$$

$\Rightarrow$ specific functional form (for example, Cobb–Douglas, Box–Cox transformation, CES, translog),[9]   (12.1)

where the arrows show the 'direction of causation'. This implies that $a_t \equiv \alpha_t$ and $(1 - a_t) \equiv \beta_t \equiv (1 - \alpha_t)$. As we have noted, economists try to find a specific mathematical functional form that will closely fit the data generated by the equation $V_t = f(L_t, J_t, t)$ and hence, by implication, the underlying identity. If, *and only if*, the weighted average of the growth rates of the wage and profit rates are a constant, and factor shares are also constant, will a conventional Cobb–Douglas relationship fit this criterion. If they are not constant, then a more flexible functional form that contains the Cobb–Douglas as a special case, such as a Box–Cox transformation, CES, or the translog, will be required. But these mathematical transformations should not be regarded as aggregate production functions. Consequently, the argument does not apply solely to the case where the aforementioned assumptions hold, *pace* Temple. As this has been quite generally emphasised throughout the literature on the subject, and especially in Felipe and McCombie (2010b), it is surprising that Temple should think otherwise. This is especially true as Felipe and McCombie (2001a) show this explicitly for the case of the CES and Felipe and McCombie (2003) for the case of the translog (see Chapter 2).

To reiterate: the argument is consequently a matter of methodology and logic. What we show are the conditions under which a given form of the production function, say the Cobb–Douglas, would yield good results in terms of the usual statistical diagnostics. This is very different from claiming that specific assumptions or some structure must be imposed for the critique to hold. In fact, an implication of the accounting critique is that unless factor shares and $a_t \hat{w}_t + (1 - a_t) \hat{r}_t$ are approximately constant, the estimation of the equation $V_t = A_0 e^{\lambda t} L_t^{\alpha} J_t^{\beta}$ using time-series data will most likely yield poor results. That is to say, implausible estimates of the factor elasticities that are very different from the values of the factor shares and may even be negative. The identity shows that a better fit can be obtained by both a more flexible functional form and a time trend. But if these stylised facts hold, then the goodness of fit will potentially be unity and the estimated elasticities must equal the factor shares.

Given this, why has the Cobb–Douglas proved so durable, and why does it so often give a good statistical fit to the data? We have shown that if we integrate the dynamic form of the accounting identity, we obtain

---

[9]   See also Chapter 2. As we have shown in Chapter 9, the *AK* model is not immune from this critique.

$V \equiv a^{-a}(1 - a)^{(1-a)}w^a r^{(1-a)}L^a J^{(1-a)}$. This is not an approximation, but an isomorphism: it holds exactly for any particular year, whether it is for, say, the UK economy or an individual firm.[10] As it is a stylised fact (not an *ad hoc* assumption) that factor shares do not change greatly between firms in the same industry, and wages and profits show little variation compared to L and J, estimating cross-section production functions gives a good fit with a surprisingly high R^2 of over 0.9, and the estimated output elasticities equal the factor shares (Douglas, 1976). Time-series data often yield worse results, not because factor shares change dramatically over time (they do not), but because $a\ln w_t + (1 - a) \ln r_t$ is often not well approximated by a linear time trend, or $a\hat{w}_t + (1 - a)\hat{r}_t$ by a constant, as they are subject to procyclical fluctuations.

To summarise: Temple's reasoning is based on a simple logical confusion. To argue that if the stylised facts of constant factor shares hold, the accounting identity will give a good fit to the Cobb–Douglas functional form, does *not* imply that the critique holds only in this restrictive case. Temple has provided no convincing proof to the contrary.

2. The Mankiw, Romer and Weil (1992) Growth Model is Merely a Misspecified Identity

Related to the above argument, further evidence of Temple's (2010, pp. 689–90) misunderstanding on this point is given by his following statement:

> As in Simon and Levy (1963) and Simon (1979b) they [Felipe and McCombie] examine the cross-section implications of the identity and show that it could lead to a (spurious) production relationship. The argument requires factor shares to be constant and the levels of factor prices to be similar across units. Felipe and McCombie relate this to international data [the Mankiw–Romer–Weil model, 1992] *even though the assumption that factor prices are similar across countries is highly implausible.*
>
> This does not strike Felipe and McCombie as a problem: 'the critique does not rest on this assumption and so nothing depends upon whether or not it is correct. If the actual data do not have this property, then researchers who estimate the Cobb Douglas form . . . will not obtain a very good statistical fit'.

---

[10] Alternatively, as we have discussed in Chapter 2, consider the accounting identity and take a particular point on it, say V', J' and L'. Expand both the Cobb–Douglas and the accounting identity in the neighbourhood of these points using a Taylor-series expansion (that is, the hypothetical Cobb–Douglas is at the point of the tangency to the accounting identity at this point). The resulting two equations are formally equivalent. Consequently, as we know the accounting identity must exist, it is this that *causes* the Cobb–Douglas specification and not the other way around. This was essentially the method and insight of Simon and Levy (1963).

But their argument has veered off course. In these more general and plausible circumstances, a researcher no longer finds that Cobb–Douglas is a good fit. Instead the researcher concludes appropriately that a Cobb–Douglas technology does not provide a good explanation of the data in question. So what is the problem here? The proposed 'tyranny of the accounting identity' seems part-time, at best. (Emphasis added)

The quotation above shows that Temple also misunderstands our arguments concerning the Mankiw et al. (hereafter MRW) paper. Let us restate MRW's procedure. They posit a 'world' aggregate production function that is a Cobb–Douglas. They see no problems in, say, aggregating Indian agriculture with the plough and oxen, the highly mechanised agricultural sector of the US and Europe, the aerospace industry of Europe and the US, the retailing sector with the hypermarkets in the developed countries and the bazaars of the less developed countries. They, therefore, assume that the 'world elasticity of substitution' is a meaningful concept and that all countries have access to the same level of technology. Common sense (and a cursory acquaintance with aggregation theory) would suggest that this is not a sensible approach.

But nevertheless, MRW find that estimating their specification gives, in these circumstances, a reasonably good statistical fit in terms of the R^2, and the coefficients are statistically significant. As they use a (neoclassical) Cobb–Douglas production function and assume initially that growth is at its steady-state rate, they implicitly assume a constant capital–output ratio. Later in the paper they introduce a specification purporting to capture the non-steady-state growth behaviour of the countries.

The question is why do the data give such a reasonably good fit? Is it that the data have not refuted their assumptions underlying the concept of world production function? The answer is 'no'. The reason is that MRW use value data, and cannot escape the fact that the series of value added, employment and capital are related through the accounting identity. Looking at their dataset, it is apparent that factor shares are roughly constant. This is an empirical observation or one of Kaldor's stylised facts, not a 'maintained hypothesis' as Temple asserts. In Solow's (1970, p. 2) words, 'the ratio of capital to output shows no systematic trend'.

What we show is that the initial relatively poor fit of the MRW model is not because the capital–output or factor shares show considerable variation, but because the wage rate varies considerably between countries. MRW assume a constant level of technology, A_t, but, from the identity, we know that $A_t \equiv B w_t^a r_t^{(1-a)}$. We are fully aware that the 'assumption that factor prices are similar across countries is highly implausible' as Temple

(2010, p. 689) notes in the above quotation, implicitly criticising us. Indeed, we discuss this at length in both our critique of MRW in Chapter 7 (see also Felipe and McCombie, 2005b, 2010b).

Moreover, it is a central tenet of our critique that the identity shows that the statistical fit of the MRW model will be improved if factor prices are allowed to vary between countries. As the accounting identity holds separately for each country (both advanced and less developed nations), then we know immediately that the specification of the MRW model with a constant level of 'technology', will not lead to a particularly good statistical fit. This indeed proves to be the case. As we point out (Felipe and McCombie 2010b, p. 676), the identity shows that the assumption of both a constant 'technology' and a spatially invariant rate of 'technical progress' (that is, which are simply $a \ln w + (1 - a) \ln r$ and $a \hat{w} + (1 - a) \hat{r}$, respectively) by MRW, will produce a less than perfect statistical fit. If the capital–output ratio did show considerable variation, then the identity shows that MRW's specification is likely to give a poor fit to the data, not that we can suddenly be confident that we can find a specification where the data are actually estimating a 'true' production function.

MRW improve the fit by including a human capital variable derived from school enrolment rates. As this is likely to be correlated with the wage rate, it acts as a proxy for the latter in the identity. Once the variation in factor prices is allowed for by regional dummies or is explicitly included in the regression, the Cobb–Douglas gives a good fit without, in the latter case, the need to include human capital, which MRW are forced to resort to (Felipe and McCombie, 2005b). Moreover, the estimated neoclassical speed of convergence becomes infinite.

But our argument does not impose a priori the assumptions that factor shares are constant, or of a constant capital–output ratio. We know from the data, given that these stylised facts hold, that the accounting identity tells us that the MRW model is bound to give a good statistical fit to the data (subject to the variability of the real wage rate), before a single regression is run. We confirm this by regression analysis using similar data to that of MRW. It is difficult to see any rationale for Temple's *non sequitur* that at this point our discussion 'veers off course' (Temple 2010, p. 690). Empirically, if factor shares did vary considerably and we found another functional form that provides a better approximation to the identity than the Cobb–Douglas, it does not mean, as we have repeatedly emphasised, that we can now be confident that we are estimating an aggregate production function.

The concluding sentences of the above quotation of Temple (p. 690) demonstrate a fundamental confusion and it is worth repeating them:

> In these more general and plausible circumstances, a researcher no longer finds that Cobb–Douglas is a good fit. Instead the researcher concludes appropriately that a *Cobb–Douglas technology* does not provide a good explanation of the data in question. So what is the problem here? The proposed 'tyranny of the accounting identity' seems part-time at least. (Emphasis added)

This implies Temple considers that if the data provide a good fit to the Cobb–Douglas, the researcher can conclude that a Cobb–Douglas *technology* does provide a good explanation. The 'problem here' is that the whole point of the critique is that the existence of the accounting identity shows that no such inference can be made. The corollary is that if, for example, factor shares vary, we cannot suddenly be confident that an aggregate production function, *pace* Temple, is being estimated.[11]

Temple continues with this line of circular reasoning when he maintains that a constant capital–output ratio 'makes little sense in the context of the Solow model. The Solow model can be seen precisely as a theory of adjustment to an equilibrium capital–output ratio. It makes little sense to reject estimates of the model on the basis of a highly restrictive assumption, even less so when that assumption rules out the central mechanism of the model' (p. 690).

This is again a case of the *petitio principii* fallacy because, as we have noted, the correct measure in Solow's growth model is the *physical* capital–output ratio. Of course, because of the heterogeneity of physical output and capital goods, there is no such thing as an aggregate physical capital–output ratio. See also Simon (1986, 172–83, Appendix A, 'A Constant Long-Run K/Y Ratio is a Meaningless Observation') for a discussion of why the constant-price monetary value of the capital–output ratio will always tend to be approximately constant regardless of what is happening to the various individual physical capital–output ratios. If the data cannot show whether or not the aggregate production function exists, then the same applies to the whole Solow growth model, upon which it depends. It is not a case of rejecting the estimates of the

---

[11]   Temple (2010, p. 688) argues: 'If the data have been generated by a translog, a simpler model such as the Cobb–Douglas will be an imperfect fit. This is because the output elasticities and factor shares will not be constant over time or across production units. Even if the researcher lacks information on factor shares, standard methods can be used to detect and investigate parameter heterogeneity that has been left unmodelled. The only way Felipe and McCombie can get around these arguments is to rule them out, by assuming that production relationships never exist, and factor shares behave in particular ways'. The point to notice is that Temple again *assumes* that an aggregate production function exists in the form of a translog, which entirely begs the question under discussion. If the shares do show variability then, of course, the Cobb–Douglas relationship (not 'production function') will give an imperfect fit and a more flexible functional form (not 'production function') is needed.

parameters of the model – we know exactly what the estimates of the model are; they are the factor shares, but they cannot be interpreted as the physical aggregate output elasticities. Again, Temple misunderstands the argument.

It is difficult to understand the implications of Temple's remark noting the fact that the MRW model can be expressed as a function of the logarithm of the aggregate labour share. He comments 'But that quantity has been assumed constant across countries, so their [Felipe and McCombie's] suggested reinterpretation seems internally inconsistent' (Temple, 2010, fn 7, p. 691). This result was actually proved by Felipe and McCombie (2005b, p. 375) and discussed there. Felipe and McCombie prove that if the stylised facts mentioned in their paper hold, then the MRW model reduces to the logarithm of the aggregate labour factor share. But note that this share does not have to be constant *across* countries. This theoretical result arises from the fact that the accounting identity is replicating the MRW model, which assumes *identical* output elasticities (and, hence, from the identity, identical factor shares). The same result arises for each country if we start from the case where the elasticities and, hence the shares, *differ* between the individual countries, although this will reduce the goodness of fit of the cross-country regressions. It is difficult to see how this is in any way internally inconsistent. (The only interpretation we can make is that Temple is implicitly assuming that if factor shares differ between countries for some unspecified reason, the regressions are estimating a 'true' aggregate production function.)

To summarise: all that Felipe and McCombie (2005b) do is to show using the identity, the circumstances under which the augmented Solow model (the specification that MRW estimated) will lead to good results. We do not claim that the assumptions about the constancy of the wage and profit rates, the factor shares, the capital–output ratio, are correct theoretically or empirically (although some of them, as we have argued, are stylised facts in the literature). What we argue is that MRW's regression will work *if and only if* these conditions are met. In fact, what we implied in our discussion about the identity was that their poor initial results derived from the fact that all these stylised facts about the data were not met (especially the constancy of the level and growth of 'TFP'). If these assumptions about the data are not correct, then the equation that MRW estimated, will give a poor statistical fit. This is exactly what originally happened, and our point was that this can be seen without the need for estimating any regression to explain why. The identity also tells us how to improve the goodness of fit.

3. The Solow Residual is Definitionally the Weighted Growth of the Factor Inputs

Temple also discusses the distinction between the Solow residual and TFP growth. Temple (2006, p. 306) notes that the equation:

$$\hat{V}_t - [a_t\hat{L}_t + (1-a_t)\hat{J}_t] \equiv T\hat{F}P_t \equiv a_t\hat{w}_t + (1-a_t)\hat{r}_t \qquad (12.2)$$

is simply an illustration of the 'dual' growth-accounting results, namely that TFP growth can be calculated either from quantities (the primal) or from factor prices (the dual). The rationale for the dual interpretation is established from the cost function.[12] This is correct, but the explanation is incomplete. While neoclassical economists are aware of the accounting identity (12.3), the interpretation of primal and dual estimates of TFP growth takes place in the context of neoclassical production function theory and the usual neoclassical assumptions (see, for example, Jorgenson and Griliches, 1967). This means that the neoclassical interpretation of $a_t\hat{w}_t + (1-a_t)\hat{r}_t$ as measuring technical change (or, more generally, the growth of TFP) *does* require the assumptions of constant returns, perfect competition and that factors are paid their marginal products. Temple does not emphasise here perhaps the most important assumption of the growth-accounting approach, namely, that an aggregate production function must also exist. In the discussion of the relationship between the aggregate production function and the dual, Temple implicitly makes use of Euler's theorem and the usual neoclassical assumptions.

As is well known, Solow (1957) came to the 'startling' result (Solow, 1988, p. 313) that the growth of factor inputs for the US explained less than one-eighth of the growth of labour productivity, while the rate of technical progress (which is how Solow loosely interpreted the residual) explained the remaining seven-eighths. Far from being startling, as we show in Chapter 5, a back-of-the-envelope calculation with the identity shows that this result is inevitable. TFP growth is defined as $T\hat{F}P_t \equiv a\hat{w}_t + (1-a)\hat{r}_t$. The neoclassical assumptions are the existence of an aggregate production function and that factor shares are equal to the aggregate output elasticities. If factor shares are roughly constant (with a labour share of about 0.75) and the rate of profit does not vary systematically over time, by using value data the growth of TFP will equate to 75 per cent of the rate

---

[12]   It is also straightforward to show that the interpretation of the dual derived from the cost function suffers from the same problem, namely, that it is determined solely by the accounting identity (Chapter 2).

of growth of productivity.[13] In fact, Solow found the proportion slightly larger than this, because the rate of profit declined over the period under consideration.

Temple ironically agrees that the growth-accounting approach requires the existence of a well-behaved production relationship, but argues that a more general approach would be needed when there is no longer equality between marginal and factor products. As examples, he cites the work of Basu et al. (2006), Temple and Wöβmann (2006) and Fernald and Neiman (2010). It is difficult to see any relevance of these articles to the present debate because all commence by explicitly *assuming* that an aggregate production function exists and use value data. Fernald and Neiman (2010) actually specify a Cobb–Douglas production function! Again a case of *petitio principii*.

4. The Problem Cannot be Solved by Disaggregating the Value Measures of Capital (and Output)

Temple (2006), repeated in Temple (2010), makes the argument that with sufficient disaggregation the aggregate production function may (or presumably may not) exist and all that remains is a statistical problem of correctly specifying its functional form. Related to this is Temple's (2006, p. 308) comment that 'if aggregation is not possible, the obvious solution must be to disaggregate'. He continues: 'In the case of growth accounting, there is nothing to stop the researcher writing down $Y = F(K_1, K_2, . . ., K_M, L_1, L_2, . . ., L_N)$ where there are M different types of capital input and N different types of labour input'. He points out that production functions and growth theory do not, in principle, need aggregation. 'Instead, it is lack of data that will typically restrict the applied researcher to simpler methods'.

Unfortunately, this confuses the aggregation and the accounting identity problem. First, if the researcher has *physical* data for output and all the different types of inputs, individual capital goods and structures, then it just might be possible to estimate a production function. But as soon as it is necessary to use different types of output and capital measured using

---

[13] Note that growth of labour productivity is given by:

$$\hat{V}_t - \hat{L}_t \equiv a\hat{w}_t + (1-a)\hat{r}_t + (1-a)(\hat{J}_t - \hat{L}_t) \equiv T\hat{F}P_t + (1-a)(\hat{J}_t - \hat{L}_t).$$

The growth-accounting approach normally calculates TFP growth over several years and given that factor shares are not constant, uses the average value of the shares (based on the Tornqvist approximation to the Divisia index).

constant-price data because of heterogeneity, then the identity is simply written as:

$$V \equiv w_1 L_1 + w_2 L_2 + \ldots w_N L_N + r_1 J_1 + r_2 J_2 + \ldots r_M J_M, \qquad (12.3)$$

where V and Js are constant-price value data. The accounting identity argument follows through, even though there are several categories of labour and capital. The use of two-sector production function models to disaggregate the economy into agricultural and non-agricultural sectors (see Temple, 2006, p. 309) does not escape the critique.[14]

Aggregation poses a problem not for the reasons that Fisher (1992) set out (important though these are), but because suitable physical data are not normally available to the researcher, who then has to resort to value data. It should be noted that this is true even for industries at the level of the three- and four-digit SIC. Disaggregating by industry, rather than by input, does not prevent the problem.

Consequently, the question is not so much about disaggregation, but the type of data, value versus physical. As we have argued, although not exempt from problems, with data in physical terms it is possible to estimate the technological parameters, although subject to specifying correctly TFP. Temple argues that 'if the inputs have been disaggregated appropriately, then a production function may well exist, and the only remaining problem is a purely statistical one: can the data be used to establish the form of the relationship?' (Temple 2010, p. 687). Temple argues that, provided we sufficiently disaggregate the constant-price value data of the capital stock and employment, the resulting aggregate production function exists and therefore can be estimated using value data.[15] He does have the proviso that the correct measure of TFP is required, which he sees as a difficult, but not insuperable problem. This legerdemain occurs in his 2006 paper and he repeats it in his 2010 comment. Thus, he seems to consider that the critique rests on a 'fundamental identification problem' (Temple, 2010, p. 685). However, we have long argued that, *pace* Temple, it is not a statistical identification problem if this implies that it is possible, in principle, to specify a model where the aggregate production function

---

[14]   Temple's argument is puzzling, as he accepts that our arguments are not about input mismeasurement, but about the dangers of using value added to measure output, and constant-price value data to measure the capital stock.

[15]   Temple only concentrates on the disaggregation of inputs, although his argument must logically apply to the different outputs, which means that we have to disaggregate the aggregate production function.

can be statistically refuted. Temple (p. 687), paradoxically also recognises that 'the argument is not simply one about statistical identification'.[16]

Consequently, no matter how many inputs (and outputs) are specified and measured in value terms, the problem posed by the identity still arises. Jorgensen and Griliches (1967, p. 253) (see Felipe and McCombie, 2006) start out by *assuming* the existence of an aggregate production function, perfect competition, and that factors are paid their marginal products. They use this approach to disaggregate the constant-price value indices of the capital stock in order to try empirically to eliminate the residual. Jorgensen and Griliches (1967, footnote 2) explicitly state that because of their assumptions, their approach cannot be used to *test* the marginal productivity theory of factor pricing.

5. Economic Rents and the Actual and Virtual Accounting Identities

Temple implies that for the critique to hold (his discussion is in the context of the Solow residual), rents need to be excluded from the accounting identity (Temple, 2010, p. 688). However, the accounting identity simply shows how value added is measured. As we have seen, this is given by the identity $V \equiv W + \Pi$, where W is the wage bill and Π is the operating surplus. The latter includes all types of profits. All we do is to split the wage bill into the product of the average wage rate (w) multiplied by employment (L); and the surplus into the product of the average rate of return (r) times the value of the stock of capital (J). This implies that $V \equiv W + \Pi = wL + rJ$. This requires no economic assumptions whatsoever and holds true by definition.

Unfortunately, Temple seems to confuse the 'actual' accounting identity with what we have termed in an earlier chapter the neoclassical 'virtual' identity (Felipe and McCombie, 2007b), based upon the assumption of perfectly competitive markets and optimisation. Consequently the latter may, or may not, hold in reality. This is usually derived at the microeconomic level by applying Euler's theorem to the micro-production function, together with the assumption that the marginal theory of factor pricing holds, that is, $pQ = pF(L, K) = p(\partial Q/\partial L)L + p(\partial Q/\partial K)K = wL + \rho K$, where Q is output and K is capital, both measured in *physical* terms, and ρ is the rental price of capital. p is the price of a unit of output. This chain of reasoning is then applied seamlessly in neoclassical production theory to the macroeconomic level, regardless of the fact that output is value added

---

[16] However, from a careful reading of the text, it is not clear if he merely correctly attributes this to us, or whether he accepts that it logically follows from our critique.

(V) – not units of physical output – and capital is not the stock of homogeneous structures and equipment, but the constant-price value of the stock of capital (J).[17] If an estimate of the competitive rate of profit is used in the accounting identity, then the implied economic rents would have to be deducted from value added and the argument follows through exactly.

6.   There is no Econometric Solution to the Implications of the Critique

Temple argues that what he terms the 'statistical' critique and the 'economic' or accounting identity critique (the identity) are close. While these two critiques share some elements, they are not, however, the same thing. One implication of the 'economic' argument is that this is not an econometric problem, that is, it is not about how to identify a good proxy for TFP (given the difficulty to control for it). Nor is the problem one of finding appropriate econometric instruments to estimate the production function. The basis of the 'statistical' critique is that this is an econometric problem that has a solution. The 'economic' or accounting critique, however, says that this is not an econometric problem and that it does not have any solution.

It is not an identification problem between two separate equations, one the identity (and, thus, not a behavioural relationship) and the other the production function, as Bronfenbrenner (1971), for example, seemed to think. There is no way that the supposed aggregate production function can be identified as distinct from the identity. Temple refers to work by Olley and Pakes (1996) and Levinsohn and Petrin (2003). But this is an *ignoratio elenchi*. These papers claim to offer solutions to the problem of estimating production functions when technical efficiency is unobserved. He also cites Griliches and Mairesse (1998) who provide an accessible summary of the problems inherent in estimating aggregate production functions. However, these first two studies are irrelevant as they are based upon the assumption that the aggregate production function exists and all that is needed is to correctly estimate it by the appropriate estimating technique. We have discussed this in Felipe and McCombie (2012). Likewise, the issues raised by Griliches and Mairesse (1998) have no bearing upon the problem. Temple also cites Ackerberg et al. (2006) as an example of progress towards solving this identification problem, but again they assume the existence of an aggregate production function.

The poor statistical results are not due to standard econometric problems (the identity does not have an error term). Poor statistical fits using

---

[17]   The argument also holds for gross output by adding intermediate materials.

time-series data are often found even though factor shares are relatively constant. The problem, as noted earlier, is that $a_t\hat{w}_t + (1 - a_t)\hat{r}_t$ is not constant, but has a pronounced cyclical component.

Consequently, its approximation by the constant term in the regression in growth rates (or a linear time trend when log levels are used) is responsible for the poor results. In these circumstances, it is necessary to find the correct approximation to this equation (for example, through a different type of time trend such as a trigonometric function).[18] If factor shares vary greatly then the Cobb–Douglas form will also give a poor statistical fit. In this case, a more flexible functional form for the identity is required.

7. Simulation Results Confirm the Importance of the Critique

As part of our 2010 reply to Temple, we cite a simulation study of ours (Felipe and McCombie, 2006) where we show that with constant mark-up pricing the data will give a perfect fit to a Cobb–Douglas production function, where the estimated coefficients of the log of capital and labour are 0.75 and 0.25, respectively; while the true output elasticities were 0.25 and 0.75, respectively. We assume the existence of well-defined physical micro-production functions not because we necessarily believe they exist, but to show the implications of the critique even under these circumstances.

Temple argues that as the estimated coefficients of the log of capital and labour using value data differ markedly from the true output elasticities, there must be large differences between the rewards to factors and their marginal products: 'Those are not the usual assumptions made in interpreting the results from estimated production functions' (Temple, 2010, p.690). But any researcher with only access to the value data and interpreting the results of the estimated 'production function' would find that the estimated 'output elasticities' equal the factor shares. Thus, the neoclassical researcher would erroneously conclude that markets are perfectively competitive, constant returns to scale prevail, and that factors are paid their marginal products. This would also be the case, as we show in our simulations, when the true production function displays increasing returns, or, indeed, there is no well-defined relationship between the outputs and inputs. In the model we use, prices are determined by a mark-up on unit costs, which in turn is determined by, for example, the state of competition in the industry and the relative power of labour and capital in the wage-bargaining process. It may well differ from the physical marginal

---

[18]   Adjusting the inputs, especially capital, for differences in capacity utilisation will also have the same effect.

productivity of labour if the firm (but not the researcher) knows the true micro-production function, but so what?[19] Firms, under neoclassical assumptions, will set the rewards equal to the marginal product measured in value terms and are unlikely to know a worker's physical marginal product. (Moreover, there are vast sectors of the economy where there is no reliable independent measure of output even in constant-price value terms.)

There have been a number of other important simulation studies discussed in Chapter 3 which demonstrate how the data will give a good fit to a Cobb–Douglas, even though we know by the construction of the hypothetical data that this is not reflected in the underlying technology. These include a study where the micro-production functions deliberately violate the conditions for successful aggregation (Fisher, 1971b); where the production function has a fixed-coefficients technology (Shaikh, 2005); and where firms satisfice, rather than optimise (Nelson and Winter, 1982). (For a further discussion of these studies, see Felipe and McCombie, 2010b.)

8.   Growth Econometrics without Production Functions

Temple notes that while the inclusion of the initial level of productivity in a regression with productivity growth as the regressand can be given an interpretation based on the aggregate production function (that is, the absolute convergence regression), this need not be the case. Regressions explaining disparities can include variables that are not related to the aggregate production function and it is not necessary to rely on this as a justification for the regression. A large number of such variables can, and are, included in such Barro-type regressions. These 'everything but the kitchen sink' regressions have become popular in some quarters. But as such models, according to Temple, have nothing to do with the aggregate production function, it is clear that they cannot represent a test of the neoclassical growth model, which is the rationale for MRW's exercise (for example, the interpretation of the coefficients in terms of output elasticities) and the debate that we raise.

In our view, such regressions represent little more than 'measurement without theory'. Whether they really tell us anything about the causes of growth and why some countries have never developed is debatable.

---

[19]   Temple (2010) argues that some argue that 'no firm knows its production function' but he considers it knows its costs and that well-behaved cost functions are mirrored by the existence of production functions. But a cost function is also derived from the accounting identity and will be mirrored by a 'spurious' production function. See Chapter 2.

The regressions assume ergodicity and thereby exclude any form of path dependence; they assume homogeneity of parameters; the data are often suspect; they oversimplify complex relationships; most of the regressors are fragile; and so on (Levine and Renelt, 1992; Kenny and Williams, 2001).

It is of course possible to run regressions that attempt to explain differences of growth rates in terms of variables that are not part of the definition of value added. This is the case of, for example, growth regressions whose objective is to test the statistical significance and sign of variables such as the abundance in natural resources, the effect of a country being coastal versus landlocked, or neighbourhood effects (see, for example, Collier and O'Connell, 2007). Clearly, these regressions are not derived from a production function and they are not the subject of this debate.

Our argument is that when capital is included in the regression as a value measure, together with employment, the problem of the accounting identity arises. Moreover, if Temple's broad interpretation of growth regressions were the standard one, we wonder why neoclassical researchers waste time with pages of theoretical work involving aggregate production functions. Therefore, it is difficult within the neoclassical paradigm to defend growth econometrics without production functions.

9. And so to Lucas on Development

Temple (2006, p. 304) cites as an example of the usefulness of the aggregate production function Lucas (1990):

> In a classic paper, Lucas (1990) showed that, under conventional assumptions about the extent of diminishing returns, the vast differences we observe in labour productivity across countries cannot be explained by differences in capital intensity, without a counterfactual implication. If differences in capital intensity account for underdevelopment, the returns to investment in poor countries would have to be many times the returns in rich countries – to a far greater extent than is usually thought plausible.
>
> One response to the Lucas paper is to say that, because his conclusions are derived from an aggregate production function, it is of no value. I think that is clearly wrong: Lucas has shifted the burden of proof away from one side of the debate and towards another.

This quotation raises a number of interesting points, not least because it shows that the neoclassical paradigm, with an aggregate production function with diminishing returns, generates puzzles that have to be answered within that paradigm, while in fact the paradigm may be irrelevant.

Lucas's observation, which is hardly novel, comes from postulating a neoclassical production function. With the supposed output elasticities of labour and capital equalling 0.75 and 0.25, it is not surprising that the data will show that capital intensity can explain little in the way of differences in labour productivity, as a simple back-of-the-envelope calculation will demonstrate.

For any year, the ratio of the accounting identities of the most advanced country, the US, and a less developed country, i, can be written exactly as:

$$\frac{(V_{US}/L_{US})}{(V_i/L_i)} \equiv \frac{w_{US} + r_{US}(J_{US}/L_{US})}{w_i + r_i(J_i/L_i)}, \tag{12.4}$$

or, equivalently as (assuming that factor shares are constant, and take the same value in the US and country i):

$$\frac{(V_{US}/L_{US})}{(V_i/L_i)} \equiv \frac{a^{-a}(1-a)^{-(1-a)}w_{US}^a r_{US}^{(1-a)}(J_{US}/L_{US})^{(1-a)}}{a^{-a}(1-a)^{-(1-a)}w_i^a r_i^{(1-a)}(J_i/L_i)^{(1-a)}}. \tag{12.5}$$

Using the stylised fact that the capital–output ratio is constant (or, what comes to the same thing, that the rate of profit does not differ between countries) and the definition $w \equiv a(V/L)$ the ratio may be written as:

$$\frac{(V_{US}/L_{US})}{(V_i/L_i)} \equiv \frac{w_{US}^a}{w_i^a} \cdot \frac{(J_{US}/L_{US})^{(1-a)}}{(J_i/L_i)^{(1-a)}} \equiv \frac{(V_{US}/L_{US})^a}{(V_i/L_i)^a} \cdot \frac{(J_{US}/L_{US})^{(1-a)}}{(J_i/L_i)^{(1-a)}}. \tag{12.6}$$

The relative contributions, in a purely mathematical and not economic sense, of the two expressions on the right-hand-side of equation (12.6) are reported in Table 12.1.

Of course, if labour's share a *differs* from 0.75, or if there are disparities in this value between countries, this will affect the contribution of columns (ii) and (iii). This is also true if we allow the rate of profit to vary. Nevertheless, the picture is clear. From the accounting identity, the increasing difference in the ratio of productivity levels is largely explained by the increasing value of the ratio of the wage rates. For example, when the productivity of the US is 50 times greater than that of the less developed country, the 'explanation' of the differential in productivity provided by the ratio of the wage rates is seven times larger than that provided by the value of the capital–labour ratio. These results do *not* require the assumption of a production function with diminishing returns to capital, all factors used technically efficiently and factors paid their marginal products, all highly dubious assumptions especially for the less developed countries. The production function approach assumes that column (ii) is

Table 12.1   *Contributions of the ratio of the real wage rate and of the capital–labour ratio to the ratio of productivity levels*

(i)	(ii)	(iii)	Ratio of (ii)/(iii)
$\dfrac{(V_{US}/L_{US})}{(V_i/L_i)}$	$\left(\dfrac{w_{US}}{w_i}\right)^a$	$\left(\dfrac{J_{US}/L_{US}}{J_i/L_1}\right)^{(1-a)}$	
1	1.00	1.00	1.00
10	5.62	1.78	3.16
20	9.46	2.11	4.47
30	12.82	2.34	5.48
40	15.91	2.51	6.32
50	18.80	2.66	7.07

Notes:
The figures are calculated using equation (12.6).
The value of a is 0.75 and column (ii) is equal to $[(V_{us}/L_{us})/(V_i/L_i)]^a$

the measure of relative level of technology or TFP. However, through the accounting identity it becomes obvious that it is not necessary to assume diminishing returns to show the relative unimportance of the relative capital–labour ratio.

CONCLUSIONS

The Cambridge capital theory controversies and the related aggregation problems have had no influence on the use of the aggregate production function, which continues to be widely and uncritically used. We suggest that the answer to this conundrum is the instrumental justification that in practice the aggregate production function 'works'. However, the fact that very simple functional forms and two highly aggregate variables (with the constant-price value of the capital stock in particular subject to all kinds of statistical measurement errors) can often explain over 90 per cent of the variation in output is due simply to the fact that the three variables are definitionally related. This explanation does not depend upon any specific assumptions such as constant factor shares, a constant level or growth of the weighted average of the growth rate of the wage rate and profit rate, or a constant capital–output ratio, *pace* Temple (2006, 2010). Allowing these to vary does not mean that all the aggregation problems and the problems posed by the accounting identity simply disappear, and that we can be confident of estimating a technological relationship.

We have considered, in particular, Temple's arguments in detail as he has taken the critique seriously and presented some criticisms that need answering.

The key disagreement between Temple and us is that we argue that using value data, a researcher can always eventually find a perfect fit to the data, with the estimated coefficients equal to the factor shares (and not only when these are constant), even though no aggregate production function exists. Temple does not share this conclusion. We have shown that the only reason why factor shares and the output elasticities may differ is that the specific functional form estimated does not accurately track the accounting identity. Temple unwittingly concedes our case when he states: 'Moreover, the production function *may* appear simple and well-behaved even when no *stable relationship* exists and the true extent of the misspecification may never be detected' (Temple 2010, p. 689, emphasis added).

This accurately summarises our position, although we argue that it is not a case of 'may', but of 'will'; and furthermore, that the statement 'no stable relationship' includes the case when plausibly the aggregate production function does not exist. An implication of the above quotation is that the researcher can never know whether or not the estimates of the aggregate production function mean anything. As we noted above, Temple correctly states, 'the argument is not simply one of statistical identification' (p. 687), but then inconsistently and erroneously states that 'to the extent that a researcher can control for the variation in TFP and takes care over the specification, the simultaneous existence of the value added identity does not invalidate these methods'.

We may summarise the position as follows:

- The aggregation literature and the Cambridge capital theory controversies have shown that, for all practical purposes, aggregate production functions do not exist, *even as approximations*.
- The use of value data means that, because of the underlying accounting identity, it is always possible to obtain a close statistical fit to the Cobb–Douglas, CES and other more flexible functions, such as the translog, with the output elasticities equal to the factor shares.
- These results cannot be interpreted as a test of the existence of the aggregate production function. And the estimates obtained are not the underlying aggregate technological parameters of the economy.
- Therefore, theoretical models that use the aggregate production function are untestable in the sense that they cannot be statistically refuted and therefore the results tell us nothing relevant.
- The accounting identity critique does *not* depend upon the assump-

tion that factor shares, the capital–output ratio, and the weighted growth of the wage rate and profit rate are constant.

- Disaggregation, *per se*, does not invalidate the critique unless physical units are used in measuring output and the various items of machinery and structures.

The criticisms of Temple have ironically, if anything, only served to confirm the validity and importance of the critique. But as Samuelson (1966, p. 583) once famously remarked in another, but related, context 'if all this causes headaches for those nostalgic for the old time parables of neoclassical writing, we must remind ourselves that scholars are not born to live an easy existence. We must respect and appraise the facts of life'.

References

Abbott, T.A., Griliches, Z. and Hausman, J.A. (1998), 'Short Run Movements in Productivity: Market Power versus Capacity Utilization', in Z. Griliches (ed.), *Practicing Econometrics: Essays in Method and Application*, Cheltenham, UK and Lyme, NH, USA: Edward Elgar.

Abramovitz, M. (1956), 'Resource and Output Trends in the United States since 1870', *American Economic Review, Papers and Proceedings*, vol. 46(2), pp. 5–23.

Acemoglu, D. (2009), *Introduction to Modern Economic Growth*, Princeton, NJ: Princeton University Press.

Ackerberg, D.A., Caves, J.K. and Frazer, G. (2006), 'Structural Identification of Production Functions', available at: http://folk.uio.no/rnymoen/Ackerberg_Caves_Frazer.pdf.

Aghion, P. and Howitt, P. (1998), *Endogenous Growth Theory*, Cambridge, MA: MIT Press.

Aghion, P. and Howitt, P. (2009), *The Economics of Growth*, Cambridge, MA: MIT Press.

Ahmad, S. (1991), *Capital in Economic Theory: Neo-classical, Cambridge and Chaos*, Aldershot, UK and Brookfield, VT, USA: Edward Elgar.

Alexander, W.R.J. (1990), 'The Impact of Defence Spending on Economic Growth', *Defence Economics*, vol. 2(1), pp. 39–55.

Alexander, W.R.J. (1994), 'The Government Sector, the Export Sector and Growth', *De Economist*, vol. 142(2), pp. 211–20.

Antras, P. (2004), 'Is the U.S. Aggregate Production Function Cobb–Douglas? New Estimates of the Elasticity of Substitution', *Contributions to Macroeconomics*, vol. 4(1), ISSN (Online) 1534-6005, DOI: 10.2202/1534-6005.1161.

Anyadike-Danes, M. and Godley, W. (1989), 'Real Wages and Employment: A Sceptical View of Some Recent Empirical Work', *Manchester School of Economics and Social Studies*, vol. 57(2), pp. 172–87.

Arrow, K.J. (1962), 'The Economic Implications of Learning by Doing', *Review of Economic Studies*, vol. 29(1), pp. 155–73.

Arrow, K.J., Bernheim, B.D., Feldstein, M.S., McFadden, D.L., Poterba, J.M. and Solow, R.M. (2011), '100 Years of the *American Economic Review*: The Top 20 Articles', *American Economic Review*, vol. 101(1), pp. 1–8.

Arrow, K.J., Chenery, H.B., Minhas, B.S. and Solow, R.M. (1961),

'Capital-Labor Substitution and Economic Efficiency', *Review of Economics and Statistics*, vol. 43(3), pp. 225–50.

Bairam, E. (1987), 'Soviet Postwar Industrial Growth and Capital Labour Substitution', *Economic Letters*, vol. 24(4), pp. 331–34.

Baldone, S. (1984), 'From Surrogate to Pseudo Production Functions', *Cambridge Journal of Economics*, vol. 8(3), pp. 271–88.

Barro, R.J. (1999), 'Notes on Growth Accounting', *Journal of Economic Growth*, vol. 64(2), pp. 119–37.

Barro, R.J. and Sala-i-Martin, X. (1995 [2003]), *Economic Growth* (2nd edition) New York: McGraw-Hill.

Basu, S. (1996), 'Procyclical Productivity: Increasing Returns or Cyclical Utilisation?', *Quarterly Journal of Economics*, vol. 111(3), pp. 719–51.

Basu, S. and Fernald, J.G. (1995), 'Are Apparent Spillovers a Figment of Specification Error?', *Journal of Monetary Economics*, vol. 36(1), pp. 165–88.

Basu, S. and Fernald, J.G. (1997), 'Returns to Scale in U.S. Production: Estimates and Implications', *Journal of Political Economy*, vol. 105(2), pp. 249–83.

Basu, S., Fernald, J. and Kimball, M. (2006), 'Are Technological Improvements Contractionary', *American Economic Review*, vol. 96(5), pp. 1418–48.

Bean, E., Layard, R. and Nickell, S. (1986), 'The Rise in Unemployment: A Multi-Country Study', *Economica*, vol. 53(210), Supplement, pp. S1–S22.

Bernanke, B. (1987), 'Comment', *National Bureau of Economic Research, Macroeconomics Annual 1987*, Cambridge, MA: MIT Press.

Birner, J. (2002), *The Cambridge Controversies in Capital Theory: A Study in the Logic of Theory Development*, London: Routledge.

Biswas, B. and Ram, R. (1985), 'Military Expenditures and Economic Growth in Less Developed Countries: An Augmented Model and Further Evidence', *Economic Development and Cultural Change*, vol. 34(2), pp. 361–72.

Blaug, M. (1974), *The Cambridge Revolution: Success or Failure?*, London: Institute of Economic Affairs.

Blaug, M. (1978), *Economic Theory in Retrospect* (3rd edition), Cambridge: Cambridge University Press.

Blaug, M. (1992), *The Methodology of Economics: Or, How Economists Explain*, Cambridge: Cambridge University Press.

Blaug, M. (2009), 'The Trade-off between Rigor and Relevance: Sraffian Economics as a Case in Point', *History of Political Economy*, vol. 41(2), pp. 219–47.

Blinder, A.S. (1989), 'In Honour of Robert M Solow: Nobel in Laureate in 1987', *Journal of Economic Perspectives*, vol. 3(3), pp. 99–105.

Bliss, C.J. (1975), *Capital Theory and the Distribution of Income*, Amsterdam: North-Holland.

Bliss, C.J., Cohen, A. and Harcourt, G.C. (2005), *Capital Theory* (3 volumes), Cheltenham, UK and Northampton, MA, USA: Edward Elgar.

Bodkin, R.G. and Klein, L.R. (1967), 'Nonlinear Estimation of Aggregate Production Functions', *Review of Economics and Statistics*, vol. 49(1), pp. 28–44.

Bresnahan, T.F. (1989), 'Empirical Studies of Industries with Market Power', in S. Strøm (ed.), *Econometrics and Economic Theory in the 20th Century: The Ragnar Frisch Centennial Symposium*, Cambridge: Cambridge University Press.

Briscoe, G., O'Brien, P. and Smyth, D.G. (1970), 'The Measurement of Capacity Utilisation in the United Kingdom', *Manchester School of Economics and Social Studies*, vol. 5(2), pp. 91–117.

Brock, W.A. and Durlauf, S.N. (2001), 'What Have We Learned from a Decade of Empirical Research on Growth? Growth Empirics and Reality', *World Bank Economic Review*, vol. 15(2), pp. 229–72.

Bronfenbrenner, M. (1944), 'Production Functions: Cobb–Douglas, Interfirm, Intrafirm', *Econometrica*, vol. 12(1), pp. 35–44.

Bronfenbrenner, M. (1971), *Income Distribution Theory*, London: Macmillan.

Bronfenbrenner, M. and Douglas, P.H. (1939), 'Cross-section Studies in the Cobb–Douglas Function', *Journal of Political Economy*, vol. 47(6), pp. 761–83.

Brown, M. (1966), *On the Theory and Measurement of Technological Change*, Cambridge: Cambridge University Press.

Brown, M. (1980), 'The Measurement of Capital Aggregates: A Postreswitching Problem', in D. Usher (ed.), *The Measurement of Capital*, Chicago, IL: University of Chicago Press.

Bureau of Labor Statistics (BLS) (2006), *Multifactor Productivity: Overview of Capital Inputs for BLS Multifactor Productivity Measures*, Washington, DC: US Bureau of Labor Statistics, available at: http://www.bls.gov/mfp/home.htm.

Burmeister, E. (1977), 'On the Social Significance of the Reswitching Controversy', *Revue d'Économie Politique*, vol. 87, pp. 330–50.

Burmeister, E. (1980), 'Comment', in D. Usher (ed.), *The Measurement of Capital*, Chicago, IL: University of Chicago Press.

Cabballero, R.J. and Lyons, R.K. (1989), 'The Role of External Economies in U.S. Manufacturing', *National Bureau of Economic Research*, working paper no. 33.

Caballero, R.J. and Lyons, R.K. (1992), 'External Effects in U.S. Procyclical Productivity', *Journal of Monetary Economics*, vol. 29(2), pp. 209–25.

Carr, J. (1989), 'Government Size and Economic Growth: A New Framework and Some Evidence from Cross-Section and Time-Series Data: Comment', *American Economic Review*, vol. 79(1), pp. 267–71.

Carter, S. (2011a), 'C.E. Ferguson and the Neoclassical Theory of Capital: A Matter of Faith', *Review of Political Economy*, vol. 23(3), pp. 339–56.

Carter, S. (2011b), '"On the Cobb–Douglas and all that . . .": The Solow–Simon Correspondence over the Aggregate Neoclassical Production Function', *Journal of Post Keynesian Economics*, vol. 34(2), pp. 255–74.

Chambers, R.G. (1988), *Applied Production Analysis*, Cambridge: Cambridge University Press.

Christensen, L.R., Jorgenson, D.W. and Lau, L.L. (1973), 'Transcendental Logarithmic Production Frontiers', *Review of Economics and Statistics*, vol. 55(1), pp. 28–45.

Clark, J.B. (1899), *The Distribution of Wealth: A Theory of Wages, Interest and Profits*, New York: Macmillan.

Clark, J.M. (1928), 'Inductive Evidence on Marginal Productivity', *American Economic Review*, vol. 18(3), pp. 450–67.

Clark, K.B. and Freeman, R.B. (1980), 'How Elastic Is the Demand for Labor?', *Review of Economics and Statistics*, vol. 62(4), pp. 509–20.

Cobb, C.W. and Douglas, P.H. (1928), 'A Theory of Production', *American Economic Review* (Supplement), vol. 18(1), pp. 139–65.

Cohen, A. (1984), 'The Methodological Resolution of the Cambridge Controversies', *Journal of Post Keynesian Economics*, vol. 6(4), pp. 614–29.

Cohen, A. and Harcourt, G.C. (2003), 'Retrospectives: Whatever Happened to the Cambridge Capital Theory Controversies?', *Journal of Economic Perspectives*, vol. 17(1), pp. 199–214.

Cohen, A. and Harcourt, G.C. (2005), 'Introduction, Capital Theory Controversy: Scarcity, Production, Equilibrium and Time', in C. Bliss, A. Cohen and G.C. Harcourt (eds), *Capital Theory*, 3 volumes, Cheltenham, UK and Northampton, MA, USA: Edward Elgar.

Collier, P. and O'Connell, S.A. (2007), 'Opportunities and Choices', in B.J. Ndulu, S.A. O'Connell, R. Bates, P. Collier, And C.C. Soludo (eds), *The Political Economy of Economic Growth in Africa, 1960–2000*, Cambridge: Cambridge University Press.

Cornwall, J. (1977), *Modern Capitalism: Its Growth and Transformation*, London: Martin Robertson.

Cotis, J.P., Renaud, M. and Sobczak, N. (1998), 'Le Chômage d'Équilibre en France: Une Évaluation', *Revue Économique*, vol. 49(3), pp. 921–35.

Crafts, N. and Toniolo, G. (1996), *Economic Growth Since 1945*, Cambridge: Cambridge University Press.

Cramer, J.S. (1969), *Empirical Econometrics*, Amsterdam, North-Holland.

Cripps, T.F. and Tarling, R.J. (1973), *Growth in Advanced Capitalist Economies: 1950–70*, Cambridge: Cambridge University Press.

Cyert, R.M. and March, J.G. (1963 [1992]), *A Behavioral Theory of the Firm* (2nd edition), Englewood Cliffs, NJ: Prentice-Hall.

Cyert, R.M. and Simon, H.A. (1971), 'Theory of the Firm: Behavioralism and Marginalism', unpublished working paper, Carnegie-Mellon University, Pittsburgh, PA.

Daly, P. and Douglas, P.H. (1943), 'The Production Function for Canadian Manufacturing', *Journal of the American Statistical Association*, vol. 38(222), pp. 78–86.

Daly, P., Olsen, E. and Douglas, P.H. (1943), 'The Production Function for Manufacturing in the United States', *Journal of Political Economy*, vol. 51(1), pp. 61–5.

Davidson, P. (1983), 'The Marginal Product Curve is not the Demand Curve for Labor and Lucas' Labor Supply Function is not the Supply Curve for Labor', *Journal of Post Keynesian Economics*, vol. 6(1), pp. 105–17.

de Marchi, N. and Gilbert, C. (1989), 'Introduction' to History and Methodology of Econometrics', *Oxford Economic Papers*, vol. 41(1), pp. 1–11.

Denison, E.F. (1962), *The Sources of Economic Growth in the United States and the Alternatives Before Us*, New York: Committee for Economic Development.

Denison, E.F. (1967), *Why Growth Rates Differ: Postwar Experience in Nine Western Countries*, Washington, DC: Brookings Institution.

Denison, E.F. (1972a), 'Some Major Issues in Productivity Analysis: An Examination of Estimates by Jorgenson and Griliches', *Survey of Current Business*, vol. 52 (Part II), pp. 37–63.

Denison, E.F. (1972b), 'Final Comments', *Survey of Current Business*, vol. 52 (Part II), pp. 95–110.

Diamond, P., McFadden, D. and Rodriguez, M. (1978), 'Measurement of the Elasticity of Factor Substitution and Bias of Technical Change', in M. Fuss and D. McFadden (eds), *Production Economics: A Dual Approach to Theory and Applications, Vol. II, Applications of the Theory of Production*, Amsterdam: North-Holland.

Dixit, A.K. and Stiglitz, J.E. (1977), 'Monopolistic Competition and Optimum Product Diversity', *American Economic Review*, vol. 67(3), pp. 297–308.

Dobb, M. (1973), *Theories of Value and Distribution Since Adam Smith:*

Ideology and Economic Theory, Cambridge: Cambridge University Press.

Domowitz, I., Hubbard, R.G. and Petersen, B.C. (1988), 'Market Structure and Cyclical Fluctuations in U.S. Manufacturing', *Review of Economics and Statistics*, vol. 70(1), pp. 55–66.

Douglas, P.H. (1934), *The Theory of Wages*, New York: Macmillan.

Douglas, P.H. (1948), 'Are There Laws of Production?', *American Economic Review*, vol. 38(1), pp. 1–41.

Douglas, P.H. (1967), 'Comments on the Cobb–Douglas Production Function', in M. Brown (ed.), *Theory and Empirical Analysis of Production*, Studies in Income and Wealth, 31, Cambridge, MA: National Bureau of Economic Research, pp. 15–22.

Douglas, P.H. (1972), *In the Fullness of Time: The Memoirs of Paul H. Douglas*, New York: Harcourt, Brace, Jovanovich.

Douglas, P.H. (1976), 'The Cobb–Douglas Production Function Once Again: Its History, Its Testing, and Some New Empirical Values', *Journal of Political Economy*, vol. 84(5), pp. 903–15.

Dow, S.C. (1980), 'Methodological Morality in the Cambridge Controversies', *Journal of Post Keynesian Economics*, vol. 2(3), pp. 368–80.

Dowrick, S. and Wells, G. (2004), 'Modelling Aggregate Demand for Labour: A Critique of Lewis and MacDonald', *Economic Record*, vol. 80(251), pp. 436–40.

Durand, D. (1937), 'Some Thoughts on Marginal Productivity, with Special Reference to Professor Douglas's Analysis', *Journal of Political Economy*, vol. 45(6), pp. 740–58.

Durlauf, S.N. and Johnson, P.A. (1995), 'Multiple Regimes and Cross-Country Growth Behavior', *Journal of Applied Econometrics*, vol. 10(4), pp. 365–84.

Durlauf, S.N. and Phillips, P.C.B. (1988), 'Trends Versus Random Walks in Time Series Analysis', *Econometrica*, vol. 56(6), pp. 1333–54.

Easterly, W. (2001), *The Elusive Quest for Growth: Economists' Adventures and Misadventures in the Tropics*, Cambridge, MA: MIT Press.

Easterly, W. and Levine, R. (2001), 'What Have We Learned from a Decade of Empirical Research on Growth? It's Not Factor Accumulation: Stylized Facts and Growth Models', *World Bank Economic Review*, vol. 15(2), pp. 177–219.

Eden, B. and Griliches, Z. (1993), 'Productivity, Market Power and Capacity Utilization when Spot Markets are Complete', *American Economic Review, Papers and Proceedings*, vol. 83(2), pp. 219–23.

Estrin, S. and Laidler, D. (1995), *Introduction to Microeconomics*, Hemel Hempstead: Harvester Wheatsheaf.

Fabricant, S. (1954), *Economic Progress and Economic Change*, 34th Annual Report, New York: NBER.

Fagerberg, J. (1987), 'A Technology Gap Approach to Why Growth Rates Differ', *Research Policy*, vol. 16(2), pp. 87–99.

Feder, G. (1982), 'On Exports and Economic Growth', *Journal of Development Economics*, vol. 12(1-2), pp. 59–73.

Felipe, J. (1998), 'On the Constancy of the Parameters of the Cobb–Douglas Production Function', mimeo, Asian Development Bank, Manila.

Felipe, J. and Adams, F.G. (2005), '"A Theory of Production". The Estimation of the Cobb–Douglas Function: A Retrospective View', *Eastern Economic Journal*, vol. 31(3), pp. 427–46.

Felipe, J. and Fisher, F.M. (2003), 'Aggregation in Production Functions: What Applied Economists Should Know', *Metroeconomica*, vol. 54(2–3), pp. 208–62.

Felipe, J. and Fisher, F.M. (2006), 'Aggregate Production Functions, Neoclassical Growth Models and the Aggregation Problem', *Estudios de Economia Aplicada*, vol. 24(1), pp. 127–63.

Felipe, J. and Holz, C. (2001), 'Why do Aggregate Production Functions Work? Fisher's Simulations, Shaikh's Identity, and Some New Results', *International Review of Applied Economics*, vol. 15(3), pp. 261–85.

Felipe, J. and McCombie, J.S.L. (2001a), 'The CES Production Function, the Accounting Identity, and Occam's Razor', *Applied Economics*, vol. 33(10), pp. 1221–32.

Felipe, J. and McCombie, J.S.L. (2001b), 'Biased Technical Change, Growth Accounting and the Conundrum of the East Asian Miracle', *Journal of Comparative Economics*, vol. 29(3), pp. 542–65.

Felipe, J. and McCombie, J.S.L. (2002), 'A Problem with Some Recent Estimations and Interpretations of the Markup in Manufacturing Industry', *International Review of Applied Economics*, vol. 16(2), pp. 187–215.

Felipe, J. and McCombie, J.S.L. (2003), 'Methodological Problems with Neoclassical Analyses of the East Asian Miracle', *Cambridge Journal of Economics*, vol. 54(5), pp. 695–721.

Felipe, J. and McCombie, J.S.L. (2005a), 'How Sound are the Foundations of the Aggregate Production Function?', *Eastern Economic Journal*, vol. 31(3), pp. 467–88.

Felipe, J. and McCombie, J.S.L. (2005b), 'Why Are Some Countries Richer than Others? A Sceptical View of Mankiw–Romer–Weil's Test of the Neoclassical Growth Model', *Metroeconomica*, vol. 56(3), pp. 360–92.

Felipe, J. and McCombie, J.S.L. (2006), 'The Tyranny of the Accounting

Identity: Growth Accounting Revisited', *International Review of Applied Economics*, vol. 20(3), pp. 283–99.

Felipe, J. and McCombie, J.S.L. (2007a), 'What Can the Labour Demand Function Tell Us about Wages and Employment? The Case of the Philippines', in J. Berg and D. Kucera (eds), *Cultivating Justice: Labour Institutions and Employment in Developing Countries*, Geneva and London: ILO and Palgrave Macmillan.

Felipe, J. and McCombie, J.S.L. (2007b), 'On the Rental Price of Capital and the Profit Rate: The Perils and Pitfalls of Total Factor Productivity Growth', *Review of Political Economy*, vol. 19(3), pp. 317–45.

Felipe, J. and McCombie, J.S.L. (2007c), 'Is a Theory of Total Factor Productivity Really Needed?', *Metroeconomica*, vol. 58(1), pp. 195–229.

Felipe, J. and McCombie, J.S.L. (2009a), 'Why the Data Tell Us Nothing about Returns to Scale and Externalities to Capital in Economic Growth', *Economiae Sociedade*, vol. 17, pp. 655–75.

Felipe, J. and McCombie, J.S.L. (2009b), 'Are Estimates of Labour Demand Functions Mere Statistical Artefacts?', *International Review of Applied Economics*, vol. 23(2), pp. 147–68.

Felipe, J. and McCombie, J.S.L. (2010a), 'On Accounting Identities, Simulation Experiments and Aggregate Production Functions: A Cautionary Tale for (Neoclassical) Growth Theorists', in M. Setterfield (ed.), *Handbook of Alternative Theories of Economic Growth*, Cheltenham, UK and Northampton, MA, USA: Edward Elgar, pp. 189–207.

Felipe, J. and McCombie, J.S.L. (2010b), 'What Is Wrong with Aggregate Production Functions? On Temple's "Aggregate Production Functions and Growth Economics"', *International Review of Applied Economics*, vol. 24(6), pp. 665–84.

Felipe, J. and McCombie, J.S.L. (2012), 'The Tyranny of the Accounting Identity Works Full Time: A Comment on Temple', CCEPP WP 01-12, Cambridge Centre for Economic and Public Policy, Department of Land Economy, University of Cambridge.

Felipe, J., McCombie, J.S.L. and Hasan, R. (2008), 'Correcting for Biases when Estimating Production Functions: An Illusion of the Laws of Algebra?', *Cambridge Journal of Economics*, vol. 32(2), pp. 441–59.

Ferguson, C.E. (1963), 'Cross-section Production Functions and the Elasticity of Substitution in American Manufacturing Industry', *Review of Economics and Statistics*, vol. 45(3), pp. 205–13.

Ferguson, C.E. (1968), 'Neoclassical Theory of Technical Progress and Relative Factor Shares', *Southern Economic Journal*, vol. 34(4), pp. 490–504.

Ferguson, C.E. (1969), *The Neoclassical Theory of Production and Distribution*, Cambridge: Cambridge University Press (reprinted 1971).

Ferguson, C.E. (1971), 'Capital Theory Up to Date: A Comment on Mrs. Robinson's Article', *Canadian Journal of Economics*, vol. 4(2), pp. 250–54.

Ferguson, C.E. (1972), 'The Current State of Capital Theory: A Tale of Two Paradigms', *Southern Economic Journal*, vol. 39(2), pp. 160–76.

Ferguson, C.E. and Allen, R.F. (1970), 'Factor Prices, Commodity Prices, and Switches of Technique', *Economic Inquiry*, vol. 8(2), pp. 95–109.

Fernald, J.G. and Neiman, B. (2010), 'Growth Accounting with Misallocation: Or Doing Less with More in Singapore', NBER Working Paper 16043, Cambridge, MA.

Fisher, F.M. (1965), 'Embodied Technical Change and the Existence of an Aggregate Capital Stock', *Review of Economic Studies*, vol. 32(4), pp. 263–88.

Fisher, F.M. (1969), 'The Existence of Aggregate Production Functions', *Econometrica*, vol. 37(4), pp. 553–77.

Fisher, F.M. (1971a), 'The Existence of Aggregate Production Functions Reply', *Econometrica*, vol. 39(2), p. 405.

Fisher, F.M. (1971b), 'Aggregate Production Functions and the Explanation of Wages: A Simulation Experiment', *Review of Economics and Statistics*, vol. 53(4), pp. 305–25.

Fisher, F.M. (1987), 'Aggregation Problem', in J.L. Eatwell, M. Milgate and P. Newman (eds), *The New Palgrave. A Dictionary of Economics*, vol. 1, Basingstoke: Macmillan, pp. 53–5.

Fisher, F.M. (1992), *Aggregation. Aggregate Production Functions and Related Topics* (Monz, J., ed.), London: Harvester Wheatsheaf.

Fisher, F.M. (2005), 'Aggregate Production Functions – A Pervasive, but Unpersuasive, Fairytale', *Eastern Economic Journal*, vol. 31(3), pp. 489–91.

Fisher, F.M., Solow, R.M. and Kearl, J.M. (1977), 'Aggregate Production Functions: Some CES Experiments', *Review of Economic Studies*, vol. 44(2), pp. 305–20.

Flux, A.W. (1894), 'Review of Wicksteed's "Essay on the Co-ordination of the Laws of Distribution"', reprinted in W.J. Baumol and S.M. Goldfeld (eds) (1968), *Precursors in Mathematical Economics*, London: LSE.

Frankel, M. (1962), 'The Production Function in Allocation and Growth: A Synthesis', *American Economic Review*, vol. 52(5), pp. 996–1022.

Friedman, M. (1953), 'The Methodology of Positive Economics', in M. Friedman (ed.), *Essays in Positive Economics*, Chicago, IL: Chicago University Press.

Gallaway, L. and Shukla, V. (1974), 'The Neoclassical Production Function', *American Economic Review*, vol. 64(3), pp. 348–58.

Gandolfo, G. (2008), 'Comment on "C.E.S. Production Functions in the Light of the Cambridge Critique"', *Journal of Macroeconomics*, vol. 30(2), pp. 798–800.

Garegnani, P. (1976), 'The Neoclassical Production Function: Comment', *American Economic Review*, vol. 66(3), pp. 424–7.

Gomulka, S. (1971), *Inventive Activity, Diffusion and Stages of Economic Growth*, Aarhus: Institute of Economics and Aarhus University Press.

Goodwin, R.M. (1967), 'A Growth Cycle', in C.H. Feinstein (ed.), *Socialism, Capitalism and Economic Growth: Essays Presented to Maurice Dobb*, Cambridge: Cambridge University Press.

Gorman, W. (1959), 'Separable Utility and Aggregation', *Econometrica*, vol. 27(3), pp. 469–810.

Griliches, Z. (1996), 'The Discovery of the Residual: A Historical Note', *Journal of Economic Literature*, vol. 34(3), pp. 1324–30.

Griliches, Z. and Mairesse, J. (1998), 'Production Functions: The Search for Identification', in S. Strøm (ed.), *Econometrics and Economic Theory in the 20th Century*, Cambridge: Cambridge University Press, pp. 169–203.

Grossman, P.J. (1988), 'Growth in Government and Economic Growth: The Australian Experience', *Australian Economic Papers*, vol. 27(50), pp. 33–43.

Grossman, P.J. (1990), 'Government and Growth: Cross-sectional Evidence', *Public Choice*, vol. 65(3), pp. 217–27.

Gunn, G.T. and Douglas, P.H. (1941), 'The Production Function for American Manufacturing in 1919', *American Economic Review*, vol. 31(1), pp. 67–80.

Gunn, G.T. and Douglas, P.H. (1942), 'The Production Function for American Manufacturing for 1914', *Journal of Political Economy*, vol. 50(4), pp. 595–602.

Haavelmo, T. (1944), 'The Probability Approach in Econometrics', *Econometrica*, vol. 12, Supplement, pp. 1–118.

Hacche, G. (1979), *The Theory of Economic Growth: An Introduction*, London: Macmillan.

Hahn, F.H. and Matthews, R.C.O. (1964), 'The Theory of Economic Growth: A Survey', *Economic Journal*, vol. 74(296), pp. 799–902.

Hall, R.E. (1986), 'Market Structure and Macroeconomic Fluctuations', *Brookings Papers on Economic Activity*, vol. 2, pp. 285–322.

Hall, R.E. (1987), 'Productivity and the Business Cycle', *Carnegie-Rochester Conference Series on Public Policy*, vol. 27, pp. 421–44.

Hall, R.E. (1988a), 'The Relation between Price and Marginal Cost in U.S. Industry', *Journal of Political Economy*, vol. 96(5), pp. 921–47.

Hall, R.E. (1988b), 'Increasing Returns: Theory and Measurement with Industry Data', mimeo, National Bureau of Economic Research, Cambridge, MA.

Hall, R.E. (1990), 'Invariance Properties of Solow's Productivity Residual', in P. Diamond (ed.), *Growth/Productivity/Employment*, Cambridge, MA: MIT Press.

Hall, R.E. and Jones, C.I. (1999), 'Why Do Some Countries Produce so Much More Output than Others?', *Quarterly Journal of Economics*, vol. 114(1), pp. 83–116.

Hamermesh, D.S. (1986), 'The Demand for Labor in the Long Run', in O. Ashenfelter and R. Layard (eds), *Handbook of Labor Economics*, vol. 1, Amsterdam: North-Holland, pp. 429–71.

Hamermesh, D.S. (1993), *Labor Demand*, Princeton, NJ: Princeton University Press.

Han, Z. and Schefold, B. (2006), 'An Empirical Investigation of Paradoxes: Reswitching and Reverse Capital Deepening in Capital Theory', *Cambridge Journal of Economics*, vol. 30(5), pp. 737–65.

Handsaker, M.J. and Douglas, P.H. (1937), 'The Theory of Marginal Productivity Tested by Data for Manufacturing in Victoria', *Quarterly Journal of Economics*, vol. 52(1), pp. 1–36.

Hansen, L.P. and Sargent, T.J. (1990), 'Recursive Linear Models of Dynamic Economies', NBER Working Paper 3479, Cambridge, MA.

Hansen, L.P. and Sargent, T.J. (1991), 'Recursive Linear Models of Dynamic Economies', Unpublished manuscript.

Harcourt, G.C. (1969), 'Some Cambridge Controversies in the Theory of Capital', *Journal of Economic Literature*, vol. 7(2), pp. 369–405.

Harcourt, G.C. (1972), *Some Cambridge Controversies in the Theory of Capital*, Cambridge: Cambridge University Press.

Harcourt, G.C. (1976), 'The Cambridge Controversies: Old Ways and New Horizons – Or Dead End?', *Oxford Economic Papers*, vol. 28(1), pp. 25–65.

Hartley, J.E. (2000), 'Does the Solow Residual Actually Measure Changes in Technology?', *Review of Political Economy*, vol. 12(1), pp. 27–44.

Heathfield, D.F. and Wibe, S. (1987), *An Introduction to Cost and Production Functions*, London: Macmillan.

Hildebrand, G. and Liu, T.C. (1965), *Manufacturing Production Functions in the United States, 1957*, Ithaca, NY: Cornell University Press.

Hogan, W.P. (1958), 'Technical Progress and Production Functions', *Review of Economics and Statistics*, vol. 40(4), pp. 407–11.

Hoover, K.D. (2012), *Intermediate Applied Macroeconomics*, Cambridge: Cambridge University Press.

Houthakker, H.S. (1955–56), 'The Pareto Distribution and the Cobb–Douglas Production Function in Activity Analysis', *Review of Economic Studies*, vol. 23(1), pp. 27–31.

Hsieh, C.-T. (1999), 'Productivity Growth and Factor Prices in East Asia', *American Economic Review, Papers and Proceedings*, vol. 89(2), pp. 133–8.

Hsieh, C.-T. (2002). 'What Explains the Industrial Revolution in East Asia? Evidence from Factor Markets', *American Economic Review*, vol. 92(8), pp. 502–26.

Hsieh, C.-T. and Klenow, P.J. (2009), 'Misallocation and Manufacturing TFP in China and India', *Quarterly Journal of Economics*, vol. 124(4), pp. 1403–48.

Hsing, M. (1992), 'On the Measurement of Aggregate Production Functions', *Cambridge Journal of Economics*, vol. 16(4), pp. 463–74.

Hulten, C.R. (1980), 'The Measurement of Capital', in E.R Berndt and J.E. Triplett (eds), *Fifty Years of Economic Measurement: The Jubilee of the Conference on Research in Income and Wealth*, Studies in Income and Wealth, Vol. 54, Chicago, IL: University of Chicago Press for the National Bureau of Economic Research, pp. 119–52.

Intriligator, M.D. (1978), *Econometric Models, Techniques and Applications*, Englewood Cliffs, NJ: Prentice-Hall.

Islam, N. (1992), 'Growth Empirics: A Panel Data Approach', unpublished paper, Harvard University.

Islam, N. (1995), 'Growth Empirics: A Panel Data Approach', *Quarterly Journal of Economics*, vol. 110(4), pp. 1127–70.

Islam, N. (1999), 'International Comparisons of Total Factor Productivity: A Review', *Review of Income and Wealth*, vol. 45(4), pp. 493–518.

Jevons, W.S. (1871), *The Theory of Political Economy*, London: Macmillan.

Jones, C.I. (1997), 'Convergence Revisited', *Journal of Economic Growth*, vol. 2(2), pp. 131–53.

Jones, C.I. (1998 [2002]), *Introduction to Economic Growth* (2nd edition), New York: W.W. Norton.

Jones, H.G. (1975), *An Introduction to Modern Theories of Economic Growth*, Middlesex: Nelson.

Jorgenson, D.W. (1963), 'Capital Theory and Investment Behavior', *American Economic Review, Papers and Proceedings*, vol. 53(2), pp. 247–59.

Jorgenson, D.W. (1974), 'Investments and Production: A Review', in M.D. Intriligator and D.A. Kendrick (eds), *Frontiers of Quantitative Economics*, Vol II, Amsterdam: North-Holland, pp. 341–75.

Jorgenson, D.W. (1995), *Productivity: Post-war U.S. Economic Growth*, Cambridge, MA: MIT Press.

Jorgenson, D.W., Gollop, F.M. and Fraumeni, B.M. (1987), *Productivity and US Economic Growth*, Cambridge, MA: Harvard University Press.

Jorgenson, D.W. and Griliches, Z. (1967), 'The Explanation of Productivity Change', *Review of Economic Studies*, vol. 34(3), pp. 249–83.

Kaldor, N. (1955–56), 'Alternative Theories of Distribution', *Review of Economic Studies*, vol. 23(2), pp. 83–100.

Kaldor, N. (1957), 'A Model of Economic Growth', *Economic Journal*, vol. 67(268), pp. 591–624.

Kaldor, N. (1961), 'Capital Accumulation and Economic Growth', in F.A. Lutz and D.C. Hague (eds), *The Theory of Capital*, London: Macmillan, pp. 177–222.

Kaldor, N. (1966), *The Causes of the Slow Rate of Economic Growth in the United Kingdom: An Inaugural Lecture*, Cambridge: Cambridge University Press.

Kennedy, C. and Thirlwall, A.P. (1972), 'Technical Progress: A Survey', *Economic Journal*, vol. 82(325), pp. 11–72.

Kenny, C. and Williams, D. (2001), 'What Do We Know About Economic Growth? Or, Why Don't We Know Very Much?', *World Development*, vol. 29(1), pp. 1–22.

Keynes, J.M. (1936), *The General Theory of Employment, Interest and Money*, London: Macmillan.

Keynes, J.M. (1939), 'Professor Tinbergen's Method', *Economic Journal*, vol. 49(195), pp. 558–68.

Kim, J.-I. and Lau, L.J. (1994), 'The Sources of Economic Growth of the East Asian Newly Industrialised Countries', *Journal of the Japanese and International Economies*, vol. 8(3), pp. 235–71.

Kincaid, H. (1996), *Philosophical Foundations of the Social Sciences: Analyzing Controversies in Social Research*, Cambridge: Cambridge University Press.

Kincaid, H. (2009), 'Explaining Growth', in H. Kincaid and D. Ross (eds), *The Oxford Handbook of Philosophy of Economics*, Oxford: Oxford University Press.

Klein, L.R. (1946a), 'Macroeconomics and the Theory of Rational Behavior', *Econometrica*, vol. 14(2), pp. 93–108.

Klein, L.R. (1946b), 'Remarks on the Theory of Aggregation', *Econometrica*, vol. 14(4), pp. 303–12.

Klenow, P.J. and Rodriguez-Clare, A. (1997), 'The Neoclassical Revival in Growth Economics: Has It Gone Too Far?', in B.S. Bernanke and J.J. Rotemberg (eds), *NBER Macroeconomics Annual 1997*, Cambridge, MA and London: MIT Press, pp. 73–103.

Knowles, S. and Owen, P.D. (1995), 'Health Capital and Cross-Country Variation in Income per Capita in the Mankiw–Romer–Weil Model', *Economics Letters*, vol. 48(1), pp. 99–106.

Kohli, I. and Singh, N. (1989), 'Exports and Growth: Critical Minimum Effort and Diminishing Returns', *Journal of Development Economics*, vol. 30(2), pp. 391–400.

Krugman, P. (1991), 'Increasing Returns and Economic Geography', *Journal of Political Economy*, vol. 99(3), pp. 483–99.

Krugman, P. (2009), 'The Increasing Returns Revolution in Trade and Geography', *American Economic Review*, vol. 99(3), pp. 561–71.

Kuhn, T. (1962 [1970]), *The Structure of Scientific Revolutions*, (2nd edition, with postscript), Chicago, IL: University of Chicago Press.

Landau, D. (1983), 'Government Expenditure and Economic Growth: A Cross-Country Study', *Southern Economic Journal*, vol. 49(3), pp. 783–92.

Landes, D.S. (1998), *The Wealth and Poverty of Nations: Why Some Are So Rich and Others So Poor*, London: Abacus.

Lau, E. and Vaze, P. (2002), 'Accounting Growth: Capital, Skills and Output', Occasional Paper PROD05, Office for National Statistics, available at: http://www.statistics.gov.uk/articles/nojournal/paper_5_TFP.pdf.

Lavoie, M. (2000), 'Le Chômage d'Équilibre: Réalité ou Artefact Statistique?', *Revue Économique*, vol. 51(6), pp. 1477–84.

Lavoie, M. (2008), 'Neoclassical Empirical Evidence on Employment and Production Laws as Artefact', Economía Informa, No.351, pp. 9–36.

Lawson, T. (2004), 'Philosophical Under-labouring in the Context of Modern Economics: Aiming at Truth and Usefulness in the Meanest of Ways', in J.B. Davis, A. Marciano and J. Runde (eds), *The Elgar Companion to Economics and Philosophy*, Cheltenham, UK and Northampton, MA, USA: Edward Elgar.

Layard, R., Nickell, S.J. and Jackman, R. (1991), *Unemployment: Macroeconomic Performance and the Labour Market*, Oxford: Oxford University Press.

Lazzarini, A. (2011), *Revisiting the Cambridge Capital Theory Controversies: A Historical and Analytical Study*, Pavia: Pavia University Press.

Lee, F.S. (1998), *Post Keynesian Price Theory*, Cambridge: Cambridge University Press.

Lee, J.-W. and Hong, K. (2012), 'Economic Growth in Asia: Determinants and Prospects', *Japan and the World Economy*, vol. 24(2), pp. 101–13.

Leibenstein, H. (1966), 'Allocative Efficiency vs. "X-Efficiency"', *American Economic Review*, vol. 56(3), pp. 392–415.

Leontief, W.W. (1947a), 'Introduction to a Theory of the Internal Structure of Functional Relationships', *Econometrica*, vol. 15(4), pp. 361–73.

Leontief, W.W. (1947b), 'A Note on the Interrelationship of Subsets of

Independent Variables of a Continuous Function with Continuous First Derivatives', *Bulletin of the American Mathematical Society*, vol. 53(4), pp. 343–50.

Leser, C.E.V. (1954), 'Production Functions for the British Industrial Economy', *Applied Statistics*, vol. 3(3), pp. 174–83.

Levhari, D. (1965), 'A Nonsubstitution Theorem and Switching of Techniques', *Quarterly Journal of Economics*, vol. 79(1), pp. 98–105.

Levine, H.S. (1960), 'A Small Problem in the Analysis of Growth', *Review of Economics and Statistics*, vol. 42(2), pp. 225–8.

Levine, R. and Renelt, D. (1992), 'A Sensitivity Analysis of Cross-country Growth Recessions', *American Economic Review*, vol. 82(4), pp. 942–63.

Levinsohn, J. and Petrin, A. (2003), 'Estimating Production Functions Using Inputs to Control for Unobservables', *Review of Economic Studies*, vol. 70(2), pp. 317–41.

Lewis, P.E.T. and MacDonald, G. (2002), 'The Elasticity of Demand for Labour in Australia', *Economic Record*, vol. 78(240), pp. 18–30.

Lewis, P.E.T and MacDonald, G. (2004), 'Modelling Aggregate Demand for Labour: A Reply to Dowrick and Wells', *Economic Record*, vol. 80(251), pp. 441–4.

Lucas, R.E. (1970), 'Capacity, Overtime, and Empirical Production Functions', *American Economic Review*, vol. 60(2), pp. 23–7.

Lucas, R.E. (1988), 'On the Mechanics of Economic Development', *Journal of Monetary Economics*, vol. 22(1), pp. 3–42.

Lucas, R.E. (1990), 'Why Doesn't Capital Flow from Rich to Poor Countries?', *American Economic Review, Papers and Proceedings*, vol. 80(2), pp. 92–6.

Lutz, F.A. and Hague, D.C. (1961), *Theory of Capital: Proceedings of a Conference Held by the International Economic Association*, London: Macmillan.

Maddison, A. (1982), *Phases of Capitalist Development*, Oxford: Oxford University Press.

Maddison, A. (1987), 'Growth and Slowdown in Advanced Capitalist Economies: Techniques of Quantitative Assessment', *Journal of Economic Literature*, vol. 25(2), pp. 649–98.

Maddison, A. (1995), *Monitoring the World Economy, 1820–1992*, Paris: OECD.

Mainwaring, L. and Steedman, I. (2000), 'On the Probability of Reswitching and Capital Reversing in a Two-sector Sraffian Model', in H.D. Kurz (ed.), *Critical Essays on Sraffa's Legacy in Economics*, Cambridge: Cambridge University Press.

Mankiw, N.G. (1995), 'The Growth of Nations', *Brookings Papers on Economic Activity*, 1, pp. 275–325.

Mankiw, N.G. (1997), 'Comment', in B.S. Bernanke and J. Rotemberg (eds), *NBER Macroeconomics Annual 1997*, Cambridge, MA: MIT Press, pp. 103–7.

Mankiw, N.G (2010), *Macroeconomics* (7th edition), New York: Worth.

Mankiw, N.G., Romer, D. and Weil, D.N. (1992), 'A Contribution to the Empirics of Economic Growth', *Quarterly Journal of Economics*, vol. 107(2), pp. 407–37.

Marshak, J. and Andrews, W.H. (1944), 'Random Simultaneous Equations and the Theory of Production', *Econometrica*, vol. 12(3/4), pp. 143–205.

Massell, B.F. (1962), 'Another Small Problem in the Analysis of Growth', *Review of Economics and Statistics*, vol. 44(3), pp. 330–32.

Matthews, R.C.O. (1988), 'The Work of Robert M. Solow', *Scandinavian Journal of Economics*, vol. 90(1), pp. 13–16.

May, K. (1946), 'The Aggregation Problem for a One-Industry Model', *Econometrica*, vol. 14(4), pp. 285–98.

May, K. (1947), 'Technological Change and Aggregation', *Econometrica*, vol. 15(1), pp. 51–63.

McCombie, J.S.L. (1987), 'Does the Aggregate Production Function Imply Anything about the Laws of Production? A Note on the Simon and Shaikh Critiques', *Applied Economics*, vol. 19(8), pp. 1121–36.

McCombie, J.S.L. (1996), 'On Hsing's Critique of Solow's "Technical Change and the Aggregate Production Function"', *Cambridge Journal of Economics*, vol. 20(6), pp. 785–95.

McCombie, J.S.L. (1998a), '"Are There Laws of Production?": An Assessment of the Early Criticisms of the Cobb–Douglas Production Function', *Review of Political Economy*, vol. 10(2), pp. 141–73.

McCombie, J.S.L. (1998b), 'Paradigms, Rhetoric, and the Relevance of the Aggregate Production Function', in P. Arestis (ed.), *Method, Theory and Policy in Keynes: Essays in Honour of Paul Davidson*, Vol. III, Cheltenham, UK and Lyme, NH, USA: Edward Elgar.

McCombie, J.S.L. (1999), 'A Problem with the Empirical Neoclassical Analysis of Economic Growth', in M. Setterfield (ed.), *Growth, Employment and Inflation: Essays in Honour of John Cornwall*, Basingstoke: Macmillan, pp. 127–48.

McCombie, J.S.L. (2000), 'Regional Production Functions and the Accounting Identity: A Problem of Interpretation', *Australasian Journal of Regional Studies*, vol. 6(2), pp. 133–55.

McCombie, J.S.L. (2000–01), 'The Solow Residual, Technical Change and Aggregate Production Functions', *Journal of Post Keynesian Economics*, vol. 23, pp. 267–97. (Errata, vol. 23(3), p. 544.)

McCombie, J.S.L. (2001), 'What do Aggregate Production Functions

Show? Second Thoughts on Solow's "Second Thoughts on Growth Theory"', *Journal of Post Keynesian Economics*, vol. 23(4), pp. 589–615.

McCombie, J.S.L. and Dixon, R. (1991), 'Estimating Technical Change in Aggregate Production Functions: A Critique', *International Review of Applied Economics*, vol. 5(1), pp. 24–46.

McCombie, J.S.L., Pugno, M. and Soro, B. (eds) (2002), *Productivity Growth and Economic Performance: Essays on Verdoorn's Law*, Basingstoke, UK and New York: Palgrave Macmillan.

McCombie, J.S.L. and Thirlwall, A.P. (1994), *Economic Growth and the Balance-of-Payments Constraint*, Basingstoke: Macmillan.

Meier, G.M. (2001), 'The Old Generation of Development Economists and the New', in G.M. Meier and J.E. Stiglitz (eds), *Frontier of Development Economics*, World Bank and Oxford University Press, Oxford: pp. 13–50.

Mendershausen, H. (1938), 'On the Significance of Professor Douglas' Production Function', *Econometrica*, vol. 6(2), pp. 143–53. (Correction, vol. 7, p. 1938.)

Menger, C. (1871), *Grundsätze der Volkswirthschaftslehre*, Wien: Wilhelm Braumiller.

Metcalfe, J.S. (2001), 'Institutions and Progress', *Industrial and Corporate Change*, vol. 10(1), pp. 561–85.

Michl, T. (1987), 'Is there Evidence for a Marginalist Demand for Labour?', *Cambridge Journal of Economics*, vol. 11(4), pp. 361–73.

Morgan, M.S. (1990), *The History of Econometric Ideas*, Cambridge: Cambridge University Press.

Moroney, J.R. (1972), *The Structure of Production in American Industry*, Chapel Hill, NC: University of North Carolina Press.

Muth, J.F. (1961), 'Rational Expectations and the Theory of Price Movements', *Econometrica*, vol. 29(3), pp. 1–23.

Nadiri, I.M. (1970), 'Some Approaches to the Theory and Measurement of Total Factor Productivity: A Survey', *Journal of Economic Literature*, vol. 8(4), pp. 1137–77.

Nataf, A. (1948), 'Sur ‧la Possibilité de Construction de Certains Macromodèles', *Econometrica*, vol. 16(3), pp. 232–44.

Nelson, C. and Kang, H. (1984), 'Pitfalls in the Use of Time as an Explanatory Variable in Regressions', *Journal of Business and Economic Statistics*, vol. 2(1), pp. 73–82.

Nelson, R.R. (1973), 'Recent Exercises in Growth Accounting: New Understanding or Dead End?', *American Economic Review*, vol. 63(3), pp. 462–8.

Nelson, R.R. (1998), 'The Agenda for Growth Theory: A Different Point of View', *Cambridge Journal of Economics*, vol. 22(4), pp. 497–520.

Nelson, R.R. and Winter, S.G. (1982), *An Evolutionary Theory of Economic Change*, Cambridge, MA: Harvard University Press.

Nonneman, W. and Vanhoudt, P. (1996), 'A Further Augmentation of the Solow Model and the Empirics of Economic Growth for OECD Countries', *Quarterly Journal of Economics*, vol. 111(3), pp. 943–53.

Norrbin, S.C. (1993), 'The Relation between Price and Marginal Cost in U.S. Industry: A Contradiction', *Journal of Political Economy*, vol. 101(6), pp. 1149–64.

O'Mahony, M. and de Boer, W. (2002), *Britain's Relative Productivity Performance: Updates to 1999*, London: National Institute of Economic and Social Research.

OECD (2001), *Measuring Capital: OECD Manual: Measurement of Capital Stocks, Consumption of Fixed Capital and Capital Services*, Paris: OECD.

OECD (2004), *Understanding Economic Growth: Macro-level. Industry-level. Firm-level*, Paris: OECD and Basingstoke: Palgrave Macmillan.

Oi, W. (1962), 'Labour as a Quasi-Fixed Input', *Journal of Political Economy*, vol. 70(6), pp. 538–55.

Olley, S. and Pakes, A. (1996), 'The Dynamics of Productivity in the Telecommunications Equipment Industry', *Econometrica*, vol. 64(6), pp. 1263–98.

Oulton, N. and O'Mahony, M. (1994), *Productivity and Growth: A Study of British Industry, 1954–1986*, Cambridge: Cambridge University Press.

Parente, S. and Prescott, E.C. (1994), 'Barriers to Technology Adoption and Development', *Journal of Political Economy*, vol. 102(2), pp. 298–321.

Pasinetti, L.L. (1994), 'The Structure of Long-Term Development: Concluding Comments', in L.L. Pasinetti and R.M. Solow (eds), *Economic Growth and the Structure of Long-Term Development*, Proceedings of the IEA conference held in Varenna, Italy, IEA Conference Volume, no. 112, New York: St. Martin's Press; London: Macmillan in association with the International Economic Association, pp. 353–62.

Pasintetti, L.L. and Scazzieri, R. (2008), 'Capital Theory (Paradoxes)', in S.N. Durlauf and L.E. Blume (eds), *The New Palgrave Dictionary of Economics* (2nd edition) Basingstoke: Palgrave Macmillan, and The New Palgrave Dictionary of Economics Online, Palgrave Macmillan, available at: http://www.dictionaryofeconomics.com/article?id=pde2008_C00 0042doi:10.1057/9780230226203.0196 (accessed 4 February 2013).

Peierls, R.E. (1960), 'Wolfgang Ernst Pauli, 1900–1958', *Biographical Memoirs of Fellows of the Royal Society*, vol. 5 (February), pp. 174–92.

Pertz, K. (1980), 'Reswitching, Wicksell Effects, and the Neoclassical

Production Function: Note', *American Economic Review*, vol. 70(5), pp. 1015–17.

Pesaran, M.H. and Shin, Y. (1999), 'An Autoregressive Distributed Lag Modelling Approach to Cointegration Analysis', in S. Strøm (ed.), *Econometric and Economic Theory in the 20th Century: The Ragnar Frisch Centennial Symposium*, Cambridge: Cambridge University Press.

Pesaran, M.H., Shin, Y. and Smith, R.J. (2001), 'Bounds Testing Approaches to the Analysis of Long-Run Relationships', Working Paper 9907, Department of Applied Economics, University of Cambridge.

Petri, F. (2000), 'On the Likelihood and Relevance of Reverse Capital Deepening', Department of Political Economy, no. 279, University of Siena.

Phelps Brown, E.H. (1957), 'The Meaning of the Fitted Cobb–Douglas Function', *Quarterly Journal of Economics*, vol. 71(4), pp. 546–60.

Pigou, A.C. (1933), *The Theory of Unemployment*, London: Macmillan.

Prescott, E.C. (1998), 'Needed: A Theory of Total Factor Productivity', *International Economic Review*, vol. 39(3), pp. 525–52.

Pritchett, L. (1997), 'Divergence, Big Time', *Journal of Economic Perspectives*, vol. 11(3), pp. 3–17.

Ram, R. (1986), 'Government Size and Economic Growth: A New Framework and Some Evidence from Cross-section and Time-series Data', *American Economic Review*, vol. 76(1), pp. 191–203.

Ram, R. (1987), 'Exports and Economic Growth in Developing Countries: Evidence from Time-series and Cross-section Data', *Economic Development and Cultural Change*, vol. 36(1), pp. 51–72.

Ram, R. (1989), 'Government Size and Economic Growth: A New Framework and Some Evidence from Cross-section and Time-series Data: Reply', *American Economic Review*, vol. 79(1), pp. 281–4.

Rao, V.V.B. (1989), 'Government Size and Economic Growth: A New Framework and Some Evidence from Cross-section and Time-series Data: Comment', *American Economic Review*, vol. 79(1), pp. 272–80.

Rashid, S. (2000), *Economic Policy for Growth: Economic Development is Human Development*, Boston, MA: Kluwer Academic Press.

Rebelo, S. (1991), 'Long-Run Policy Analysis and Long-Run Growth', *Journal of Political Economy*, vol. 99(3), pp. 500–521.

Reder, M.W. (1943), 'An Alternative Interpretation of the Cobb–Douglas Function', *Econometrica*, vol. 11(3/4), pp. 259–64.

Ricardo, D. (1821), *The Principles of Political Economy and Taxation*, London: John Murray.

Robinson, J.V. (1933), *The Economics of Imperfect Competition*, London: Macmillan.

Robinson, J.V. (1953–54), 'The Production Function and the Theory of Capital', *Review of Economic Studies*, vol. 21(2), pp. 81–106.

Robinson, J.V. (1956), *The Accumulation of Capital*, London: Macmillan.

Robinson, J.V. (1970), 'Capital Theory up to Date', *Canadian Journal of Economics*, vol. 3(2), pp. 309–17.

Robinson, J.V. (1975), 'The Unimportance of Reswitching', *Quarterly Journal of Economics*, vol. 8(11), pp. 32–9.

Romer, P.M. (1986), 'Increasing Returns and Long-run Growth', *Journal of Political Economy*, vol. 94(5), pp. 1002–37.

Romer, P.M. (1987), 'Crazy Explanations for the Productivity Slowdown', *NBER Macroeconomics Annual 1987*, Cambridge, MA, pp. 163–201.

Romer, P.M. (1990), 'Endogenous Technical Change', *Journal of Political Economy*, vol. 98(5), Part 2, S71–S102.

Romer, P.M. (1994), 'The Origins of Endogenous Growth', *Journal of Economic Perspectives*, vol. 8(1), pp. 3–22.

Romer, P.M. (2001), 'Comment on "It's Not Factor Accumulation: Stylized Facts and Growth Models"', *World Bank Economic Review*, vol. 15(2), pp. 225–7.

Rowthorn, R.E. (1999), 'Unemployment, Wage Bargaining and Capital–Labour Substitution', *Cambridge Journal of Economics*, vol. 23(4), pp. 413–25.

Salter, W.E.G. (1966), *Productivity and Technical Change*, (2nd edition), Cambridge: Cambridge University Press.

Salvadori, N. (2000), 'Comment', in H.D. Kurz (ed.), *Critical Essays on Sraffa's Legacy in Economics*, Cambridge: Cambridge University Press, pp. 354–7.

Samuelson, P.A. (1962), 'Parable and Realism in Capital Theory: The Surrogate Production Function', *Review of Economic Studies*, vol. 29(3), pp. 193–206.

Samuelson, P.A. (1963), 'Problems of Methodology – Discussion', *American Economic Review, Papers and Proceedings*, vol. 53(2), pp. 231–6.

Samuelson, P.A. (1966), 'A Summing Up', *Quarterly Journal of Economics*, vol. 80(4), pp. 568–83.

Samuelson, P.A. (1979), 'Paul Douglas's Measurement of Production Functions and Marginal Productivities', *Journal of Political Economy*, vol. 87(5), pp. 923–39.

Sandelin, B. (1976), 'On the Origin of the Cobb–Douglas Function', *Economics and History*, vol. 20(2), pp. 117–25.

Sargent, J.R. (1985), 'Employment and Real Wages in UK Manufacturing, 1955–1980', in Bank of England Panel Paper No. 2, *Employment, Real Wages and Unemployment in the United Kingdom*, London.

Sato, K. (1975), *Production Functions and Aggregation*, Amsterdam: North-Holland.

Scazzieri, R. (2008), 'Reswitching of Technique', in S.N. Durlauf and L.E. Blume (eds), *The New Palgrave Dictionary of Economics* (2nd Edition), Basingstoke: Palgrave Macmillan, and The New Palgrave Dictionary of Economics Online, Palgrave Macmillan, available at: http://www.dictionaryofeconomics.com/article?id=pde2008_R000126 doi:10.1057/9780230226203.1430 (accessed 4 February 2013).

Schefold, B. (2008), 'C.E.S. Production Functions in the Light of the Cambridge Critique', *Journal of Macroeconomics*, vol. 30(2), pp. 783–97.

Scott, M.F.G. (1989), *A New View of Economic Growth*, Oxford: Clarendon.

Sen, A. (1974), 'On Some Debates in Capital Theory', *Economica*, vol. 41(163), pp. 328–35.

Shaikh, A. (1974), 'Laws of Production and Laws of Algebra: The Humbug Production Function', *Review of Economics and Statistics*, vol. 56(1), pp. 115–20, pp. 80–96.

Shaikh, A. (1980), 'Laws of Production and Laws of Algebra: Humbug II', in E.J. Nell (ed.), *Growth, Profits and Property*, Cambridge: Cambridge University Press.

Shaikh, A. (1987), 'Humbug Production Function', in J. Eatwell, M. Milgate and P. Newman (eds), *The New Palgrave: A Dictionary of Economic Theory and Doctrine*, vol. 2, London: Macmillan, pp. 690–91.

Shaikh, A. (2005), 'Nonlinear Dynamics and Pseudo-Production Functions', *Metroeconomica*, vol. 31(3), pp. 447–66.

Sheehey, E.J. (1990), 'Exports and Growth: A Flawed Framework', *Journal of Development Studies*, vol. 27(1), pp. 111–16.

Simon, H.A. (1979a), 'Rational Decision-Making in Business Organizations', *American Economic Review*, vol. 69(4), pp. 493–513. (Nobel Memorial Lecture, 8 December, 1978.)

Simon, H.A. (1979b), 'On Parsimonious Explanations of Production Relations', *Scandinavian Journal of Economics*, vol. 81(4), pp. 459–74.

Simon, H.A. and Levy, F.K. (1963), 'A Note on the Cobb–Douglas Function', *Review of Economic Studies*, vol. 30(2), pp. 93–4.

Simon, J.L. (1986), *Theory of Population and Economic Growth*, Oxford: Basil Blackwell.

Smith, A. (1776), *An Inquiry into the Nature and Causes of the Wealth of Nations*, Edwin Cannan, ed. 1904, Library of Economics and Liberty, available at: http://www.econlib.org/library/Smith/smWN.html (accessed 15 January 2013).

Solow, R.M. (1955–56), 'The Production Function and the Theory of Capital', *Review of Economic Studies*, vol. 23(2), pp. 101–8.

Solow, R.M. (1956), 'A Contribution to the Theory of Economic Growth', *Quarterly Journal of Economics*, vol. 70(1), pp. 65–94.

Solow, R.M. (1957), 'Technical Change and the Aggregate Production Function', *Review of Economics and Statistics*, vol. 39(3), pp. 312–20.

Solow, R.M. (1958a), 'Technical Progress and Production Functions: Reply', *Review of Economics and Statistics*, vol. 40(4), pp. 411–13.

Solow, R.M. (1958b), 'A Skeptical Note on the Constancy of Relative Shares', *American Economic Review*, vol. 48(4), pp. 618–63.

Solow, R.M. (1966), 'Review of *Capital and Growth*', *American Economic Review*, vol. 56(5), pp. 1257–60.

Solow, R.M. (1974), 'Laws of Production and Laws of Algebra: The Humbug Production Function: A Comment', *Review of Economics and Statistics*, vol. 56(1), p. 121.

Solow, R.M. (1975), 'Cambridge and the Real World', *Times Literary Supplement*, 14 March, pp. 277–78.

Solow, R.M. (1987), 'Second Thoughts on Growth Theory', in A. Steinherr and D. Weiserbs (eds), *Employment and Growth: Issues for the 1980s*, Dordrecht: Martinus Nijhoff.

Solow, R.M. (1988), 'Growth Theory and After', *American Economic Review*, vol. 78(3), pp. 307–17.

Solow, R.M. (1994), 'Perspectives on Growth Theory', *Journal of Economic Perspectives*, vol. 8(1), pp. 45–54.

Solow, R.M. (1997), 'Is There a Core of Usable Macroeconomics We Should All Believe In?', *American Economic Review*, vol. 87(2), pp. 230–32.

Solow, R.M. (2001), 'What Have We Learned from a Decade of Empirical Research on Growth? Applying Growth Theory Across Countries', *World Bank Economic Review*, vol. 15(2), pp. 283–8.

Sraffa, P. (1960), *Production of Commodities by Means of Commodities: Prelude to a Critique of Economic Theory*, Cambridge: Cambridge University Press.

Srinivasan, T.N. (1994), 'Data Base for Development Analysis: An Overview', *Journal of Development Analysis*, vol. 44(1), pp. 3–27.

Srinivasan, T.N. (1995), 'Long-run Growth Theories and Empirics: Anything New?', in T. Ito and A.C. Krueger, (eds), *Growth Theories in Light of the East Asian Experience*, Chicago, IL: University of Chicago Press, pp. 37–70.

Steedman, I. (2003), 'On "Measuring" Knowledge in New (Endogenous) Growth Theory', in N. Salvadori (ed.), *Old and New Growth Theories: An Assessment*, Cheltenham, UK and Northampton, MA, USA: Edward Elgar, pp. 127–33.

Stiglitz, J. (1974), 'The Cambridge–Cambridge Controversy in the Theory of Capital: A View from New Haven: A Review Article', *Journal of Political Economy*, vol. 82(4), pp. 893–903.

Summers, R. and Heston, A. (1984), 'Improved International Comparisons of Real Product and its Composition: 1950–80', *Review of Income and Wealth*, vol. 30(2), pp. 207–62.

Summers, R. and Heston, A. (1991), 'The Penn World Table (Mark 5): An Expanded Set of International Comparisons, 1950–1988', *Quarterly Journal of Economics*, vol. 106(2), pp. 327–68.

Swan, T.W. (1956), 'Economic Growth and Capital Accumulation', *Economic Record*, vol. 32(2), pp. 334–61.

Sylos Labini, P. (1995), 'Why the Interpretation of the Cobb–Douglas Production Function Must Be Radically Changed', *Structural Change and Economic Dynamics*, vol. 6(4), pp. 485–504.

Tatom, J.A. (1980), 'The "Problem" of Procyclical Real Wages and Productivity', *Journal of Political Economy*, vol. 88(2), pp. 385–94.

Temple, J.R.W. (1999), 'The New Growth Evidence', *Journal of Economic Literature*, vol. 38(1), pp. 112–56.

Temple, J.R.W. (2005), 'Dual Economy Models: A Primer for Growth Economists', *Manchester School*, vol. 73(4), pp. 435–78.

Temple, J.R.W. (2006), 'Aggregate Production Functions and Growth Economics', *International Review of Applied Economics*, Vol. 20(3), pp. 301–17.

Temple, J.R.W. (2010), 'Aggregate Production Functions, Growth Economics, and the Part-time Tyranny of the Identity: A Reply to Felipe and McCombie', *International Review of Applied Economics*, Vol. 24(6), pp. 685–92.

Temple, J.R.W. and Wößmann, L. (2006), 'Dualism and Cross-Country Growth Regressions', *Journal of Economic Growth*, vol. 11(3) pp. 187–228.

Thirlwall, A.P. (1993), 'The Renaissance of Keynesian Economics', *Banca Nazionale del Lavoro Quarterly Review*, no. 186, pp. 327–37.

Thirlwall, A.P. (2002), *The Nature of Economic Growth: An Alternative Framework for Understanding the Performance of Nations*, Cheltenham, UK and Northampton, MA, USA: Edward Elgar.

Thomas, R.L. (1993), *Introductory Econometrics* (2nd edition), London: Longman.

Thünen, J.H. von. (1826), *Der Isolierte Staat in Beziehung auf Landwirtschaft und Nationalökonomie* (1966 reprint, Stuttgart: Gustav Fischer).

Tinbergen, J. (1939), *Statistical Testing of Business-Cycle Theories, Vol. 1: A Method and Its Application to Business Cycle Theories*, Geneva: League of Nations.

Tinbergen, J. (1942), 'On the Theory of Trend Movement' (in German),

Weltwirtschaftliches Archiv, Reprinted in J. Tinbergen (1959), *Selected Essays*, L.H. Klassen, L.M. Koyck and H.J. Witteveen (eds), Amsterdam: North-Holland.

Turner, M.S. (1989), *Joan Robinson and the Americans*, Armonk, NY: M.E. Sharpe.

Valdés, B. (1999), *Economic Growth: Theory, Empirics and Policy*, Cheltenham, UK and Northampton, MA, USA: Edward Elgar.

Von Weizsäcker, C.C. (1971), 'Ender einer Wachstumtheoroie? Zu Hajo Rieses Missverstandnissen über die "Neoklassische" Theorie', *Kyklos*, vol. 24(1), pp. 97–101.

Waldman, R.J. (1991), 'Implausible Results or Implausible Data? Anomalies in the Construction of Value-Added Data and Implications for Estimates of Price-Costs Mark-ups', *Journal of Political Economy*, vol. 99(6), pp. 1315–28.

Wall, B. (1948), 'Cobb–Douglas Function for U.S. Manufacturing and Mining, 1920–40', *Econometrica*, vol. 16(2), pp. 211–13.

Wallis, K.F. (1979), *Topics in Applied Econometrics*, Lectures in Economics, 5, London: Gray-Mills.

Walras, L. (1874), *Éléments d'Économie Politique Pure: Ou Théorie de la Richesse Sociale*, Paris: R. Pichon & R. Durand-Auzias; Lausanne: F. Rouge.

Walters, A.A. (1963a), 'Production and Cost Functions: An Econometric Survey', *Econometrica*, vol. 31(1–2), pp. 1–66.

Walters, A.A. (1963b), 'A Note on Economies of Scale', *Review of Economics and Statistics*, vol. 45(4), pp. 425–7.

Wan, H.Y. (1971), *Economic Growth*, New York: Harcourt Brace Jovanovich.

Weil, D.N. (2005), *Economic Growth* (2nd edition), Englewood Cliffs, NJ: Prentice-Hall.

Whiteman, J.L. (1988), 'The Efficiency of Labour and Capital in Australian Manufacturing', *Applied Economics*, vol. 20(2), pp. 243–61.

Wibe, S. (1984), 'Engineering Production Functions: A Survey', *Economica*, vol. 51(204), pp. 401–11.

Wicksell, K. (1893), *Value, Capital and Rent* (tr. G.L.S. Shackle, 1954), London: George Allen & Unwin.

Wicksell, K. (1895), *Zur Lehre von der Steuerincidenz*, Upsala.

Wicksell, K. (1900 [1958]), 'Om Gränsproduktiviteten Säsom Grundval För den National ekonomiska Fördelningen', *Economisk Tidskriff*, pp. 305–37. English translation 'Marginal Productivity as the Basis for Distribution in Economics', in E. Lindahl (ed.) (1958), *K Wicksell, Selected Papers on Economic Theory*, London: George Allen & Unwin.

Wicksteed, P. (1894), *An Essay on the Co-ordination of the Laws of Distribution*, London: Macmillan.

Wilson, D.J. (2009), 'IT and Beyond: The Contribution of Heterogeneous Capital to Productivity', *Journal of Business and Economic Statistics*, vol. 27(1), pp. 52–70.

Woit, P. (2006), *Not Even Wrong: The Failure of String Theory and the Search to Unify the Laws of Physics*, New York: Basic Books.

Young, A. (1928), 'Increasing Returns and Economic Progress', *Economic Journal*, vol. 38(152), pp. 527–42.

Young, A. (1992), 'A Tale of Two Cities: Factor Accumulation and Technical Change in Hong Kong and Singapore', in O. Blanchard and S. Fischer (eds), *NBER Macroeconomics Annual*, Cambridge, MA: MIT Press, pp. 13–63.

Young, A. (1995), 'The Tyranny of Numbers: Confronting the Statistical Realities of the East Asian Growth Experience', *Quarterly Journal of Economics*, vol. 110(3), pp. 641–80.

Zambelli, S. (2004), 'The 40% Neoclassical Aggregate Theory of Production', *Cambridge Journal of Economics*, vol. 28(1), pp. 99–120.

Zellner, A., Kmenta, J. and Drèze, J. (1966), 'Specification and Estimation of Cobb–Douglas Production Function Models', *Econometrica*, vol. 34(4), pp. 784–95.

Index

Abbott, T. 268
Abramovitz, M. 155, 178
accounting identity
  aggregate production function
    criticisms *see* aggregate
    production function criticisms,
    reasons for ignoring, and
    accounting identity implications
  aggregate production functions
    as *see* aggregate production
    functions, behavioural
    relationship or accounting
    identity?
  and Cobb–Douglas production
    function *see* aggregate
    production function,
    behavioural relationship
    or accounting identity?,
    accounting identity and Cobb–
    Douglas production function
  and cost functions *see* aggregate
    production function,
    behavioural relationship or
    accounting identity?, cost
    functions and accounting
    identity
  critique, first appearance of 152–4,
    155–7
  linear 54–6, 58–9
  observed and virtual *see* aggregate
    production function,
    behavioural relationship or
    accounting identity?, accounting
    identities, observed and virtual
  problems, neoclassical dual-sector
    growth model 242–5
  problems, *see* Mankiw–Romer–Weil
    (MRW) test of neoclassical
    growth model
  simulation studies *see* simulation
    studies, aggregate production
    function and accounting
    identity

Solow and total factor productivity
  measurement 205–7
and Solow's 'Technical Change
  and the Aggregate Production
  Function' paper *see* Solow's
  'Technical Change and the
  Aggregate Production Function'
  paper, and accounting identity
accounting identity for estimation
  of degree of market power and
  mark-up, problems with 266–83
  Bureau of Economic Analysis (BEA)
    and high mark-ups in non-
    manufacturing industries 270
  Caballero and Lyons extension of
    Hall's procedure 279–81
  Caballero and Lyons extension of
    Hall's procedure, externality
    effect in production 279–80
  empirical illustration of Hall's results
    273–6
  gross output use 282–3
  Hall's estimation procedure 271–4,
    279–80
  Hall's method of estimating mark-
    up 267–71, 276–9
  literature survey 268–71
  marginal cost 266, 267–8, 269, 270,
    274, 279
  monopoly profits 271, 278–9
  nondurable goods industry 276,
    277–8
  production function use 267–8
  Solow residual, increasing returns
    to scale, and revenue and cost
    shares 276–9
Acemoglu, D. 6
Ackerberg, D. 338
Adams, F. 133
advanced countries, neoclassical dual-
  sector growth model, problems
  with 240, 246, 247, 248,
  249